Eating God's Sacrifice

The Lord's Supper Portrayed In Old Testament Sacrifice

Daniel J. Brege

2010

Scripture references from
HOLY BIBLE, NEW AMERICAN STANDARD BIBLE
Copyright © The Lockman Foundation 1960, 1962, 1963, 1968, 1972, 1973, 1975

Copyright © 2010 by Daniel J. Brege
4520 W 750 N   Decatur, IN   46733

All rights reserved. No part of this book may be reproduced, stored in a retrieval system, or transmitted by any means or in any form—electronic, mechanical, digital, photocopied, recorded, or any other—except brief quotations (of a page or less) in pertinent papers or printed reviews, without the prior written permission of Daniel J. Brege. Electronic retrieval of the book may be purchased through a vendor authorized by Daniel J. Brege.

Printed by Lulu, Morrisville, NC, USA
Published by Daniel J. Brege
ISBN-13: 978-0-578-07680-5

In cherished memory of my
Christ-minded parents:
Reverend Robert and Edna Brege

And to my loving, supportive wife:
Lynn

Deep appreciation is extended to those who encouraged and assisted in the completion of this book. The following were instrumental:

Rev. Dr. Arthur Just
Rev. William Brege
Rev. Peter Cage
Rev. Richard Tino
Rev. Floyd Smithey
Maj. Heidi Clark
Rev. John Wurst
Lloyd Wittenmyer

CONTENTS

Introduction..9

1. **Beginning to Sense the Lord's Supper from the Old Testament......17**
   General and Specific Sacramental Eating............................. 18
   An Overview of Hebrew Sacrifice... 20
   A Biblical Chart of Sacrificial Eating..................................... 30
   Beginning to Sense Sacred Eating....................................... 30
   Christ, the Antitype... 32
   A General History of Sacrificial Eating.................................37
   Christ Related His Supper to Hebrew Sacrifice....................... 40
   Cautiously Revealing the Lord's Supper................................. 45
   Liturgy.. 47
   Warning Against Sacramental Hypocrisy..............................56
   Names for the Lord's Supper.. 58
   What About Baptism?... 60

2. **The Passover, Preface to the Lord's Supper............................... 62**
   The Importance of the Passover Feast................................. 64
   Deliverance Through the Lamb's Body and Blood................... 70
   The Church of the Firstborn..77
   God Requires Faith... 80
   Memorial Meals 81
   Does the Lord's Supper Replace the Passover?...................... 85
   Christ Dining With Us... 88
   The Leader of the Feast ("Paterfamilias")............................... 93
   Connecting the Passover to Specific Sacrifices....................... 96
   Eating Requirements.. 99

3. **The Tabernacle, Template of Christ and His Supper....................102**
   The Heavenly Tabernacle..105
   Jesus: God Tabernacling Among Us.................................. 107
   Christ: Pattern of the Earthly Tabernacle.............................109
   Christ and His Church, Today's Temple..............................113
   The Basics of the Hebrew Tabernacle.................................114
   Tabernacle Diagram.. 115
   The Outer Court of the Tabernacle......................................116
   Christ and His Sacraments: Antitypes of the Outer Court...........120
   The Holy Place.. 134
   Christ and His Sacraments: Antitypes of the Holy Place............ 136
   The Most Holy Place (Holy of Holies).................................. 141
   Christ and His Sacraments: Antitypes of the Most Holy Place.... 143
   Christ, Anointed Tabernacle..147

4. **The Burnt Offering, a Link to the Sacrament of the Altar...............149**
   The Meaning of the Burnt Offering...................................... 151
   Holocaust and Communion Sacrifices 155
   God Ignited the Sacrificial Fire.. 157
   Public and Private Burnt Offerings...................................... 159
   Sacrificial Blood...160

	Man as Physical Being	169
	God Eats	171
	Why Would God Eat?	175
	Pagan Communion	178
	The Burnt Offering: Love	183
	The Burnt Offering: Ascension	186
	The Burnt Offering: "Do This"	188
	Salting the Sacrifice	190
5.	**The Sin and Guilt Offerings, Keen Shadows of the Sacrament**	**193**
	Sin and Guilt Offerings Contrasted	198
	Public and Private Sin Offerings	203
	The Sprinkled Blood Now Internalized	206
	Eating the Public Sin Offering Today	210
	Holy and Most Holy Meals	215
	Absolution	221
	Christ's Supper and Isaiah 53	229
	Special Occasion Sin Offerings	233
6.	**The Peace Offering, Portrayer of the Eucharist**	**237**
	Sacrifice of the Peace Offering	239
	The Peace Offerings	242
	The Priestly Meal	244
	Holy Things Eaten by the Laity	247
	God Communes with His People	251
	Connecting Holy Communion to the Peace Offering	254
	Other Peace Offering Connections	257
	Public and Private Peace Offerings	259
	Sacrificial Meals and John 6	262
	Eating the Peace Offering with Joy	268
	The Special Passover Peace Offering	270
	The Thank Offering: "Eucharist"	272
	A Unique Thank Offering Bread	276
	Rendering Thanks Today in the Eucharist	277
	The Votive Peace Offering	280
	Christ's Eucharist in Psalm 22	282
	Malachi and the Lord's Supper	289
	Was Isaiah Predicting the Eucharist?	293
	The Free-will Offering	295
	The Covenant (Testament) Sacrifice	296
	Covenant Inauguration by Moses and Jesus	299
	Feasting Implications of Jeremiah's Covenant Prediction	301
	The Death of the Testator	303
	The Sacrifice of Completion	306
	The "Salvation" Sacrifice	307
	The Sacrifice of Praise	310
	The Confession Sacrifice	312
	Eating of the Tithe and the Firstborn	315
	The Consecration Sacrifice	317
	Pagans and Peace Offering Meals	320
	Sharing a Meal with the Poor	325

7. **The Grain Offering, Food of Holy Communion**........................ 329
        Grain Offering Directives... 330
        The Feast of First-fruits... 335
        Priestly Eating of the Grain Offering....................................... 337
        Public and Private Grain Offerings.. 341
        Sacrificial Flesh and Bread Eaten Together............................. 343
        The "Minchah" (Bread and Wine) of the Inner Court................. 346
        Eating the Bread of the Presence... 347
        Wine Next to the Bread of the Presence................................ 350
        The Wine with the Blood.. 351
        Wine with Peace Offerings... 357
        Memorial Bread Rituals... 359

8. **Hebrews, Epistle of Sacrifice and Sacrament**........................... 368
        The Author of Hebrews Identifies His Purpose........................ 375
        What Does It Mean that Christ is Priest, Mediating
            a Better Covenant?.. 376
        Christ, Priest of the Peace Offering....................................... 377
        Christ, Priest of the Sin Offering... 391
        What Does It Mean that Christ is at the Right Hand
            in the Tabernacle Pitched by God?................................ 395
        What Does It Mean that Christ is a "Minister"?.......................... 421
        What Are the Gifts and Sacrifices Offered by Christ,
            and How Does He Offer them?..................................... 425

Bibliography.. 436

Glossary with Index.. 445

Biblical Index... 462

Introduction

> *"For if you believed Moses, you would have believed Me; for he wrote of Me."*
> *John 5:46*

As a young man I considered the Old Testament to be of little or no value. Such thinking is nothing new. Within a hundred years of Christ a cult leader named Marcion tried to bring perverse teachings into the Christian church, and one of these perverse teachings was that the Old Testament was of little or no value. Several years after becoming a pastor, I was taken aback—because it dawned on me that my view of the Old Testament had been something like his! I believe this Marcion mindset is prevalent among Christians today.

Before coming to realize the importance of the Old Testament I would have thought Martin Luther to have been somewhat crazy when he brazenly asserted, "We should let the worthless babblers go who despise the Old Testament and say it is of no further use, when, as a matter of fact, we must derive the ground of our faith from it alone."[1] Derive the ground of our faith from the Old Testament *alone*? Luther must have been exaggerating, right?

As I further studied the Old Testament (OT), I observed that time and again God's OT saints ate sacrificial portions when they gathered to worship. Could it be that God had established an ancient precedent for worship-related eating? And could Martin Luther have been correct, that the ground of our faith—even concerning the Lord's Supper—must really be derived *from the Old Testament alone*?

Upon investigating sacrificial practices I came to realize that the OT indeed testifies to a longstanding precedent for worship-oriented, sacrifice-related eating. Nearly all OT sacrifices not only involved eating, but they also

---

[1] Edward M. Plass, comp., *What Luther Says*, 3 vols. (St. Louis: Concordia Publishing House, 1959), vol. 2, 995.

presented worship-related nuances whereby the Lord's Supper is seen to have a profound depth that far exceeds what one might perceive simply from the New Testament (NT) texts. So when Jesus invited the eating and drinking of His body and blood, this made a certain amount of sense to those familiar with OT worship; God had given prescriptions for sacrificial flesh and blood. When instituting the Lord's Supper Jesus was not inventing the practice of worship-related eating, but He was establishing a meal that was both the continuation and the consummation of what had been done for centuries before Him. This readily explains why the early church effortlessly took Christ's Words of Institution literally, and with near unanimity professed to be eating Christ's true body and blood in the Lord's Supper. This belief—that Christ's actual body and blood are truly present and eaten with the mouth in the Lord's Supper—is called the belief in the *Real Presence*.[2] Such a belief naturally maintains the rhythm of OT sacrificial practice.

Jesus himself presented the basic rule for studying the OT when He explained to the Jewish theologians, "You search the Scriptures, because you think that in them you have eternal life; and *it is these that bear witness of Me*."[3] By the word "scriptures" Jesus was here identifying what Christians commonly call the *Old Testament*. Thus *the* rule for Bible study is simply *look for Christ, because the Bible is ultimately about Him.*[4]

This declaration of Jesus should cause one to seek Christ more diligently in the *entire* OT scriptures. More germane to our current study, however, is that while He walked this earth Christ guided His followers especially to the writings of Moses. For example in John 5, after stating that the "scriptures" testify of Him, Jesus said, "If you believed *Moses,* you would

---

[2] This belief is held by the branches of Christendom with the most ancient roots: The Orthodox Church and the Roman Catholic Church. Confessional Lutherans and some other protestants also believe in the *Real Presence*.

[3] John 5:39, *The Holy Bible, New American Standard Version*, (Copyright 1975 The Lockman Foundation). All Bible quotes will be from the NASB, unless otherwise noted.

[4] The Greek word in John 5:39 for "search" is the word used by the Jews for Midrash. A Midrash was an "official" commentary on Old Testament texts. Thus this verse is giving *the* hermeneutical directive, that the right way to interpret the OT is to seek Jesus therein! Since the NT is *obviously* about Jesus, then He is at the heart of the entire Bible.

believe Me; for *he wrote of Me.*"[5] Again, in Christ's parable of the rich man and Lazarus, the testimony of salvation is said to reside in "*Moses* and the prophets."[6] Note the priority of Moses.[7] Then the parable concludes, "If they do not listen to *Moses* and the Prophets, neither will they be persuaded if someone rises from the dead."[8] Once again after His resurrection Christ explained the necessity of His death and resurrection—"beginning with *Moses.*"[9] Jesus consistently directed people to view the writings of *Moses* as the primary beacon illuminating Himself. These writings of Moses are called the *Pentateuch*, the first five books of the Bible.[10]

The Pentateuch contains many things, and indeed these books of the Bible are foundational to all theology. Within these first five books of the OT it is abundantly clear that through the great prophet Moses God instituted and repeatedly referenced the worship-related sacrificial rites. God's ordained sacrificial rites are clearly a central topic of the Pentateuch.

Numerous Christians have perceived the importance of the OT sacrificial rites. Alfred Edersheim, a devout nineteenth century Jew who converted to Christianity, is one such person. His writings demonstrate his superlative knowledge of Jewish belief and tradition, and today's scholars still value his insights. From his extensive studies Edersheim recognized that "sacrifices constitute the center of the Old Testament."[11] With this sacrifice-centered perception, the writings of Moses must then be the pulsating heart of the OT. Is Christ to be found in these sacrificial rites recorded in the

---

[5] John 5:46.
[6] Luke 16:29.
[7] It is true that Jews always perceived the priority of Moses. Jesus, however, maintains this priority when explaining that the OT points to Him.
[8] Luke 16:31.
[9] Luke 24:27.
[10] The Pentateuch was also called the *Torah*, which is Hebrew for "teaching." *Torah* can be used beyond referring to the Pentateuch, and is often translated "Law". However, "Law of Moses" usually identifies the Pentateuch.
[11] Alfred Edersheim, *The Temple, Its Ministry and Services*, updated edition (Peabody, MS: Hendrickson Publishers, 1994), 75. The book of Leviticus must then be extremely important, for it contains the majority of information in the Pentateuch pertaining to sacrifice. See John W. Kleinig, *Leviticus*, (St. Louis: Concordia Publishing House, 2003), 25ff.

Pentateuch? He said the OT scriptures—emphatically Moses' writings—testify of Him. If the OT is about Christ, and if sacrificial talk permeates the foundational books of the OT (the Pentateuch), it would be strange indeed if this sacrificial talk were not about Christ. Clearly the New Testament (NT) testifies that Christ is the person in the portrait painted by the OT sacrificial rites—rites ordained in the Pentateuch.

Because the NT possesses a seemingly all-encompassing authority among current Christians, some today have viewed the Pentateuch as nonessential. It is, however, essential—especially because it is foundational. Its value should not be underestimated, for certain aspects of Christ's person and work cannot be realized without a study of the OT sacrificial rites founded in the Pentateuch.[12]

Even as the Pentateuch enables a clearer picture of Christ, so it accomplishes the same task in relation to the Lord's Supper. As students of the Pentateuch begin to realize that the Jewish sacrificial rites involved substantial *sacred eating*, they will attain a deeper appreciation for the *sacred eating* of the Lord's Supper. They will also better understand why Christians have always worshiped by gathering to join in *sacred eating*.[13] When God's people learn to relate the OT both to Christ and to His Holy Supper, they will better perceive the consistency and continuity of God's ways. Such students will realize that God's pattern for worship naturally flowed from the OT into Christ's institution of the Lord's Supper, and that through sacred meals God

---

[12] We will expand upon this throughout the book. It is summarized well by John Leighton, *The Jewish Altar: An Inquiry into the Spirit and Intent of the Expiatory Offerings of the Mosaic Ritual*, (New York: Funk and Wagnalls, 1886), 113: "But viewing the sacrifices of Moses as typical in the sense of containing and enforcing all the great principles underlying the gospel of salvation, the record of those principles can never be safely left out of sight."

[13] Tibor Horbath, *The Sacrificial Interpretation of Jesus' Achievement in the New Testament Historical Development and Its Reasons*, (New York: Philosophical Library, 1979), 88: "Thus the question of the real presence is connected with the validity of the application of sacrificial terms to the Eucharistic celebration." S. C. Gayford, *Sacrifice and Priesthood*, (London: Methuen & Co. LTD., 2nd ed. 1953), 54: "So when our Lord came to 'fulfill the Law,' His Sacrifice was the fulfillment not of one only but of all four types of Sacrifice under the Old Covenant. He gathers into one Sacrifice the intentions of Sin Offering, Trespass Offering, Burnt Offering, and Peace Offering: atonement, satisfaction for sin, dedication, communion."

blessed and still blesses His people. They will then come to appreciate the Lord's Supper both in worship and in application to their day-to-day living.[14]

Though I seek to point readers to the Lord's Supper, this is not my main purpose. A primary premise in this book is that *the teaching of the Jewish sacrificial rites do not exist primarily to enhance one's understanding of the Lord's Supper—they exist to point to Christ Jesus.* Only secondarily do such sacrificial rites instruct God's people about the Lord's Supper.

Doctrine is like health food for the soul. God wants His people to have the very best nutrition to sustain them in a life where spiritual disease and injury perpetually attack the vigor of their faith in Christ.[15] The more correct doctrine one possesses, the more resistant one will be to spiritual disease and injury. Someone without the basic doctrine of Christ is dead; faith in Christ's person and work is the essence of the Christian's spiritual life. Indeed all doctrine, including that pertaining to the Lord's Supper, will ultimately magnify Christ's person and work. Correct doctrine surrounding the Lord's Supper promotes Christian vitality. Correct doctrine pertaining to the Lord's Supper also engenders proper use of the Sacrament. Proper use of the Sacrament of the Lord's Supper provides several invigorating "vitamins" and "minerals" for the believer, promoting spiritual healing and strength. If in their study of the OT, Christians obtain a deeper understanding of *both* Christ *and* His Supper, then the richness of their blessing will be greatly multiplied. By faith in Jesus they will not only have the bread that gives life, but in their godly reception of the Lord's Supper they will also have a truly potent spiritual health food to nourish them on their journey through life.

Primarily this book will seek to explore the relationships between the OT sacrificial practices and Christ. Such a relationship will then be shown to have a direct bearing upon one's understanding and use of the Lord's Supper.

---

[14] This was the basis of the author's doctoral thesis: Daniel J. Brege, "The learning of Old Testament sacrificial concepts will enhance one's appreciation for the Lord's Supper." Concordia Theological Seminary, Ft. Wayne, Indiana, 2002.

[15] Temptations to sin, tragedy, false doctrine cleverly promoted by false teachers, loss of physical or mental heath—these and other such evils are used by Satan to ravage the Christian's soul.

Ultimately the goal of this book is to demonstrate that God-ordained, sacrifice-related meals have always been an integral part of worship, as can be traced from OT rituals to the present celebration of the Lord's Supper. And all such true worship finds its center in Christ—crucified (sacrificed) and risen.

It has been my observation that many do not realize that the Lord's Supper possesses a vital connection both to God's unchanging plan of salvation and to what happens in worship. Thus many do not see the importance of Holy Communion, its need for frequent reception, and its application to their lives. Pastors cannot merely command their people to "commune regularly"; they must *teach their people* to recognize the tremendous importance and value of The Lord's Supper.[16] Hence this book. It is hoped that both clergy and laity will find this book useful for their own personal growth pertaining to Holy Communion, and also useful for assisting them as they instruct others who are preparing to receive the Holy Supper.[17]

While researching this book it became apparent to me that theologians from various persuasions have perceived connections between OT sacrifice and NT Holy Communion.[18] I am currently a pastor in a conservative Lutheran synod.[19] Throughout Lutheran history there have been Lutheran theologians who have realized the connection between OT sacrifice and NT sacrament.[20] We conservative Lutherans maintain allegiance to our

---

[16] Martin Luther wrote in his *Large Catechism*: "In order that the common people and the weak, who also would like to be Christians, may be induced to see the reason and the need for receiving the sacrament...on this subject we must be persistent in preaching." Theodore G. Tappert, ed., *The Book of Concord* (Philadelphia: Fortress Press, 1959), "The Large Catechism," 451.

[17] Most technical theology will be relegated to the footnotes. Those with a theological aptitude are encouraged to reference these. We pray that the main text remains user-friendly to the laity.

[18] It is intriguing to me that theologians especially wrote about this connection in the late 19th century. As the 20th century dawned, theological treatises connecting OT sacrifice and NT sacrament appear to be less frequent. I believe this is so because of the profound influence of higher critical methodology, which especially took root at various seminaries in the early 20th century. Nevertheless, even many current higher critical scholars have maintained a sacrifice-sacrament connection, and if they do not contradict Scripture we may quote their insights.

[19] The *Lutheran Church—Missouri Synod* is currently Bible based and confession oriented.

[20] Because of the Roman Catholic doctrine of the Sacrifice of the Mass, Lutherans have been hesitant to relate OT sacrifice to NT sacrament. This does not mean they have failed to recognize the connection.

confessional statement, *The Book of Concord* (compiled in 1580), in which there are also references to the sacrifice-sacrament connection—references that include important warnings about taking such connections too far.[21] I have however not limited my references to Lutheran theologians; Lutherans by no means have a corner on this theology. There have been early church fathers, several non-Lutheran Protestant scholars, Orthodox teachers and liturgies, as well as many Roman Catholic theologians who have discerned proper connections between OT sacrifice and NT sacrament.[22] I have not ignored theological insights that draw valid conclusions from God's Word.

As our present era finds an anti-sacramental theology permeating Protestantism around the globe, God's people need to be ready to *defend* the thoroughly biblical truth that the Supper of Christ is at the heart of worship. Additionally they must be prepared to *explain* why they believe Christ's body and His blood are true yet supernatural food, and that through eating Christ's body and blood one personally receives the blessings earned by Christ at the cross and verified by Christ at the empty tomb. My hope and prayer is that the following chapters will serve to assist Christians in such defense and explanation.

Daniel J. Brege, 2008

---

[21] Theodore G. Tappert, ed., *The Book of Concord* (Philadelphia: Fortress Press, 1959), "Apology of the Augsburg Confession," 252ff. Especially within this section of the Apology ("Sacrifice, Its Nature and Types") one finds discussion about sacrifice and its relation to Holy Communion. However, neither this section nor any other section of the Confessions was intended to be exhaustive on particular doctrinal issues.

[22] It should be noted at the outset that we do not agree with the sacrifice of the Mass—that Christ is re-sacrificed, nor do we agree that extra-biblical tradition has the same authority as Holy Scripture. Additionally the reader should realize that just because an author is quoted, it does not mean total agreement with that author.

> *"Look at the nation Israel, are not those who eat the sacrifices in communion with the altar?"*
> *I Corinthians 10:18*

Chapter One

BEGINNING TO SENSE THE LORD'S SUPPER FROM THE OLD TESTAMENT

Eating has been and continues to be an important, if not necessary, part of worship. As St. Paul explained in the above quote, Israelites ate of the temple sacrifices and as such they were communing with God at His altar. When Christians now gather to worship, they still find—appropriately—that the eating of sacrifice-related food remains foundational to communing with God.

When Jesus invited His Apostles to eat His body and drink His blood, these Jewish followers would have made sense of such an invitation by drawing from their understanding of related temple directives. Such OT worship directives, which almost always involved sacred eating, had been officially practiced from Moses onward, and had been ingrained in the lives of Jewish men such as the Apostles. For God's people today to better grasp the intended meaning and ramifications of the Lord's Supper, they must attempt to cultivate an apostolic mindset, a mindset that quite naturally relates Jesus' words to the OT, and, more specifically, to the worship rites established through Moses.

In this the first chapter, these rites of Moses will only be summarized, and thus the reader can expect this first chapter to generate unanswered questions about sacrifice. In the remaining chapters we will strive to answer many of these questions by exploring and explaining the Mosaic rites, especially as they relate to Christ and His Holy Supper.

General and Specific Sacramental Eating

> *"And all ate the same spiritual food; and drank the same spiritual drink...Is not the cup of blessing which we bless a sharing in the blood of Christ? Is not the bread which we break a sharing in the body of Christ?"*
> *I Corinthians 10:3,4a,16*

In the above quote Saint Paul presented the OT accounts of the eating of the heaven-sent manna and the drinking of the water that supernaturally flowed from the rock. He then utilized these OT accounts as a diving board, preparing his readers to plunge into a consideration of the Lord's Supper. There are many Biblical accounts that involve miracles associated with eating. Following Paul's example, we suggest that eating-related miracles can be instructive concerning the Lord's Supper. All such miracle-related eating and/or drinking we will loosely refer to as "sacramental."

To enable a more efficient discussion of such "sacramental" eating in the Bible, the following two categories are here defined: *General Sacramental Eating* and *Specific Sacramental Eating*. *Specific Sacramental Eating* is the supernatural eating only found in the Lord's Supper. *General Sacramental Eating* is any other miracle-related eating. In *General Sacramental Eating* there is, as presently defined, a dining in which God has created something supernatural in or surrounding the meal. We believe that by recognizing *General Sacramental Eating*, God's people will obtain a better sense for the *Specific Sacramental Eating* of Christ's body and blood in the Lord's Supper.

When we here rather loosely speak of "sacrament" we do not intend to make the church acknowledge additional sacraments, but to direct the

Beginning to Sense the Lord's Supper from the Old Testament

reader to *General Sacramental Eating*.[1] The word "sacrament" is not in the Bible, and various Christian denominations have defined it differently. In the Lutheran Church a "sacrament" is usually defined as a God ordained NT rite in which He connects His Word to tangibles (water, bread, wine), to convey the salvation earned by Christ.[2] Holy Communion and Holy Baptism are the two sacraments usually identified by Lutherans. Since our focus is mainly on sacramental *eating*, Holy Baptism will be considered particularly when it relates to Holy Communion. In our definition of *General Sacramental Eating*, we maintain the presence of actual food. In *General Sacramental Eating*, contrasted with the Lord's Supper, the miracle of the forgiving presence of Christ's body and blood is replaced with *any* miracle associated with a meal. Such miracles were always the result of God's Word connected to a given food. That word from God could have been a word of blessing, a word of invitation, a promise or even a threat connected with eating.

The first example of General Sacramental Eating was Adam's encounter with the forbidden fruit in the Garden of Eden.[3] Adam and Eve were not harmed by some physical poison in the fruit, but they were harmed in this "sacramental" eating because God had *said* there was death in eating such fruit. Similarly when the OT priests consumed portions of animal flesh, they participated in General Sacramental Eating to convey forgiveness and atonement. How could such eating be connected with forgiveness? God said so! God invited the children of Israel to eat the manna from heaven and drink water from the rock.[4] He invited the multitudes to dine on the bread and fish

---

[1] Charles Porterfield Krauth, *The Conservative Reformation and Its Theology: as represented in the Augsburg Confession, and in the History and Literature of the Evangelical Lutheran Church*, (Philadelphia: The United Lutheran Publication House, n. d.), 585ff. Krauth sees the beginning of "sacramental eating" to have been the two trees in Eden.

[2] The Confessions of the Lutheran Church identify Baptism and Holy Communion as the two basic sacraments, but sometimes Holy Absolution is also considered a sacrament. The Confessions would also not object to calling Ordination a sacrament, if the preaching office is being considered.

[3] Genesis 2,3. See Krauth in footnote 1.

[4] Exodus 16 and 17.

miraculously multiplied by the blessing of Jesus.[5] These are a few of the many examples of General Sacramental Eating. Simply put, there was something supernatural associated with these meals. God loves to involve miracle related food as He fellowships with man.

As our book progresses, it will become apparent that the greatest example of General Sacramental Eating is the eating that permeated the sacrificial system of the OT. We label such eating as the "greatest example" because this General Sacramental Eating was the closest practice in the OT to the Specific Sacramental Eating of the Lord's Supper. In the eating of the OT sacrifices God involved His people with the two merciful elements of *forgiveness* and *communion* with Him; these are also two of the basic blessings of the Lord's Supper.

An Overview of Hebrew Sacrifice

> *"And there you shall bring...your sacrifices [...]. There also you and your households shall eat before the Lord your God..."*
> *Deuteronomy 12:6a,7a*

This section is but a summary of sacrificial information to be further explained and applied in later chapters. The reader may want to return to this summary to review the basics of OT sacrificial understanding.

Through Moses, God officially established a sacrificial system. There were mainly three reasons to bring sacrifices to God's house: when needing *forgiveness* from God, when desiring to demonstrate *dedication* to God, and when desiring to offer formal *thanksgiving* to God. Priests were appointed by God to properly present sacrificial portions upon and around His altars. Either an individual would bring to God such sacrifices for *forgiveness*, for *dedication*

---

[5] E.g. John 6:1-14.

or for *thanksgiving*; or the priests on behalf of the entire nation of Israel would bring them.[6]

The priests officiated numerous prescribed sacrifices on behalf of the nation of Israel. For instance, there were the daily sacrifices, the weekly (*Sabbath*) sacrifices and the monthly (*New Moon*) sacrifices.[7] Several different creatures were sacrificed to God at these appointed times, with the lamb being the primary creature. In addition, God instituted three sacred festivals that every Hebrew man was required to attend: the *Feast of Unleavened Bread*, the *Feast of Weeks* and the *Feast of Booths*.[8] Traveling to these festivals, Hebrew families participated in special sacrificial rites, rites that were led by the priests, rites that involved worship-related eating.

Our emphasis will not be upon the special days and festivals during which sacrifices were offered, with the exception of the Passover. The Passover, to be discussed in our second chapter, initiated the *Feast of Unleavened Bread*.[9] The *Feast of Unleavened Bread*, unlike the other two Jewish feasts, is uniquely related to the Lord's Supper because Jesus instituted The Supper while celebrating the Passover.

The following is a sketch of the content and general application of sacrifices, but not a discussion of appointed occasions for Jewish sacrifices.

Blood, Fat and Flesh

When a creature was sacrificed, the life-related elements drawn from that creature had special significance. The three life-related elements from an

---

[6] The men were responsible to bring such sacrifices for their families. Kleinig is convinced a woman could also approach the tabernacle with certain sacrifices. John W. Kleinig, *Leviticus*, (St. Louis: Concordia Publishing House, 2003), 99. Occasionally a king would supply sacrificial creatures for the entire nation.
[7] Numbers 28:1-15.
[8] Deuteronomy 16:16. The feasts are described in Leviticus 23, Numbers 28,29 and in Deuteronomy 16. These three feasts are frequently further subdivided. During the history of the nation of Israel there were also special occasions at which God directed various sacrifices to be offered either by a leader (e.g. Moses, Samuel, Solomon) or by the official priests. Two examples of such special feasts are Aaron's ordination and the dedication of the tabernacle.
[9] See e.g. Mark 14:12.

animal sacrifice were *blood, fat* and *flesh.*

First consider sacrificial blood. To realize the value of blood, it must be understood that blood was directly associated with life. As it was linked with life, sacrificial blood was considered the atoning element in the sacrificial process, which meant that it conveyed forgiveness before God.[10] Even today the term "life-blood" is in use, and from such a term people continue to vaguely associate life with blood. Blood was too valuable to be burned upon God's altar, and drinking it in OT times was absolutely forbidden.[11] Sacrificial blood was usually returned to God by being reverently placed upon the outer part of and around the base of His altar.[12] There are abundant NT references to the blood of Christ, and these are more fully understood by considering God's blood-rituals ordained through Moses.[13]

Consider now the fat drawn from a sacrifice. A creature's fat included its fat-laden organs. The fat-laden organs in and of themselves possessed a degree of sacredness, but they were most likely included as part of the fat-sacrifice because the fat could not easily be separated from such organs. These fat-laden organs were included under the term *fatty (fat) portions.*[14]

The fat, like the blood, was deemed a highly sacred sacrificial element, being symbolic of wealth.[15] Even today this meaning can easily be grasped since a fat creature is one that has obviously been blessed with more than sufficient food, as well as a measure of good health. Abundant fat upon

---

[10] Leviticus 17:11,14. Forgiveness could be *conveyed* because of Christ's retroactive death.
[11] Leviticus 17:11ff.
[12] There were two altars in God's House, the Bronze Altar and the Altar of Incense. In addition to placing sacrificial blood upon or around these, sacred blood was also sprinkled toward the Mercy Seat on the Day of Atonement. Blood of any non-sacrificial creature, such as a deer, was to be poured upon the ground.
[13] Sacrificial blood will be further explained in chapter four.
[14] See e.g. Leviticus 7:3-5. J. H. Kurtz, *Offerings, Sacrifices and the Worship of the Old Testament*, trans. James Martin (Peabody, MA: Hendrickson Publishers, Inc., 1998), 222: "The fat portions, as contrasted with the rest of the flesh, can only be regarded as the noblest, best and most sublimated portion, the *flos carnis...* "
[15] See e.g. Deuteronomy 31:20. The innards of a creature were also used by pagans for divination. Burning these on the altar prevented the Jews from using them for this purpose. Kleinig, *Leviticus...*, 89.

a creature was not necessary, but it demonstrated that God had provided a cushion, more than was necessary for survival. Fattened livestock indicated that God had truly blessed the owner with more than he needed. God was the source of such life-supporting super-abundance, so when a creature was sacrificed it made a certain amount of sense that its fat, like its blood, uniquely belonged to God—the giver of life and sustenance. Because sacrificial blood and fat belonged only to God, no Israelite was allowed to eat these.[16] Unlike the blood, however, the fat of a sacrifice was almost always burned upon God's altar.

Anything burned upon God's altar was understood to have been eaten by God.[17] God was never hungry, nor was His eating a case of chewing and swallowing. By eating, God demonstrated His loving desire to commune with man. Such eating by God presents a unique category of General Sacramental Eating. Some do not want to say that God "ate" what was burned on His altar.[18] As will be discussed in subsequent chapters, the Scriptures indeed say that God, unlike false gods, truly ate at His altar. The altar is called God's table, the items burned are called His food (bread), and the fire—icon of God's presence—is said to literally eat that which was being burned. Other than the daily burnt offerings, fat was the most common element burned (eaten) on God's altar.

There is no *specific* NT application for the OT sacrificial fat. However, the slaying of the "fatted calf" in the parable of the prodigal son surely indicated the Jewish conviction that God was participating in this celebration as *He* ate the fat and *the people bringing the sacrifices* ate the flesh of the

---

[16] Leviticus 3:17. See Kleinig, *Leviticus*, 85: "Many pagan religions believed that just as the "life" of an animal was found in its blood, its spiritual power and strength lay in its fat. Those who ate these parts supposedly gained supernatural power by eating the fat from animals that had been sacrificed to a deity." Similar beliefs were held concerning the sacrificial blood (p. 89). Thus God excised this pagan belief by forbidding the eating of fat or blood.

[17] Andrew Jukes, *The Law of the Offerings in Leviticus I. - VII Considered as the Appointed figure of the Various Aspects of the offering of the Body of Jesus Christ* (London: James Nisbet & Co., 13th ed., 1883), 49: "The altar is the 'table of the Lord:' whatever was put upon it was 'the food of God.'"

[18] E.g. Kleinig, *Leviticus*, 93.

calf.[19]

The third and final significant element drawn from a sacrificed animal was its flesh. A creature's flesh was its identity. Without its blood, a creature, identified by its fleshly presence, was dead. The flesh of a *burnt offering* was totally consumed by God via the fire of His altar. For all other kinds of animal sacrifices God's people usually consumed the flesh as a holy, special-occasion food.[20] The special occasions for such sacred feasting can be generally identified as either a time of forgiveness, when the priests alone ate the flesh; or a time of thanksgiving, when both priests and laity consumed the sacrificial flesh. The parable of the prodigal son is a NT reference describing a time of thanksgiving, a time when the fatted calf would be slain and the flesh feasted upon by those with thankful hearts.[21]

Compared to today's American diet, the Jewish common person ate far less meat. One reason for this is that once a lamb, goat or bovine had been sacrificed it no longer could provide wool or milk for its owner. In addition, wealth was determined by the size of one's herd, and thus to eat too many animals from a man's herd was literally to consume his wealth. The Jews also ate less meat because, at least with the directives for the original tabernacle, *any* livestock slain for its meat was considered a type of *peace offering.*[22] For this reason a Jew could not simply butcher his ox or lamb in his barn. The blood of any "butchered" livestock had to be reverently poured at God's altar, the fat had to be burned upon God's altar, and the priests had to be given their portion of the flesh before the laity could eat their portion. Again referencing the parable of the prodigal son, one can see how the fatted

---

[19] Luke 15:11ff. The Greek for slaying the fatted calf is a common word for "sacrifice." Since the fatted calf was a peace offering (see below), its fat was considered God's food, and its flesh was to be eaten in a celebrative communion meal. In chapter six we will consider this further.
[20] The public sin offering was the exception. Its flesh was totally burned outside the camp.
[21] Luke 15:11ff.
[22] Leviticus 17:1-6. Livestock thus slain were considered peace offerings. As God fulfilled His promise and extended Israel's borders, those who were too distant from the tabernacle/temple were given permission to ceremonially slay livestock on their property (Deuteronomy 12:20-23). This will be elucidated in chapter six.

calf was a form of sacrifice, and indeed the Greek word for killing the fatted calf in this parable is the usual word for "sacrifice."[23]

When a Jew consumed sacrificial flesh it served two purposes. The food first established communion with God, but then it also served as the main ingredient of a nutritious meal. More than any other type of sacrifice the *peace offering* emphasized a nutritional aspect to sacrificial participation. This was demonstrated by the fact that people bringing peace offerings were at times commanded to nourish the poor with such a meal.[24] Even though the poor were frequently nourished by a peace offering meal, still such poor folk had to be ceremonially clean to eat of this sacrificial flesh.[25] This demonstrated that any peace offering feast still possessed a degree of holiness.

Priestly food was considered too holy to be shared outside of a priest's household. Sacrifice-related priestly food was labeled either *holy* or *most holy*. Of the *holy* flesh apportioned to a priest, only the priest's *family* could eat of it; of the *most holy* sacrificial portions, only the *priests* themselves could eat. This holiness connected to the OT priestly food aptly prefigured the holiness of the Lord's Supper, which also is a sacred meal intended for the NT priesthood. All NT believers are priests, and they are eligible to receive the Lord's Supper after being baptized and catechized (officially instructed) in the Christian faith, and then also—as learned in their catechesis—they should approach the holy meal with a repentant attitude.[26]

There were four types of sacrifice wherein an animal's life was taken and from which the priests reverently applied a creature's blood, fat and

---

[23] Luke 15:23. See Johannes Behm, "θυω, θυσια, θυσιαστηριον," vol. III, *Theological Dictionary of the New Testament*, ed. Gerhard Kittel and Gerhard Friedrich, trans. Geoffrey W. Bromiley (Grand Rapids: Wm. B. Eerdmans Publishing Co., 1968), 180ff.
[24] Deuteronomy 14:22,23,28,29. The tithe was a category of peace offering.
[25] Alfred Edersheim, *The Temple, Its Ministry and Services* (Peabody, MS: Hendrickson Publishers, updated edition 1994), 101.
[26] Such requirements parallel the OT requirements of circumcision and cleanliness required to eat sacred meals. Future chapters will consider this further.

flesh.[27] These sacrifices were the *sin offering,* the *guilt offering,* the *burnt offering* and the *peace offering.* Such sacrifices consisted of livestock (e.g. goats, bulls, lambs), but never wild game such as deer or antelope.[28] Since livestock was essential for a family's sustenance, to sacrifice these creatures established a personal relationship between God and the giver. To offer one's livestock was, in a sense, to offer one's self.[29] In addition to the four types of animal sacrifice, there was also the grain offering.

The Sin and Guilt Offerings

Recall that sacrifices were offered for three reasons: to receive *forgiveness,* to demonstrate *dedication,* or to offer *thanksgiving.* The need for *forgiveness* was what motivated both the sin and guilt offerings. A *sin offering,* as the name implies, was sacrificed when an individual or the nation became aware of sin and thus realized the need for forgiveness. This offering involved various types of livestock, depending on the status of the offender; those who were very poor could even present flour as a sin offering.[30] The blood of the loftiest sin offering was sprinkled toward a holy location in the tabernacle. The blood from all sin offerings was ceremonially daubed upon the horns and outer walls of one of God's two altars, with the remaining blood poured (shed) at the base of the bronze altar.[31] The fatty portions of a sin offering were then burned upon God's bronze altar. When the sin offering was not being sacrificed on behalf of the high priest, a priest was then *required* to cook and eat the flesh as a *most holy* meal. If, however, the sacrifice was for the sins of the high priest, then the sacrificial flesh had to be

---

[27] We will consider the sacrifice of the Red Heifer to be an intensified sin offering. Some of these sacrifices also had subcategories of sacrifice.
[28] Leviticus 1:2. An exception to the use of wild game appears to be the dove/pigeon (Lev. 5:11). However these creatures may have been domesticated as well. An exception to the sacrifice of an animal was the sin offering of flour given by the poor.
[29] Andrew Jukes, *The Law of the Offerings...*, 38: "The offering, whatever it might be, stood for, and was looked upon as identical as the offerer."
[30] Leviticus 5:11ff.
[31] On the Day of Atonement, sin offering blood was sprinkled toward the Mercy Seat. Ezekiel uniquely mentions the placement of sin offering blood upon the doorposts.

burned outside the camp, and the priests ate none of it.[32] Usually such sin offerings burned outside the camp were not only sacrificed for the high priest, but for the entire nation as well, and as such they have been called "public" sin offerings.[33]

It is believed that the *guilt offering* was a subordinate kind of sin offering.[34] The rules directing the private sin offering also applied to the guilt offering, with the following exceptions. Unlike the sin offering, there were no "public" guilt offerings. The guilt offering additionally required paying back any debt owed to God or man, and thus some have called the guilt offering a trespass offering or a reparation offering.[35] The guilt offering was *always* a ram, and its flesh was *always* to be cooked and eaten by an officiating priest.[36] This constant priestly-eating of guilt offerings must certainly have been on the minds of those early Christian Jews when they partook of the Lord's Supper.

The Burnt Offering

Dedication to God was demonstrated by giving a burnt offering. The *burnt offering*, as its name also implies, was totally burned upon God's altar—of course with the exception of the blood.[37] The blood, as with all animal sacrifices, was sacredly applied to and around the base of God's Bronze Altar. The burning of this offering signified the *dedication* on the part of those bringing it because such a sacrifice completely belonged to God; no man participated in this sacrifice by eating a meal drawn from it. To completely

---

[32] It was especially (probably only) when the *high priest* was in need of forgiveness that the sin offering was burned outside the camp.
[33] Alfred Edersheim, *The Temple...*, 96ff. Edersheim labels such offerings as "outer" and "inner" sin offerings. We use "public" and "private" to be consistent with the variations surrounding the other kinds of sacrifices.
[34] J. H. Kurtz, *Offerings, Sacrifice...*, 248.
[35] E.g. Kleinig, *Leviticus...*
[36] On some occasions the guilt offering is referred to as a male sheep. There is little difference between this and a ram.
[37] The skin of a burnt offering was not burned as well; it was given to the priests (Leviticus 7:8).

burn such a sacrifice was a mark of extreme faith and dedication. How many Christians today would bring their money to church only to have it totally burned upon God's altar? Thus, if a common person (layman) brought a burnt offering, it signified his wholehearted dedication to God; and when the burnt offerings were sacrificed on behalf of the nation of Israel this indicated the nation's dedication to God.

The Peace Offering

The concluding sacrifice in the sacrificial process was the *peace offering*. This sacrifice established a statement of *thanksgiving* to God. Even though both the blood and the fat of this offering were treated similar to that of a sin offering, yet the peace offering was not sacrificed primarily to create peace but because there already was peace with God.[38] Eating the flesh of this sacrifice was crucial in the sacrificial process. The flesh of the peace offering was not eaten solely by the priests, but by the families of the priests, *and by the common people (laity) as well*. Such eating corresponds with the eating of NT Holy Communion. Along with eating, praising God was also uniquely linked to the peace offering. The peace offering was so intimately associated with praise and thanksgiving, that godly celebration and songs of praise were routinely expressed with this sacrifice. The Psalms frequently reference this fact.[39]

The Grain Offering

In addition to the sacrifice of livestock, there was also the *grain offering*. This sacrifice, once again as the name implies, involved the sacred burning of grain upon God's altar. Before bringing it to God's altar, a grain offering would usually be crushed and mixed with olive oil to render it into a simple form of unleavened bread. God prescribed that the unleavened bread

---

[38] Like all other sacrificial blood, the peace offering blood offered atonement; however atonement was not the emphasis of the peace offering.
[39] Such references will be identified in our peace offering chapter, chapter six.

of a grain offering be burned whenever a burnt offering or peace offering was sacrificed.[40] However, only a portion of the grain offering was thus burned. That part of the grain offering burned upon God's altar was called God's *memorial portion*, and after burning the memorial portion—which consisted of a mere handful—the rest of the grain offering was baked as unleavened bread for a *most holy* meal consumed solely by the priests.[41] An association with the Lord's Supper is found in this worship-related consumption of unleavened bread.

Upon entering the promised land, Israel's grain offerings were always united with drink offerings ("libations"). OT Jewish libations consisted of grape wine, which would not be mixed with the bread of the grain offering but would be sacredly poured at the altar's base.[42] Relative to the Lord's Supper, wherein Christ's blood is conveyed via wine, it is of value to realize that the wine was poured at the same place where much of the sacrificial blood was poured.[43]

Concerning the consumption of wine, the laity drank it in relation to worship, especially in conjunction with the peace offering. But they did not drink from the official libation wine.[44] Even though the priests were *required* to eat a major portion of the grain offering, yet they were strictly *prohibited* from drinking the libation or any alcoholic beverage in God's courts.[45]

The following chart shows the basics of what was eaten in the sacrificial process.[46] Sacrificial blood was never eaten nor was it burned on God's altar.

---

[40] Alfred Edersheim, *The Temple...*, 101. Edersheim maintains that at times the grain offering was burned alone.
[41] Leviticus 6:16 shows how the priestly portion was indeed unleavened bread. Leviticus 2:4ff describes God's unleavened portion.
[42] Though almost exclusively wine, the libation also apparently included "strong drink", which Kleinig is convinced was beer. Kleinig, *Leviticus...*, 231.
[43] Numbers 15:2ff describe the importance of the libation after entering the Promised Land.
[44] E.g. 1 Chronicles 29:22 records the "drinking" associated with the eating of the peace offering at the temple's dedication. See also Isaiah 62:9 for the use of wine in God's courts.
[45] Leviticus 10:9 records God's command concerning priestly imbibing.
[46] For a thorough set of charts see Kleinig *Leviticus...*, 37ff.

Beginning to Sense the Lord's Supper from the Old Testament

Type of Sacrifice	Eaten by God* (On His Altar)	Eaten by People (Priests, Laity)	Biblical Institution** Leviticus:
Burnt Offering	Flesh /Fat Portions***	None	1:1-17; 6:8-13; 21:6
Public Sin Offering	Fat Portions	None	4:1-21
Private Sin Offering	Fat Portions	Priests, Flesh	4:21-5:13; 6:24-30
Guilt Offering	Fat Portions	Priests, Flesh	5:14-6:7; 7:1-6
Peace Offering	Fat Portions	Priests & Laity, Flesh	3:1-17; 7:11-34
Grain Offering	"Bread" Portions	Priests, "Bread"	2:1-16; 6:14-18

*Anything burned on God's altar was considered to have been eaten by Him.

**Additional directives are given in Exodus, Numbers and Deuteronomy.

***The "fat portions" included also those internal organs that were fat-laden. Such internal organs apparently also carried a degree of sacredness.

Beginning to Sense Sacred Eating

> *"But I have this against you, that you...eat things sacrificed to idols."*
> *Revelation 2:20*

Why would Christ be troubled over the Christians at Thyatira eating things sacrificed to idols? (Rev. 2:20) Does it make sense to say that God's people truly eat and drink Christ's body and blood in the Lord's Supper?

Specific Sacramental Eating, though foreign in that it dealt with *human* flesh and blood, nonetheless made sense to early Jewish Christians because of their familiarity with the General Sacramental Eating that involved *animal* flesh and blood in their worship practices.

The Lord's Supper also made a degree of sense to many *pagans* as well! F. C. N. Hicks explains how the participation in sacrificial-meals was even more than a Jewish worship activity, for it was practiced in regions around the world:

> We begin with the known fact that in practically every quarter of the globe religion as it emerges as such in a recognizable form is bound up with sacrificial practice. And this practice has one marked feature. For whatever reason, it centers upon a solemn act of eating and drinking.[47]

In *practically every quarter of the globe* worship revolved around *a solemn act of eating and drinking!* This common practice lends support to the belief that God Himself instituted worship-related eating even before Moses. Though man's sinful yearning for other gods twisted and warped the recognition of the true God, yet it should come as no surprise that vestiges of true worship were retained among pagans the world over, and one such vestige was the practice of worship-related eating. The fact that worship involves eating truly stands out prominently even in the study of pagan religions. Both the OT and the NT warn that eating such idol-related meals is a form of crass idolatry.

This meal-oriented "sense" of worship, clearly set forth in the OT and repeated in the NT, is missing in many Christian churches today. Many modern Christians have lost this "sense" for the sacred eating that had been retained even by many pagans, and thus such Christians fail to perceive the timeless importance of eating within the worship setting. Part of the problem may be that God's people have rarely been instructed in the basics of OT worship.

The Book of Concord, the Lutheran confessional document established in 1580, asserts: "The Old Testament had pictures or shadows of what was to come; thus this depicted Christ *and the whole worship of the New Testament.* [emphasis added]"[48] Could it really be true that the OT shadows

---

[47] F. C. N. Hicks, *The Fullness of Sacrifice* (London: Macmillan & Co.: 1946), 33.
[48] *The Book of Concord*, trans. & ed. T. Tappert (Philadelphia: Fortress Press, 1959), 257.

depicted *the whole worship of the New Testament*?

Immediately after the Christian Pentecost-event, the Lord's Supper was deemed to be so important that Christians included it in at least every weekly worship service. Joachim Jeremias explains what he and other scholars have observed concerning worship in early Christianity: "The earliest community celebrated the Lord's Supper daily, later weekly."[49] No doubt one reason for such frequency is found in the fact that Jesus lovingly included "often" in His command to do the Lord's Supper. Additionally, this frequent reception of the Lord's Supper naturally flowed from the daily and weekly Jewish sacrifices that had been eaten for centuries in a worship setting. Early Christians needed no one to explain to them that *worship involved sacrifice-related eating*. From the very beginning they naturally sensed the centrality of The Lord's Supper in weekly worship, simply because they were familiar with the OT liturgy of daily and weekly sacrifice.[50]

Christ, the Antitype

> "......*Christ our Passover also has been sacrificed....*"
> *I Corinthians 5:7*

Frequently the Old Testament has only been used to single out *direct prophecies* of Jesus Christ. A *direct prophecy* of Christ is a prediction that speaks *only* of Him.[51] As such it has no other application. Though identifying direct prophecy has merit (since the NT often does this), yet one can seek

---

[49] Joachim Jeremias, *The Eucharistic Words of Jesus*, trans. Norman Perrin (Philadelphia: Trinity Press International: 1966), 137.
[50] We will reference such regular eating in subsequent chapters.
[51] E.g. Genesis 3:15 was given by God as a direct prophecy of Christ. It spoke of no one else as the devil-crushing seed of the woman.

and find more than direct prophecy in the drama of the OT.[52] In addition to direct prophecies, there are OT "shadows" of NT realities.

The NT relates that there are prophetic shadows found in activities, people, places and objects in the OT, and these shadows foretold something about Christ.[53] Such prophetic shadows are often called *types* and the NT things being foreshadowed are then *antitypes*. A *type*, by definition, foreshadowed something that would possess similar but magnified qualities, and that thing being foreshadowed is considered an *antitype*. This is perhaps confusing to some since "anti" usually means "against" or "opposed to." A good way to grasp the meaning of *antitype* is to realize that once the *antitype* arrived on the scene, the *type* either had to fade away or be subordinated to its *antitype*. Thus the *anti*type is in a way *against* the type, because the type ceases to be the main thing. For instance Moses ceases to be the main man, for Christ is his antitype; the Passover feast is replaced and ceases to be necessary, for now Christians have the Lord's Supper as its antitype; temple sacrifices cease to exist altogether, for the sacrifice of Christ is their antitype; the eating of the temple sacrifices would also cease, for the antitype of the Lord's Supper makes such eating obsolete. The type must give way to its antitype. OT types or NT antitypes are recognized as such by their explicit or implicit identification in the NT.[54]

Consider, for example, Paul's statement in which Christ is identified as the Passover Lamb: "Christ our Passover [Lamb] has been sacrificed for

---

[52] Such "direct" prophecies of Christ and Christ alone are called *rectilinear*. One observes from the book of Hebrews as well as from other NT books that the OT worship rites were not rectilinear predictions of Christ. They first served the people of the OT in various capacities, then additionally they portrayed something similar but far greater yet to come. Thus they would not be called *rectilinear* but they would be called *typical*.

[53] E.g. when John the Baptist cried out, "Behold the Lamb of God who takes away the sin of the world," he was identifying a sin offering lamb as a shadow (type) of Christ. He was citing no particular verse but generally all sin offerings and the many OT references relating such.

[54] E.g. in 1 Peter 3:21 Baptism is the *antitype* of Noah's salvation. In Romans 5:14, Adam is said to be a *type* of Christ. Often the NT will speak of the OT types as shadows or portrayals of what was to come, frequently not using the words *type/antitype* yet truly conveying the technical meaning of *type/antitype*. See e.g. Colossians 2:16,17. Note also that *type* and *allegory* are not the same; *allegory* often employed imagination to create symbolic meaning.

us, let us therefore celebrate the feast..."⁵⁵ The Passover *lamb* thus served as a *type* and *Christ* is the *antitype* of the lamb. In addition, the Passover *feast* served as a *type*, and the *feast* of the Lord's Supper is its *antitype*. The Passover was not a *direct prophecy* of Jesus, because other than pointing to Jesus, the Passover served to remind the Israelites of the time when God miraculously led them out of the land of Egypt. The Passover event and meal were indeed types. When the antitype of the Passover *meal* arrived, the OT Passover *meal* had to fade as a shadow fades in the noonday sun. Today Christians need not celebrate the Passover meal, for it was a type, a shadow. The antitype, the Lord's Supper, makes the Passover meal unnecessary.⁵⁶

An activity, a person, a place or an object could serve as a *type*. As such it fulfilled an immediate God-given purpose, and frequently those experiencing such a *type* had no realization that it had any predictive quality. For instance, when God's people celebrated the Passover they had little or no realization how it stood as a *type* of Christ's sacrifice and His Holy Supper.

As another example consider a ram sacrificed as a guilt offering, which served to convey forgiveness to OT Jews. Many Jews perceived this conveyance of forgiveness to be the *only* purpose of a guilt offering, and thus they viewed the guilt offering not so much as a prediction or shadow of anything but solely as a worship statute ordained by God.⁵⁷ However it truly portrayed (*typified*) Christ. The guilt offering ram was thus a *type* of Christ,

---

⁵⁵ 1 Corinthians 5:7.
⁵⁶ Though we cease celebrating the Passover, yet it is very appropriate to continue to study it and to recognize what it stood for. This is also true, for instance, with Moses. Christ is the greater Moses, but this does not mean we now totally ignore Moses. On the contrary, we study Moses that we might learn the more about Christ. A type should be studied to grasp God's OT works and, even more importantly, to understand its NT antitype even better. Temple sacrifices have ceased. Andrew E. Steinmann, *Daniel*, (St. Louis: Concordia Publishing House, 2008), 475, shows how Daniel 9:27 was likely predicting this cessation of OT sacrifice. Yet we still study such sacrifice—else our book would be useless!
⁵⁷ Until Isaiah 53:10 was divinely penned, it is doubtful that Jews connected the guilt offering with the coming Savior. There perhaps was speculation, but most Jews no doubt only looked at the guilt offering as a statute instituted by God for their forgiveness.

and Christ is the *antitype*.[58] Additionally, the sacred *eating* of a guilt offering served as a *type*, and the *eating* of the Lord's Supper is now the *antitype* of the eating of the guilt offering.[59] General Sacramental Eating, which in this case was the eating of the guilt offering flesh, frequently served as a type of Specific Sacramental Eating (eating the Lord's Supper).

Recall the assertion from the *The Book of Concord*: "The Old Testament had pictures or shadows of what was to come; thus this depicted Christ and the whole worship of the New Testament."[60] These OT "pictures or shadows" are really nothing other than what theologians have called "types." In penning our present book there will be no attempt to delineate all of the many pictures and shadows (types) of Christ. Nonetheless in the midst of such prophetic pictures it will be demonstrated that there is a striking portrait of Christ painted with the brush of the Jewish sacrificial system. The hues for this portrait were derived from the palette of Moses' writings. This portrait of Christ is not only colored by the various practices surrounding Jewish sacrifice, but additional details and richness in the portrait are provided by the *place* of sacrifice, the tabernacle. This OT portrait of Christ is what this author hopes he can enable the reader to behold with increasing clarity. The portrait was the type; Jesus is the antitype—that which the portrait portrayed. John Kleinig explains the portrait painted by the OT types:

> As Moses and Aaron are types of Christ and ancient Israel is a type

---

[58] W. W. Washburn, *The Import of Sacrifice in the Ancient Jewish Service*, (New York: Phillips & Hunt, 1883), 37: "They [Jewish sacrifices] were a type--a type being a visible representation of a future truth, a truth yet to be revealed, as a symbol is a visible representation of a present truth. A type is a sensuous prediction, an acted prophecy." "Now, it is of the very nature of a type to signify the same thing, to teach the same truth, as its antitype, though under a different form and in a different way." (49). For additional explanation of Jewish sacrifices as "types" see John Leighton, *The Jewish Altar: An Inquiry into the Spirit and Intent of the Expiatory Offerings of the Mosaic Ritual*, (New York: Funk & Wagnalls, 1886). See also Kleinig, *Leviticus*, 28ff.

[59] Kurtz, *Offerings, Sacrifices...*, 285, footnote 1: "No doubt the sacrificial worship of the Old Testament does present a type of the Lord's Supper...simply in the sacrificial meal."

[60] Tappert, *The Book of Concord*, 257. NB that the Old Testament foreshadowed the *whole worship* of our New Testament time.

of the NT church, so also the various sacrifices and offerings are ordained by God as types for the sacramental and sacrificial aspects of the Divine Service. Everything that God offered to his people through the daily service at the tabernacle resembles, however imperfectly, what he offers through his Son in the ministry of Word and Sacrament...The offices and ritual enactments in Leviticus therefore prefigure [typify] the celebration of the Lord's Supper in the church.[61]

Not only is this detailed portrait of Christ displayed for Christians so that they regard with awe the wonderful prophetic nature of the OT, but in reality many important aspects of Christ's death remain veiled without the OT sacrificial portrait.[62] How, for instance, can one fully understand the purpose for Christ's death? John Leighton insightfully concludes, "...the volume containing the great facts of a Savior's death is accompanied by an authoritative key—the divine record of the law and practice of the Jewish Altar."[63] This *practice of the Jewish Altar* is a matchless key enabling Christians to unlock otherwise unknowable truths of Christ's work and words. With this key one can now better understand such things as the meaning of Christ's blood, the meaning of payment for sin, and the meaning of communing through a sacrifice-related meal. Since an OT type laid the foundation and prepared the way for its antitype, by studying a type a person can gain greater insights concerning its antitype. Unless a Christian grasps OT types, certain NT texts and concepts will remain partially or fully veiled.

---

[61] Kleinig, *Leviticus*, 30.
[62] E.g. Kleinig, *Leviticus*, (St. Louis: Concordia Publishing House, 2003), 25: "Leviticus cannot be sidelined as easily as that, for much of the NT is rightly interpreted only in its light. We depend on Leviticus for the proper understanding of Christ's death for sinners and the doctrine of his vicarious atonement which is at the heart of the NT Gospels and epistles."
[63] Leighton, *The Jewish Altar*..., 112. 113: Leighton profoundly concludes that "any treatment of gospel facts which does violence to the impress made by the Mosaic ritual is false to the truth of God and damaging to the high interests of salvation. [...] But viewing the sacrifices of Moses as typical in the sense of containing and enforcing all the great principles underlying the gospel salvation, the record of those principles can never be safely left out of sight."

But then conversely Christ Himself is the key whereby one rightly grasps the depth of meaning and the power of God in the OT rituals. For instance, how could an OT sin offering bring forgiveness? It could do so because Christ's sacrifice at the cross reaches back to endow these OT rituals with the very power of God. This is not circular reasoning, but rather it reveals how tightly Christ is woven into the fabric of the entire Bible, and indeed into the fabric of human history.

A General History of Sacrificial Eating

> *"Then Jacob offered a sacrifice on the mountain, and called his kinsmen to the meal; and they ate the meal and spent the night on the mountain."*
> **Genesis 31:54**

When Moses requested of Pharaoh that the Jews be given permission to leave Egypt and offer sacrifices, he made it clear that such sacrificing had to involve *feasting*. Moses said to Pharaoh, "Thus says the Lord God of Israel, 'Let my people go that they may celebrate a *feast* to Me in the wilderness.'"[64] This pre-Passover request, to *feast* upon sacrifice, occurred *before* God had established the official Jewish sacrificial system. This demonstrates the point made earlier, that sacrifice and sacrificial feasting reach back in history long before Moses stood before Pharaoh.

Sacrificial practices can be traced back to Adam and Eve. Sacrifice apparently began when God utilized animal skins to cloth Adam and Eve.[65]

---

[64] Exodus 5:1; see then Exodus 3:18 where God's command is to go out and offer sacrifice.
[65] Genesis 3:21. Alfred Cave, *The Scriptural Doctrine of Sacrifice and Atonement*, (Edinburgh: T & T Clark, 1890), 39. Cave (and others) sees the skins used to clothe Adam and Eve to have been from the first sacrifice. Some early church fathers considered these "animals skins" to be a reference to the fact that now the skin of Adam and Eve was the skin of animals; after the fall man seems to be but one of the animals! Even this explanation relates to sacrifice as it gives explanation as to how an animal could stand in for a human.

To obtain such skins the animals had to be sacrificed. Shortly thereafter Cain and Abel offered sacrifices to God.[66] Noah offered sacrifices, Abraham offered sacrifices, and the ancient book of Job, which obviously predates the Jewish sacrificial system, likewise records Job offering sacrifices for the sins of his family.[67]

Did such sacrifices involve eating? Some are convinced that many or even most of them did involve eating, but the records usually do not indicate one way or another.[68] One of the first specific examples of sacrificial eating is recorded in Genesis 31:54, which relates the patriarch Jacob hosting a sacrifice-related meal: "Then Jacob offered a sacrifice on the mountain, and called his kinsmen to the meal; and they ate the meal and spent the night on the mountain."[69] This record of Jacob's "sacrifice" utilizes the same Hebrew word for "sacrifice" that Moses used 400 years later in his pre-Passover request of Pharaoh to go into the wilderness to perform a "sacrifice."[70] Such sacrifices were to involve eating. It is clear already in these ancient records from Genesis and Exodus that *sacrifice* at least sometimes involved *eating*. Recall that the Jews, the Egyptians and many others around the globe knew that sacrifice, worship *and eating* were legitimately conjoined.

Interestingly the Israelites *did* get to leave Egypt, and they *did* sacrifice and they *did* eat of the sacrifice! Such sacrificial eating by the Jews,

---

[66] Genesis 4:2-8. Alfred Cave, *The Scriptural Doctrine...*, 37: "One feature of Abel's act is abundantly clear. His offering was eucharistic." We are not sure why this is "abundantly clear", but a eucharistic offering was eaten. Perhaps Cave is emphasizing thanksgiving.
[67] Job 1:5. Only the burnt offering is mentioned. It is likely that also the peace offering was sacrificed since these two, as will be explained later, are the most ancient kinds of sacrifice.
[68] One of the most ancient of sacrifices was the peace offering, which had the communion meal as its main feature. S.C. Gayford, *Sacrifice and Priesthood*, (London: Methuen & Co. LTD., 2nd ed. 1953), 32: "The Peace Offering was the most primitive form of Semitic Sacrifice." The burnt offering was the other ancient kind of sacrifice. Genesis 8:21 tells of the sweet aroma of Noah's burnt offering, an indication that God was "eating" such a sacrifice.
[69] Even before this, Genesis 26:26-30 records a covenant sealed by a sacrificial meal.
[70] Robert J. Daly, *Christian Sacrifice*, (Washington, D.C.: The Catholic University of America Press, 1978), 22: "In Gen. 31,54....the zebah is a covenant-sealing festive sacrificial meal between Jacob and Laban....In Gen 46,1 (J) Jacob offers zebahim at Beersheba.....The Exodus tradition of Exod 3,18; 5,3.8.17; 8,8.21-25 (J) uses the verb zebah for the Israelites' demand for permission to sacrifice in the desert."

officially begun at the Passover, was performed in subsequent centuries through God's sacrifice-related ordinances, which He instituted for worship within His tabernacle.

God's institution of a sacrificial system for the Jews solidified the practice of worship-related eating, and thus when the Jews participated in their sacrificial rites they knew that someone was going to eat of a sacrifice. Such eating would be done at times by laymen, more frequently by priests, and always, strange as it may sound, by God.

Consider the eating of the *sin offering* and the *guilt offering*. If the priests who officiated sin or guilt offerings were not the offenders, they were required to cook and eat the flesh from these two kinds of offerings. The directions for the *sin offering* mandated, "The priest who offers it for sin shall eat it. It shall be eaten in a holy place, in the court of the tent of meeting."[71] And of the *guilt offerings* the priests were directed, "Every male among the priests may eat of it. It shall be eaten in a holy place; it is most holy."[72] Note well the most holy eating done by the priests.

The *burnt offering*, and in fact each sacrificial portion burned upon God's altar, was considered God's "food" or, frequently in the Hebrew, God's "bread." Thus Leviticus 21:6 directs, "They [the priests] shall be holy to their God...for they present the offerings by fire to the Lord, *the bread of their God*, so they shall be holy." Note well the sacred eating done by God.

A *peace offering* was normally eaten by both priests and laity (non-priests). For instance, the laity was instructed: "Now when you offer a sacrifice of peace offerings to the Lord, you shall offer it so that you may be accepted. It shall be eaten..."[73] Note well the holy eating done by the laity.

After part of a *grain offering* was burned upon God's altar, the remainder was a most holy memorial-related food to be eaten only by the priests. The priests were directed, "And what is left of it [the grain offering]

---

[71] Leviticus 6:26.
[72] Leviticus 7:6.
[73] Leviticus 19:5,6a.

Aaron and his sons are to eat. It shall be eaten as unleavened cakes in a holy place; they are to eat it in the court of the tent of meeting."[74] Again note well the most holy eating done by the priests.

As present day worship is considered, God's people have been given the honor to eat and drink Christ's body and blood. This sacred dining will continue until Christ returns.[75] The crucified Christ *and His Holy Supper* have been revealed as the antitypes of the sin offering, guilt offering, burnt offering, peace offering and grain offering.

Christ Related His Supper to Hebrew Sacrifice

> *"Take eat; this is my body. [...] Drink from it, all of you; for this is my blood..."*
> **Matthew 26:26-28**

Many Christians today are aware of the fact that the Passover is fulfilled in Christ's death upon the cross, and that the Passover meal is directly linked to the Lord's Supper.[76] What many apparently do not realize is that Christ's institution of the Lord's Supper points beyond the Passover and into the Jewish sacrificial system. John Stephenson explains that when Jesus spoke His words of institution, "Christ deliberately took His vocabulary from the divinely instituted sacrificial cultus..."[77] *Sacrificial cultus* refers to the *worship rites* of the OT.

Certainly Christians agree that the OT sacrificial system generally pointed to *the* sacrifice of God's Son, Jesus Christ. This alone should cause Christians to relate the Jewish sacrificial system to the Lord's Supper. Christ, however, also established *specific* connections between the Lord's Supper

---

[74] Leviticus 6:16.
[75] 1 Corinthians 11:26.
[76] Such Passover relationships will be discussed in Chapter Two.
[77] John R. Stephenson, *The Lord's Supper* (St. Louis: The Luther Academy, 2003), 52.

and the OT sacrificial rites simply by the words and the ingredients He chose when He instituted His holy meal. The following discussion of Christ's institution of Holy Communion presents those specific elements that connect the Lord's Supper to OT sacrifice.

Christ Indicated the Peace Offering

Consider how in Matthew's record of the Words of Institution Jesus says of the sacramental cup of wine, "This is my blood of the covenant."[78] By speaking of His *blood of the covenant*, Christ was leading His followers beyond the domain of the Passover, because neither the institution of the Passover nor its subsequent celebrations were considered primarily *covenant* meals.[79] On the other hand, a covenant meal was directly linked to the type of sacrifice called the *peace offering*.[80] Covenants were routinely sealed by a meal drawn from a *peace offering*, and indeed the peace offering was often simply called the *covenant sacrifice*.[81]

Christ Jesus was in fact directing His hearers to a specific peace offering event. His *blood of the covenant* wording directed His Jewish audience to that lofty peace offering sacrificed by Moses on Mt. Sinai, and precisely to the very words used by Moses at the sealing of the covenant upon Mt. Sinai: "Behold, the blood of the Covenant."[82] This blood (which in the OT was never eaten), and the meal that followed upon that holy mountain, were drawn from the *peace offering* that Moses had just sacrificed. Christ's covenantal words not only identify with that special Mt. Sinai peace offering, but they demonstrate the general fact that Jesus described His death under a

---

[78] Matthew 26:28.
[79] Though there are definite covenantal associations with the Passover, to be noted in later chapters, there are no *direct* covenantal connections established at the institution of the Passover.
[80] Daly, *Christian Sacrifice*, 22: (describing particularly Genesis 31,54) "The zebah [often a type of peace offering] is a covenant-sealing festive sacrificial meal..." Daly maintains (90,93) that "selamim," a technical word for peace offering, is really best described as "covenant sacrifice."
[81] This will be explained as the peace offering is further explored in later chapters.
[82] Alfred Cave, *The Scriptural Doctrine*..., 280.

sacrificial aspect.[83] Christ was pointing beyond the Passover, clearly inferring the Mt. Sinai event, which was the seed of the Jewish sacrificial system.[84] Thus from Jesus' Words of Institution it behooves Christians to learn what the *peace offering* was about.

Christ Referenced the Sin Offering

Similarly Christ steered His Apostles and all subsequent believers beyond the Passover, as His Words of Institution bespoke forgiveness of sins. When Christ offered the consumption of His blood, He predicted that it was to be "shed on behalf of many *for the forgiveness of sins*."[85] This was definitely not a Passover theme. In the Passover celebration there was no specific offer of forgiveness connected to the blood of the lamb, but this was precisely God's offer in the Jewish *sin offering*. To the Jewish Apostles Christ's blood-related reference to forgiveness was an unmistakable indication that His Supper was to be understood in terms of the *sin offering* sacrifice. Observe how the *sin offering*, described in Leviticus 4:25,26b, clearly parallels Jesus' wording in the institution of the Lord's Supper:

> Then the priest is to take some of the *blood of the sin offering*...and its *blood* he shall pour out *["shed"]* at the base of the altar of burnt offering...Thus the priest shall make atonement for him in regard to his sin, and he *shall be forgiven*. [italics added].

This is not a Passover directive but a directive pertaining to the *sin offering*. Christ's Last Supper leads His followers to consider sin offering prescriptions such as the one just cited. When one realizes that priests were required to eat of most sin offerings, the relevance to the Lord's Supper is even more enhanced. Additionally, since all mature Christians may eat of

---

[83] Ibid.
[84] Exodus 24:4-8; Hebrews 9:18-20. Chapters six & eight will further elucidate "covenant".
[85] Matthew 26:28.

Christ's sin offering, the priesthood of believers must be considered as well.

Christ Implied the Guilt Offering

In the institution of the Lord's Supper, Jesus not only predicted his imminent death but He directed God's people to the OT when He said that His blood would be "*shed* on behalf of many." The word *shed* is in itself a technical sacrificial word.[86] Joachim Jeremias explains that the word *shed* "is taken from the language of sacrifice. It is linked with... Isaiah 53:12, 'because he poured out [shed] his life to death...'"[87] As will be explored in chapter five, Isaiah 53 specifically predicted Jesus as the *guilt offering*, not as the Passover sacrifice. Moreover, as one recognizes that priests always ate the flesh of guilt offerings, then once again one perceives an unmistakable link between OT sacrifice and the Lord's Supper.

Christ Used Burnt Offering Terminology

In addition to the above references, one finds other wording in the institution of the Lord's Supper that could easily have led the attentive Jew beyond the Passover and into his sacrificial thinking and practices. Some believe Christ's words "Do this in memory of me" connote the Jewish sacrificial system. K.O. James explains that the specific words *do* and *memory* "were related to the morning and evening sacrifice in Judaism."[88] Such morning and evening sacrifices were the daily *burnt offerings*.[89] Thus in addition to directing His hearers to the *peace*, *sin* and *guilt* offerings, Christ's

---

[86] Daly, *Christian Sacrifice*, 221. Et al.

[87] Jeremias, *The Eucharistic...*, 226. Jeremias explains how this was first set forth in second century Christianity. See also Darwell Stone, *A History of the Doctrine of the Holy Eucharist*, (London: Rivingtons, 1909), 11,12: "...the word ["shed"] suggests the pouring out of the blood of the slain victim at the base of the altar in the Jewish sacrifices, rather than the shedding of the blood in death."

[88] K.E.O. James, *Sacrifice and Sacrament* (New York: Barnes and Noble, Inc., 1962), 207,208. James gives references in footnote 56: "Ex. xxix,39; cf. Lev. ix,7; xxiv,7; Num. x,10; Ps. lxvi,15; Lock, *Theology*, 1923, vii, 284ff." Darwell Stone, *A History of the Doctrine*, 9: "'This do' may well be regarded as indicating....a sacrificial element in the rite instituted."

[89] The memorial nature was due to the grain offering that was burned with burnt offerings.

institution of the Lord's Supper has connections to a fourth type of sacrifice, the *burnt offering*.[90] Once again Jesus, in His institution of the Lord's Supper, employed wording that would have drawn a Jew to consider OT sacrificial practices. These four types of sacrifices (*peace, sin, guilt, burnt*) encompassed all of the Jewish blood-sacrifices.

Christ Used Grain Offering Ingredients

Beyond these OT blood-sacrifices, there was the *minchah* ("minka"). This was a Hebrew word usually used to reference the ingredients associated with the *grain offering*.[91] The *minchah* primarily consisted of two foods: unleavened bread and wine. Though bread and wine were also chief ingredients of the Passover, yet when the Words of Institution associated such ingredients to the peace offering, the sin offering, the guilt offering and the burnt offering, then one realizes that Christ's selection of bread and wine was not incidental. S. C. Gayford explains the connection: "He took Bread and Wine, the materials of the minchah; He spoke of them in terms of Body and Blood, the objects of the offering of animal sacrifices..."[92]

It is clear then, that with a careful selection of words and ingredients Jesus instituted the Lord's Supper to point beyond the Passover and into the Hebrew sacrificial system. However, even though the Jewish Passover and the Jewish sacrificial system may be viewed as distinct, yet the two are no doubt related. It is highly probable that the Jewish sacrificial system was *designed* to remind the Jews of the Passover, and the Passover was that seed that took root and, by God's design, grew into the Jewish sacrificial

---

[90] Undeniably, this link with the burnt offering is weak. Many theologians do not consider "This do" to have any sacrificial connotation. Even if this burnt offering link is not accepted, the links to the other sacrifices are quite solid.
[91] The word *minchah* was also at times used to speak of sacrifice generally, but in later Jewish history it became a technical term for the grain offering ingredients.
[92] Gayford, *Sacrifice and Priesthood*, 161.

system.[93] Such a line of thinking will be considered in future chapters.

Cautiously Revealing the Lord's Supper

> *"Do not give what is holy ["holy things"] to the dogs, and do not throw your pearls before swine..."*
> Matthew 7:6

When discussing the Lord's Supper, the early church was very secretive. Scholars today acknowledge that the early church practiced the "discipline of the secret." This secretive "discipline" was the practice of holding the Lord's Supper in such high regard that only those who had developed a sufficient level of Christian maturity could be taught the details of such a "holy thing."[94] One reason for this secretive practice was that non-Christians were hearing of the consumption of Christ's body and blood, and they were then accusing Christians of cannibalism.[95] Non-Christians did not realize nor were they prepared to believe that a miracle was occurring every time the Lord's Supper was celebrated. Only thorough Christian instruction ("catechesis") would enable a convert to realize the miracle of the Lord's Supper. Christians were truly eating Christ's body and blood with their mouths—but in a supernatural, non-cannibalistic fashion. Who would believe this sacramental reality except someone carefully instructed in the faith?

The early church derived such a secretive practice partly from Jesus' words, "Do not give what is holy [holy things] to the dogs, and do not throw

---

[93] Edersheim, *The Temple*..., 184: "In a sense it [the Passover], may be said to have been the cause of all later sacrifices of the Law, and of the Covenant itself."

[94] James Swetnam, ""The Greater and More Perfect Tent". A Contribution to the Discussion of Hebrews 9,11," *Biblica* 47, (1966), 96: "The fact that the early Church was under the 'Discipline of the Secret', i.e., was not allowed to speak openly about the cult of the Church, seems to be at least partially responsible for the vagueness of references [to the Lord's Supper] where references are found, and the relative lack of testimony in general." The church practiced this secretive discipline partly because pagans were accusing Christians of being cannibals!

[95] Stephenson, *The Lord's Supper*, 12,13.

your pearls before the swine..."[96] There is a very ancient Christian document called *The Teaching of the Twelve Apostles*. Often simply called the *Didache* ("didakay")—meaning *teaching*—this writing is so ancient that some believe it was composed partly by the Apostles themselves.[97] The *Didache*, which calls Holy Communion the *Eucharist*, instructs: "Let no one eat and drink of your Eucharist but those baptized in the name of the Lord; to this, too, the saying of the Lord is applicable: *Do not give to dogs what is sacred [holy].*"[98]

Like certain OT sacrificial meals, the Lord's Supper was indeed one of those "holy things" which had certain restrictions or parameters. It was not to be liberally sown like the more general Gospel message.[99] The general Gospel proclamation was to be distributed generously, like water to every thirsty soul. But the worship-oriented Gospel of the Lord's Supper was to be distributed like fine wine, only to those who had acquired the taste for it. The early church understood the danger of allowing the uninstructed and/or unrepentant to join in their sacred meal.[100] They did not want any of this sacred information to fall into the wrong hands, with the result that the faith be compromised, Christ mocked, or Christians persecuted. Once Christianity became a "legal" religion, the secretive attitude surrounding the Lord's Supper was relaxed, because the teaching of the Lord's Supper became more or less public. Nevertheless, it was and still is realized that the uninstructed and/or the unrepentant should be lovingly prohibited from receiving Christ's body and

---

[96] Matthew 7:6. The term for "holy things," (το αγιον) came to be used in ancient liturgies to mean Holy Communion. It was also used in Lev. 22:10,14 and elsewhere to refer to the flesh of the sacrifice which was to be eaten. This will be explored in chapters five & six.

[97] Johannes Quasten & Joseph C Plumpe, ed.; James E Kleist, trans. and annotator, *Ancient Christian Writers*, No. 6 (New York: Paulist Press, nd, copyright 1948), 5: "It is impossible to disprove the statement of some scholars that the *Didache* was written, if not in whole, at least in part, between 60 and 70."

[98] Ibid., 20.

[99] Jesus showed such "careless" casting of the Gospel in His parable of the sower (e.g. Matt. 13:3-23).

[100] Ezekiel 44:6,7 demonstrate from the OT the evil of allowing other faiths to God's altar. Note also St. Paul's warnings in 1 Corinthians 11.

Beginning to Sense the Lord's Supper from the Old Testament

blood in the Eucharist.[101]

Even though the earliest Christian churches did not want to publicly distribute information about the Lord's Supper, yet it is apparent that certain ancient leaders would continue to publicly teach the faithful through cleverly concealed instruction about Holy Communion in their sermons and writings. Such concealed instruction was easily recognized by those mature in the faith, but it remained hidden to non-Christians. In chapter eight, when the Lord's Supper is discussed in relation to the epistle to the Hebrews, some of this concealed instruction will be identified.

Another reason why there appears to be little written about the Lord's Supper in early Christian history is that in that era of the Church God's people needed less instruction about Holy Communion than today's catechumens. Early Christians needed less instruction pertaining to the Lord's Supper because sacrifice-related eating was commonly practiced by most of the religions of the day. Particularly to the Jews, who were familiar with the OT, the Lord's Supper not only made sense but it needed little additional explanation; OT sacrificial practice led right into this Holy Meal.[102]

Liturgy

> *"But you [Aaron] and your sons with you shall attend to your priesthood for everything concerning the altar and inside the veil, and you are to perform service ["liturgize the liturgy"]."*
> **Numbers 18:7**

A *liturgy* is a regular, constant formula or pattern used to do worship. A *liturgy* framed OT sacrificial rites, and it likewise frames today's celebration

---

[101] See St. Paul's warnings in 1 Corinthians 11:27-29.
[102] F. Gavin, *The Jewish Antecedents of the Christian Sacraments*, (New York: The Macmillan Co., 1928), 23: "...the essential germinal principles of a sacramental outlook on the universe were not only tolerated by Judaism, but even lay at its centre."

of the Lord's Supper. God ordained the basics of the OT liturgy. Liturgical scholars have noted how the OT liturgy gave birth to the NT liturgy.[103] When the Jews practiced their sacred washings and sacrifices, when they taught God's truths, and when they prayed, they were exercising the OT counterparts of the NT practices surrounding Baptism, the Lord's Supper, preaching and the prayers. To administer such OT and NT ordinances God's people utilized and continue to utilize a *liturgy*. In our study of OT sacrifice, it will be important for the reader to understand what *liturgy* is.

Liturgy: Service/Giving

The word *liturgy* especially means *service*, and in a religious sense it identified that service performed in relation to the worship of God. It is, however, not simply an identification of *man's* service to God, but frequently the word *liturgy* describes *God's* service to man.[104] Strange as it may seem, the first thing that happens through liturgy is that God serves His people! He comes to His people and gives them the blessings that flow from the Savior. This is very important to realize; worship begins with and is mainly about God giving, not man giving. Though praise and thanksgiving are an integral part of worship, these are secondary, occurring as the proper response to God's gifts that flow from His Word and Sacraments.

When the Jews used the Greek word *liturgy*, they used it almost exclusively to refer to the work of the priests and Levites as they, on God's behalf, performed God's prescribed temple rituals so the people could be forgiven, offer their prayers, commune with God and the like.[105] Through this work of the priests, God was doing "service"—bestowing blessings upon His

---

[103] See below, Aidan Kavanagh.
[104] See e.g. Aidan Kavanagh, *On Liturgical Theology*, (Collegeville, Minnesota: The Liturgical Press, 1984), 8. Note who serves, Luke 22:27, in the context of the Lord's Supper. Also 12:37.
[105] Hermann Strathmann, "λειτουργια," vol. IV, *Theological Dictionary of the New Testament*, ed. Gerhard Kittel and Gerhard Friedrich, trans. Geoffrey W. Bromiley (Grand Rapids: Wm. B. Eerdmans Publishing Co., 1968, 220: "Apart from the two pagan [biblical] instances, ...the [Greek Old Testament] reference is always to the worship of Yahweh performed by the priests and Levites either in the tabernacle or in the temple."

people. The Levites' part of the liturgy even involved such God-ordained tasks as the orderly dismantling and carrying of God's dwelling place—the tabernacle.[106] The priests performed the liturgy as they followed prescribed rituals for sacred washings, for slaying animals, for applying sacrificial portions, for burning incense, for speaking the prayers, for eating sacred meals, for speaking God's truths, etc. Such activity involved movement, clothing, locations in the temple, sacred furniture, what to say, and when to speak. The repeatedly used words, actions and elements surrounding these items made up the liturgy. Hebrew laity did liturgical "service" in the temple precincts as they responded to and participated in the liturgy of the priests and Levites, particularly as they offered their praise and thanksgiving. [107]

God had dictated many elements of this OT liturgy.[108] He commanded Aaron and his sons: "But you and your sons with you shall attend to your priesthood for everything concerning the altar and inside the veil, and you are to *perform service.*"[109] In the Jew's Greek version of the OT, the words *perform service* are literally *liturgize the liturgy.*[110] To *liturgize the liturgy* meant that the priests *administered* what might be called *Word and Sacrament* to God's people.[111] This *administration* is really *liturgy.* The liturgy

---

[106] E.g. Numbers 4:21-28.

[107] Some examples: The people responded with officially designated Psalm verses and with the official liturgical word, "Amen." They also responded by their posture, e.g. raising their hands in supplication, and kneeling. When incense was burned on the altar of incense, they offered their prayers to God. Official Psalm sections were repeated in the temple and at home during unique seasons of the liturgical calendar. Two major sections of the Psalms thus utilized were the Greater Hallel (Psalms 120-136) and the Lesser (or "Common" or "Egyptian") Hallel (Psalms 113-118). These and other practices will be referenced in future chapters.

[108] E.g. God informed the priests what clothing to wear, when and where to perform certain rites, as well as movements within and furnishings for the tabernacle/temple. Such specifics have not been given to us in the NT era.

[109] Numbers 18:7

[110] λειτουργειν τασ λειτουργιας.

[111] Herman Sasse, *This is My Body* (Augsburg Publishing House, 1959; revised edition, Adelaide: Lutheran Publishing House, 1977), 19, 20, footnote 10: "The Lutheran Church has the freedom to apply the term 'sacrament' also to Old Testament rites. [However] the New Testament sacrament is infinitely more than what would be called a sacrament in the Old Testament."

does not equal God's Word and Sacraments, but it was and is the *administration* of such Word and Sacraments.[112]

Liturgy: The Worship Setting of Ritual

Human beings (and even to a degree animals!) are ritual creatures.[113] A ritual is a meaningful bodily action that has become standardized; by definition a ritual is habitual. Concerning worship ritual, John Kleinig has noted the extremely important fact that "Religious ritual engages people bodily."[114] This cannot be emphasized enough—that worship involves the location, posture, movement and other decorum of worshiping *bodies*; it also includes the sounds, smells and food that go into those *bodies*, and the expressions proceeding from a worshiper's mouth.[115] Ritual engages the body, and liturgy helps to standardize such bodily actions.[116] The liturgy administers God's rituals in an orderly, standardized way.

God Himself established the basic worship rituals for His people both before and after Christ. When Aaron's sons, Nadab and Abihu, tried to re-invent God's OT rituals, they were struck dead![117] This was a stark reminder that the God-ordained OT liturgy/ritual was not a trifling matter.

In the OT God inaugurated numerous rituals, including bodily actions surrounding the many different sacrifices. Though *ritual* and *liturgy* are words that might be interchanged, yet the word *liturgy*—as we use it—particularly

---

[112] The word "Sacrament" is a term usually used to describe a sacred ordinance instituted by God whereby God offers His salvation. Since the term has no biblical explanation, it can be used by various church bodies for any number of sacred ordinances. The Lutheran Church usually designates Baptism and the Lord's Supper as the Sacraments. Occasionally Absolution is called a Sacrament, and occasionally (as Luther was fond of doing) the Lord's Supper is simply called, "*The* Sacrament."

[113] Kleinig, *Leviticus*..., 20ff.

[114] Kleinig, 22.

[115] Many in our Western culture have totally "spiritualized" worship so that the influence upon the "heart" is considered the only necessary part of worship, and bodily action is ignored altogether; worship ritual—even the Lord's Supper—may then be spurned.

[116] Various eastern religions—frequently being adopted today—emphasize the mind and meditation. Though God indeed desires to engage our minds, he fervently desires to engage our bodies in worship.

[117] Leviticus 10:1-3.

involves the administration of God's rituals. The Jews then appropriately added to God's ordained OT liturgy by generating secondary words and actions to administer God's ordained rituals. Some of this secondary liturgy—reverently generated by the OT church—is revealed in the OT Scriptures, and some of it was orally passed down from generation to generation. Even one thousand years after the temple was destroyed in 70AD, certain Jews could recite parts of this secondary, extra-biblical temple liturgy.[118]

God gave the Jews detailed rituals (bodily actions) in worship, and—not just incidentally—much of that ritual involved eating. Feeding one's body is of course essential to survival in this life; life implies eating. It makes sense that God would then ordain eating to be the core ritual in worship, for God is granting the eternal life-food via His worship-oriented meals.

Kleinig rightly observes that now in NT times, "When Christ commanded us to do the Lord's Supper in remembrance of him, he instituted our central ritual."[119] Though preaching, praying, confessing, praising and absolving are important components of worship, it should be noted that there is no God-ordained ritual (bodily action) associated with these, other than the words that come from the mouth. In performing these components of worship a NT liturgy was developed that—rightly so—drew from the OT liturgy.[120] The NT church, like the OT Jews who generated their secondary liturgy, has reverently generated a liturgy to administer worship ritual. The Christian's loftiest worship ritual, however, remains the eating of the Lord's Supper; Christ *did* establish this ritual (bodily action) as central to worship. The Bible and Christian history attest to this fact. This NT worship-related eating certainly parallels the OT worship rituals that involved eating as well. NT

---

[118] The Jewish scholar Maimonedes, who lived one thousand years after Christ, is one such Jew, whose writings will be referenced in later chapters.

[119] Kleinig, *Leviticus...*, 22. Some might argue that Baptism is a NT worship ritual. However Baptism frequently has occurred outside of the worship setting, and Christians can worship for months, perhaps years, without a Baptism; it is not a weekly ritual.

[120] E.g. bowing the head and folding the hands for prayer, burning incense, making the sign of the cross, kneeling, facing a certain direction to speak the creed.

liturgy is thus organized around this pivotal ritual of the Lord's Supper, drawing from OT precedent.

The Liturgy of the Household

OT Hebrew liturgy was practiced outside of the work of the priests and Levites who served in the temple, even as today's liturgy must go beyond the worship service on Sunday mornings. Jewish families had their own liturgy in their family life, because worship was a way of life. The liturgical response of the laity carried over into their public lives and into their homes.

Jewish home-liturgy done by the laity would at times be called *seder*.[121] When the Jews speak of their "Passover *Seder*" they are citing their household liturgy whereby God's ordained Passover rituals would be administered in their homes. The head of the household led such liturgy, utilizing many ritual movements and liturgical phrases. The Passover *seder* ("liturgy") in Christ's day administered such rituals as the bread-baking, the slaying and cooking of the lamb, the candle-lighting, the story telling, leading the Passover, singing certain Psalms, blending the wine, and blessing both the bread and the cups of wine. It is important to realize that Jews also practiced a prayer-"seder" (liturgy) at every meal, not just at the Passover.[122]

OT Liturgy Leads to NT Liturgy

At the very inception of Christianity the notion and use of "liturgy" was

---

[121] *Seder* was a fairly broad word, sometimes even indicating the set lectionary reading from the Pentateuch. Generally it is appropriate to understand *seder* as a word for liturgy. *Seder* is the Hebrew word for "order".

[122] Today, the ideal in Christian homes would be the observance of a regular home-liturgy—a seder. Martin Luther suggested this when in his *Small Catechism* he added the section entitled, "How the Head of the Household Should Teach His Family to Pray." Luther recognized, as established among God's OT people, that a regular pattern (liturgy/seder) for family prayer is extremely valuable and important.

natural and automatic.[123] Thus the *Didache*, that ancient apostolic document referenced earlier, calls the leaders of NT worship "liturgists."[124] In doing so, this ancient document was identifying a connection between NT worship and OT worship.

Today, when the Word and Sacrament are administered both in the church setting and in the family setting, there is liturgical precedent. The Christian Church and the Christian home did not have to re-invent how to administer God's ritual to His people. Liturgical expert Aidan Kavanagh thus writes, "Before any books of the Christian Bible had been produced, Christian liturgy had already been not only conceived within the womb of Judaism but had also been born and had grown into a vigorous youth."[125] Thus today one finds ancient liturgical texts that date to the time of the Apostles, and portions of these texts are even found in the Bible.[126]

Though OT liturgy did not dictate NT liturgy, yet it established the flow of NT liturgy. OT liturgy also instructs Christians about Christ. "While the law of Moses does not prescribe what we do in the Divine Service," Kleinig explains, "it helps us to understand how God interacts with us in Christ..."[127] Thus disciples of Christ are to be schooled by OT liturgy and rituals, as was recognized especially in the early history of Christianity.

Jewish liturgy was consistently lofty, solemn and joyous. It was not frivolous, entertaining or self-centered; but it was God-centered and reverent,

---

[123] Romans 9:4 indicates that "liturgy" is part of the heritage from the Jews. Hicks, *The Fullness...*, 226, also identifies the likely liturgical reference in Acts 13:2 which speaks of Barnabas and Saul "*liturgizing* to the Lord." On p. 292 Hicks observes (as others have noted): "In form and content they [Eucharistic Prayers] are Jewish; and the introductory dialogue between priest and people, beginning with 'The Lord be with you', and continuing with 'Lift up your hearts', and 'Let us give thanks', seems to have...a Jewish background."
[124] *Ancient Christian Writers*, James Kleist trans., 24, Didache 15. Though NT pastors should not be seen as the equivalent of OT priests, yet they should be seen as "liturgists," leading the *service*, administering God's ritual.
[125] Kavanagh, *On Liturgical Theology*, 111. Kavanagh also presents the fact that such Jewish liturgy is continually referenced in the New Testament. See also Sasse, *This is...*, 15.
[126] Probable examples: Hebrews 12:22-24 ; 1 Timothy 3:16; the many references to the "holy kiss"; frequent usage of the phrase, "The grace of our Lord Jesus Christ be with you..."
[127] Kleinig, *Leviticus*, 25.

employing the best of music and the best of public reading, and employing sacred texts to frame all rituals. This attitude flowed naturally into the NT Service of Holy Communion. The Psalms stand as a significant part of the liturgical framework employed by both OT and NT worshippers.[128]

The Christian liturgy has been firmly established through the centuries as the best way to administer God's ritual, and liturgical practice does not require regular or major revision. The nature of Christian liturgy is that it "stays put,"[129] creating a sense of historical continuity, of unity and of familiarity.[130] The liturgy demonstrates the fact that the church is not a recent development; its roots extend into the OT—before Christ's incarnation. This durable character of the liturgy then gives the intended sense that the church will outlast every fad. By dropping its liturgical heritage and adopting current fads to frame its worship, a congregation places itself on a path whereby its future *could* be cut off even as its past has been amputated.[131]

Though the OT liturgy gave birth to the NT liturgy, there are notable differences, because the OT *type* gave way to the NT *antitype*. The antitype is similar to yet greater than its type. Certainly a major difference between OT and NT liturgy is that NT liturgy is not bound by law. Christians will not be

---

[128] As will be noted later, specified "sections" of Psalms were to be sung by the Jews at certain festivals. Today Christian liturgies utilize the Psalms in liturgical responsories such as the Introit and Gradual, and additionally numerous other versicles and responses.

[129] We believe such an expression is ascribed to C. S. Lewis.

[130] It is interesting that people especially sense this concerning the *Lord's Prayer*; its *old English* wording remains constant even when other liturgical portions receive language updates, and it stands unchanged when new liturgies are attempted. The liturgy also should stay put. One six year old explained, "Its so the pastor knows what he's doing."

[131] As it stays put, the liturgy then remains familiar to children, to mothers wrestling with children, to the elderly and to others who find it difficult to read. Rote is the mother of education, and through repetition the liturgy effectively teaches key Bible passages, the Lord's Prayer, the Creeds and the like. Since it stays put, the liturgy also demonstrates that the church is not of the world, for the world craves novelty and change. If a congregation gives in to novelty and change, striving to repeatedly change its liturgical format to fit each generation's cravings, such a church can feel obligated to entertain. Entertainment cannot tolerate guilt. In entertainment oriented churches the central theme of repentance will then cease to be heard, and the Gospel—the good news of forgiveness—will ultimately fade away.

Beginning to Sense the Lord's Supper from the Old Testament

struck dead, like Nadab and Abihu, for altering liturgical practices.[132] The biggest difference is that NT liturgy directly connects people to Christ. OT liturgy, though it foreshadowed Him, did not *directly* connect worshipers to Christ; they were not specifically thinking of Christ when they did their liturgy. Another major difference between OT liturgy and NT liturgy is that today's pastors are *not* the equivalent of OT priests. Pastors today, we believe, are almost like a hybrid between priest and household father.[133] Today all Christians are priests and many are heads of their family's households, yet not all are nor can be pastors.

Liturgy: Like the Administration of a Feast

To grasp liturgy relative to worship, imagine for the moment that God's Word and Sacraments are food that must be distributed in a kingly court. Liturgy is then the total means by which that food is distributed. Liturgy is like the administration of a feast that involves several courses. One course of the feast is the absolution, another course is the reading of Scripture, another is the sermon, another is the public prayer and another is the Lord's Supper, which happens to literally involve eating. There are other courses of the feast as well.[134]

These different "courses" are the various worship rituals, with the Lord's Supper as the central ritual. The liturgy then becomes the proper preparation of those food items that need preparation, the method of serving the food to the hungry, the dinner-ware that carries the food, the placement of table and chairs, the timing of the various courses, the communication and apparel of the servers, the seating of the guests, the proper dining etiquette

---

[132] Nonetheless, note how some Corinthians became ill because they treated Communion as common. (1 Corinthians 11:30) Communion is the ritual ordained by Christ; it is not an optional element of worship.

[133] The New Testament does not have a priestly office paralleling the OT priestly office. Field, *The Apostolic Liturgy*..., 211-224, claims that the early church (e.g. Clement) uses the word "liturgus" to describe the work of the Pastor, whereas "Priest" is applied to all believers. All participate in the liturgy, but one who leads it is the "liturgus."

[134] E.g. Invocation, Creed, hymns, Baptism, reception of new converts.

taught then practiced, and even the "clean-up" when the meal is finished. The liturgy, consisting of repeated formulas and actions, insures that everything that needs to get done indeed gets done—in an orderly fashion.

As one today thinks of how the sermon is prepared and presented, how the readings are chosen, how these are read and set in the service, how one "conducts" the Lord's Supper, how the pastor is clothed and moves, how the church is designed, how sacred furniture identifies the basics of worship, how laity and pastor are situated, how certain elements of worship magnify the reception of God's Word and Sacrament, how the service is held together and flows via responsive Psalm verses, how the service ends—all of these and other practices form the *liturgy*, the means for distributing God's "feast" of Word and Sacrament. Within these NT liturgical elements there are parallels to OT liturgical elements.[135]

Warning Against Sacramental Hypocrisy

> *"Do not trust in deceptive words, saying, 'This is the temple of the Lord, the temple of the Lord, the temple of the Lord.'"*
> Jeremiah 7:4

As God instituted sacred ordinances (often rituals) for His people in both Testaments, a warning must be vigilantly heeded. It is powerfully tempting to place such high regard upon God's ordinances that *doing* them can become a person's primary source of hope. In other words, God's people must stand warned lest the very performance of God's sacred

---

[135] Though we are not commanded to have liturgical elements like pastoral vestments, altar, lectern, baptismal font, church building, etc., yet such elements make perfect sense when viewing OT parallels.

ordinances become what is worshiped.[136] Whenever God gives a means through which he offers His blessings, sadly that thing can be venerated as a sort of mechanical or magical means whereby one merits God's favor.[137]

Demonstrating such an attitude, God's OT people came to rely on the temple and on their sacrifices, instead of employing these to rely on God Himself. Strangely, they came to ignore God's unique presence in their worship even though they continued to faithfully participate in offering their sacrifices within God's temple. As they ignored God's holy presence they became haughty and unrepentant. In Jeremiah's day the people claimed invading armies could not destroy them because they were still "doing" the temple things. God warned, "Do not trust in deceptive words, saying, 'This is the temple of the Lord, the temple of the Lord, the temple of the Lord.'"[138] Similarly, as they trusted in unrepentantly *doing* their sacrifices God had to warn, "Your burnt offerings are not acceptable, and your sacrifices are not pleasing to Me."[139]

The people of Jeremiah's day had begun to think that their wickedness didn't matter, as long as they were "doing" the temple rituals.[140] The same attitude can prevail today. One of the chief signs of sacramental hypocrisy today is when people, like their OT counterparts, become convinced that their sinful lifestyles make little difference, as long as they have been baptized and are at least occasionally "doing" the Lord's Supper. God can just as easily say to such Christians today, "You have denied your

---

[136] Indeed Christ's uniquely wonderful presence should be worshipped in the celebration of the Eucharist. However, when people or pastor consider *their* sacramental activity to be meritorious, then the sacrament and even the people themselves become what is worshipped. At such times Christ's presence is in fact ignored.

[137] The Latin, *ex opera operato*, refers to such "doing" of the ordinance to merit God's favor. The *Book of Concord* repeatedly warns against such practice.

[138] Jeremiah 7:4

[139] Jeremiah 6:20. This is also no doubt the warning found in Psalm 50:7ff.

[140] See e.g. Jeremiah 7:8-10; Proverbs 15:8; Psalm 51:16-19; Hosea 6:6; 8:12-14; Amos 4:4,5; 5:21,22; Micah 6:6-8.

Baptism and your reception of the Lord's Supper is not pleasing to Me."[141]

The key then to rightly using God's sacraments is an attitude of repentance, a repentance that is not merely a one-time act but a lifelong attitude. Repentance can only be generated by God through His Word, and such repentance is an essential part of the "sacrifice" offered to God when Christians gather to worship. King David was inspired to expertly explain this repentance-sacrifice: "The *sacrifices* of God are a broken spirit, a broken and a contrite heart—These, O God, You will not despise."[142] Such sacrifice—the sincerely repentant attitude—will occur only when one is making every effort to keep God's Holy Law, and it is generated by God through His Word. When a person strives to keep God's Law, sin will continually be exposed, and that person's need for forgiveness will then be heartily realized. Forgiveness, indeed distributed through Christ's Word and Sacrament, will then cause the sin-struck heart to rejoice in Christ's cross and empty tomb.[143]

Names for the Lord's Supper

> *"And they were continually devoting themselves to the apostles' teaching, and to the breaking of bread communion, and to the prayers."*
> Acts 2:42

The Lord's Supper has over the years developed several names and titles. Many of these names, as will be shown in subsequent chapters, have

---

[141] 2 Peter 2:12-22. In verse 13 such deceivers "eat with" Christians. In Jude 10-13 feasting is referenced in verse 12. In Hebrews 6:1-8, there is "tasting" referenced in vv. 4,5. We believe these and other references likely describe the wrongful participation of hypocritical Christians in Holy Communion.

[142] Psalm 51:17. The exhortation to repent is pan-biblical. It is this repentant attitude that the godly bring to God (Psalm 32:3-6; Isaiah 66:1,2; Matthew 5:3-6; 1 John 1:7-10; etc.). Martin Luther grasped this fact as the first of his 95 theses stated that repentance is the continual lifelong attitude of the Christian.

[143] E.g. Romans 3:20ff; 7:7; 1 Corinthians 15:56.

direct connections to the Jewish sacrificial system. As revealed in the quote highlighted above, in apostolic times the Lord's Supper was immediately called the *breaking of bread*. In the Scriptures the Lord's Supper is referred to as "Breaking of Bread,"[144] "(Holy) Communion,"[145] "The Cup of Blessing,"[146] "The Table of the Lord,"[147] "The Cup of the Lord,"[148] "The Lord's Supper,"[149] "The Body (or Flesh) and Blood of the Lord."[150] Additionally, in the early history of Christianity, and—some argue, in the text of the New Testament—there are references to the Lord's Supper as "Holy Thing,"[151] "Mystery,"[152] "Eucharist,"[153] and that which is eaten from "The Altar," (thus "Sacrament of the Altar").[154] Through the centuries a popular word for Communion was "Mass," probably derived from the *dismiss*al of people before and after Communion was celebrated.[155] There are yet other titles for The Supper, but in subsequent chapters the most frequently used titles for Christ's Supper will be *The Lord's Supper, (Holy) Communion*, and *Eucharist*. We will use these interchangeably.

---

[144] E.g. Acts 2:42; 20:7,11.
[145] E.g. 1 Corinthians 10:16. The word translated "sharing" or "participation" is the word, "Communion." Acts 2:42 is likely another reference to The Supper as Communion.
[146] 1 Corinthians 10:16
[147] 1 Corinthians 10:21. As will be noted later, the "table" was another way of saying "altar".
[148] 1 Corinthians 10:21,
[149] 1 Corinthians 11:20; also called simply *The Supper*, or *The Sacrament*.
[150] John 6:53-56 and Hebrews 10:19,20 are debated as to whether they refer to the Lord's Supper. They will be discussed, to a degree, in later chapters.
[151] Matthew 7:6 has been, as stated already, connected to the Lord's Supper.
[152] 1 Corinthians 4:1. The early church so connected such "mysteries" to the Sacrament that in the Latin text for this verse the Greek word for mystery is translated "sacramentum".
[153] "Eucharist" became the most common title for the Lord's Supper in the second century. It is quite plausible that texts such as 2 Corinthians 9:11-15 and Hebrews 13:15 are using "eucharist" to obliquely reference the Lord's Supper.
[154] Hebrews 13:10. See also the comparison made in 1 Corinthians 10:18 to the Jewish "altar".
[155] Non eligible people were dis*miss*ed before Communion was celebrated. After receiving Holy Communion, Christians were also "dis*missed*" to go and live as Christ.

What About Baptism?

> *"And he placed the laver between the tent of meeting and the altar, and put water in it for washing."*
> *Exodus 40:30*

Though this book is not primarily about the "other" Sacrament, Baptism, yet there are times when Baptism is related to OT sacrificial rites. There are also texts that connect Baptism with the Lord's Supper. These two sacraments are indeed interconnected and both are depicted by OT types.

When the tabernacle is discussed in our third chapter, it will be shown that the Laver, a sacred basin resting between the Bronze Altar and the Holy Place, created obvious associations with Christian Baptism—associations noted in the NT.

At the time of Christ Jews practiced Baptism to initiate those converted to Judaism. The Jews considered such a sacred washing to be so important that shortly after the time of Christ Jewish leaders would actually debate whether Baptism or Circumcision was the essential rite of initiation into Judaism.[156]

In 1 Corinthians 10:1-2 the Apostle Paul describes how there was an OT type of "baptism" when the children of Israel were saved at the Red Sea. It is no coincidence that later in this chapter of First Corinthians the Apostle Paul then explains a connection between the Lord's Supper and OT sacrifice. In this section of First Corinthians the Apostle says of Baptism, "For I do not want you to be unaware, brethren, that our fathers were all under the cloud, and all passed through the sea; and all were baptized into Moses in the cloud and in the sea."[157] This text declares that children of Israel were *baptized into Moses*, which indicates that they were connected to Moses and his deliverance.

---

[156] F. Gavin, *The Jewish Antecedents...*, 31. On p. 52 Gavin shows how Jews considered Baptism to be the source of new birth, thus shedding light on Jesus words in John 3.
[157] 1 Corinthians 10:1,2.

From the NT descriptions of Baptism, one can say that every time someone is baptized, something like a "Red Sea deliverance" occurs, only it is a deliverance based on and drawn from Jesus, not Moses. The NT thus appropriately declares that instead of being baptized *into Moses*, God's people are baptized *into Christ*. Thus in Baptism Christians are connected to Christ and to His deliverance.[158] Moses and the Red Sea deliverance are types; Christ and NT Baptism are their antitypes.

While this book emphasizes the Lord's Supper, this does not mean Baptism is unimportant. Through Baptism God places a person into Christ's lifeboat, and through Holy Communion God feeds that person as he is tossed about on the perilous ocean of life. The lifeboat entered into by Baptism is, so to speak, the floating cross of Christ, to which, at times, Christians must be lashed or even nailed for their own good. Through Baptism God conforms a Christian's life to Christ's.[159] While in this lifeboat the Christian's heavenly food is the flesh and blood of the Crucified One, miraculously multiplied to sustain and encourage all Christians—especially when they feel they are adrift. Each Christian will make it through the storms of this life because the Crucified One made it, having risen victorious; through the Sacraments every Christian is one with Christ.

By Baptism God's children have "entered" Christ. By eating the Eucharist He "enters" them. This dual entrance fulfills Christ's seemingly impossible prediction, "In that day you will know that I am in My Father, and *you in Me, and I in you.*"[160] How can Christ be in us and simultaneously we in Him? The two Sacraments become the weaver's shuttles whereby Jesus lovingly and powerfully weaves Himself into the body-and-soul fabric of each Christian. He then is woven into us and we are woven into Him, and the result is that nothing, not even the grave, can hold a Christian from heaven.

---

[158] E.g. Romans 6:34; Galatians 3:27; Colossians 2:12.
[159] Romans 6:1ff.
[160] John 14:20.

> "I have earnestly desired to eat this Passover with you before I suffer."
> Luke 22:15

Chapter Two

THE PASSOVER, PREFACE TO THE LORD'S SUPPER

It is essential to relate the Lord's Supper to the Passover feast, because the night Jesus instituted the Lord's Supper He was leading twelve of His Jewish brethren in precisely that feast.[1] There is therefore a distinct correlation between the Passover and the Lord's Supper. Christ's deliverance of mankind is the antitype of the Passover *deliverance*, and the Lord's Supper is the antitype of the Passover *meal*. Saint Matthew introduced that night of the Lord's Supper by explaining, "Now on the first day of the Feast of Unleavened Bread the disciples came to Jesus saying, 'Where do you want us to prepare for you to eat the Passover?'"[2]

The evening when Christ instituted the Lord's Supper came to be called Maundy Thursday. "Maundy" was likely derived from the Latin, *mandatum*, a commandment of God.[3] On that night, one of Christ's primary

---

[1] There is scholarly debate whether Jesus instituted the Last Supper during a Passover feast. Many biblical scholars yet agree that Jesus was leading a Passover celebration, and the synoptic texts fully support this. For a review of scholarly opinions see Jerome Kodell, *The Eucharist in the New Testament*, (Collegeville, MN: The Liturgical Press, 1988), esp. 22ff. "For the Synoptics the Supper is a Passover meal, taking place on the first evening of Passover..." (19). For a defense of the Passover position see Alfred Edersheim, *The Temple:Its Ministry and Services* (Peabody, MS: Hendrickson Publishers, 1994), 311ff.
[2] Matthew 26:17. The Passover marked the beginning of the Feast of Unleavened bread.
[3] That night Jesus gave several commands. E.g., to love, to pray, to do as He did with the washing of the feet; but especially we think of the Eucharistic command, "Do this."

commands was, "Do this." He gave this gospel mandate concerning the meal He was instituting. Christians henceforth were to do *this* holy meal, as opposed to doing the Passover meal.

In Saint Luke's Maundy Thursday account Jesus highlighted the importance of eating the Passover on that particular night by declaring, "I have earnestly desired to eat *this* Passover with you before I suffer."[4] Jesus instituted the Lord's Supper near the end of that Passover meal. This is demonstrated by the fact that Luke describes Christ sharing one of the official Passover cups of wine before presenting that unique cup of the new testament.[5]

Several books and studies have been compiled in recent years maintaining that Christ is portrayed in the *modern* Passover rituals.[6] The problem with such studies, however, is that some (perhaps many) of the Passover rituals performed at the time of Christ are unknown, and in fact numerous scholars are convinced that several of the Passover rituals of Christ's day were significantly different from today's Passover rituals.[7] As a major example, consider that at the time of Christ all Passover lambs were sacrificed in the temple, but in today's orthodox Jewish Passover celebrations *no lambs are sacrificed or eaten!* Jews do not eat Passover lambs today

---

[4] Luke 22:15.

[5] Luke 22:17. This was likely the first of four Passover cups of wine. See further discussion below.

[6] Though the Passover Seder was not perceived to be predictive, yet the feast did communicate the ever-pervasive Messianic hope of the Jews. Many Jews did view the Christ as a main topic of the OT, but they did not see their Passover or any other sacred ritual to be typical of Christ. This is why they totally missed the centrality of His crucifixion. Alfred Edersheim, *The Temple: Its Ministry and Services* (Peabody, MS: Hendrickson Publishers, 1994), 181: "No other service contains...so many allusions to the Messianic hope, as the liturgy for the night of the Passover now in use among the Jews [a remolded remnant of what was in use in Christ's time]." As Christ's death and resurrection unfolded it became clear to early Christians that the Passover and other Jewish rituals were shadows of Christ (Colossians 2:16,17)

[7] Edersheim, *The Temple*..., 182: "The present Passover liturgy contains comparatively very few relics from New Testament times, so also the present arrangement of the Pascal table evidently dates from a time when sacrifices had ceased."

because there is no temple in Jerusalem.[8]

Certain rituals found in modern Passover celebrations are intriguing, and surely some—perhaps most—of these rituals have roots extending back to Christ. Yet because of a lack of clear evidence, we will not try to connect the details of the modern Passover rituals with Christ.[9]

The Importance of the Passover Feast

> *"...You shall celebrate it as a feast to the Lord; throughout your generations you are to celebrate it as a permanent ordinance."*
> *Exodus 12:14*

To the Israelites the feast of Passover was extremely important. Since the Lord's Supper replaces[10] the Passover feast, then the Lord's Supper must be supremely important. In the following discussion follow the logic that if the *type* was perceived to be great, then its *antitype* must be tremendous.

The Passover feast was instituted by God to be a memorial meal reminding God's people that He miraculously delivered them from Pharaoh and from slavery to the Egyptians.[11] After the Israelites had lived in Egypt for four hundred years, God sent a deliverer—Moses—who approached Pharaoh with a simple request: "Thus says the Lord, the God of Israel, 'Let my people

---

[8] Though it is true that in some places Jews eat lamb at Passover, yet *no lambs are officially sacrificed in the Jewish temple*, for this cannot happen. Orthodox Jews strictly forbid eating lamb at today's Passover meals.

[9] Kevin Howard and Marvin Rosenthal, *The Feasts of the Lord,* (Printed in the United States, no printer specified, 1997), 60ff. Howard and Rosenthal give evidence that the Jewish Passover was in fact Christianized in the first century to reflect its fulfillment in Jesus of Nazareth! E.g. "afikomen" is Greek (not Hebrew!), meaning, "I came", (p. 61).

[10] From other perspectives the Lord's Supper can be seen to *fulfill* the Passover or to *continue* it on a higher plane.

[11] Exodus 12:1ff

go that they may celebrate a feast to me in the wilderness.'"[12] In this request, Moses asked for a *feast*, a sacred dinner. Moses later expanded upon this request by explaining to Pharaoh, "Thus says the Lord, 'Let my people go that they may serve [worship] Me.'" Serving God was often equated with worshiping Him.[13] These requests to *feast* and to *serve* were united in the concept of *sacrifice*; for God had originally told Moses to ask Pharaoh, "The Lord, the God of the Hebrews, has met with us. So now, please, let us go a three days' journey into the wilderness, that we may *sacrifice* to the Lord our God.'"[14] These petitions that Moses presented to Pharaoh illustrate a critical point in our study—that *feasting and worshiping are bound together in sacrifice*.[15] Moses' requests additionally demonstrate that even before the Passover there was the reality of sacrifice-derived, worship-related eating. The requests are also significant to our study of Holy Communion, because they demonstrate that the showdown between God and Pharaoh was put into motion over the right and necessity of the Israelites to worship God by eating a sacrifice-related meal.

After God sent nine plagues upon Egypt, Pharaoh still would not let God's people go to celebrate a sacrificial feast. So finally God gave a tenth plague, which would also be the awesome event generating the commemorative feast of *Passover*. Embedded in this final plague was God's command that Jewish families each eat a Passover lamb, and through this lamb and his blood they would experience deliverance. When the tenth plague fell upon the Egyptians, death *passed over* the homes of the faithful Jews, but death entered the homes of the faithless Egyptians, and all of their

---

[12] Exodus 5:1. The word used for "feast" in this verse was employed in the Scriptures for the subsequent Passover feasts (Exodus 12:14) and other sacred feasts (Exodus 23:14).

[13] Exodus 8:1, 20; 9:1. Moses repeats this request. The Hebrew for "serve" is used at times as a synonym for "worship."

[14] Exodus 3:18; 5:3, 8, 17; 8:8, 21-25. The Hebrew word used in these verses for *sacrifice*, (here a verb, also often in noun form) was commonly used for the peace offering sacrifice. The primary characteristic of Peace Offerings is that *they were eaten* by the offerer. The word (as a noun) is first used in Scripture in Genesis for the covenant-sealing sacrifice and subsequent meal shared by Jacob and Laban (Gen. 31:54).

[15] See also Exodus 10:23-26.

firstborn died. At the heart of this deliverance were the issues of life and death, belief and unbelief. After this fateful plague, Pharaoh literally drove the Jews from the land of Egypt. The Passover was God's monumental act of deliverance, and it marked the beginning of the official Jewish sacrificial feasts ordained by God. With that first Passover feast, the sacrificial feasting requested by Moses was begun.

The following ten points mark the tremendous importance attached to the Passover deliverance:

1. The Passover deliverance had been predicted by God 500 years before it happened.[16]

2. God himself performed the deliverance, not Moses or Aaron.[17]

3. God emphasized the importance of this Passover deliverance when He recast the Jewish calendar, making the month of the Passover the beginning of every year.[18]

4. When God gave the directives for the initial Passover deliverance, He declared that the children of Israel should observe a yearly feast as a memorial of it.[19]

5. God would further draw attention to the Passover deliverance as He singled out the firstborn. Since the firstborn of Egypt were stricken, and by God's grace the firstborn of Israel were saved, God declared that henceforth all Israel's firstborn males, of man and beast, belonged to Him. With God now owning these firstborn sons of Israel, they had to be redeemed (bought from or else given back to God) by the child's parents.[20]

---

[16] Genesis 15:13,14.
[17] Exodus 7:5
[18] Exodus 12:1-13. The Jews recognized both an ecclesiastical new year (beginning with the Passover month, Nisan) and a civil new year, Rosh Hashana, which began with the seventh ecclesiastical month, Tishri. Edersheim, *The Temple...*, 158.
[19] Exodus 12:14. For those unable to celebrate it on its usual date, God allowed the Passover to be celebrated one month later (Numbers 9:1-14 ; 2 Chronicles 30:2,15). This allowance was granted for no other Jewish festival, again demonstrating the primacy of the Passover.
[20] Exodus 13:13b-15. The price of "redemption" was later transferred to the Levites who were wholly dedicated to God, and the redemption of a firstborn son who was not a Levite amounted to 5 shekels, this money then going to the Levites. Numb. 3:44-51.

The Passover, Preface to the Lord's Supper

6. Again God would emphasize the Passover by declaring that the tabernacle responsibilities delegated to the Levites were founded upon the Passover deliverance of the firstborn.[21]

7. As will be discussed throughout this book, Israel's sacrificial system was cast in the shadow of the Passover deliverance.[22] The sacrificial rites were thus, to a degree, derived from the Passover. From this alone one perceives the far-reaching influence of the Passover.

8. Throughout the OT, God would repeatedly remind His people of His Passover deliverance. Perhaps the most notable reminder is the introduction to the Ten Commandments: "Then the Lord spoke all these words saying, 'I am the Lord your God, who brought you out of the land of Egypt, out of the house of slavery."[23] What should motivate God's people to obey His commandments? The motivation would be God's unprecedented Passover deliverance, at which Israel was really born as a nation.

9. The Jews demonstrated the importance of the Passover by their view of history. As the Jews reviewed their past, they concluded that many of the noteworthy events associated with Judaism occurred at the very time of the Passover.[24] Thus it was believed to have been the time of Passover when Abraham encountered the heavenly guests, when the walls of Jericho fell, when Assyria was miraculously overtaken, when Daniel interpreted the handwriting on the wall, etc.[25]

10. Finally, the importance of the Passover deliverance was magnified as

---

[21] Numbers 3:12,13

[22] For example Edershiem, *The Temple*, 184: "In a sense it [the Passover] may be said to have been the cause of all the later sacrifices of the Law, and of the Covenant itself [no doubt referring to Exodus 24]." Later in this chapter the Passover connections with the sacrificial system will be summarized.

[23] Exodus 20:1,2

[24] Robert J. Daly, *Christian Sacrifice* (Washington, D.C.: The Catholic University of America Press, 1978), 203. Daly points to the fact that Abraham's offer of Isaac (The "Akedah") was foundational to the understanding of the Passover (175ff). Daly contends the "Akedah" was foundational to all Jewish theology, and, "The Eucharistic inaugurative command...must be seriously considered as possibly drawing on the richness of the Akedah." (185).

[25] Edersheim, *The Temple*, 180-181.

it was woven into the Jewish understanding of the end times. Concerning the end times, the original Passover...

> is taken by the Jewish tradition to be the model or archetype of the final salvation event to take place at the end of history. This theme was taken up and developed further by post-biblical Judaism until it had become a religious commonplace by the time of Christ and the Apostles.[26]

It seems that one cannot overestimate the value placed by the Jews upon their Passover deliverance. As amazingly important as the Passover was, Christ, by His crucifixion and resurrection, was fulfilling and then displacing the Jewish Passover in terms of importance! The antitype displaces its type.

The value connected to the Passover *feast* correlated with the value placed upon the Passover *deliverance*. If the original Passover feast and subsequent Passover feasts were so highly esteemed, then the feast of the Lord's Supper must be superlatively important as it replaces this ancient, highly regarded memorial meal. Even as Christ's deliverance via the cross and empty tomb is the antitype of the Passover deliverance, so too the Lord's Supper is the antitype of the Passover feast. The type must give way to the antitype. The Lord's Supper is as much greater than the Passover feast as Christ is greater than His shadow.[27]

To eat the original Passover meal was to eat deliverance. To eat of subsequent Passover feasts was to communicate God's powerful Passover deliverance, but none of these later Passover feasts actually conveyed

---

[26] Daly, *Christian Sacrifice*, 202. "The Paschal Christology of the Early Church was deeply indebted to the Jewish understanding of this feast, especially for the idea of the Passover as a sacrifice involving the meta-historical dimensions of past, present and future..." (207).
[27] Colossians 2:16,17

deliverance.[28] Every Lord's Supper, however, actually conveys deliverance! Unlike the yearly Passover feasts, to eat of *any* Lord's Supper at *any time* in history, is to eat of the deliverance at the cross, a deliverance that frees people from sin, Satan and everlasting condemnation. The reason the Lord's Supper conveys deliverance is found in the fact that in *every* Lord's Supper the partakers are actually receiving the very body and blood of *the* Passover Lamb, Jesus; for this is what He had promised. If the OT Passover was the great *deliverance* of the Israelites, how much greater is the *deliverance* given by the body and blood of Jesus Christ through His death upon the cross? Now Christ's once-sacrificed body and blood, miraculously given to His people to eat in the Eucharist, deliver them from enemies that far transcend the enemies from which the Passover delivered the Israelites. The deliverance from sin, eternal death and the power of the devil, should cause one to marvel at the value of the Lord's Supper, which—every time it is celebrated—conveys the salvation of the cross.

It was obviously no coincidence that the Lord's Supper was instituted on the night the Jewish Passover was being celebrated. It was God's plan. It was God's fulfillment. It was God's way of magnifying Christ *and* His new sacred meal.

---

[28] Such recollection in the Passover feasts was more than a mere mental exercise. Daly explains: "The [Passover] liturgy, however, did not merely recall, it also actualized or "made present" the exodus event, making of it in a real sense, a present reality for those taking part in the feast. . . . Dt. 16,3 and 6 reinforce the idea that the participants in the rite of the Pasch are by that fact themselves participants in the historical Exodus." (199, *Christian Sacrifice*). We add, however, that each Passover meal following the original was *not a deliverance meal*; it had *no power* to deliver from anything. This understanding fit OT sacrifices as well.

Deliverance Through the Lamb's Body and Blood

> *"And they shall eat the flesh that same night, roasted with fire, and they shall eat it with unleavened bread and bitter herbs."*
> Exodus 12:8

Deliverance is certainly the key theme of the Passover. Consider now God's means of deliverance, the lamb.

On the night of the actual Passover (Ex. 12:1-13), God directed each family of the Children of Israel to take a flawless, yearling lamb. After slaying it, they were to place its blood on the doorposts and lintel of their home, and then roast and eat the lamb's flesh. As a result, death would "pass over" their homes, and the firstborn would be spared. Note well that God had commanded each Passover lamb to be a male in its prime (a year old), without blemish—which meant it could have no deformities, scars, broken bones, or other imperfections.

This Passover lamb was a type of Christ Jesus. He is without blemish, only in a far greater sense in that He is without sin. Jesus is "one who has been tempted in all things as we are, yet without sin."[29] The Apostle Peter identified Jesus as the unblemished sacrificial lamb when he was inspired to write, "…you were not redeemed with perishable things like silver or gold from your futile way of life inherited from your forefathers, but with the precious blood, as of a *lamb unblemished and spotless*, the blood of Christ."[30] John the Baptist identified Jesus as the perfect sacrificial lamb when he declared, "Behold the *lamb of God* who takes away the sin of the world."[31] It is true that these two verses just cited only generally depict Christ as a sacrificial lamb. Yet the connection between the Passover and the Jewish sacrificial system justifies applying such verses to any sacrificial lamb,

---
[29] Hebrews 4:15b
[30] 1 Peter 1:18,19. The Passover deliverance required that henceforth a firstborn donkey, an unclean beast of burden, had to be *redeemed by a lamb*. (Ex. 13:13). Is this teaching something about us?
[31] John 1:29.

including but not limited to the Passover lambs. Moreover, Saint Paul explicitly identified Christ as the Passover lamb when he explained, "Christ, our Passover [lamb] has been sacrificed for us."[32]

Christ's death upon the cross was depicted by the prescribed treatment of the Passover lambs. The Passover lamb could have no broken bones, either before or during the meal. "You are not...to break any bone of it," the Israelites were directed.[33] St. John records Jesus' death as a fulfillment of this prophetic picture: "For these things came to pass that the Scripture might be fulfilled, 'Not a bone of Him shall be broken.'"[34] When the Apostle John also highlighted the piercing of Christ's heart, this too was likely a Passover referent, because the Jewish prescription for sacrificing the Passover lambs was to "slit the heart and let out its blood."[35]

There was a set household liturgy for the Passover, and this liturgy was called the *Seder*. According to one understanding of the Passover Seder of Christ's day, the last thing eaten had to be the lamb; no other solid food was to enter the mouth. Alfred Edersheim represents this viewpoint, and he explains that after eating the lamb "nothing was to be eaten, so that the flesh of the Paschal Sacrifice might be the last meat partaken of."[36] According to this viewpoint, when the Jews had thus finished eating the lamb, the head of the household concluded the meal with the third Passover cup of wine (the *Cup of Blessing*).[37] Jesus, according to Edershiem, after *completing* the

---

[32] 1 Corinthians 5:7
[33] Exodus 12:46; Numbers 9:12
[34] John 19:36. Daly, *Christian Sacrifice*, 207, calls this "the very obvious Paschal reference." John may have been referencing Psalm 22:17 and Psalm 34:20 as well.
[35] Daly, *Christian Sacrifice*, 206: "The piercing of Christ side in John 19:34 recalls the Mishnah prescription to 'slit the heart and let out its blood'---Tamid 4.2. [ref. Danby, 585]." Whether this slew the lamb or was prescribed to drain its blood, we do not know. It must be understood that the Roman soldier, a professional killer, knew just where to thrust his spear into Christ's side so that His heart would be pierced and His death would be assured.
[36] Edersheim, *The Temple,* 191. Edershiem notes how this again marks a difference with post-temple Passover meals. In such meals, precursors of modern Passover celebrations, the last thing eaten was the *aphikomen*, the final unleavened cake.
[37] The fourth cup of wine would be consumed while joining in the final hymn—the concluding Hallel of Psalm 115-118 (The entire Hallel was 113-118). See Edersheim, *The Temple*, 192.

Passover meal, but before the third cup was consumed, invited the disciples to eat additional food, unleavened bread. Of that bread Jesus said, "Take, eat; this is my body." Jesus *seemed* to be breaking Seder regulations, but in reality He was not breaking the Seder rubric. For still the last thing being eaten was *the* Lamb, *the body* of the Passover victim, Jesus Himself! This is so because Jesus had declared, "This is my body."

Others maintain that Jesus instituted the bread related portion of the Eucharist toward the end of, but still during, the eating of the Passover meal.[38] If this was the case, then Jesus again broke from strong Passover tradition. According to this timing for the institution of the Lord's Supper, Jesus spoke when he should have remained silent. Joachim Jeremias explains, "During the distribution [of the Passover meal], which normally took place in silence, Jesus spoke the words of interpretation."[39] Such speaking by Jesus, as Jeremias notes, would have drawn stark attention to what He was saying, for there should have been silence. Thus the bread-related words of the Lord's Supper, whether spoken after or during the final stage of the Passover meal, stood out quite prominently to the Jewish Apostles present that evening. By such timing in the Passover Seder, Jesus emphasized the reality of His declaration, that they were truly eating His body, the body of the Passover Lamb.[40]

Another important connection between Christ's sacramental bread and the Passover lamb is again found in Jesus' seemingly simple words, "This is my body." Certain knowledgeable Jews would have readily related such a statement to the Passover lamb, because in rabbinic circles the

---

[38] The common translation of Matthew 26:26 supports this view: "While they were eating..."
[39] Joachim Jeremias, *The Eucharistic Words of Jesus,* (London: SCM Press, 1966), 109.
[40] Shortly after instituting the bread-related meal in which His body is miraculously consumed, Christ then took the third Passover chalice of wine, the *Cup of Blessing,* and invited all present to drink of it, for it is His blood. The fourth and final cup of wine was then consumed as they joined in the closing hymn, which the seder prescribed to be Psalms 115-118. Matthew 26:30 is likely referencing this common Hallel hymn of Psalms 115-118.

Passover lamb was at times designated simply as "his body."[41] We, like the disciples, eat of the Lamb ("His Body") when we eat the bread of the Lord's Supper!

Jesus is the Passover Lamb, and, consistent with the OT Passover celebrations, His family truly feasts upon the Lamb. If Christ wanted merely to *symbolize* (not really eat) His body in the Lord's Supper, He no doubt would have continued to require that Christians eat literal lamb (mutton), the substance that clearly typified Christ in every Passover meal.

Eating Christ's body in The Supper transcends the kind of eating that occurred when God's people ate the OT Passover lambs. Those partaking of Christ do not taste or chew or digest his flesh as if they were cannibals. Communicants taste and chew and digest the bread of His Supper, and while doing so they reverently trust Christ's words that in some transcendent way their mouths consume His true body as they eat of the bread.[42]

Martin Luther, reflecting the belief of early church Fathers, explained that, consistent with Jesus' own words, each Christian should believe that the *entire* body of Christ is consumed every time an individual eats the Eucharist:

> When you receive the bread from the altar, you are not tearing an arm from the body of the Lord or biting off his nose or a finger; rather, you are receiving the entire body of the Lord; the person who

---

[41] Edersheim, *The Temple*, 182: "But the words [of Institution]...come with strange sound when we find in Rabbinical writings the 'Passover Lamb' designated as 'His body'..." Edersheim then footnotes, "The Words of the *Mishnah* (Pes. x.3) are: 'While the Sanctuary stood, they brought before him his body of (or *for*) the Passover.'"

[42] The Greek word for "bread" is a masculine noun. In normal usage, *this*, in referring to the bread, should also be masculine. When Jesus held the bread and said of it, "*This* is my body," the Greek reflects a strange change in gender. In all four accounts the Gospel writers put Jesus' words into Greek by using the *neuter* word for "this" instead of the *masculine*. Such wording was grammatically inconsistent, unless "this [bread]" means that "this" is a new thing, *more than just bread*. The Greek for "body" is indeed neuter. *This* "bread" is now to be recognized as His body! Thus Jesus is implying that "this" bread is something new! It is sacramental bread, it is Christ's body. Luther stated it this way: "It is no longer mere bread of the oven but bread of the flesh, or bread of body, that is, bread which is sacramentally one with Christ's body." For this quote and discussion see R.C.H. Lenski, *The Interpretation of St. Matthew's Gospel*, (Minneapolis: Augsburg Publishing House, 1943), 1025, 1026.

comes after you also receives the same entire body, as does the third and the thousandth, on forever and ever.[43]

Tasting, chewing and digesting all imply consuming, breaking down and using up nutrients for physical nourishment. Communicants of course do this with the bread of Holy Communion, but they do *not* need Christ's flesh for physical nutrition, and He does not offer it to His people for this purpose. People need His flesh for eternal salvation. This is why He gives believers His flesh, so that when they eat His body in the Sacrament their souls *and bodies* are uniquely nourished unto eternal life. But the nourishment is not with nutrients for the body's upkeep, but with the transcendent nutrition of forgiveness, life, salvation and the guarantee of bodily resurrection.[44] These are conveyed by the very flesh of Jesus, the sacrificed Lamb, into the body and soul of all who eat this sacred meal.

Even as eating the original Passover lamb conveyed deliverance, but *not* by virtue of nutritional value, so the eating of Christ's body conveys an even greater deliverance, a deliverance based upon absolutely no earthly nutrients contributed to the body. We neither eat Christ's body for taste nor for physical nutrition, but that we might eat salvation. In relation to this it is insightful to realize that the Lord's Supper has *never* been celebrated with a dead Christ. Thus He is not to be viewed so crassly as a piece of meat from a sacrificed, dead lamb. He is to be viewed as the Lamb, slain from the foundation of the world—the Lamb that was slain but is now alive forevermore![45] Of *this* Lamb God's people miraculously eat, and, as with the bread that fed the 5,000, He is not depleted.[46]

---

[43] See John R. Stephenson, *The Lord's Supper* (St. Louis: The Luther Academy, 2003), 248ff for this quote and further discussion.
[44] Stephenson, *The Lord's Supper*, 200ff; 201: "Luther [and the ancient Fathers] proclaimed the bodily benefit imparted in the sacrament of the altar, which will be manifested on the Last Day, and which is now received in faith and hope." This describes the resurrection of the body.
[45] Revelation 1:18; 13:8
[46] John 6:1ff

In addition to lamb's flesh, the original Passover event dealt with lamb's blood—but the people were forbidden to drink such blood. Only God, the giver of life, had the right to receive a creature's life-blood back to Himself.[47] For the original Passover, the lambs' blood was placed on the doorposts and lintel of Jewish homes. For the Passover celebrations thereafter, it is apparent that no blood would be placed upon the doorjambs of a person's home. After the tabernacle (and later the temple) was erected, God directed that the slaying of Passover lambs be an official sacrificial rite to be carried out in God's House, with the Passover blood reverently shed at the base of the Bronze Altar.[48] Such a practice surely demonstrated the connectedness of the Passover with the Jewish sacrificial rites. Thus the blood of Passover lambs, together with the "left over" blood of other temple sacrifices, had to be poured at the base of God's altar.[49] In this way God received back unto Himself the life of these creatures as He received their blood.

Exodus 12:22 gives detailed direction concerning the application of the Passover blood for the *original* Passover event: "And you shall take a bunch of hyssop and dip it in the blood which is in the basin, and apply some of the blood that is in the basin to the lintel and the two doorposts." The hyssop was a bushy, hairy-leafed plant with a minty aroma.[50] After the basin of the lamb-blood was placed on the floor in the doorway, the leafy hyssop would be placed in the blood. Then the blood-drenched hyssop would be lifted to draw the blood from the basin and raise it to daub the *lintel*—the top of the door frame. The blood-drenched hyssop would then be waved side-to-side to daub *the two doorposts*. By this movement, the hyssop was actually making the sign of the cross in the doorway, with the blood of the Passover

---

[47] Leviticus 17:11
[48] Deuteronomy 16:2.
[49] Particularly the blood of the sin offering was described as "shed" at the altar's base.
[50] The hyssop was later employed in certain sacrificial rites (See e.g. Lev. 14:4,6; Psalm 51:7), thus making another apparent connection between the Passover and the sacrificial system.

lamb.[51] The cross is the center of all theology. The blood of the Passover lamb was typical of the blood of Jesus Christ, and it is His blood that Christians are now privileged to drink. God has now declared that this blood of salvation belongs to Christ's people; they may now take it through the portal of the body, the mouth.[52] As the actual mouths of God's people now receive the actual *blood* of Christ, they partake of His *life*. The result is that eternal death *passes over* these believers, as surely as the OT lamb's blood caused death to *pass over* those firstborn Jews whose fathers made the bloody marks on their doorways.

Another connection between Christ and the Passover lamb is explained in the writings of Justin Martyr, an early Christian layman born around 100AD. Recall that God had commanded the Passover lamb be wholly roasted over a fire. The ancient method for roasting a Passover lamb was to affix its body lengthwise to a wooden spit. Then, to prevent the body from slipping on the spit, the Jews connected a cross piece at the shoulders of the lamb.[53] Observe then that the Passover lamb was affixed to a cross! Concerning this ancient practice, Justin Martyr wrote: "... the lamb which was commanded to be wholly roasted was a symbol of the suffering of the cross which Christ would undergo. For the lamb, which is roasted, is roasted and dressed upon the form of the cross."[54] The Scriptures had specified that Passover lambs be roasted. Even though no specific directives for cross-wise roasting may be found in Scripture, nonetheless early Christians such as Justin Martyr realized that this ritual fit the antitype of Christ's crucifixion.

---

[51] This was pointed out to the author in a class taught by Rev. Professor John Saleska at Concordia Theological Seminary, Ft. Wayne, IN.
[52] Christ declared that we are to drink of the chalice *for* it is His blood. (Matt. 26:27). "For" is in the Greek, but some translators—strangely—leave it out (e.g. NIV)!
[53] Robert J. Daly, *Christian Sacrifice*, 206: "...the animal [was] pierced length wise with a wooden spit -- Pesahim 7,1 [....] but [then] the custom of [placing] a cross-piece at the shoulder height to keep the carcass from slipping on the spit would give the animal the shape of a cross."
[54] Daly, *Christian Sacrifice*, 206, footnote to Justin's *Dialogue With Trypho* 40,3.

The Church of the Firstborn

> *"But you have come to Mount Zion...to the general assembly and church of the firstborn who are enrolled in heaven."*
> *Hebrews 12:22,23*

Recall again who died and who was spared in the original Passover. The firstborn of the Egyptians died, and the Passover lamb died. The firstborn of the faithful Jews were, by grace, spared.[55] Some fifteen centuries after that first Passover, God's Son, the firstborn from eternity, was born of the Virgin Mary to become the world's redeemer. The writer of the epistle to the Hebrews identifies Christ's firstborn status by explaining, "And when He [God the Father] again brings the firstborn into the world, He says, 'And let all the angels of God worship Him.'"[56] This firstborn dies as if He were an Egyptian firstborn, and He dies as the Passover lamb. The result is that all people might now become the fully redeemed firstborn, the ones given life and deliverance.

The Levites were the only men privileged to perform the temple liturgy. God had founded the Levitical office on the deliverance of the Passover firstborn.[57] Every Levite was considered a replacement for the firstborn of Israel, and every firstborn son who was not a Levite had to be redeemed.[58] In addition, all firstborn creatures belonged to God.[59] Robert Daly explains the depth of the Passover relationships created by these firstborn regulations. In the following quote as well as in other quotes, realize that "Paschal" and its other similar forms (*Pasch, Pascha*) are simply words that mean *Passover,* frequently identifying specifically the Passover lamb. Daly writes:

---

[55] All of Israel was identified as "firstborn" as well; Exodus 4:22.
[56] Hebrews 1:6
[57] Numbers 3:12,13.
[58] Exodus 13:13.
[59] Exodus 13:12-15.

What is of significance is that the OT ordinances concerning the dedication, etc. of the first-born (and therefore concerning also the ransom-redemption and substitution ideas) are associated without exception with the Paschal feast.[60]

What shall we now say of the "new and improved" Paschal feast of the Lord's Supper? Shall it not also be associated with the firstborn and with the redemption and substitution themes even as the Passover it supplants?

God's Word declares that every Christian (male or female!) is a "firstborn son."[61] Christ has given His firstborn status and His life to every Christian. This is by grace, which means it is an undeserved gift, as surely as God's deliverance of the children of Israel was an undeserved gift. They did not deserve deliverance, for they were "a stiff-necked people."[62] So too are all people. Though all were born in sin (Psalm 51:5), and all deserved death like the firstborn Egyptians, yet now Christ Jesus, God's "firstborn," dies so that His people might be called the "firstborn." A Christian's firstborn status is identified by the fact that God offers to each the inheritance as the "sons of God."[63] In the Jewish community, the firstborn son was to receive the main inheritance, and now each Christian is marked as that heir! When Holy Scripture speaks of the Christian's eternal inheritance, this identifies the Christian's firstborn status.

The Christian's firstborn status not only marks him/her as heir, but the OT Passover additionally identifies the need for the Christian's deliverance. Although death passed over *all* the faithful Jews on that first Passover, yet it was imperative that it particularly pass over the firstborn, for they were the ones under the sentence of death. So too now, though all of the children of Adam are under the sentence of death, yet by the blood of Christ they are not

---

[60] Robert Daly, *Christian Sacrifice*, 205.
[61] E.g. Galatians 3:26,27; Romans 8:14. Hebrews 12:23 calls Christ's people "the church of the firstborn."
[62] Exodus 32:9; 33:3; etc.
[63] Galatians 4:4,5,7; Romans 8:16,17.

only redeemed that they might *become* God's firstborn, but by that same blood they are *delivered* so that eternal death passes over these firstborn. The firstborn (all Christians) are delivered from sin, death and Satan's stranglehold.

As identified in certain ancient liturgies, a Christian's firstborn status relates directly to the Lord's Supper. There was an ancient Communion liturgy called *The Liturgy of St. James*, in which there is an important *firstborn* reference in the "Prayer of the Veil." Bear in mind that this prayer immediately preceded the reception of the Lord's Supper. Part of the prayer reads as follows:

> It is very meet...to give thanks unto Thee...whom the heavens are hymning, ... the heavenly Jerusalem, the general assembly and *church the firstborn* written in heaven, spirits of righteous men and prophets, souls of martyrs and Apostles, angels and archangels [Emphasis added]...[64]

This liturgical excerpt, dating back perhaps to the very writing of the New Testament, connects the Passover theme of "firstborn" to the celebration of Holy Communion.[65] Such a liturgy drew from or was the source for Hebrews 12:23, which, with the same wording, described the church as "the general assembly and *church of the firstborn* who are enrolled in heaven." These firstborn are enrolled in heaven because the Lamb, Jesus, has

---

[64] John Edward Field, *The Apostolic Liturgy and the Epistle to the Hebrews* (Waterloo Place, London: Rivingtons, 1882), 376.

[65] Field, *The Apostolic Liturgy...* Throughout his book, Field presents logical reasons why the *Liturgy of Saint James* should be understood to have preceded the New Testament documents. In his preface,iii, Field states that his secondary purpose is to "examine the important subject of alleged quotations from the Greek Liturgy of S. James in the New Testament."

redeemed God's children, declaring them all to be "firstborn sons."[66] The Church of Christ, by definition, is made up of those declared to be firstborn; she is the *church of the firstborn*! Certain ancient Christian Communion liturgies recognized this Passover-related fact.

God Requires Faith

> *"Without faith it is impossible to please Him."*
> **Hebrews 11:6**
> *"Let us draw near with a sincere heart and full assurance of faith."*
> **Hebrews 10:22**

In all of these matters God desires, requires and inspires faith. The faithful Jews were those who *believed* God's Word concerning the Passover lamb. Because they believed, they sacrificed the lamb, they put its blood on their doorways, and they ate of its flesh. Consequently they were spared. To those who have never heard of God's ways, this may sound ridiculous. For how can there be deliverance in eating a lamb's flesh and in applying its blood to one's doorway? But this is God's way, because "God has chosen the foolish things of the world to shame the wise."[67]

Even in the beginning God chose a fruit tree and told Adam that if he ate of it he would surely die. Many years later God told Moses that if he lifted up a brass serpent on a pole, whoever looked to it would be healed from poisonous snakebites.[68] Throughout the Bible there are examples of God choosing simple, earthly things and then connecting His Word of promise or

---

[66] There were basically two Hebrew concepts for *redeem*, utilizing two different Hebrew words. One recognized the Passover-based redemption of the *firstborn*, the other recognized the redemption of a person out of *slavery*. The Passover is connected by God to the concept of *firstborn*, but the original Passover dealt with deliverance from *slavery* as well. Both uses of *redeem* find their antitype in Christ's redemption at the cross.
[67] 1 Corinthians 1:27
[68] Genesis 2:17; Numbers 21:6-9.

threat to them. In such instances God desires and calls forth one thing, *faith*! Thus the *faith*ful Jews at that first Passover were those who *believed* His promise and followed His lamb-related instructions.

"Accordingly the sacrament requires faith," declared the Lutheran Confessors, "and without faith it is used in vain."[69] God has chosen to save mankind through the body and blood of His Son. Those who believe this wonderful fact are indeed saved! Additionally, Christ has invited His followers to eat and drink of bread and wine, promising "this is my body, this is my blood...given and shed for you for the remission of sins." The *faith*ful one is he who *believes* it just as God has said it. Christians are truly invited to eat of the Lamb! One who does not *believe* is not benefited.

Memorial Meals

> *"Now this day will be a memorial to you, and you shall celebrate it as a feast."*
> *Exodus 12:14*
> *"This is my body, which is for you; do this in remembrance of Me."*
> *I Corinthians 11:24*

When He held the bread of the Last Supper Jesus commanded, "Do this in *remembrance* of Me," and with the wine, "Do this as often as you drink it in *remembrance* of Me."[70] Jesus wants the Lord's Supper to be a *memorial meal*, a meal done in remembrance of Him.[71]

The Passover was God's first memorial meal. God had commanded, "Now this day will be a *memorial* to you, and you shall celebrate it as a feast to the Lord; throughout your generations you are to celebrate it as a

---

[69] *The Book of Concord*, trans. & ed. T. Tappert (Philadelphia: Fortress Press, 1959), 59.
[70] From 1 Corinthians 11:23-25.
[71] In chapter seven we will discuss Jesus' unique memorial language.

permanent ordinance."[72]

The Passover and the Lord's Supper are meals designed to bring God's people to remember God's remarkable acts of deliverance. Concerning the Passover feast and the redemption of the firstborn, God explained one aspect of its memorial nature: "And it shall be when your son asks you in time to come, saying, 'What is this?' then you shall say to him, 'With a powerful hand the Lord brought us out of Egypt, from the house of slavery.'"[73] By this required recitation, the people *remembered* God's wondrous act of deliverance performed at the first Passover.

When God's people would remember God's acts of deliverance, God would come and bless them. This attitude of God is summarized when He explains in Exodus 20:24, "Where I cause My name to be remembered I will come to you and bless you." When God gives a memorial token, such as the Passover, He causes His name to be remembered with that token. Then, as promised, He comes and blesses His people. This is also true of the Lord's Supper. In Holy Communion, God is causing His name to be remembered, and as such He is coming and blessing His people.

Jesus said that His Supper is a meal in remembrance *of Him*. Saint Paul explained such sacramental remembrance by declaring, "For as often as you eat this bread and drink the cup, you proclaim the Lord's death until He comes."[74] When partaking of the Lord's Supper, Christians are especially to remember and proclaim *Christ's death*.

In Saint Paul's wording—"proclaim the Lord's death"—Holy Communion again crosses the path of the Passover feast. The Greek word for "proclaim" is in fact precisely the technical word the Jews used for their Passover proclamation! In Hebrew, this proclamation is called the Haggadah. During the Passover celebration there was to be the "Haggadah," the "proclamation" of God's Passover deliverance. In this Haggadah, the Jews

---

[72] Exodus 12:14
[73] Exodus 13:14
[74] 1 Corinthians 11:26

were remembering God's deliverance by proclaiming a summary of that account. Alfred Edersheim explains, "The very term for the Passover liturgy, the 'Haggadah,' which means 'showing forth,' is exactly the same as that used by St. Paul in describing the service of the Lord's Supper! (I Cor. 11:23-29)."[75] The sermon, the entire liturgical setting, and the Words of Institution surrounding the Lord's Supper are the "Haggadah," the "Passover" proclamation. In these there is the proclamation of Christ's death, and the Lord's Supper then causes the worshipers to have a proper remembrance of Him.

Probably many Christians today consider the memorial nature of the Lord's Supper to indicate simply a personal or a corporate recollection, a calling to mind of what Jesus had done. Though this truly happens, the Jews of Jesus day would have understood biblical memorial language to indicate that *God* remembers! Joachim Jeremias explains that when the Jews observed a religious memorial, such as the Passover, they realized in their common use of memorial terminology that "it is almost always God who remembers."[76] Certainly God never forgets, but when God *remembers* something in a positive way, it means that He applies His grace and blessings. Thus the Psalmist declares, "May *He remember* all your meal offerings and find your burnt offerings acceptable."[77] With such a remembrance on God's part, the Psalmist then implied that God would answer His people in the day of trouble. God indeed instituted rituals for His people so that when they performed such rituals they were to be assured that God was remembering.

With this line of thinking, when Jesus lovingly commanded that the Lord's Supper be done in *remembrance of Him*, this would have been understood by the Jews to mean that when Holy Communion is celebrated, *God* has a *remembrance of Him*! The thing that God specifically remembers

---

[75] Edersheim, *The Temple*, 182. See also Jeremias, *The Eucharistic Words of Jesus*, 59.
[76] Jeremias, *The Eucharistic Words of Jesus*, 252. See 246ff for further discussion.
[77] Psalm 20:3. Also e.g. Psalm 119:49.

of Christ is His spectacular self-sacrifice, the fountain of all eternal blessings.

In summary, from the Passover we learn that the memorial nature of the Lord's Supper is a coin with two distinct sides. One side of the coin is the comforting remembrance of Christ's death for man's salvation, a recollection focused by the worship proclamation. God's people perform this remembrance. On the other side of the memorial coin, God remembers. He remembers His Son's substitutionary death; from this remembrance, God looks with favor upon His redeemed people. Christ's cross is the coin. On one side Christians are remembering, and on the other side, God remembers.

Though both the Passover and the Eucharistic celebrations through the centuries were memorial meals, yet they are profoundly different from each other. The Passover meals through the years have *only* been memorial meals, only proclaiming (and in a sense re-living) the deliverance at the original Passover.[78] However, the meals of the Lord's Supper have not only been memorial meals, but they have each been in and of themselves *deliverance meals*. Thus Christians not only *proclaim* Christ's death every time they celebrate the Eucharist, they also literally *partake* of His death, eating the body and blood given and shed on the cross for man's redemption. Christians eat of the Passover lamb at *every* Lord's Supper! Christians partake of forgiveness at *every* Eucharistic meal! Thus when Christ said of the Lord's Supper, "This is my body," and, "This is my blood," He meant it. Every single Lord's Supper conveys the very body and blood of the one and only deliverance-Lamb. Every Lord's Supper is a deliverance-meal, similar to yet surpassing the *original* Passover as a deliverance-meal. To eat of the Lord's Supper is to eat and drink of deliverance as surely as the children of Israel ate of deliverance on that first Passover evening.

---

[78] Such Passover recollections were more than a mere mental exercise. See footnote 28.

Does the Lord's Supper Replace the Passover?

> *"Do not think that I came to abolish the Law or the Prophets; I did not come to abolish, but to fulfill."*
> *Matthew 5:17*

In the study of Christian doctrine it is extremely important to realize that Christianity did not cancel Judaism, but it is the proper continuation of it. It is not inappropriate to make the overarching statement that OT Judaism was the *type* and NT Christianity is the *antitype*. This is so because Christ did not come to abolish the Law and the Prophets, but He came to fulfill.[79]

The Passover and the subsequent deliverance at the Red Sea (Ex. 14) are often highlighted as *the* memorable acts of God's deliverance upon the children of Israel, repeatedly referenced in the OT. God still desires that these accounts be remembered.[80] Now, however, God has established an even greater historical act of deliverance in Christ's death and resurrection. Christ has established the Lord's Supper so that those eating may literally receive the fruit of His stupendous work, not merely commemorate it. Christians now continually feast upon the one and only deliverance lamb.

The early church reflected the belief that the Lord's Supper *continues* the Passover celebration on a higher plane. This belief was attested by the fact that frequently early church writers and preachers would adopt the title of "Passover" (or "Pasch") for the Lord's Supper.[81] Christians on the one hand quickly adopted Passover terminology for Holy Communion, then on the other hand they soon ceased celebrating the Jewish Passover altogether. The Lord's Supper had thus become *the* central feast of God, the greater Passover. Robert Daly explains, "The Christian Eucharist came to be looked

---

[79] Matthew 5:17.
[80] These accounts prefigured Christ's deliverance. E.g. 1 Corinthians 10:1-2; 1 Corinthians 5:7.
[81] At times the Lord's Supper would be called the "Pasch", which means *Passover* or *Passover Lamb*. E.g. Melito of Sardis (2nd century theologian) thus commonly used the word.

upon in the Early Church as the new Pasch."[82] Alfred Edersheim rightly explains that the earliest Christians perceived the Lord's Supper to be the "better Passover."[83] Appropriately, the antitype displaces its type.

In 1 Corinthians 5:7,8, the Apostle Paul wrote that, "Christ our Passover [lamb] has been sacrificed. Let us therefore celebrate the feast with the unleavened bread of sincerity and truth." What feast were the Corinthians here being encouraged to celebrate? With the reference to Christ as the *Passover lamb* and with the context being that of unleavened bread, the *feast* for the Corinthians was assuredly a "Passover" feast.[84] However the Corinthians who were being told to "celebrate the feast," were not, for the most part, Jewish.[85] Thus the Corinthians were likely *not* being directed to celebrate the *Jewish* Passover. Instead, these Christians were being encouraged to celebrate the antitype of the Passover, the Lord's Supper. Since Paul prefaces his directive by stating, "Christ our Passover has been sacrificed for us," and since it is the very next verse wherein the Corinthians are being directed to reverently celebrate the feast of *the* Passover Lamb, then with Christ as the Passover Lamb it is apparent that the Christians of Corinth were being encouraged to celebrate the feast of the Lord's Supper.[86] In his commentary on the epistles to the Corinthians, M. F. Sadler agrees with this understanding. In the following quote Sadler not only connects St. Paul's Passover-feast reference to the Lord's Supper, but he explains that the sacrificial feasts permeating the OT are typical of Holy Communion as well:

"Let us keep the feast." In order to realize this, we must remember

---

[82] Daly, *Christian Sacrifice*, 196.
[83] Edershim, *The Temple*, 169f.
[84] R. C. H. Lenski, *The Interpretation of St. Paul's Fist and Second Epistles to the Corinthians* (Minneapolis: Augsburg Publishing House, 1963), 224. Lenski and others "spiritualize" this feast referred to by St. Paul. Why are Lenski and other commentators hesitant to refer this text to the Lord's Supper, especially in light of 1 Corinthians 10 & 11?
[85] This is inferred throughout the epistles to the Corinthians as well as from the fact that St. Paul was the Apostle to the Gentiles.
[86] In 1 Corinthians 5, St. Paul's desire for church discipline fits the traditional understanding of excommunication, banning from Holy Communion.

that every Jewish sacrifice (except one, the burnt-offering) was partaken of, either by the priests or the sacrificers. In the case of the Passover, the whole was eaten as a Feast by the people. If, then, the offering of Christ be a true Sacrifice, there must be means ordained whereby it is to be partaken of; and so there are. Christians have by Christ's own ordinance a means by which they may perpetually partake of Him as their Paschal Lamb... As the outward Passover was to them a figure of the true Passover, so its appendages were figures of the reality which we this day possess. If, therefore, we would wish to feed on Christ's Flesh and Blood, let us bring to this feast sincerity and truth.[87]

In his recent book, *The Lord's Supper*, John Stephenson explains how renowned theologians such as Luther and Krauth also maintained this Eucharistic interpretation of First Corinthians 5:7,8. Stephenson agrees with Luther and Krauth as well.[88]

Recall that the Passover received its name because death *passed over*. As the original Passover was only complete when death passed over, so too the Christian celebration of Christ's death is only complete when Christ's resurrection is part of the celebration, for in His resurrection death has surely passed over. With this in mind, certain liturgical propers for Easter Sunday have rightly appropriated Saint Paul's wording, "Christ our Passover has been sacrificed for us...Let us therefore celebrate the feast."[89] What a grand feast Easter should be as God's people eat of The Lamb, celebrating

---

[87] M. F. Sadler, *The First and Second Epistles to the Corinthians* (London: George Bell and Sons, 1898), 79f. "So the Lord's table in our churches is...an altar...[...] Christ our Passover has been slain,...and there at our altars we keep the feast." (160).
[88] Stephenson, *The Lord's Supper*, 112.
[89] E.g. *The Lutheran Hymnal*, (St. Louis: Concordia Publishing House, 1941),68, the Gradual for Easter.

the complete Passover of death![90] Still today many churches highlight Easter by igniting a traditional "Paschal" candle, a candle of Passover. Can Easter properly be observed without the Lord's Supper? This is our Paschal feast!

The Lord's Supper is the fully blossomed *continuation* of the Passover feast. Yet the early church saw Holy Communion as *more than* a Passover celebration, and that is why without hesitation they celebrated it at least weekly. Joachim Jeremias describes the frequent reception of the Lord's Supper in the early church: "The earliest community celebrated the Lord's Supper daily, later weekly."[91] This weekly celebration went beyond the prescribed practice of the Jewish Passover, which was celebrated but once a year.[92] Such weekly celebrations of Holy Communion perhaps purposely reflected the fact that the Eucharist was related to the weekly sacrificial rites performed in the temple.[93]

Christ Dining With Us

> *"I will not drink of this fruit of the vine from now until that day when I drink it new with you in my Father's kingdom."*
> *Luke 22:18*

While Jesus explains that His people will continue the Passover celebration as they partake of His body and blood, He also indicates that He is not only the supernatural *food* for the meal, but He is also the *host* of the meal, dining with His people in a new way. Such explanations and indications are set forth in the context of His Last Supper.

---

[90] The Jewish Passover has also been called Easter. *The Book of Concord*, trans. Tappert, 176: "The apostles had commanded their churches to celebrate the *Passover* with the brethren who had been converted from Judaism....they say that no one should mind if his brethren do not correctly compute the time in celebrating *Easter*. [emphasis added]"
[91] Jeremias, *The Eucharistic Words of Jesus*, 137.
[92] In the early church some tried to celebrate the Eucharist but once a year at Passover. These were called quartodecimarians, because Passover was on the 14th of Nisan.
[93] This will be explored in later chapters.

First consider Christ's references to *drinking*. In Luke's account of the institution of the Lord's Supper there is the somewhat mystical promise of Jesus, "I will not drink of the fruit of the vine from now on until the kingdom of God comes."[94] Matthew and Mark report Jesus' statement in this way: "I will not drink of this fruit of the vine from now on until that day when I drink it new with you in my Father's kingdom."[95] The key word here is *until*. When He says He will not drink it *until* the kingdom comes, Jesus implies that at some future date He *will drink* it again. By these statements Jesus indicates that at some future point, when the kingdom is established, He will indeed join His people with a worship-related cup of wine.

When in Matthew's account Jesus says, "I will not drink of this fruit of the vine from now on until that day when I drink it new," He is using *this fruit of the vine* as a liturgical reference to the *Passover wine*.[96] The phrase "fruit of the vine" was liturgical language, identifying the uniquely blessed wine of Passover.[97] By using such liturgical Passover language, the institution of the Lord's Supper is given a ritual, liturgical flavor; therefore the Lord's Supper was to be worship-related.

Within this liturgical context Jesus is promising to drink again of the "Passover" wine in a new way in His Father's kingdom. Clearly such "Passover" wine would be the wine of the new supper He is in the process of instituting. Christ is thus promising to join His people in their future worship-meals. Is this to happen already in our present era, or is this describing Christ's communion when His people join Him in heaven?

---

[94] Luke 22:18. Luke reports this statement before the institution of the Lord's Supper.
[95] Matthew 26:29
[96] Edersheim, *The Temple*..., 185, explains the extreme importance of wine in the Passover celebration: "The use of wine in the Paschal Supper....was strictly enjoined by tradition. According to the Jerusalem Talmud, ...even the poorest must have 'at least four cups, though he were to receive the money for it from the poor's box' (*Pes.* X.1)." Edersheim (and others) show the liturgical understanding of *fruit of the vine*.
[97] Edersheim, *The Temple*,187. Precisely such wording is still used in today's Jewish Passover prayers spoken over cups of Passover wine. E.g. over the first cup the paterfamilias prays, "Blessed art Thou, Jehovah our God, who hast created the *fruit of the vine*. [emphasis added]" There appears to be agreement that the basics of such prayers date to before Christ.

The word "new," as recorded in Matthew and Mark, is a word in the Greek that especially means "in a new way." Thus *An American Translation* renders Jesus' words as, "I will not drink again of this product of the vine till that day when I drink it with you in a new way in My Father's kingdom."[98] What could Jesus mean when He says that at the coming of the kingdom He would drink Passover wine *in a new way* with His disciples? In the Lord's Supper Christians are indeed drinking *in a new way,* and for the glorified Christ to join in this fruit of the vine, He must also be drinking *in a new way*!

So far the references cited in this section have only spoken of *drinking*. However *eating* is the topic of Luke 22:15,16. Here Jesus similarly promises, "I have earnestly desired to eat this Passover with you before I suffer; for I say to you, I shall never again eat it until it is fulfilled in the kingdom of God." Now, instead of referring to *drinking* of the Passover cup in the kingdom, Jesus speaks of *eating* the Passover, and, as with the drinking, He relates His future eating to the kingdom. When He says He will not eat it *until* it is fulfilled in the kingdom, He implies, as with the wine, that at some future date He *will* eat it again.

Christ said He would again both eat and drink the Passover with His disciples when the Passover was 1) *fulfilled* in the kingdom and 2) when the kingdom would *come*. Though *fulfillment* and *coming* of the kingdom may be describing the same event, consider the following differentiation. The Passover was *fulfilled* in the kingdom when Jesus, the Passover Lamb, was sacrificed, and when death passed over in His resurrection. Christ's gifts of salvation were fully generated with this fulfillment. The kingdom of God would then *come* when Jesus, the great King, began to give His gifts of salvation to His people. This coming of the kingdom would begin in earnest when Pentecost arrived, at which time the Holy Spirit was uniquely bestowed, and

---

[98] *The Holy Bible, An American Translation*, William F. Beck, trans. (New Haven, Missouri: Leader Publishing Company, 1976), Matthew 26:29.

then the kingdom of God came in its fullest pre-Judgment Day measure.[99] Though God's kingdom came on that Pentecost Sunday, this was not the end of the coming of the Kingdom of God, only the beginning. Today the Kingdom continues to come as God sends the Holy Spirit through the sacred ordinances of Preaching, Baptism, Absolution and the Lord's Supper. As the kingdom would thus come, Christ said He would eat and drink with His people.[100] With this understanding, then—from Pentecost to the present—Christ has been joining His people at His greater "Passover" feast, eating and drinking with them in some wondrous way!

Whenever God's kingdom comes through Holy Communion it is apparent from Jesus' own words that He is in a "new way" drinking the fruit of the vine and eating the Passover with His disciples. Alan Stibbs thus remarks:

> We remember that at its institution the Lord looked forward and spoke of a coming day of fulfillment, and of the triumph feast in which He, obviously alive again from the dead, would join with them in fellowship [feasting]. So our eating and drinking at His table are the occasion to realize the spiritual fellowship with the risen Christ.[101]

Holy Communion must be truly remarkable, for not only is this sacred meal the fulfillment and continuation of the Passover feast, but Christ Himself

---

[99] Martin Luther Scripturally explained that the kingdom comes when God sends His Spirit.

[100] See John 7:37-39. John 20:22,23 indicate that He breathed forth the Spirit to empower His Church to remit sins (absolve). See Acts 2:14 concerning the Spirit-powered preaching. Read Acts 2:38 concerning the Spirit-powered Baptism. Read Acts 2:42 concerning the basics of Spirit-powered Christianity, including the "breaking of bread," which is the Lord's Supper. See also Matthew 12:28.

[101] Alan M. Stibbs, *Sacrament, Sacrifice and Eucharist* (London: Billing and Son LTD., 1961), 56-57. Stibbs here references Matthew 26:29 and Mark 14:25. O. Cullmann and F.J. Leenhardt, *Essays on the Lord's Supper* (London: Lutterworth Press, 1958). Cullman maintains the early church first perceived Christ only as Eucharistic guest. After St. Paul's influence, "no longer will it be a matter of eating with Christ, but of eating Christ." (20).

The Passover, Preface to the Lord's Supper

is, in some sense, dining with His people, giving unto them a foretaste of the heavenly banquet.

Some might wonder at this point how Christ can on the one hand be offering His body and blood for His people to eat and drink in the Sacrament, while at the same moment He is there eating and drinking with His people as well. Recall that when Christ first instituted the Lord's Supper this is precisely what happened! He was hosting the event when *simultaneously* He invited His Apostles to eat of His body and drink of His blood at His table. Should it not still be so today as Christians celebrate the Eucharist? In the Lord's Supper, Christ's people should perceive Christ as both the meal *and* the host, as both the Sacrificed One *and* the Risen One. The *Sacrificed One*, the Lamb, is present as miraculous *food*, and the *Risen One* is present as the meal's divine *host*. They are one and the same person, the Lord Jesus Christ.

The Christian faith is full of such apparent paradoxes. Consider, for instance, Christ's work of salvation. On the one hand He is the sacrificial lamb, and on the other hand He is the great High Priest who offers up the lamb.[102] If Christ is both the sacrificial lamb and the priest, can't He offer the eating of Himself as lamb and yet dine with His people as priest as well?[103] It may seem strange that while Christians eat and drink of Christ's body and blood in the Lord's Supper He is there dining with them. But is it any more peculiar that He is both the victim and the Priest, both the Shepherd and the lamb[104], and both God and man?[105] The Sacrament of the Altar stands as a perpetual reminder of these foundational gospel-mysteries.

Christ predicted, "And they will come from the east and west and from the north and south and will recline at table in the kingdom of God."[106] Truly

---

[102] Hebrews 7:26,27.
[103] In relation to this, as will be detailed in future chapters, Hebrew priests were often *obligated* to eat of certain sacrifices, and Christ, as explained in Hebrews, is the great "high priest."
[104] Revelation 7:17.
[105] Isaiah 9:6; John 1:1,14; etc.
[106] Luke 13:29.

this is already happening in the Lord's Supper, as people of all nations are hearing Christ's voice and He is dining with them and they with Him.[107] In the Lord's Supper the saints are, as seen by the eyes of faith, receiving a foretaste of heaven, dining with their Savior, at His table.

The Leader of the Feast ("Paterfamilias")

> *"Jesus took some bread, and after a blessing, He broke it and gave it to the disciples...and He took a cup and gave thanks and gave it to them..."*
> Matthew 26:26,27

When the Jews celebrated their Passovers it usually occurred in a family's home. Whether it occurred in a family's home or whether it was a non-family group, as was the case with Jesus and His Apostles, the Passover celebration required that one person be the leader. This leader received the designation *Paterfamilias* ("potterfameeleeus"). This is Latin for *family father*. It was the responsibility of the *Paterfamilias* (family father) to perform certain duties of Seder leadership. As such he would be the one to bless and to break the bread, this being an official liturgical act performed by the *Paterfamilias*.[108] The *Paterfamilias* would similarly hold aloft the liturgical cups of wine and speak the official blessing over each of them.[109]

There was great significance attached to the blessings spoken over the bread and wine by the *Paterfamilias*. After such blessings the family members responded with "Amen," and then they ate/drank of such bread/wine. However, these family Seder-rituals were not viewed as mere prayers before the meal, but they were viewed as fellowship around the blessing just spoken by the *Paterfamilias*. Joachim Jeremias explains that

---

[107] Revelation 3:20.
[108] Jeremias, *The Eucharist Words...*, 109, explains that "the paterfamilias [would] break from the cake a piece at least the size of an olive for each participant..." See also 232,233.
[109] Jerermias, *The Eucharist Words...*, 110. Such words of blessing elicited official liturgical responses from those at table with him.

when the family members ate of the blessed bread, "the meaning of the action is that each of the members is made a recipient of the blessing by this eating...The same is true of the 'cup of blessing'... drinking from it mediates a share in the blessing."[110] When the Apostles gathered for that special Passover, Jeremias has shown that such thinking "was therefore a familiar and self-evident idea to the disciples from their earliest childhood." They knew that the eating of the broken bread and the drinking of the wine established "a share in the blessing which was spoken over the bread or the wine before the distribution."[111] What strange and awesome blessing Jesus spoke over the bread and wine: *This is my body; this is my blood!* To eat and drink was then to share in these blessed words spoken by *the* Paterfamilias, the Lord Jesus Christ.

The connection is obvious. When Jesus, as the *Paterfamilias*, spoke the unique and powerful blessings over the broken bread and over the chalice of wine, promising the very reception of His body and His blood, the Apostles knew intuitively that they were receiving those very blessings as they ate and drank. Jeremias explains: "When immediately afterwards he gave this same bread and wine to his disciples to eat and drink, the meaning is that by eating and drinking He gives them a share in the atoning power of his death."[112] When one adds to this the worship-related fact that the Jews commonly realized that divine gifts are communicated by eating and drinking, then the Lord's Supper becomes something a Jew would have *expected* from the Christ.[113]

At His Last Supper Jesus told His *Apostles,* "Do this." In order for the Apostles to fully "do this" as individuals, they would have to go forth and execute the role of the *Paterfamilias.* John Stephenson summarizes: "...the imperative 'This do in remembrance of Me' authorized them henceforth to act

---

[110] Jeremias, *The Eucharistic Words...*, 232,233. This was true, as Jeremias points out, at special family meals beyond the Passover.
[111] Ibid., 233.
[112] Ibid., 233.
[113] Ibid., 233.

as the visible representatives of Christ."[114] Thus the Apostles, as *Paterfamilias* ordained by Christ, were to speak Christ's words of blessing over the bread and wine, and by His Word their "families" (congregations) would then partake of such blessings. In so doing Christ would be giving His people "a share in the atoning power of his death."

Thus the Jews would have had a *Paterfamilias*-understanding of St. Paul's explanation in I Corinthians 10:16: "Is not the cup of blessing which *we bless* a sharing in the blood of Christ? Is not the bread which *we break* a sharing in the body of Christ?" The "we" doing the Seder blessing and the "we" doing the Seder bread-breaking in this text would naturally have been understood to be the Paterfamilias—who first were the Apostles and then later those who would lead the worship liturgy.[115]

When Christ instituted the Lord's Supper He demonstrated a very important facet of the Office of the Public Ministry: Paterfamilias. Consistent with this concept of *Paterfamilias*, the New Testament also reflects the movement of the place of worship from "temple" to "household." The *Paterfamilias* was not a temple-related position, but a family-related one. Saint Luke especially emphasizes this transition from temple to house in the movement of Judaism into Christianity. John Elliot explains:

> Houses and households constitute not only the settings for the reception of the good news in Luke-Acts. As house churches, they also represent the basic social organization through which the gospel advances from Palestine to Rome. Literally, the church

---

[114] Stephenson, *The Lord's Supper*, 84. Stephenson also here identifies the Apostles as the first laity to receive the Supper.

[115] Observe how in Acts 20:11 the Greek relates that he (singular, St. Paul) broke the bread. Sadler, *The First and Second Epistles...*, 156: "By a very large number of modern expositors and commentators we are told that the "we" involved in ευλογουμεν refers not to the Apostle....but to the Apostle or minister associated with the congregation of laymen [...]. Now this view seems to me to be totally incompatible with the original institution... [Christ] afterwards sent His Apostles to act in His place, not as the representatives of the people but as His representatives, when He said, 'As my Father sent me, so send I you.'"

spread "from house to house." [...] In Luke-Acts the household plays a paramount role in the ministry, teaching, and mission of Jesus and his followers.[116]

Christ no longer needed the Jewish temple. As clearly attested in Scripture, Jesus is the temple, and similarly His people, who are His body, can be identified as His temple as well.[117] The church "family" could gather in homes, synagogues or wherever, as long as they worshiped in spirit and in truth.[118] When they thus gathered in Jesus' name, however, they were not chaotic mobs, but they were orderly "families" led by a *Paterfamilias*, a pastor. In such worship the paterfamilias kept order and continuity as he utilized the liturgical forms that had been conceived in the womb of Judaism.

Connecting the Passover to Specific OT Sacrifices

> *"Behold the Lamb of God who takes away the sin of the world."*
> John 1:29

As already noted, in Christ's day the Passover lambs were sacrificed at the temple. God gave this directive when He anticipated the construction of His tabernacle: "And you shall sacrifice the Passover to the Lord your God from the flock and the herd, in the place where the Lord chooses to establish His name."[119] The place where God chose to establish His name was the tabernacle, and later the temple. The Jewish historian Josephus explained that at the time of Christ there would have been, at a given Passover, over

---

[116] Jerome H. Neyrey, ed., *The Social World of Luke-Acts*, (Peabody, MS: Hendrickson Publishers, 1991), chapter 8, John H. Elliot, "Temple Versus Household in Luke-Acts: A Contrast in Social Institutions," 226, 229.
[117] E.g. John 2:19ff; 1 Corinthians 3:16
[118] John 4:23.
[119] Deuteronomy 16:2.

250,000 lambs sacrificed at the temple in Jerusalem![120] Because it was entirely poured at the *base* of the Bronze Altar, with none of it being placed on the sides or horns of the altar, such lamb-blood was not directly viewed as atoning blood. Yet the slaying of the Passover lamb and the pouring of its blood had come to be viewed as an official sacrificial rite of the temple.[121] It is apparent that through the sacrifice of Passover lambs, the priesthood of the nation of Israel was recognized, because through such sacrifices each household was allied with priestly work.[122]

Subsequent chapters will explain the Lord's Supper in light of the Jewish sacrificial system. It is of value however at this point to grasp the basic connections that existed between the Passover and the temple sacrifices. In the temple there were three basic types of blood-related sacrifice: the peace offering, the sin offering and the burnt offering.[123] Consider now the Passover in light of each of these.

The Passover, a Kind of Peace Offering

The Passover sacrifice was viewed especially as a category of peace offering. S. C. Gayford simply says that the "Passover [was] a sacrifice belonging to the class of Peace Offering."[124] People of the Middle East sacrificed and ate of peace offerings long before the actual Passover deliverance, as demonstrated by Moses' request that Pharaoh allow the Hebrews to have a sacrificial feast. Even as the peace offerings did not emphasize atonement, neither did the Passover. Even as the laity were usually invited to eat of OT peace offerings, so too the laity consumed the Passover meals. And finally, even as peace offerings were sacrificed and

---

[120] Edersheim, *The Temple*...,168.
[121] Since the Temple's destruction in 70AD Jews ceased eating lamb at their Passover feasts.
[122] The NT priesthood of believers eats of the Passover Lamb like their OT counterparts. It is, we believe, important to realize that the priesthood of believers in the NT is demonstrated by the eating of the sacrifice—not just the Passover. This will be explored in later chapters.
[123] We here include the guilt offering under the category of sin offering.
[124] S.C. Gayford, *Sacrifice and Priesthood*, (London: Methuen & Co. LTD., 2nd ed. 1953), 72.

eaten as a celebration of salvation, so too the Passover was sacrificed and eaten as a celebration of salvation.[125]

The Passover Relates to the Sin Offering.

The Passover was also considered a cousin of the sin offering. Alfred Edersheim explains that the Passover "was neither exactly a sin-offering nor a peace-offering, but combined them both."[126] Though the Passover did not convey forgiveness, its relationship to the sin offering is likely found in the fact that the original Passover was a deliverance-meal. Man's greatest deliverance-need is the deliverance from sin.[127] Sin offering lambs, and indeed sacrificial lambs associated with any type of sacrifice, were thus logically linked to the lambs of Passover. John the Baptist appropriately identified Christ as a sin offering lamb when he declared, "Behold the Lamb of God who takes away the sin of the world."[128] The prophet Ezekiel connected the sin offering to the Passover by giving a Passover-like prescription to certain sin offering blood: "And the priest shall take some of the blood from the sin offering and put it on the door posts..."[129] This peculiar prescription for a sin offering, only found in Ezekiel, supports the underlying understanding that the Jewish sacrificial system was related to the Passover, for at the original Passover the lamb's blood was also placed upon the door posts.[130]

The Passover and the Daily Burnt Offering

As far as the burnt offering is concerned, its relationship to the Passover is found in the *daily* version of the burnt offering. Every day a *lamb*

---

[125] Such concepts will be expanded upon in the chapter dealing with the peace offering.
[126] Edersheim, 184.
[127] This need for sin-deliverance permeates both Testaments. The OT sacrificial system was set in motion to *convey* sin-deliverance; to *create* sin-deliverance God's Son became incarnate.
[128] John 1:29
[129] Ezekiel 45:19.
[130] It is no coincidence that in the midst of explaining the Jewish sacrificial system God spoke of the Passover: "And they shall know that I am the Lord their God who brought them out of the land of Egypt, that I may dwell among them..." Exodus 29:46.

was required as a burnt offering in the morning, and then another one in the evening. Robert Daly observes:

> Since the lambs for the daily burnt offerings are to be year-old males without blemish (Num. 28,3), just as the Paschal lamb is required to be (Exod. 12,5), it is not surprising that the lamb came to be looked upon as the sacrificial animal par excellence. The rabbis, for example, like to compare the morning and evening tamid [Burnt Offering] with the Pasch [Passover].[131]

Thus the morning and evening sacrifice of the burnt offering was specifically connected to the sacrifice of the Passover lamb.

Passover Ingredients Parallel the Grain Offering

In addition to having such relationships to the OT blood-sacrifices, the Passover also had connections to the unbloody sacrifice, the grain offering. From the grain offering the priests consumed *unleavened bread,* after a handful of it had been burned as a *memorial* before God.[132] The fact that the grain offering was both unleavened bread and a memorial offering, had to remind worshippers of the Passover, for like the grain offering it too had a memorial status and it likewise consisted especially of unleavened bread. In addition, even as wine was considered a key element of the Passover, so too with the grain offering, wine became a necessary ingredient.[133]

In these ways the towering Jewish Passover cast its shadow onto the sacrifices performed continually in the Jewish temple.[134] Such a shadow finds

---

[131] Daly, *Christian Sacrifice*, 204, referencing Fuglister, 51.
[132] This will be further explored in the chapter dealing with the grain offering.
[133] This was true only after the entrance into the Promised Land.
[134] Alfred Edersheim, *The Life and Times of Jesus the Messiah*, (McLean, VA: MacDonald Publishing Co. nd), Book V, 492: "[The Passover] in a sense was the cause and the foundation of all the Levitical Sacrifices...And it could not be classed with either one or the other of the various kinds of sacrifices, but rather combined them all, and yet differed from them all."

its reality in Christ crucified, and all of the sacrifice-related meals find their antitype in the Lord's Supper.

Eating Requirements

> "All the congregation of Israel are to celebrate this.... But no uncircumcised person may eat of it."
> Exodus 12:47,48

Consider the prerequisites for eating the Passover. Exodus 12:43,44,47,48 outlines these basic requirements:

> And the Lord said to Moses and Aaron, 'This is the ordinance of the Passover: no foreigner [literally: "son of a stranger"] is to eat of it; but every man's slave purchased with money, after you have circumcised him, then he may eat of it...all the congregation of Israel are to celebrate this. But if a stranger sojourns with you, and celebrates the Passover to the Lord, let all his males be circumcised, and then let them come near to celebrate it; and he shall be like a native of the land. But no uncircumcised person may eat of it.[135]

God here commands that for any given Passover, one *had to celebrate* it if he was of the congregation of Israel. On the other hand, one *could not celebrate* it unless he was a member of the congregation—the sign of membership in Israel being circumcision.

Prerequisites for the Lord's Supper run parallel to such Passover requirements. One *should celebrate* Holy Communion if he/she is a Christian, and a person who is not a Christian should not join at the meal. The sign of

---

[135] These rules were loosened as the years rolled on.

being a Christian is now not circumcision, but *Baptism*.[136]

Immediately before His ascension, Christ's commission outlined these requirements: "Go therefore and make disciples of all nations, *baptizing* them in the Name of the Father and of the Son and of the Holy Spirit, teaching them [the baptized] *to observe all that I commanded you.*"[137] Disciples of Christ are first to be established through the Sacrament of *Baptism*, and then they are to be taught to *observe all that He commanded the Apostles.* What had Christ commanded the Apostles to observe? Specifically, on Maundy Thursday, Jesus commanded that His disciples *observe* His Supper; for He said, "Do this."

The *Book of Concord* appropriately connects Christ's Supper to His Great Commission:

> And so that no misunderstanding could creep in, he [Jesus] explained things more clearly by adding the words, "given for you, shed for you." He let his disciples keep this simple and strict understanding and *commanded* them *to teach all nations to observe all that he had commanded them (that is, the apostles).*[138]

Christ, our Passover lamb has been sacrificed for us. Let us now observe what Christ commanded His Apostles; let us celebrate the feast!

---

[136] See Colossians 2:11ff where circumcision is specifically compared to Baptism. Later God specified that no unclean person was to eat of the Passover, paralleling the fact that no unrepentant person eat of the Lord's Supper.
[137] Matthew 28:19,20a
[138] *The Book of Concord*, trans. & ed. T. Tappert (Philadelphia: Fortress Press, 1959), 578. Italics added.

> *"And I will consecrate the tent of meeting and the altar; I will also consecrate Aaron and his sons to minister as priests to Me. And I will dwell among the sons of Israel and will be their God."*
> *Exodus 29:44.45*

Chapter Three

THE TABERNACLE, TEMPLATE OF CHRIST AND HIS SUPPER

Through Moses God had established detailed furnishings and methods for worship. This involved a portable structure called the *tabernacle*. In this chapter we will demonstrate how this structure, its furnishings and the activities associated with it, portrayed Christ, frequently also foreshadowing something about the Lord's Supper.

The OT tabernacle and the worship therein presented an unassembled jigsaw puzzle of the coming Christ. Many families today have enjoyed the challenge of a jigsaw puzzle, but those who put together the very complex puzzles realize that these are nearly impossible to assemble unless the picture on the box can be referenced. The OT tabernacle-puzzle, however, had no picture to assist in its assembly. The OT Jews were one big family, regularly beholding these tabernacle-related puzzle pieces scattered on their dining room table, but with no picture to reference, they couldn't complete the puzzle. Even the Hebrew prophets struggled to piece together the puzzle, but, alas, it could not be done.[1] In spite of having no picture to reference, there were still the "easy" pieces that could be assembled. Thus these OT believers, as God's revelation progressed, perceived assembled

---
[1] 1 Peter 1:10,11.

The Tabernacle, Template of Christ and His Supper

parts of their puzzle picture; God's OT people could discern that there was something about Christ in their worship activities.[2]

Finally these OT puzzle-pieces could be completely pieced together when the full picture could be referenced. The full picture could be referenced when the person and work of Christ Jesus became a matter of history.[3] After His death and resurrection, the Jews then had a picture enabling them to assemble their OT puzzle, enabling them to see how all they had been doing for centuries in the tabernacle really portrayed Christ!

There are now two versions of this glorious picture, and they both portray the same thing. Whether painted by the eyewitnesses of Christ's work of salvation, or whether portrayed by the fully assembled OT puzzle, each presents a portrait of the Redeemer. This divine portrait of Christ was fully unveiled when the Holy Spirit was poured forth on Pentecost. That picture continues to be displayed today whenever the Gospel is faithfully proclaimed. When completely assembled and displayed, the OT puzzle-picture vividly portrayed the death and resurrection of Jesus Christ, but in the background of this tabernacle-portrait of Christ one could see that the Lord's Supper was clearly portrayed as well. Once pieced together, the OT puzzle showed that God's OT people had partaken of a forerunner of communion in Christ, through the types ordained in their tabernacle liturgy.

The Jewish tabernacle—a portable house of worship—was the first dwelling-like structure established by God for His worship.[4] The Hebrew (or Greek) word for *tabernacle* can simply be translated *tent*. God not only directed Moses concerning the specific design of this tent and its furnishings,

---

[2] This seems especially true of the priesthood. E.g. Psalm 110 describes Christ as priest. The high priest Joshua is said to be a picture of the Branch, the coming Messiah (Zech. 3:8,9). In Zech. 6:12,13, the Branch (Christ) will build the temple and will be both king and priest. Isaiah 53 connected the coming Christ to the guilt offering.

[3] God purposely kept His OT revelation just out of focus, just beyond the grasp of even the greatest OT theologians. Two likely reasons were: 1) It kept His people constantly wrestling with His Word. 2) It made the person and works of Christ the ultimate revelation enabling His previous Word to come into focus, thus confirming all in Christ.

[4] God had previously encouraged the construction of altars in the open. (e.g. Genesis 12:8).

but He also directed the "how," the "when" and the "why" of the worship that was to take place within it. God gave the directives for the tabernacle structure and for tabernacle worship to Moses while he met with God on Mount Sinai for forty days.[5] The writer of the epistle to the Hebrews speaks of this divine structure and worship: "Now even the first covenant had regulations of divine worship and the earthly sanctuary. For there was a tabernacle prepared..."[6] Moses, as a faithful servant, was pointing forward to Christ. Hebrews 3:5 explains, "Now Moses was faithful in all His house as a servant, for a testimony of *those things which were to be spoken later.*" What would be spoken later? The Gospel of the Lord Jesus!

Probably most people are more familiar with the Jew's temple than with their tabernacle. Though both the Jewish *temple* and *tabernacle* served the same purpose, yet the Jewish temple was quite different, for it was a non-portable, permanent structure built centuries after the tabernacle's construction. Whereas the *tabernacle* was built around 1400BC, the first *temple* wasn't constructed until around 900BC.[7] After the temple's completion, the tabernacle was no longer necessary. The temple possessed the same basic characteristics as the tabernacle, only it was a larger, non-mobile version. God did not direct the temple's construction as He did the tabernacle's construction, and thus the tabernacle, the initial prescribed dwelling place of God, will be the heart of our present discussion.[8]

The purpose of this chapter is to show how the sacred implements and the worship within the tabernacle have an earthly *and a heavenly* reality centering in Christ, a reality often finding expression in the Lord's Supper. There is a continuity of the tabernacle flowing into Christ and His worship. Thus, the configuration of Christianity's acts of worship, as James Swetnam

---

[5] Exodus 24:12-32:19. Such tabernacle-related information would then be further explained in the subsequent books of the Pentateuch.
[6] Hebrews 9:1,2. Refer to chapter eight for a more detailed discussion of the Lord's Supper in the book of Hebrews.
[7] The dates are debated. These rounded figures are close enough.
[8] Regrettably, it is beyond the scope of this chapter to utilize many of the special biblical references to "temple" or "tabernacle." Thus, e.g., little of Ezekiel will be referenced.

would summarize, has been "viewed as being related to the tent."[9]

The Heavenly Tabernacle

> *"For Christ did not enter a holy place made with hands, a mere copy of the true one, but into heaven itself, now to appear in the presence of God for us."*
> Hebrews 9:24

The main feature of the tabernacle, simply put, is that it is the identifiable dwelling place of God, whether in heaven or on earth.[10] Though God is present everywhere, His worship-related presence is specifically found in His tabernacle. Indeed the Scriptures indicate that the tabernacle on earth had a counterpart in heaven. When God directed Moses to construct an *earthly* tabernacle, He dictated its pattern because there was already a *heavenly* tabernacle, a *heavenly* "dwelling place" of God. The writer of the epistle to the Hebrews makes a major issue of this heavenly pattern. In Exodus 25:40 God had commanded the earthly tabernacle to be patterned after the *heavenly* tabernacle. Hebrews 8:5 references this directive:

> [The priests in the tabernacle] serve a *copy and shadow of the heavenly things*, just as Moses was warned by God when he was about to erect the tabernacle; for, "See," He says, "That you make all things according to *the pattern* which was shown you on the mountain." [italics added]

---

[9] James Swetnam, "'The Greater and More Perfect Tent.' A Contribution to the Discussion of Hebrews 9,11," *Biblica* 47 (1966): 91-106. On p 95f. Swetnam quotes Alfred Adam, "Ein vergessener Aspekt des fruhchristlichen Herrenmahles. Eiene Beitrag zur Geschichte des Abendmahlsverstandnisses der Alten Kirche," *Theologische Literaturzeitung* 88 (1963) cols. 9-20: "[Alfred] Adam has collected evidence which indicates that there was a tradition in the early church according to which the configuration of her cult acts was viewed as being related to the tent."
[10] See e.g. Habakkuk 2:20

The *pattern* for the earthly tabernacle was the heavenly tabernacle. The author of Hebrews again presents a description of this "heavenly tabernacle" in Hebrews 9:23,24:

> Therefore it was necessary for the *copies of the things in the heavens* to be cleansed with these [blood of lambs, goats, etc.], but the *heavenly things* themselves with better sacrifices than these. For Christ did not enter a holy place made with hands, a *mere copy of the true one*, but into heaven itself, now to appear in the presence of God for us. [italics added]

Observe how the earthly tabernacle and its accoutrements were mere *copies* of the heavenly tabernacle, *the true one*. The existence of a heavenly tabernacle is a doctrine abundantly attested in Jewish theology.[11] It cannot be ascertained whether the Jews considered this "heavenly tabernacle" to be what one might consider a physical place, but its reality in the minds of the Jews and, more importantly, in Holy Scripture is beyond doubt. That it and its earthly counterpart have to do with Christ, worship, and salvation is a certainty—as the Scriptures and other Jewish writings attest.[12]

In early Christianity the celebration of the Lord's Supper was considered the miraculous admittance of Christians into God's heavenly tabernacle.[13] Certain ancient liturgies profess this, as will be shown when we discuss the Holy of Holies.

---

[11] James L. Kugel, *The Bible As It Was*, (London: Belknap Press, 1997), 420. Kugel gives several examples.

[12] This will be demonstrated throughout this chapter.

[13] In Revelation 7:14,15 the saved reach their goal—the *temple*—and the Lord spreads His *tabernacle* over them. The first result named in verse 16 is that they hunger and thirst no more. They are in perfect communion! This is what happens when one enters the temple of God.

Jesus: God Tabernacling Among Us

> *"And the Word became flesh and dwelt ["tabernacled"] among us, and we beheld His glory, glory as of the only begotten from the Father, full of grace and truth."*
> John 1:14

In the above verse, John 1:14, observe that the word "dwelt" is literally the word "tabernacled."[14] Thus St. John is declaring that the Son of God (the "Word") *tabernacled* among men when He became flesh. Such a statement would have been especially significant to the Jews, since they were quite familiar with God's presence in their earthly tabernacle. Through the prophet Zechariah the Son of God had predicted, "Sing for joy and be glad, O daughter of Zion; for behold I am coming and I will dwell [tabernacle] in your midst..."[15]

The OT tabernacle was a place of God's unique presence on earth. In this place God "tabernacled." Though God is present everywhere, yet He chose to be *found* in this "tent." There He would express Himself, and there He would be worshipped. As an illustration, consider the fact that television waves surround everyone; however one can only *find* the expression of such waves by being in the presence of a turned on, tuned in television. In an infinitely greater way God fills heaven and earth, but He chose to have Himself *found* in the earthly tabernacle of the Jews. Thus the function of the tabernacle can be figuratively compared to a turned on, tuned in television.

Though God should indeed be approached everywhere through prayer, yet uniquely at His designated place one can find the distribution of

---

[14] Greek, εσκηνωσεν.
[15] Zechariah 2:10. The word for *dwell* in the LXX is κατασκηνωσω. See also Amos 9:11.

His gracious gifts of salvation.[16] During certain periods of OT history, it was in approaching the earthly tabernacle that God's people worshiped Him, finding there His gracious gifts of salvation. At the tabernacle their thirst for forgiveness was quenched. At the tabernacle God's people could commune with Him. One *knew* God was found in the tabernacle, so one went there to worship, as God Himself had directed: "But you shall seek the Lord at the place which the Lord your God shall choose...to establish His name there for His dwelling, and there you shall come."[17]

Upon His conception in Mary's womb, the Son of God chose His grace-giving presence to be found where His flesh and blood were present. Not that God's Son merely possessed or entered Jesus, but the Son of God *became* flesh, and in this way He set up a *permanently* indwelt tent among humanity. Like the OT tabernacle, which was a portable tent filled with God's presence, so too Jesus was a portable, moving tent, filled with God's presence.[18] In finding the man Jesus, one finds God tabernacling among us, for Jesus is Immanuel, "God with us."[19]

Christ has not left the tent of His flesh and blood. He bodily rose from the grave and He bodily ascended into heaven. We cannot visibly locate Him now, but we can identify His presence. Today the Lord's Supper serves the same purpose as the OT tabernacle, which is the same purpose as the thirty-three odd years Jesus walked this earth. That purpose is the revelation of the localized grace-giving presence of God. At the Lord's Supper the Christian's thirst for forgiveness is quenched. At the Lord's Supper God's people can commune with Him. Even though Christ Jesus is present everywhere, yet He has chosen to be *found* where His body and blood are truly present. In the Christian era, Christ's presence is wherever Christ *promises* it to be so. Uniquely, Christ is thus found in the Sacrament of the Altar, wherein He

---

[16] Even OT prayer, after the temple's construction, was to be directed facing the location of the temple. E.g. 1Kings 8:29,30, 35-38; Daniel 6:10.
[17] Deuteronomy 12:5; Exodus 20:24.
[18] Colossians 1:9.
[19] Matthew 1:23.

The Tabernacle, Template of Christ and His Supper

promised His body and blood to be actually present.[20] In the Lord's Supper there is God's body and blood; God is tabernacling among His people, and there they may find Him.[21] In this sacrament Christ's disciples may even internalize Him, and thus also His salvation.[22]

Associated with the OT tabernacle was a *visible* manifestation of God's presence. It was called the "Glory of the Lord," which was a radiance streaming from God because He is God. God possessed such glory even without any radiance seen by man. The "Glory of the Lord" in the tabernacle was a visible aura or glow, and it was nothing less than God in visible form. Exodus 40:35 speaks of this Glory: "And Moses was not able to enter the tent of meeting because the cloud had settled on it, and the Glory of the Lord filled the tabernacle."[23] The Apostle John, near the beginning of his Gospel, clearly connects this tabernacle-glory to Christ. Once again realize that the Son of God in this passage of John's Gospel is called *the Word*: "And the Word became flesh and *tabernacled* among us, and we beheld *His glory, glory* as of the only begotten from the Father, full of grace and truth."[24] In Christ, God truly *tabernacled* among men. Moreover, in Christ, as in the OT tabernacle, the *glory of the Lord* is revealed. Keep this *glory of the Lord* in mind. We will return to it in our discussion of the Holy of Holies.

---

[20] Christ has promised (or implied) His presence also in Baptism and in the proclamation of His Word, but uniquely in the Eucharist one encounters the tabernacled presence of God.

[21] Swetnam, "The Greater..." Swetnam's main point is that the "greater and more perfect tent" in Hebrews 9:11-12, in 10:19-20 and in 10:29 is really the body of Christ in the Lord's Supper.

[22] It is interesting that within the Roman Catholic church there has been, since around 1200AD, the tradition of placing the consecrated host from the Lord's Supper into an ornate box called a "tabarnacle." Unfortunately such practice elicited worship directed to the tabernacle. See Herman Sasse, *This is My Body* (Augsburg Publishing House, 1959; revised edition, Adelaide: Lutheran Publishing House, 1977), 54.

[23] See also e.g. Exodus 16:7,10; 24:16,17; Leviticus 9:6,23; Numbers 14:10,21; 16:19,42.

[24] John 1:14. In His transfiguration Christ was no doubt visibly revealing this glory He possessed by nature (Luke 9:28ff).

Christ: Pattern of the Earthly Tabernacle

> "And now, glorify Thou Me together with Thyself, Father, with the glory which I had with Thee before the world was."
> John 17:5

Christ fulfills the figures of the tabernacle that God directed Moses to construct. However, instead of merely recognizing that Christ *fulfills* the figures of the Jewish tabernacle, it is important to also realize that Christ is at least one expression of the pre-existent heavenly *pattern* for the earthly tabernacle. Concerning Christ's pre-existence, the Scriptures appropriately describe Him has having been "slain from the foundation of the world."[25] Of the glory that was observed in the tabernacle, Jesus explained that His glory existed with His Father "before the world was."[26]

Though Christ and His work of salvation occurred at a specific time, yet from God's perspective they span all of time, even as God's glory spans all of time. Such a reality reflects the existence of the Son of God from eternity. Christ's death and resurrection, though occurring in the fullness of time, nevertheless reached back in time and actually bestowed through the OT tabernacle sacrifices God's gift of forgiveness.[27] It is thus fitting that Christ be considered the *pattern* for the earthly tabernacle.

Christ, however, is not a mere physical pattern like an architect's blueprint. Instead, each of the compartments, the furnishings and the liturgy surrounding the earthly tabernacle are expressing something about Christ. At least one ancient Jewish document maintained that the earthly tabernacle identified a man, a man who is called the "Heavenly Man."

Now *just as the human body* possesses many organs, higher and

---

[25] Revelation 13:8; 1 Peter 1:19,20.
[26] John 17:5.
[27] Some only want to say that the OT sacrifices *assured* people of forgiveness. No, it is clear that through them God actually *offered* forgiveness, as will be discussed in future chapters.

lower, some being internal and not visible, while others are external and visible, and yet they all form one body, *so also was it with the tabernacle*: all its individual parts were formed in the *pattern of that above*, and when they were all properly fitted together "the tabernacle was one." [...] The mystery of the tabernacle, which thus consists of members and limbs all ascending into the mystery of the *Heavenly Man*, is after the pattern of the commandments of the Torah, which are also in the mystery of *Man*, both Male and Female, which, when united, form *one mystery* of Man. (Zohar, IV, 162b.) [italics added][28]

Though this "Heavenly Man" is, from a Jewish perspective, associated most particularly with the "Adam" of the first chapter of Genesis, yet clearly the tabernacle was perceived by some to have been patterned after *a man*. Such a concept, from the Christian perspective, is most aptly applied to *the* Heavenly Man, Jesus Christ, the New Adam.[29] In Him the earthly tabernacle finds its pattern.

Many times God the Son would appear in the Old Testament as a *heavenly man*.[30] Recall for instance the appearances to Abraham (Gen. 18:1ff), to Jacob (Gen. 32:24ff), to Manoah and his wife (Judges 13:33ff), and to Joshua (Josh. 5:13ff).[31] When the Son of God thus appeared, He frequently was called the "Angel of the Lord" or the "Angel of God's Presence." Such appearances, the texts demonstrate, were not appearances

---

[28] W. Gunther Plaut, *The Torah: A Modern Commentary*, Exodus Commentary, (New York: Jewish Publication Society, 1983), 442.
[29] 1 Corinthians 15:45 identifies Christ as the New Adam. Certain Jewish writings also identified the coming Christ as the New Adam.
[30] Such appearances of Christ are likely part of what St. John had in mind when he wrote John 1:18: "No man has seen God at any time; the only begotten God, who is in the bosom of the Father, He has explained [shown, presented] Him."
[31] Charles A. Gieschen, *Angelomorphic Christology*, (Leiden: Brill, 1998), 68: "[...] God can manifest himself in visible form ranging from a fire, to a cloud, to a man. [To be manifest as a man] is by far the most prominent part of these epiphanic traditions..."

of created angels but of God Himself.[32] It is of value to realize that in Aramaic, which was the common language of Christ's day, the Jews would speak of this Angel of the Lord as the "*Word* of the Lord."[33] Such terminology presents one likely reason why John would begin his Gospel by declaring, "In the beginning was the *Word*, and the *Word* was with God, and the *Word* was God...And the *Word* became flesh and tabernacled among us...and we beheld His glory..."[34] Truly the "angel of the Lord," understood to be the Son of God, became flesh, and thus He pitched the most fabulous tent ever among men.

God's Son would not be satisfied to merely *appear* in human form, as He had done numerous times in the Old Testament. Through Mary He would actually *become* human, for through her He has actually, permanently taken into Himself flesh and blood. After His incarnation, to label Christ as "tabernacle" or "temple" was appropriate not only because His humanity housed God, but also because He is readily perceived to have been the "pattern" for the OT earthly tabernacle. William Brown thus identifies Christ as God's ultimate tabernacle:

> God dwells...in Christ...more gloriously than elsewhere. 'In Him dwelleth all the fullness of the Godhead bodily.' He is the 'true tabernacle which the Lord pitched and not man,' –a shrine altogether lovely, and a pre-eminently meet habitation for the Deity.[35]

The Son of God can be viewed from the beginning as the "pattern" for the earthly tabernacle. But on the other hand, when He entered history as the

---

[32] Thomas B. Falls, trans., *Writings of Saint Justin Martyr*, (New York: Christian Heritage, Inc., 1948), 231-244. Justin uses the Angel of the Lord already in the first century after Christ to explain Christ's deity to the Jew, Trypho.
[33] Gieschen, *Angelomorphic Christology*, 100ff.
[34] John 1:1,14.
[35] William Brown, *The Tabernacle: Its Priests and Its Services*, (Peabody, Mass.: Hendrickson Publishers, Inc., 1996), 39.

man Jesus, He is then the antitype of the earthly tabernacle, the One whom the tabernacle was foreshadowing. Christ is the pattern and the antitype, the beginning and the end, the alpha and the omega.

Christ and His Church, Today's Temple

> *"But He was speaking of the temple of His body."*
> John 2:22

Recall that the temple was the stationary rendition of the portable tabernacle. Most Bible students recognize the Scriptural reality that Christ is the temple and His Bride, one body with Him, is likewise identified as the temple of God.[36]

The Old Testament had predicted that the Christ would establish a new temple/tabernacle. The prophet Zechariah, who called the coming Messiah the *Branch*, predicted, "Behold a man whose name is Branch, for He will branch out from where He is; and He will build the temple of the Lord."[37] What temple would Christ build? He would build/raise up His body, the church, in His resurrection.

Near the beginning of Jesus' public ministry He declared that the "temple" would be destroyed and in three days He would raise it up. St. John then explains, "But He was speaking of the temple of His body."[38] St. John also, when beholding his ultimate vision (Revelation), saw the heavenly Jerusalem and there was no physical temple in it because "the Lord God, the

---

[36] Robert J. Daly, *Christian Sacrifice* (Washington, D.C.: The Catholic University of America Press, 1978), 247, concerning 1 Peter 2:1-10: "This is the most comprehensive of all NT texts on the theology of sacrifice, for it contains important direct witness to the first and third of the Pauline aspects of the theology of sacrifice: the idea of the Christian community as the new temple and the sacrificial nature of Christian life."

[37] Zech. 6:12. Amos 9:11—David's tabernacle raised (Acts 15:16-18). See also Haggai 2:6-9.

[38] John 2:19-22.

Almighty, and the Lamb [Christ] are its temple."[39] From such a thoroughly biblical theme alone, Christ is seen to be the antitype of the OT temple/tabernacle. It also enables one to realize why, after the temple's destruction in 70AD, Christianity no longer needed any such temple of stone, wood and other building materials. Christ, united with His bride, is the temple.[40] Now whenever two or three are gathered in His name, He is in their midst, for *there* is the tabernacle/temple.[41] How appropriate then that God's people today, like His people of old, gather in the Lord's temple to commune in a sacred feast—even though they behold neither a temple nor a sacrifice nor glory of the Lord with their eyes![42]

The Basics of the Hebrew Tabernacle

> *"And let them construct a sanctuary for Me, that I may dwell among them. According to all that I am going to show you, as the pattern of the tabernacle and the pattern of all its furniture, just so you shall construct it."*
> Exodus 25:8,9

The following floor plan of the tabernacle will assist the reader in understanding the subsequent discussions pertaining to the liturgy and furnishings within the tabernacle.

---

[39] Revelation 21:23.
[40] 1 Corinthians 3:16; 12:27; Ephesians 5:28-32.
[41] Matthew 18:20. Notice that His Name is associated with worshipful gathering. God had connected His Name to His OT tabernacle-presence (e.g. Deuteronomy 12:5).
[42] Since the temple of God is identified as each Christian's body (1 Cor. 6:19), doesn't it make sense that The Sacrifice is quite at "home" within these "temples"? Thus the sacrifice of Jesus is eaten, taken into the temples of God!

The Tabernacle, Template of Christ and His Supper

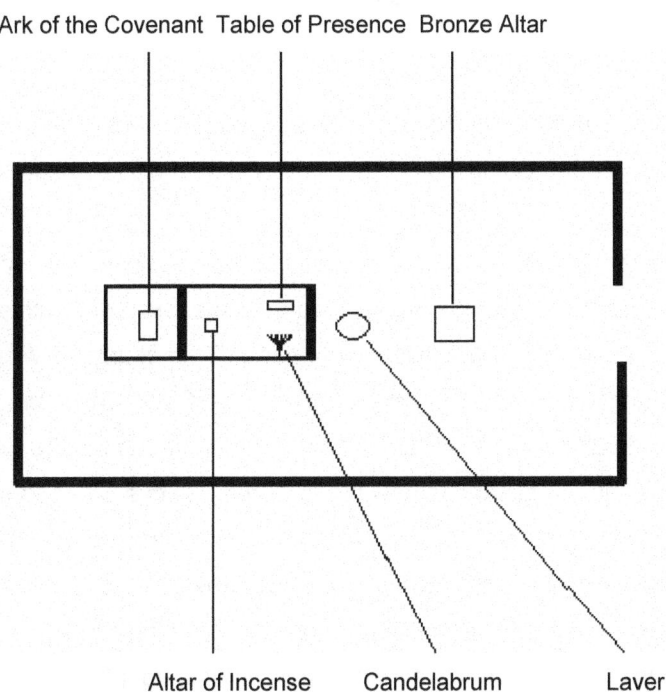

The entrance, located on the East side of the tabernacle, was the least sacred place of the tabernacle. As the priest would move from East to West he would approach holier and holier ground, until he arrived at the Ark of the Covenant. The Ark of the Covenant marked the place of the Most Holy, the place where God declared his unique presence to be located between the two gold angels that rested upon the lid of the Ark. The lid of this Ark of the Covenant was called *The Mercy Seat.* Of this place God informed Moses: "And there I will meet with you, and from above the mercy seat, from between the two Cherubim which are upon the ark of the testament, I will speak to you."[43]

The Outer Court of the Tabernacle

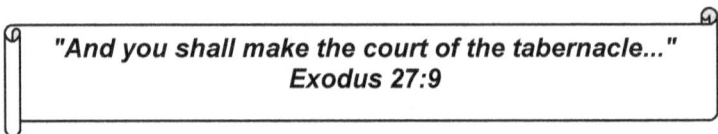

"And you shall make the court of the tabernacle..."
Exodus 27:9

The OT tabernacle had basically three compartments or sacred spaces.[44] They were the *Outer Court*, the *Holy Place* and the *Most Holy Place*.

First consider the *Outer Court*. A portable wall enclosed the entire tabernacle area. This wall, though it surrounded the other two compartments of the tabernacle, stood first to enclose a courtyard. This courtyard was at times called the *Outer Court*, or simply the *Court*.[45] The *Outer Court* was the first of the three compartments of the tabernacle. At the entrance to the outer wall encompassing this courtyard, Hebrew men peered into this Court as they brought their sacrifices to God.[46] At this entrance the offerer would come to have the priest approve him and his sacrifice. After the priest's approval—either at the entrance or on the north side of the Bronze Altar—while facing the *Holy Place*, the offerer would lay his hand on the sacrificial animal, confess his sins, and slay it.[47] The priest would then perform any necessary

---

[43] Exodus 25:22. Do the two angels at Christ's tomb relate to this (John 20:12)?

[44] Brown, *The Tabernacle*, 4ff, shows that the word "tabernacle" often referred only to the inner two compartments: the Holy Place and the Holy of Holies.

[45] Exodus 27:9-19; 38:9-20.

[46] It is debated whether women could bring sacrifices. However it is agreed that only the men could lay hands upon the sacrifice, thus representing themselves and their families. See Alfred Edersheim, *The Temple...*, 81. John Kleinig is one who believes that women also could bring sacrifices. Kleinig, *Leviticus*, 44.

[47] Edersheim, *The Temple...*, 80: "The Rabbis mention the following five acts as belonging to the offering of a sacrifice: the laying on of hands, slaying, skinning, cutting up, and washing the inwards." S. C. Gayford, *Sacrifice and Priesthood*, (London: Methuen & Co. LTD, 1924, 2nd ed. 1953). 139ff: Gayford maintains that Christ thus did not become priest until He entered the Heavenly tabernacle, because His "earthly" work was the work of the offerer, not the priest.

ceremonies with the blood, the fatty portions and the flesh of the creature.[48]

The Bronze Altar

Not far from the entrance to the Outer Court there stood the Bronze Altar. It was located exactly midway between the entrance to the Outer Court and the entrance to the Holy Place.[49] No animal was actually slain upon this altar, but it was upon this Bronze Altar that the necessary portions of sacrificial fat and flesh were burned. The blood was never burned. The priest would collect the blood and cast it, sprinkle it, daub it or pour it upon the sides, on the horns and at the base of the Bronze Altar.[50] Various sacrifices required different applications of the blood. For all animal sacrifices the blood was considered the atoning substance.[51]

The sacrifices thus burned or partially burned upon the Bronze Altar were: sin offering, guilt offering, burnt offering, peace offering and grain offering. In our present chapter we will speak of these sacrifices only generally.

The Bronze Altar was the focal point of tabernacle worship. John Kleinig describes the Bronze Altar, also called the *altar for burnt offering*, as that place where God and man met: "The people entered the courtyard to approach the Lord at the altar for burnt offering," Kleinig explains, "where he came from his 'private residence' to meet with them."[52] God's private residence was the Most Holy Place, a place that was off limits to all but the high priest. The Bronze Altar, however, was the hearth of God's house, a place for Him to meet with all of His faithful people.[53]

On the four corners of the Bronze Altar were horns.[54] These were a

---

[48] The "fatty portions" included those organs that had fat integrally connected (e.g. kidneys).
[49] Some do not agree that this altar stood in the "middle" of the Outer Court.
[50] Edersheim, *The Temple...*, 83,84.
[51] See e.g. Leviticus 17:11.
[52] Kleinig, *Leviticus*, 49. 55: "In practical terms the altar for burnt offering was the most important piece of furniture at the tabernacle."
[53] Kleinig, *Leviticus*, 55.
[54] Exodus 27:2.

common symbol for strength and power.[55] As the horns pointed upward they were comparable to today's church steeples, reaching upward to God.[56] On these horns the blood of highly sacred sin offerings was solemnly applied, indicating that such blood was brought as close to God as possible.[57]

The Jews usually offered the various sacrifices in a certain order when approaching God in worship.[58] In fact, each type of sacrifice was often perceived as a "stage" in the sacrificial process, with the final stage being the sacrificial meal.[59] When a sin-burdened Hebrew approached God he would first bring his sin offering; justification is needed first. Second the burnt offering would be sacrificed; sanctification follows justification.[60] Finally the peace offering would be sacrificed; from this offering the sacrificer drew near to God by joyfully eating a sacred meal. S. C. Gayford summarizes:

> It is significant that the three offerings (Sin, Burnt, Peace) are very frequently found in combination and almost invariably in this very order of succession (See e.g. Exod. xxix.14,18,28; Lev. v.8,10, viii.14,18, ix.7,8,12,22, xiv.19,20,22,31, xv.15,30, xvi.11,24; Numb. vi.11,16,17, viii.12; Ezek. xliii,19,27; it will be seen that sometimes the peace offering is omitted, but the sequence is not disturbed.)[61]

---

[55] E.g. 1 Samuel 2:1,10.
[56] W. W. Washburn, *The Import of Sacrifice in the Ancient Jewish Service*, (New York: Phillips & Hunt, 1883), 79.
[57] Ibid.
[58] A major exception to this "rule" occurred when the altar was dedicated (Numbers 7). The burnt offerings were brought first then the sin offering and finally the peace offerings. One explanation is that the burnt offering was the most ancient of sacrifices and was already associated with an altar. After the altar would be dedicated, the daily burnt offerings offered upon it would be the foundation for all other sacrifices.
[59] F.C.N. Hicks, *The Fullness of Sacrifice*, (First Published by Macmillan & Co., 1946, Reprinted London: S.P.C.K., 1953). Throughout Hicks relates the different kinds of sacrifice as "stages" within the single concept of sacrifice. He repeatedly emphasizes that the final stage is the sacrificial meal.
[60] Chronologically justification and sanctification are simultaneous. Logically, most specifically theologically, justification precedes sanctification.
[61] Gayford, *Sacrifice and Priesthood*, 53.

The Tabernacle, Template of Christ and His Supper

The Bronze Altar, which was the centerpiece of the *Outer Court*, was the hub of all sacrificial activity.[62] This altar was the first thing encountered when entering the tabernacle, and by contact with it, God communicated His holiness to His people.[63]

The Laver

Beyond the Bronze Altar, a person peering through the entrance of the outer wall would see a large basin. It stood just west of the Bronze Altar, between the Bronze Altar and the curtain-doorway into the Holy Place. This basin was called the *Laver*. From this Laver, water would be drawn for the priests to ceremonially wash their feet and hands, and to ceremonially wash the sacrificial portions as well.[64] Such washing performed at the Laver could be called a "baptism"—a religious washing.[65] The priestly washing was primarily a "foot washing," bathing the right hand upon the right foot and the left hand upon the left foot.[66] Perhaps this is partly what Jesus was alluding to when, on the night He instituted the Lord's Supper, He washed the disciple's priestly feet, declaring that they need only cleanse their feet.[67]

The contents of the Outer Court consisted of two furnishings, the Bronze Altar and the Laver. The primary priestly activity in the Outer Court consisted of performing God's part of the tabernacle liturgy at these two sacred sites. Beyond the Laver, still looking from the entrance into the Outer Court, one could see a curtain. This curtain covered the entrance into the second compartment, the Holy Place. Before discussing the Holy Place, consider how Christ fulfills the "types" of the Outer Court.

---

[62] When the temple was being rebuilt, the bronze altar was built and used first; Ezra 3:1-6.
[63] Kleinig, *Leviticus*, 55.
[64] Exodus 30:17-21; Leviticus 1:9. The priests particularly washed their feet, but while doing so their hands were washed as well.
[65] Thus, as will be shown in chapter eight of our present study, Hebrews 10:22 connects Christian baptism with priestly washing.
[66] Edersheim, *The Temple*, 121.
[67] John 13:3ff. Edersheim, *The Temple*, 121, makes such a suggestion in footnote 13. We suggest also that this perhaps marks the Apostles with a quasi-priestly identity.

Christ and His Sacraments: Antitypes of the Outer Court

> *"...things [of Old Testament worship] are a mere shadow of what is to come; but the substance belongs to Christ."*
> **Colossians 2:17**

Recall that the OT sacrifices were *types* and Christ is the *antitype*.[68] Christ's death and resurrection stand as the ultimate *antitypes* of the Hebrew sacrifices. The Sacraments of Baptism and the Lord's Supper stand as background *antitypes* of the OT sacrificial rites, Christ Himself being in the foreground.

The Priests Typified Christ

The OT priests, who were especially active in the Outer Court, were types of Christ. Christ is *the* ultimate priest, as the book of Hebrews repeatedly attests.[69] For the service of the tabernacle, priests were appointed by God to perform various functions. These functions mainly involved the sacred handling of sacrificial blood, the burning of various sacrificial portions, and the *presenting and eating of holy meals*. In addition, apparently especially in later years, the priests were responsible for teaching/preaching.[70] As explained in chapter one, such work of the priests was often summarized by the word "liturgy." Christ, as priest, performs this liturgy, but in relation to the Eucharist we note especially that He presents the sacrificial meal to His people.[71]

As a priest performed the sacrificial liturgy he was always aware that

---

[68] W. W. Washburn, *The Import of Sacrifice...*, 37: "They were a type—a type being a visible representation of a future truth, a truth yet to be revealed, as a symbol is a visible representation of a present truth. A type is a sensuous prediction, an acted prophecy." 49: "Now, it is of the very nature of a type to signify the same thing, to teach the same truth, as its antitype, though under a different form and in a different way."
[69] The book of Hebrews will be more thoroughly discussed in chapter eight.
[70] E.g. Nehemiah 8:4,5,9 (Levites were teaching with Ezra); Micah 3:11; Malachi 2:7.
[71] This will be more thoroughly discussed in chapter eight.

behind this liturgy was the unique presence of God within the tabernacle. Christ now fulfills all priestly functions ("liturgy") in the heavenly tabernacle.[72] He has offered the sacrificial blood and flesh to His Father, and He then offers the meal of His body and blood to His people. Generally speaking, Christ intercedes for His people, thus relating himself to all other parts of the OT priestly liturgy. As the other compartments of the tabernacle will be considered shortly, and as all three compartments involved special priestly activity, preliminarily realize that Christ is not merely a "priest" but He is the ultimate "*high* priest."

The Bronze Altar Foreshadowed NT Worship

The Bronze Altar, and the various activities surrounding it, typified Christ and His cross. By the fourth century of Christianity, the cross of Christ was called the "altar of the cross."[73] The cross itself compared with the Bronze Altar, not in appearance but in the activity surrounding it. In OT worship, sacrificial blood was repeatedly poured at and flowed to the base of the Bronze Altar. At the base of the cross, typified by the base of the Bronze Altar, the blood of Christ was poured forth ("shed") for man's atonement. And even as there was flesh burned upon the altar, so too on the cross Christ's flesh was offered to God for man's salvation. From the cross the primary ingredients of the Eucharist are derived; these are the body and blood of Christ *given* and *shed* for all. The words that Christ used to institute the Eucharist, especially the word *shed*, are sacrificial terms, thus establishing the Eucharist as an altar-concept.[74]

---

[72] Hebrews 8:6. (The word translated "ministry" in this verse is the Greek word for "liturgy.")
[73] Gayford, *Sacrifice and Priesthood*, 146, traces the phrase, *Altar of the cross*, (ara crucis) as far back as Ambrose. It likely goes back much further. Many have simply used the phrase to describe the fulfillment of OT sacrifices at the cross. Thus e.g. Cave, *The Scriptural Doctrine of Sacrifice and Atonement*, (Edinburgh: T & T Clark, 1890), 421: "The cross is the altar upon which Jesus makes His sacrifice."
[74] On "shed," see e.g. Robert J. Daly, *Christian Sacrifice*), 221. Also Joachim Jeremias, *The Eucharistic Words...*, 226. Also many have realized that when Christ spoke of His body and blood as separate elements at His Last Supper, this implied sacrifice as well.

The Tabernacle, Template of Christ and His Supper

A major difference between Christ's cross and the Bronze Altar was that no creatures were actually slain upon the altar. Christ was indeed slain upon the cross, but no animal was slain on the Bronze Altar. However, the cross is the antitype of not merely the Bronze Altar. It stands as the antitype of what was done in the entire tabernacle liturgy, including, for example, the slaying of the animal sacrifices at the Outer Court, and the application of their blood in the Holy and Most Holy Places.

As Christians supernaturally dine on the once-sacrificed Lamb of God in the Eucharist, they often have called it "The Sacrament of the Altar." In ancient times altars were the center of worship. Even before the tabernacle's construction, God regularly met with His people at various altars.[75]

The OT identifies primarily six worship-concepts associated with altars. Four of these concepts are God's *name*, God's *presence*, *sacrifice* and *eating*. Each of these four is easily identified in Deuteronomy 12:5-7:

> But you shall seek the Lord at the place which the Lord your God shall choose from all your tribes, to establish *His name* there for *His dwelling*, and there you shall come. And *there you shall bring your burnt offerings, your sacrifices*, your tithes, the contribution of your hand, your votive offerings, your freewill offerings, and the first-born of your herd and of your flock. There *you and your households shall eat* before the Lord your God... [italics added][76]

Since an altar is associated both with God's *name* and His *presence*,[77] Jesus was apparently setting forth an "altar" principle when He

---

[75] E.g. Genesis 8:20; 12:8; 13:4
[76] This quote describes the tabernacle, the place of God's altars, a place of sacrifice and eating.
[77] God's Name is associated with His worship-oriented presence throughout the Pentateuch (e.g. Ex. 20:24; Deut. 12:5; 26:2). F. Gavin, *The Jewish Antecedents of the Christian Sacraments*, (New York: The Macmillan Co., 1928), 97: Gavin explains the power in the Lord's Supper was perceived by the Jews to be "in the ancient and primitive conception of the Power of the Name recited in Thanksgiving, in conformity with the precedent and institution of Him who first spake the words..."

declared, "Where two or three of you have gathered together in my *name*, there I am *in their midst*."[78] It would then be no coincidence that the context of this verse is church discipline, a discipline that throughout Christian history has found its ultimate application at the Sacrament of the Altar.

Besides the four elements just identified as altar-concepts, *forgiveness* has been a central altar-concept. This is found throughout the Old Testament (esp. Leviticus).[79] Observe it even in the great vision of Isaiah wherein Isaiah, realizing himself to be a sinner, must have an angel approach him "with a burning coal in his hand which he had taken from the altar with tongs." As the angel touched Isaiah's mouth with the coal *from the altar* he proclaimed, "'Behold, this has touched your lips; and your iniquity is taken away, and your sin is forgiven.'"[80]

Finally, an altar is associated with the *unity* of those who approach it. As a rather unique NT example, Hebrews 13:10 explains, "We have an altar from which those who serve the tabernacle have no right to eat."[81] Christians are to be protective of their altar. They are not to welcome non-Christians to their altar, nor are Christians to join at the altar of non-Christians.[82] Similarly God's people should not commune at an altar together with those Christians who hold to false doctrines.[83] Why do some have no right to eat from a Christian altar? The altar represents what is believed, and only those in agreement with what an altar represents should approach it. The altar then becomes the place where such lines of distinction are to be drawn. It is a

---

[78] Matthew 18:20.
[79] Job (Job 1:1ff), before the Jewish tabernacle, offered sacrifices for the sins of his family.
[80] Isaiah 6:6,7.
[81] This verse will be further explored in chapter eight.
[82] 1 Corinthians 10:21.
[83] Romans 16:17. As will be discussed in later chapters, the altar is not only associated with the holy, but it conveys the holy (Matthew 23:18,19). This is true also of the Sacrament of the Altar, and it must thus be treated as holy; compromise and false doctrine must there be avoided.

place of unity, a place of common confession.[84]

As an OT example of this, in Ezekiel 44:7-9 God warns that the "uncircumcised in heart and uncircumcised in flesh" should not be allowed in His sanctuary. This would exclude both the unrepentant (uncircumcised in heart) and the non-Jews (uncircumcised in flesh). In verse 16 He then explains that only the faithful priests should "come near to My table." God's "table" was indeed His altar, the location associated with sacrifice-related food. What was prescribed for the OT priests frequently finds its antitype in the NT priesthood of believers; we NT priests may *come near to His table.*

As a NT example of such thinking, consider Saint Paul's command that Christians avoid those who caused divisions contrary to the doctrine they had learned (Romans 16:17). Through the centuries this directive has been applied by drawing the line at the Sacrament of the *Altar.* Those who caused divisions contrary to Apostolic doctrine were prohibited from joining at the same altar as those who adhered to Apostolic doctrine. The Sacrament of the Altar was identified as the place to which those of other beliefs could not go.

In relation to Romans 16:17, drawing the line at the "altar" of the Lord's Supper made sense for at least two reasons. First, the previous verse (Romans 16:16) describes greeting one another with a "Holy Kiss." It is now realized that the *Holy Kiss*—referenced five times in the New Testament—conveyed a liturgical practice marking that time in the Communion Service just before the distribution of Christ's body and blood.[85] By placing his warning to avoid those who hold to false doctrine at this point in the epistle, St. Paul implied that such people obviously could not join in the Holy Kiss nor,

---

[84] Edersheim, *The Temple*, 94. Edersheim notes that in Jesus' day non-Israelites were allowed to bring burnt offerings. These were slain and handled by the priests. Edersheim also footnotes that occasionally such burnt offerings had a peace offering status, but no meal was shared. In other words, there was never an altar-communion shared with Jews and non-Jews. Thus the Bronze Altar remained a place of unity. This would perhaps be comparable to a pagan attending a worship service in our day and putting money in the offering plate. This would not imply altar-communion.

[85] Sasse, *This is My Body*, 322 and footnotes on 235 & 324. Rom. 16:16; 1 Cor. 16:20; 2 Cor. 13:12; 1 Thess. 5:26; 1 Pet. 5:14 are the references to the Holy Kiss (also called Kiss of Peace or Kiss of Love).

even more importantly, in the reception of the Lord's Supper that followed the Holy Kiss. Second, since joining at an altar indicated unity, it made perfect sense to follow the Apostle's directive in Romans 16:17 by applying it to the Sacrament of the Altar. Those who held to different doctrines were lovingly barred from joining in the Sacrament of the Altar. This is how they were "avoided."

Since the Lord's Supper is associated with all six of the concepts frequently associated with an altar (God's Name, His Presence, Forgiveness, Unity, Sacrifice and Sacred Eating), it becomes clear why the church naturally came to refer to Christ's Supper as the "Sacrament *of the Altar*." The body and blood of the Lord was *sacrificed* on the cross for man's *forgiveness*, and when Christians join in worship, the time when God's *name* is invoked, the body and blood are to be *eaten* by those who are *united* in the faith. These are altar concepts.

The Sacrament of the *Altar* is also appropriately associated with an altar because of references such as Malachi 1:7,12. God declared in this passage:

> You are presenting defiled food upon My *altar*. But you say, 'How have we defiled Thee?' In that you say, 'The *table* of the Lord is to be despised...But you are profaning it, in that you say, 'The *table* of the Lord is defiled, and as for its fruit, its food is to be despised.' [italics added]

Malachi here uses "altar" and "table" interchangeably. Thus the Bronze Altar could be spoken of as the *table of the Lord*. Relate this then to the Apostle Paul's comparison of pagan altar-communion and Christian altar-communion in 1 Corinthians 10:21b: "...You cannot partake of the *table* of the Lord [Holy Communion] and the *table* of demons [pagan communion]." The Greek here for "table of the Lord" is identical to the Greek translation of the "table of the Lord" in Malachi 1:7,12. Thus when St. Paul calls Holy Communion the "*Table* of the Lord," such a reference would have been understood as the equivalent of saying "*Altar* of the Lord." The Apostle Paul is the first to connect Holy Communion to an altar (table)—the place associated with God's name, presence, sacrifice, eating, forgiveness and unity. Hence not by command but by association it is very proper to both *call* the Lord's Supper the Sacrament of the *Altar*, and to *use* an altar when celebrating it.

Further realize, as will be explained in our chapter dealing with the peace offering, that Malachi 1:11 was considered by many in the early church to be a *specific* prediction of the Lord's Supper. Thus when the following verse, Malachi 1:12 (quoted above), speaks of "table of the Lord," it is easy to realize why the Lord's Supper was early on in Christian history associated with an altar.

The Jewish-oriented words of Jesus in Matthew 5:23,24 are then also rightly related to the Sacrament of the Altar:

> If therefore you are presenting your offering at the altar, and there remember that your brother has something against you, leave your offering there before the altar, and go your way; first be reconciled to your brother, and then come and present your offering [at the altar].

The church through the centuries has appropriately applied this command of Christ to the Lord's Supper. Shall not Christians heed these words of their Lord and thus make every effort to make amends with a "brother" before going to the *Sacrament of the Altar*? Indeed, Jesus' words should be heeded even more diligently than in relation to the Bronze Altar, for Christians are preparing to approach the altar of the very body and blood of God's Son, the body and blood that is the foundation of all sacrifice!

It is true that Jesus neither commanded that an altar be used nor did He directly refer to the Lord's Supper as the Sacrament of the *Altar*.[86] An altar does not have to be present to celebrate the Eucharist. As already noted, there are various good reasons to connect the Lord's Supper with an *unseen* altar. An unseen altar is consistent with the fact that Christians in our present era cannot *see* the presence of a *temple*, nor can they *see* the *flesh and blood of a sacrifice*. Though these are unseen, yet early Christian liturgies demonstrated the belief that the Christian temple, the sacrificial meal of Christ's body and blood, and the altar are now more heavenly than earthly realities. Even though they are heavenly, yet they are realities that God's people can and do now participate in, even while existing in this sin-laden world. The NT sacrificial meal of Christ's body and blood is commanded to be eaten with the elements of bread and wine; this is not an option, and through such communion Christ's people miraculously encounter God's heavenly temple realities.[87]

So why construct a church building, an altar and other sacred furnishings? Even though Christ commanded neither the construction of a house of worship nor an altar for NT worship, yet such furnishings can stand as icons (sacred earthly figures) of heavenly realities, and as such they are in harmony with the celebration of the Sacrament of the Altar. Though non-essential, these visible furnishings silently yet powerfully preach to the people of God the presence of the heavenly realities.

One might ask whether the disciples on that night of the institution of the Lord's Supper were reminded of the Bronze Altar. It is doubtful that they

---

[86] As will be explained shortly, Matthew 5:23,24 may be an exception to this. Christ may indeed be here referencing altar practice for the yet to be instituted Sacrament of the Altar.

[87] R.C.H. Lenski, *The Interpretation of St. Matthew's Gospel*, (Minneapolis: Augsburg Publishing House, 1943), 1031: "The miracle of the sacrament is not that Christ makes us partakers of his glorified body and blood but of the body *given* and of the blood *shed* for us on the cross. The sacrament draws from Calvary not on heaven." Though we think Lenski is correct in emphasizing the cross in the sacrament, yet we believe Lenski creates an artificial dichotomy between the glorified and non-glorified body and blood of Christ. To partake of the body and blood given and shed at the cross in the sacrament is to gather with angels and archangels and all the company of heaven.

immediately made the connection between the Lord's Supper and an altar, even though Christ spoke of Himself as a sacrifice. Nevertheless it seems nearly certain that this reality dawned on them later, especially when Jesus' prediction of the temple's destruction became a reality. When the Romans destroyed the Jew's temple in 70 AD, God's Bronze Altar was destroyed. Where then were God's people to apply their sacrifices and to obtain their sacred meals? Where were God's presence, forgiveness, His name and the unity of His people to be uniquely found? Christians looked to the Sacrament of the Altar and there observed an unseen altar that possessed even greater realities than the Bronze Altar. The Sacrament was (and is) the "altar" directly linking God's people with the sacrifice of Jesus, even when no visible altar is present.

Blood Shed at the Altar

At Christ's cross, as had been the case also at the Bronze Altar, the blood was recognized as the key atoning element.[88] The blood of the animal sacrifices was *not burned* on the Bronze Altar, but it was poured (shed) at the altar's base—after part of it had been daubed, sprinkled or dashed upon the horns or side of the altar.[89] To say the blood was "poured out" at the base of the Bronze Altar was equivalent to saying it was "shed."[90] With this altar-related terminology, the Son of God spoke of both the Eucharist and His death when He held the chalice of wine and predicted, "...this is My blood of the covenant, which is to be *shed* (poured out) on behalf of many for forgiveness of sins."[91]

---

[88] E.g 1 Peter 1:2, 18,19; 1 John 1:7; Acts 20:28; Hebrews 9:14.
[89] Edersheim, *The Temple*, 83,84.
[90] Thus, for example, in Leviticus 4:7,18,25 the sin offering blood is shed at the altar's base. The LXX uses the same word for "shed" as Christ used in His Supper (e.g. Matt. 26:28).
[91] Matthew 26:28. The Greek can literally be translated, "...blood being shed..," thus explaining the imminence of His crucifixion. The NASB quoted above captures the fact that His blood is soon to be shed.

Shed-blood signaled the death of the sacrificial creature.[92] Such a creature's life-blood was always poured out in the sacrificial process. However the blood of a sacrificial creature was never burned, hence it was not destroyed. Thus several theologians have explained that OT worshippers believed that the blood (the life) of an OT sacrifice lived on. S. C. Gayford explains this: "'Blood' in sacrificial sense always means a 'Risen' life, one that has passed through death, but is alive."[93] Sacrificial blood was then a sign of continued life, even after the creature had died, and Christ clearly fulfills this picture in His resurrection![94] Thus as the Bronze Altar was the location of sacrificial blood, it represented *both* Christ's death for sin *and* His resurrection.[95] As it was shed, Christ's blood demonstrated His death, for His life was drained; it represented His continued life as it remained unburned, unconsumed. It is of this life-blood that Christ's people may now miraculously drink.

Wine and Water Poured at the Altar

In the tabernacle liturgy, wine was almost always poured at the base of the Bronze Altar, at the same place where the sacrificial blood was poured.[96] From this practice one observes a sacrifice-related reason why Christ chose wine to be the "vehicle" of His blood in the Lord's Supper.

Particularly at the festival called the *Feast of Tabernacles (Booths)*, water was poured with the blood and wine at the base of the Bronze Altar as

---

[92] In fact every time the Bible uses the word *shed* to refer to blood, the creature (whether man or beast) died. Hebrews 12:4 *may* be an exception to this.
[93] Gayford, *Sacrifice and Priesthood*, 170. Also, 68: "The Hebrews regarded the life-blood almost as a living thing inside the body which it quickened; and not only was it the vitalizing life while it pulsated within the body, but it had an independent life of its own, even when taken from the body."
[94] Hicks, *The Fullness of Sacrifice*, 18: "The death is vital to the sacrifice, because it sets free the blood, which is the life. But the victim is, in a true sense, operative, not as dead, but as alive 'as it had been slain'..." P. 243: "So St. Paul—brings out the backward look of death, as death, and the forward look of blood, as life—'while we were yet sinners, Christ died for us. Much more then, being now justified by His blood, shall we be saved...'"
[95] We will discuss this further in our next chapter.
[96] Kurtz, *Offerings...*, 301. Edersheim, *The Temple*, 97, 103, 220 speaks of the two "funnels".

well.[97] In Christ's day the Bronze Altar in the temple had two permanent channels at its base. Into one of these channels the blood and wine were both poured, and into the other one the water from these special ceremonies would be poured.[98] Such sacrifice-related blood and water demonstrate the significance of what was so emphatically noted by Saint John as he reported the blood and water flowing from Christ's pierced side: "But one of the soldiers pierced His side with a spear, and immediately there came out blood and water."[99] The Apostle magnified this observation by declaring, "And he who has seen has borne witness...and he knows that he is telling the truth..."[100] The foot of the cross, where blood and water flowed, thus related directly to the foot of the Bronze Altar, where likewise blood and water were officially poured into the two channels. The church through the ages has understood this highlighted blood and water passage in John's Gospel to refer to the Sacraments of Baptism and Eucharist. Robert Daly explains:

> As for Jn 19,34f, the simultaneous flowing of blood and water from the side of Christ may also be an allusion to that specific rite of the Feast of Tabernacles in which water and wine poured out simultaneously from bowls on the altar. If so, then it would serve the function of bringing in the idea of Jesus and those who follow him as the new temple, an interpretation which harmoniously supports the customary sacramental-ecclesial interpretation of the water and blood from Christ's side.[101]

Thus the water, wine and blood rituals in the temple are perceived to foreshadow the connection between Christ's pierced side and the New

---

[97] Edersheim, *The Temple*, 220.
[98] Edersheim, *The Temple*, 220ff
[99] John 19:34.
[100] John 19:35. Similar emphasis, apparently Sacrament-related, is found in 1 John 5:6-8.
[101] Daly, *Christian Sacrifice*, 291,292.

Testament Sacraments.[102] Additionally, Daly here also describes the biblical understanding, explained earlier, that Christ's people are one with Him as the "new temple."

Sacrifices

Even as the Bronze Altar foreshadowed the cross of Christ, so also each kind of sacrifice performed at the Bronze Altar foreshadowed something about Christ and His Holy Supper. Alfred Cave explains, "Every variety of the Old Testament sacrifice may be made beautifully illustrative of certain aspects of Christ's work."[103] Whether lamb, goat, ram, dove, bull or grain, Christ is being pictured.[104] Whether sin offering, guilt offering, burnt offering, peace offering or grain offering, Christ's sacrifice is being portrayed.[105] When the people of Israel or the priests then participated in the many sacrifice-related meals, these sacrifices, and the meals drawn from them, portrayed something not only about Christ's death but about His Holy Supper as well.

Brooke Westcott, speaking generally of the relationship between OT sacrificial-meals and the Sacrament of the Altar, remarks, "In this sacrament then, where Christ gives Himself as the support of His faithful and rejoicing people, the Christian has that which more than fulfills the types of Jewish ritual."[106] Subsequent chapters will detail the various sacrifices and their relationships to Christ and His Supper.[107]

The Laver, Shadow of NT Baptism

Moving now to the "Laver"—which like the Bronze Altar was located in the Outer Court of the tabernacle—recall that it was at this water-filled

---

[102] In chapter two we explained how Christ's pierced side was also seen as Passover fulfillment.
[103] Alfred Cave, *The Scriptural Doctrine...*, 424.
[104] We will not delve into the possible significance of each kind of sacrificial creature.
[105] In later chapters these kinds of sacrifices will be further explained.
[106] Brooke Westcott, *The Epistle to the Hebrews*, (Grand Rapids: Wm. B. Erdmans Publishing Co., 1973) 438.
[107] Stephenson, *The Lord's Supper,* 110. Stephenson here gives four reasons why the Eucharist is rightly related to sacrifice.

basin where priests ceremonially cleansed their feet.[108] Such cleansing enabled them to walk in God's holy places. They also ceremonially washed sacrificial portions at the Laver.

This Jewish "Laver" has been linked to Christian baptism because the Greek word for "Laver" is utilized in a couple of baptismal texts in the New Testament. For instance in Titus 3:5, the "*washing* of regeneration" is literally translated, "*Laver* of regeneration."[109] And again, the baptismal reference in Ephesians 5:26, "*washing* of water with the word," can be translated, "*Laver* of water with the word."[110] Cyril of Jerusalem, a pastor who was born in 315 AD, said simply, "...the laver had been set within the tabernacle, as a symbol of baptism."[111]

By Baptism Christians now have a priestly washing and they may now, as purified priests, walk in God's holy courts, participating in the body and blood of Christ in the heavenly holy of holies. As such, they draw near to God. Such drawing near to enter the holy of holies as priests is precisely what Hebrews 10:19-22 is about:

> Since therefore, brethren, *we have confidence to enter the holy place* [Holy of Holies] by the blood of Jesus, by a new and living way which He inaugurated for us *through the veil*, that is, His flesh, and since we have a great high priest over the house of God, *let us draw near* in full assurance of faith, having our hearts sprinkled clean from an evil conscience and our bodies *washed with pure water* [italics added].

---

[108] In the *temple* there were additional "basins" used to ceremonially wash the daily burnt offerings as well. See e.g. 2 Chronicles 4:6.

[109] Brown, *The Tabernacle...*, 57: "The priests, without washing dared not, on penalty of death, enter the house made with hands, and none but those who have been cleansed by the washing (laver) [sic] of regeneration, and renewing of the Holy Spirit, will ever enter the one 'not made with hands.'"

[110] Ephesians 5:26.

[111] Leo P. McCauley and Anthony A Stephenson, translators, *The Works of Saint Cyril of Jerusalem*, vol. 1 (Washington, D.C.: The Catholic University of America Press, 1969), 111.

The priestly "Laver-washing" of Christians—indicated in Hebrews 10:22—encourages Christians to "draw near" [a Jewish worship term][112] with their "bodies washed with pure water."[113] Only the priests were to participate in the OT Laver-washing, but this text applies it to every Christian. Because this reference implies the priestliness of all Christians, it underscores the "priesthood of believers," a doctrine delineated in the NT.[114] James Swetnam explains, "Those who are urged to 'draw near' in [Hebrews] 10:19-22 are considered to be priestly: The Christian priesthood of all Christians is the fulfillment of the Old Testament priesthood of the Levites."[115]

Recall that, in addition to the sacred washing of the priests, sacrificial portions were also ceremonially washed at the Laver. Thus as Christians are baptized they are not only cleansed of impurity but they are also prepared to be sacrificed, even as their Lord and Savior. Appropriately then St. Paul informs Christians that they are presenting their bodies to God as living sacrifices.[116] And as the Baptized live out their lives, "we are being put to death all day long; we were considered as sheep to be slaughtered."[117]

No doubt one should *first* connect the OT Laver to Christ, because He is *the* high priest and He is *the* sacrifice. Thus when Jesus was "lavered" in His Baptism, He was appropriately being prepared for His *priestly* work before God. Moreover He, as the ultimate *sacrifice*, was washed in preparation for the very sacrifice of Himself. How fitting then that John the Baptist, of Hebrew

---

[112] Franz Delitzsch, trans. Thomas Kingsbury, *Epistle to the Hebrews*, (Minneapolis: Klock and Klock Christian Publishers, 1978), 174: The Greek here "is a technical liturgical word, and sprinkling and washing are liturgical acts of preparation."

[113] Brooke Westcott, *The Epistle to the Hebrews*, 323: "The two phrases [in Hebrews 10:22] appear to contain allusions to the Christian Sacraments. That to the Eucharist is veiled: that to Baptism is unquestionable."

[114] 1 Peter 2:9; Revelation 1:6; 5:9,10.

[115] James Swetnam, "'The Greater and More Perfect Tent.' A Contribution to the Discussion of Hebrews 9,11," *Biblica* 47 (1966): 91-106, 103. Such priestly privileges are inferred by "the allusions to purification through sprinkling and ritual washing." (103).

[116] Romans 12:1.

[117] Romans 8:36, quoting Psalm 44:22.

priestly lineage, would perform this washing of Jesus in the Laver of the Jordan!

Concluding the tour of the Outer Court, one must understand that this was the only court viewed by the laity. As they looked into this court from the main entrance, the laity saw two implements: The Bronze Altar and the Laver. Observing the liturgical activities surrounding these implements, the laity realized there were primarily five substances established by God to be "utilized" in worship: Flesh, blood, unleavened bread, wine and water.[118] Flesh and blood came from the animal sacrifices, unleavened bread and wine were drawn from the grain offerings with libations, and the water was seen in the Laver. The relation to Christian worship is obvious. Christians—like their OT brethren—gather together around exactly these ingredients of worship. God's continuity is clearly recognized in these five ingredients; in Christian worship there is a continuity of God's tabernacle as His people gather around Christ's *flesh* and *blood* under the *bread* and *wine* of the Lord's Supper, having had their bodies cleansed and prepared by *water* in the Laver of regeneration.

The Holy Place

> *"And let every skillful man among you come, and make all that the Lord has commanded: ...for ministering in the holy place."*
> Exodus 34:10,19

Imagine now that you are living at the time when the tabernacle stood, and you are allowed to walk through the outer compartment of the tabernacle. In this Outer Court, which was just discussed, there is no roof over your head. You walk past the Bronze Altar, then past the Laver, and

---

[118] All of these elements will be further explored in subsequent chapters. One element that does not find an immediate clear antitype in the NT is the fat that was burned upon the altar.

soon you arrive at a heavy curtain, which is really the doorway into the second compartment. This second compartment was called the "Holy Place" and only priests were allowed to enter this sacred space behind the curtain.[119] You may now enter.

Walking into this Holy Place behind the curtain you enter a rectangular room stretched out lengthwise before you, with gilded walls to your right and to your left. Near the gilded wall on your right, you would see a gold-plated sacred table commonly called the *Table of Presence* (or just *The Table*). On this table are consecrated bread and wine, as well as consecrated incense.[120] Looking toward the gilded wall on your left you would see *The Candelabrum*, a solid gold fixture fashioned with seven solid gold branches, each branch possessing an oil-drawing wick, ignited to burn brightly in this otherwise dark room.[121] This room has a roof, and this glowing seven-fold candelabrum furnishes the only light, a light that reflects brightly from the two gold-plated walls.

Ahead, just before the next curtain, you would see a golden altar, smaller than the Bronze Altar of the Outer Court but more beautiful because it is covered not with mere bronze but with pure gold. This altar is often called the *Altar of Incense*, and it, like the Bronze Altar, has horns upon each corner.[122] Just beyond this altar you would see yet another heavy curtain. This curtain marks the entrance into the third and final compartment of the tabernacle, the Holy of Holies.[123]

In summary, upon entering this Holy Place you behold three sacred furnishings: the Table of Presence to your right, the Candelabrum to your left, and the golden Altar of Incense straight ahead of you.

---

[119] Quite often the "Holy Place" meant both the *Holy Place* and the *Most Holy Place*. As such it is often translated "sanctuary."
[120] Exodus 25:23-30; Leviticus 24:5-9
[121] Exodus 25:31-40; 37:17-24.
[122] Exodus 30:1-10; 37:25-28.
[123] Exodus 26:33.

Christ and His Sacraments, Antitypes of the Holy Place

> *"And beginning with Moses....He explained to them the things concerning Himself in all the Scriptures"*
> Luke 24:27

The Table of Presence

    The primary items upon the Table of Presence were the twelve loaves of bread that were eaten by the priests and replenished weekly. This bread was often called the *bread of the presence*, or *showbread*, and thus the table upon which it rested has been called the *Table of Showbread*. Relative to this *bread of the presence*, Alfred Edersheim explains, "Ancient symbolism, both Jewish and Christian, regarded 'the bread of the Presence' as an emblem of the Messiah."[124] Thus God's people of both testaments connected the bread of the presence to Christ, the Messiah. Since the bread of the presence was considered a kind of grain offering, further connections between Christ and the bread of the presence will be explored when the grain offering is investigated in chapter seven.

    Recall that *General Sacramental Eating* was any eating with which God performed something miraculous, beyond the ordinary, and that *Specific Sacramental Eating* is that miraculous eating found only in the Lord's Supper. The bread of the presence stands as an exceptional example of *General Sacramental Eating*, because here God chose to relate His presence with the eating of this special bread. From this OT shadow, the *Specific Sacramental Eating* of the Lord's Supper is all the more readily grasped since Christ too has chosen His presence to be found in the eating of bread. Concerning the bread of the Lord's Supper, Christ has declared, "This is my body." God the

---

[124] Edersheim, *The Temple*, 144.

Son is bodily present in the bread, and thus it is truly the bread of His presence! And the altar of the Eucharist, which is the "Table of the Lord," can then be perceived as the antitype of the Table of Presence.

The *bread of the presence* was eaten by the priests once a week. Relative to this fact, Alfred Edersheim relates an observation held by some Bible scholars: "The apostolic practice of partaking the Lord's Supper every Lord's-day may have been in imitation of the priests eating the showbread [bread of the presence] every Sabbath."[125]

Next to the bread of the presence there were flagons of wine.[126] This was wine used in sacrificial ceremonies called *libations*. Recall that such ritual wine was poured at the base of the Bronze Altar, at the identical place where the sacrificial blood was also shed. From this fact, one realizes that the wine on the Table of Presence possessed a link to sacrificial blood. With wine thus connected to the OT ritual blood, the properly catechized Christian observes an obvious correlation with the NT Eucharist.

Since bread and wine were situated side by side on the Showbread Table, these elements possessed sacrificial significance to the Jews. When Jesus then chose bread and wine as the two visible ingredients of his "sacrificial" meal, such ingredients would have reminded the Jews not only of the Passover but also of the basic worship elements located on the Table of Presence—elements regularly utilized in the sacrificial rituals. Concerning Christ's use of wine and bread together, Alfred Cave concludes, "The mere use of these symbols, after the long initiatory education of Mosaism,...would unerringly suggest that they were in some way connected with a finished atonement."[127]

Along with the bread and wine on the Table of Showbread, there was

---

[125] Edersheim, *The Temple*, 145. Daly, *Christian Sacrifice*, 368. Daly writes concerning Hippolytus: "The idea of Christ's sacrifice is also clearly presented in the instructions for private prayer (AT 41, p.90, 1-9; cf. ATC 62 p. 37). For there the OT bread of proposition [presence] is seen as a type of the body and blood of Christ."
[126] Edersheim, *The Temple*, 142.
[127] Alfred Cave, *The Scriptural Doctrine*, 468,469.

incense. This incense, as will be explained shortly, was burned particularly on the Altar of Incense.

The Candelabrum

Along the wall, directly across the room from The Table of Showbread, there stood the seven-fold Candelabrum. All of the many references to Christ as the "light" certainly reflect the fact that this shining Candelabrum foreshadowed Him. Additionally there are NT references that specifically connect Christ with the OT Candelabrum. For instance, in Revelation 1:12,13 Christ is spoken of in terms of the seven-branched Candelabrum (often plural, "lampstands") of the tabernacle:[128]

> And I turned to see the voice that was speaking with me. And having turned I saw seven golden lampstands [candelabrum]; and in the middle of the lampstands [candelabrum] one like a son of man, clothed in a robe reaching to the feet, and girded across His breast with a golden girdle.

As the text later explains in verse 20, the vision of the candelabrum is to be understood in terms of Christ's Church(es). However, verse 12 reveals that when John turned to *see the voice* he *saw* the seven-fold Candelabrum. The voice of Christ comes from the Candelabrum! Further, verse 13 explains that Christ ("son of man") is standing in the midst of the Candelabrum. Truly Christ and His Church are united, and He speaks in her midst and is her light, with His voice as a lamp to her feet and a light to her path. Within every congregation Christ's voice is uniquely heard as it reverberates, "This is my body; This is my blood." Jesus is uniquely present via the sacrament of His body and blood. How appropriate that today's churches frequently have a

---

[128] The words here in Revelation are the same words used in the LXX, Ex. 25:31-40 to describe the seven-branched candelabrum. Exodus 25:37, like the reference in Revelation, uses the plural, *lamps*, for the lampstand.

seven-fold candelabrum standing near the altar where the Eucharist is celebrated.

Though a slightly different word for "lamp" is used, some have also seen Revelation 21:22,23 to be another reference to Christ as the antitype of the OT Candelabrum. Condensing these verses, we read: "[...] the Lord God, the Almighty, and the Lamb are its *temple*,...and its *lamp is the Lamb*. [emphasis added]" The context of Revelation 21 is the tabernacle/temple (see 21:3). "Its lamp" in this verse is rightly understood to be *the temple's* lamp. The temple (or tabernacle) lamp truly typified Christ; thus St. John's Revelation appropriately says of the temple, "Its lamp *is the Lamb*."[129] In other words, the temple-candelabrum *is* Jesus!

Christ as "lamp" can also be related to the fact that many have understood both the seven-fold nature of the lamp and its oil to be references to the Holy Spirit, whom Christ "had without measure"—that Spirit of truth whom Christ pours into His churches.[130]

The Altar of Incense

The final divinely ordained furnishing in the Holy Place was the golden *Altar of Incense* (or *Golden Altar*), which shimmered in front of the curtain that served to cover the entrance into the final sacred chamber. This holy Altar of Incense was used only for highly sacred purposes. Upon it a priest was daily chosen to burn consecrated incense, and while the privileged priest performed this liturgical act the people stood outside praying. At the time of Christ there were so many priests that the burning of incense on the Golden Altar was a privilege accorded to a priest usually only once in a

---

[129] Brown, *The Tabernacle*..., 72: Brown connects the lamp of the tabernacle with Christ as lamp in Rev. 21:23.

[130] Brown, *The Tabernacle*..., 72: "With oil, a symbol of the Holy Spirit, priests and kings were anointed...." "The very number [of lamps, seven] is expressly applied to the Spirit, and one cannot help thinking that the reference is to the seven lamps of the golden candlestick: 'Grace be unto you, and peace, from Him which is, and which was, and which is to come; and from the seven Spirits which are before the throne.'" Also Kurtz, *Offerings*..., 319.

lifetime.[131] This is what Zecharias, father of John the Baptist, was doing when the angel announced to him the astounding conception of his son: "According to the custom of the priestly office, he was chosen by lot to enter the temple of the Lord and burn incense.... And the angel of the Lord appeared to him, standing to the right of the altar of incense."[132]

The sacred incense, as noted earlier, was taken from the Table of Showbread where it rested with the wine and the bread. This sacred incense clearly symbolized the prayers of God's people ascending to Him, as explained by the pleading of the psalmist, "Let my prayers be set before Thee as incense."[133] Christ is *the* mediator of all prayer, for "there is one mediator between God and man, the man Christ Jesus."[134] It is through Him that believer's prayers are able to ascend as incense to the otherwise unapproachable throne of God. The holy incense, which rested next to the bread and wine on the sacred Table, and which was then ceremonially burned on the Altar of Incense, wonderfully typified the mediatorship of Christ Jesus.

Not only did this Altar of Incense receive the burning incense, it also received the "atoning" blood on the most solemn and holy occasions. The sin offering blood that was shed for the entire nation of Israel was reverently applied to the horns on the Altar of Incense. As the loftiest example of this action, once a year, on the Day of Atonement, the high priest would place the most holy blood upon the Altar of Incense horns, and then also sprinkle some of this blood toward the Ark of the Covenant behind the final curtain. The placement of the atoning blood on the Altar of Incense apparently signified that God was forgiving His people *collectively*, and by such blood He was sanctifying this altar so they knew their prayers would ascend to Him. Correspondingly, the blood placed upon the walls and horns of the Bronze

---

[131] Edersheim, *The Temple*..., 120.
[132] Luke 1:9,11. Though this "angel of the Lord" who appeared to Zechariah was Gabriel, not the Son of God, we do know that Jesus Christ is indeed the mediator of all prayers.
[133] Psalm 141:2. See also e.g. Rev. 5:8.
[134] 1 Timothy 2:5.

Altar in the outer court signified the intercession for *individuals*. Christ is the reality here. His blood pleads not only for individuals (Bronze Altar), but also for *all* of His people collectively (Altar of Incense). Truly through the blood of Christ all people have access to God and he hears their prayers. The golden Altar of Incense pictured this.

Even as prayer and the most sacred OT sacrificial blood were both associated with the Altar of Incense, the early church would from the beginning connect the prayers of God's people to the Sacrament of the Altar wherein the holiest blood was to be found. The prayers themselves, especially prayers of thanksgiving, were considered the "sacrifices" of God's people when they celebrated the Eucharist. Robert Daly relates that within mere decades of Christ's resurrection, the "Eucharistic prayer of praise and thanksgiving was generally considered by Christians of this period to be a sacrificial act (in the spiritual sense)."[135] These prayers have been made acceptable to God by the body and blood of The One Sacrifice, the same body and blood received in the Sacrament. So yet again the NT Sacrament of the Altar, with its related prayers, is found to possess antitypical characteristics relative to the Altar of Incense. Most importantly, this Altar of Incense stands as a type of Christ, for through Him the prayers of God's people ascend as incense.

The Most Holy Place (Holy of Holies)

> *"And you shall put the mercy seat on the ark of the testimony in the holy of holies."*
> **Exodus 26:34**

The third and final compartment of the tabernacle was located behind the ultimate curtain located just beyond the Altar of Incense. It was a small

---

[135] Daly, *Christian Sacrifice*, 502.

room called the *Holy of Holies* or *Most Holy Place*. This room was so sacred that only the Jewish high priest was allowed to enter it just one day out of each year. If you could imagine yourself to be the high priest walking behind this final curtain you would find yourself entering a relatively small, cubical room about fifteen feet on a side. If you brought no light with you, the room would have been pitch black if it were not for the "glow" of the Glory of the Lord, which was present in the earlier history of the Jews. Centuries later in the temple, in which there was neither ark nor aura of God's glory, the high priest would enter the pitch dark Holy of Holies via the light from the glow of live coals taken from the Bronze Altar.[136] Whether from the glow of the Glory of the Lord or from the glow of the coals, the interior of this awesome room would be shimmering from the three gold-plated walls and from the gold-plated Ark of the Covenant.

The Holy of Holies was purposely resplendent in gold, for it was the royal room of God's enthroned presence. Here the King of the universe condescended to meet with man. Within this room the only furnishing you would see is a gilded chest called the Ark of the Covenant. If you could open this gold-plated Ark you would behold the two tablets of the Ten Commandments.[137] These Commandments are called God's *Testimony*.[138] The emphasis on the Ten Commandments is made clear when the Ark is at times called the *Ark of Testimony*,[139] and again when the entire tabernacle is similarly called the *Tabernacle of Testimony*.[140] Upon this Ark is a lid called the *Mercy Seat*, for it is here that the Merciful One is enthroned.[141] This Mercy Seat was solid gold, with two solid gold angel-figures called cherubim

---

[136] Edersheim, *The Temple*..., 250.
[137] Hebrews 9:4. Additionally the Ark held a jar of manna and Aaron's rod that budded (Ex. 16:31-34; Numbers 17:10).
[138] E.g. Exodus 31:18.
[139] E.g. Exodus 25:22. The Decalogue was also directly connected to God's covenant (Ex. 34:27,28). Thus one also realizes why the ark is also called the *Ark of the Covenant*.
[140] E.g. Numbers 1:53.
[141] Jewish writings referred to the Ark as God's "footstool," thus identifying His throne to be just above the Ark.

mounted on either end of it.[142] In 2 Samuel one reads that the Ark of the Covenant is "called by the Name, the very name of the Lord of hosts who is enthroned above the cherubim."[143] It was here, at God's *enthroned* presence upon the Mercy Seat, between the two gold angels, that sacrificial blood would be sacredly sprinkled by the high priest once a year on the Day of Atonement.[144] God would then consider the sins of the people to have been *atoned for* (covered) in the highest sense possible in the OT.

Christ and His Sacraments: Antitypes of the Most Holy Place

> "...Christ Jesus; whom God displayed publicly as a propitiation [Mercy Seat] in His blood."
> Romans 3:25

Christ, The Ultimate High Priest

Christ is all that pertains to the Holy of Holies (Most Holy Place). He is *the* high priest, as abundantly attested in the book of Hebrews. As such He can enter into this holiest room in the heavenly places, but instead of entering with sacrificial *animal* blood He does so with *His own* blood. He is thus both high priest and sacrifice, as summarized in Hebrews 9:11,12:

> But when Christ appeared as a high priest of the good things to come, He entered through the greater and more perfect tabernacle, not made with hands, that is to say, not of this creation; and not through the blood of goats and calves, but through His own blood, He entered the [most] holy place once for all, having obtained eternal redemption.

---

[142] Exodus 25:10ff.
[143] 2 Samuel 6:2.
[144] Leviticus 16; Succinct explanation is found in Edersheim, *TheTemple*..., 240ff.

This description of the *Day of Atonement*, presenting Christ as the high priest entering the Holy of Holies with His most sacred blood, is really the theme of the book of Hebrews, to be further explained when Hebrews is discussed in chapter eight.[145] Once again observe in these verses the *heavenly* tabernacle-reality, whereat the blood of Christ pleads for us.[146]

The Ark of the Covenant

Recall that the cover of the Ark was called the *Mercy Seat*. In the New Testament, when the word "propitiation" is used to describe Christ in Romans 3:24,25a, it is precisely the Greek word for "Mercy Seat." Thus Bible scholars such as George Stoeckhardt have noted that Romans 3:24,25a can legitimately be translated, "[We are] being justified as a gift by His grace through the redemption which is in Christ Jesus; whom God displayed publicly as a *Mercy Seat* in His blood through faith."[147]

Of this passage Stoeckhardt explains, "Thus Christ is compared to and appears as the Antitype of the Old Testament Mercy-seat." Stoeckhardt then summarizes Christ's all-encompassing tabernacle-like work: "In one person He is the Offering as well as the Priest and the Mercy-seat."[148] In addition to Stoeckhardt's summary, the crucial observation must be added that Christ also supplies the blood, which finds its ultimate goal to be the heavenly Mercy Seat, the presence of God! Truly Christ here desires that His gospel be fully grasped: By His mercy believers are not condemned; for He is the Mercy Seat, He offers His life-blood for man's atonement, and, as will be

---

[145] Daly, *Christian Sacrifice*, 263: "It is the Yom Kippur sin offering which easily dominates the sacrificial scenery of the letter [to the Hebrews]."

[146] Washburn, *The Import of Sacrifice...*, 81: "It will be noted that effusion of blood alone was not sufficient; atonement was not effected until it was brought to some place which God designated as his special abode. So Christ's work was completed by his entering 'with his own blood...into heaven itself, now to appear in the presence of God for us,' there executing in that 'more perfect tabernacle,' his high-priestly office."

[147] George Stoeckhardt, trans. Erwin Koehlinger, *Epistle to the Romans*, (Fort Wayne: Concordia Theological Seminary Press, 1980), 41.

[148] Stoeckhardt, *Epistle to the Romans*, 41,43.

explained shortly, He is present. All of these NT concepts find their OT expression in the liturgy of the Holy of Holies, in the presence of the Ark that houses the Ten Commandments. With the Mercy Seat remaining atop the Ark of the Covenant, the tablets of the Ten Commandments remain sealed inside this "box," and thus God's law remains contained so His people are not condemned.

With the understanding of the Mercy Seat as God's *throne* (Ps. 80:1), and with the tabernacle/temple language of Revelation 21 and 22, then the phrase "the throne of God and of the Lamb" in Revelation 22:1 is readily understood to be God the Father *and* Christ upon the Mercy Seat.[149] Again, as emphasized especially in the Epistle to the Hebrews, Christ's position at God's right hand is also understood to be His enthronement alongside God upon the Mercy Seat behind the veil.[150] Christians now have the priestly privilege of approaching God's enthroned presence in the heavenly Holy of Holies, and this is done as they receive Christ's enthroned body and blood in the Sacrament.[151] As the epistle to the Hebrews is studied in chapter eight, it will be shown that Christians enter through the veil into God's holy presence through Christ's flesh and blood, and there they find the distribution of mercy from the Mercy Seat.

The Glory of the Lord

A final point concerning the Holy of Holies, is that Christ is also perceived to *be* the "Glory of the Lord." As noted earlier, this Glory of the Lord shone forth from the tabernacle, particularly from the Mercy Seat. This

---

[149] Daly, 296: "It is from this vantage point that the seer [Saint John] experiences most of his visions, looking into the Holy Place, past the golden altar of incense and into the Most Holy Place where, in the heavenly sanctuary, the throne of God would be...E.g. the Lamb stands within the Most Holy Place as he opens successively the seven seals (5, 6:1-8)."

[150] In fact this writer has wondered whether every NT reference to Christ seated at God's right hand is directing God's people to the heavenly Mercy Seat, the Seat we may now approach in prayer and as we partake of the Eucharist.

[151] Interestingly, Christ's ultimate *earthly* throne is indeed His cross. The body and blood of Christ is that of the crucified, risen and ascended Christ.

Glory of the Lord appears to have been directly related to the Son of God who obviously allowed Himself to be manifested many times in the OT. Charles Gieschen cites biblical references where *Glory of the Lord* is shown to be God's presence as a man: "The texts in which the Glory of the Lord has the form of a man are especially important for our study..."[152] Gieschen cites Ezekiel 1:26-28 as a primary example of the *Glory of the Lord* being equated with a man. As these verses from Ezekiel are here condensed, the equation becomes obvious: "[...] High up, was a figure with the appearance of a man...Such was the appearance of the likeness of the glory of the Lord." A man here stands as the glory of the Lord!

The *Glory of the Lord* is additionally a concept and description directly connecting God to the "Angel of the Lord" who, as noted earlier, often took the form of a man. Recall that this unique God-angel both represented God and was God. By such OT appearances as a glorious man, the Son of God can thus be understood to be a "place" where God is present, sometimes demonstrating this presence in the OT as the Glory of the Lord in human form, and sometimes as the Angel of the Lord in human form. Being a "place" for God's presence, God's Son can rightly be understood as the pattern for the tabernacle, the *structural place* of God's presence.

Upon the event of His birth, Christ shows Himself to have become the antitype of the earthly tabernacle, for He was "tabernacling" among man, revealing the Glory of the Lord as a human.[153] However, strange to non-Christian ears, He uniquely revealed such Glory at the cross.[154] As the far superior antitype, the blood upon the beams of the cross, even as the blood upon the exterior of the Ark of the Covenant, pleads for man's atonement. And, further elucidating the atonement in Christ's crucifixion, at the cross one truly finds God enthroned upon His Mercy Seat, sealing off the condemnation

---

[152] Gieschen, *Angelomorphic Christology*, 80-82.
[153] Isaiah and other prophets had predicted the glory of the Lord to be revealed (Isaiah 40:5)
[154] It almost goes without saying that the central action of the tabernacle was sacrifice. Throughout the Gospel of John, Christ's glorification is associated with the crucifixion.

of the Ten Commandments. Truly the Glory of the Lord, uniquely found in the precincts of the tabernacle, has been revealed in Christ Jesus; and in Christ-crucified not merely the Jews but all flesh beholds the glory of the Lord.[155] Thus Saint Paul wrote: "God...is the One who has shone in our hearts to give the light of the knowledge of the *glory of God* in the face of Christ. [italics added]"[156] Such *glory of God*, able to be literally seen in the OT tabernacle, is presently perceived not by sight but by faith. When Christians now enter behind the veil in the reception of the Eucharist, they possess in this Sacrament "the knowledge of the glory of God in the face of Christ."

Christ, Anointed Tabernacle

> *"The Spirit of the Lord God is upon me, because the Lord has anointed me to bring good news to the afflicted...."*
> *Isaiah 61:1; Luke 4:18*

After God's tabernacle and its furnishings were ready for sacred use, and after God ordained the priesthood, He commanded that a special anointing oil be mixed and sanctified to anoint the tabernacle, its furnishings and the priests. Each article within the tabernacle was to be anointed:

> And with it you shall anoint *the tent* of meeting and *the ark* of the testimony, and *the table* and all its utensils, and *the lampstand* and its utensils, and the *altar of incense*, and the *altar of burnt offering* and all its utensils, and *the laver* and its stand. You shall consecrate them, that they may be most holy; whatever touches them shall be holy. And you shall anoint *Aaron and his sons* and consecrate them, that they may minister as priests to Me.[157]

---

[155] Isaiah 40:5.
[156] 2 Corinthians 4:6. See Gieschen, *Angelomorphic Christology*, 334.
[157] Exodus 30:26-30. Italics added. The recipe for the oil is in verses 22-25.

Edersheim relates the Jewish explanation that there is "distinct reference to the King Messiah, on whose account the anointing oil was to be used."[158] Tracing the use of this sacred anointing oil, it is likely that kings David and Solomon were christened with the same oil.[159] Early in catechism instruction Christians rightly become familiar with the terms *Christ* and *Messiah*. These are titles for Jesus, but specifically they are the Greek and Hebrew words for *anointed one*. It fits the prophetic and Christological nature of the OT to directly link the anointing of the tabernacle—including all its furnishings and priests—to *the* Anointed One, Jesus. Jesus, *the Christ*, is the anointed tabernacle, the anointed Bronze Altar, the anointed Laver, the anointed Table of Showbread, the anointed Candelabrum, the anointed Altar of Incense, the anointed Ark of the Covenant and the anointed high priest. He is *the* Christ, *the* anointed One.

From this anointing-relationship, one observes all of the tabernacle types finding their antitype in Christ, and, as has been shown, many of the tabernacle furnishings and practices then secondarily possessed typical connections to the Lord's Supper.

In conclusion, the tabernacle [later the temple] of the Jews had tremendous significance for them and for their worship. Since both Jewish and Christian sages have declared that the Jewish Scriptures are primarily about the Christ, it should come as no surprise that this Jewish tabernacle is really about Him, that He is both its pattern and its fulfillment. With such a perception one realizes both the changeless nature of God and the changeless nature of His worship, for "Jesus Christ is the same yesterday, today and forever."[160]

---

[158] Edershim, *Life and Times*, 714, commenting especially on Exodus 40:9-11 in which God repeats the command to anoint the Holy Implements and the Priests.
[159] Psalm 89:20; 1 Kings 1:39.
[160] Hebrews 13:8.

> *"If his offering is a burnt offering from the herd, he shall offer it a male without defect; he shall offer it...that he may be accepted before the Lord."*
> Leviticus 1:3

Chapter Four

THE BURNT OFFERING, A LINK TO THE SACRAMENT OF THE ALTAR

This chapter is the first of four chapters discussing specifically how OT sacrifices relate both to Christ and to the Lord's Supper. As the sacrificial process is discussed, it may be helpful to refer back to the tabernacle floor plan in the previous chapter.

In Hebrews 10:4-10, Christ identifies Himself specifically as the fulfillment of the burnt offering and the sin offering, and then generally as the fulfillment of the other kinds of sacrifices; Christ's sacrifice is indeed *the* ultimate bodily sacrifice. We have added bracketed comments in Hebrews 10:4-10 to further explain Christ's description of His sacrifice; parenthetic comments are in the text:

> For it is impossible for the blood of bulls and goats to take away sins. Therefore, when He [God's Son] comes into the world, He says, 'Sacrifice and offering [of animals & grain] Thou hast not desired, but a body thou hast prepared for Me; in whole burnt offerings and sacrifices for sin Thou hast taken no pleasure.' Then I said, 'Behold I have come (in the roll of the book it is written of Me) to do Thy will, O God.' After saying above, 'sacrifices and offerings

and whole burnt offerings and sacrifices for sin Thou hast not desired, nor hast Thou taken pleasure in them' (which are offered according to the Law), then He [Christ Jesus] said, 'Behold, I have come to do Thy will.' He takes away the first [types of sacrifices] in order to establish the second [His own sacrifice]. By this will [God's will] we have been sanctified through the offering of the body of Christ once for all. (Hebrews 10:4-10)

Christ explains, as He is the voice of this prophecy in Psalm 40, that the OT "sacrifices and offerings and whole burnt offerings and sacrifices for sin" were not what God ultimately desired.[1] Such a quote encompasses all of the various kinds of sacrifice when it succinctly lists "sacrifices and offerings and whole burnt offerings and sacrifices for sin." Whereas the *burnt offering* and the *sin offering* are specified in this quote, the *sacrifices and offerings* includes the various other kinds of sacrifices. Every kind of OT animal and grain offering was a *type* of the ultimate reality. God's grand and gracious will was that His Son become the *antitype* of all such OT sacrifices by His death upon the cross. This reference from the epistle to the Hebrews shows that the sacrifice of the body of Jesus Christ is the end of all OT sacrifices as well as their fulfillment; something like the Passover is ended and fulfilled in Christ.

When Christ addresses His Father, "...a body Thou hast prepared for Me," He is explaining to us how He needs a *body* so He can be *the sacrifice*. The *body* of Christ was sacrificed once for all, and ultimately only His bodily sacrifice is pleasing to God. Whenever God was pleased with OT sacrifices it was partly because they were given in faith, but even more so because they were expressions and shadows of the sacrifice of God's Son, the only sacrifice that truly removes sin and stands in for human beings.

In the Hebrews text just cited, Christ Jesus identified Himself with the burnt offering, the topic of our current discussion. It should be realized that out of all the Jewish sacrifices the burnt offering has the least to do with the

---

[1] The author of Hebrews uses the LXX (Septuagint) version of Psalm 40.

Lord's Supper. Nonetheless we will show that there are some clear connections between the burnt offering and the Lord's Supper. Because the burnt offering has the least to do with the Lord's Supper, this chapter will also explore the more general sacrificial themes of blood, communion and sacrificial salt.

The Meaning of the Burnt Offering

> *"Then Noah built an altar to the Lord, and took of every clean animal and of every clean bird and offered burnt offerings on the altar."*
> *Genesis 8:20*

As we initiate our discussion of sacrifice, it would seem to make sense to begin with the sin and guilt offerings since these preceded the burnt offering in the "private" sacrificial process.[2] However, our discussion about specific sacrifices begins with the burnt offering because, as Robert Daly explains, "of all the sacrificial rites of the Israelites, the burnt offering...is by far the most important."[3]

The burnt offering was perceived to be the most important sacrifice for several reasons. This sacrifice was the primary sacrifice recognized by the ancients; for instance, Genesis 8:20 records Noah offering a burnt offering.[4] Its importance was also demonstrated as it was the first sacrifice received by God when He lighted the sacred fire.[5] When God prescribed sacrificial procedure for Israel, He magnified the burnt offering by explaining it before

---

[2] S.C. Gayford, *Sacrifice and Priesthood*, (London: Methuen & Co. LTD., 2nd ed. 1953), 53. "It is significant that the three offerings (Sin, Burnt, Peace) are very frequently found in combination and almost invariably in this very order of succession [Sin, Burnt, Peace]..." Private and public offerings will be explained later in our present chapter.

[3] Robert J. Daly, *Christian Sacrifice* (Washington, D.C.: The Catholic University of America Press, 1978), 33. Daly shows the burnt offering to be the "principle sacrifice" (19). See also John W. Kleinig, *Leviticus*, (St. Louis: Concordia Publishing House, 2003), 40.

[4] The burnt and peace offerings are considered the most ancient kinds of sacrifice.

[5] This will be discussed and referenced shortly.

any other sacrifice.⁶ The burnt offering was considered to be uniquely prominent for the Israelites, because for the nation of Israel God had commanded it to be the daily, required sacrifice, and the Bronze Altar was then often called, "The altar for burnt offering." Additionally, since all other sacrifices were burned upon the *daily* burnt offerings, the *daily* burnt offerings were literally foundational for the rest of the sacrifices offered by the Jews on any given day. Finally, its importance is magnified in that the burnt offering was always to be a male creature.⁷

Exodus 29:38,39,42 explains some of the regulations concerning the daily presentation of the burnt offering:

> Now this is what you shall offer on the altar: two one year old lambs each day, continuously. The one lamb you shall offer in the morning, and the other lamb you shall offer at twilight; ...It shall be a continual burnt offering throughout your generations at the doorway of the tent of meeting before the Lord, where I will meet with you, to speak to you there.

As one considers these directions for the daily burnt offerings, one observes the use of *yearling lambs*, the same sacrificial creature prescribed for the Passover. Since *unleavened bread* (grain offering) and *wine* (libation) were also presented with the morning and evening burnt offerings, then once again anyone familiar with the OT would recognize these two ingredients as key Passover ingredients.⁸ With the elements of lamb, unleavened bread and wine being *the* essential ingredients for the burnt offering, one can see why Jewish teachers liked to compare the morning and evening burnt offering with

---

⁶ Leviticus 1.
⁷ J. H. Kurtz, *Offerings, Sacrifices and the Worship of the Old Testament*, trans. James Martin (Peabody, MA: Hendrickson Publishers, Inc., 1998), 250.
⁸ It is interesting that God had not commanded that wine be used for the Passover celebration, but by the time of Christ it was considered so essential that even the poorest of Jews had to drink of the four liturgical cups of wine. Psalm 116:13 is, some believe, referring to the essential wine of the Passover.

the Passover.⁹

Such a comparison also demonstrates why the burnt offering can be compared to the Lord's Supper. The Lord's Supper, like the Passover it supplants, also emphasizes the Passover-ingredients of *Lamb, unleavened bread* and *wine* (Christ is the Lamb.). Both the burnt offering and the Lord's Supper inherited the use of these three foundational ingredients from the Passover, thus giving the same ancestry to both of these sacred ordinances; one might say the daily burnt offering and the Lord's Supper are cousins, both descended from the Passover.

Burnt Offering Purpose

Some have wrongly concluded that the burning of the burnt offering signified God's fiery anger over sin. Those who have studied this type of Jewish offering have come to a very different conclusion. Alfred Edersheim explains:

> The common idea that the burning either of the part or the whole of the sacrifice pointed to...and symbolized the wrath of God and the punishment due to sin, does not seem to accord with Scripture... The rite symbolizes...chiefly its acceptance on the part of God.[10]

OT theologians appear to agree that the burning of the burnt offering flesh upon the altar signified the giving of oneself to God, thus demonstrating one's commitment to Him via this token of self-sacrifice. The central meaning of the burnt offering was that it was a profound statement of *dedication*; recall this word—*dedication*—when thinking of the burnt offering. Thus, for example, S. C. Gayford explains, "When the sin-caused barrier is removed [by the sin offering], he [the offerer] is free to dedicate himself afresh to God,

---

[9] Daly, *Christian Sacrifice,* 204, referencing Fuglister, 51.
[10] Alfred Edersheim, *The Temple: Its Ministry and Services,* (Peabody, Mass.: Hendrickson Publishers, Inc., 1994), 85.

and it is his duty to do so; and this was the 'intention' of the burnt offering."[11] Such *dedication* to God is rightly identified with *sanctification*, which is the godly living performed by people dedicated to God.

Whereas the blood was associated with justification (forgiveness), the body of the burnt offering burned upon the altar was associated with sanctification (godly living). The burnt offering should be understood as the offerer, having been forgiven, offering himself to God. If this is done faithfully, sincerely trusting in God's salvation, God is pleased. If it is done hypocritically, with the offerer flagrantly persisting in sin, God is neither pleased with the offerer nor with his offering. Thus, for example, God would warn through the prophet Isaiah: "What are your multiplied sacrifices to Me? ...I have had enough of burnt offerings of rams, ...I cannot endure iniquity and solemn assembly."[12] Such hypocrisy in the reception of the Lord's Supper should also be guarded against; God cannot endure someone coming to the Lord's Supper and flagrantly persisting in sin.[13]

Burnt Offering Procedure

The burnt offering had just a few basic directives for the priests. Part of the blood of the burnt offering was sacredly dashed upon the outside of the walls of the Bronze Altar to signify atonement, and the remainder was poured at the base of it.[14] Note preliminarily that the blood of the burnt offering was not sprinkled. In later chapters we will explain how the more sacred blood of a sin offering would have been the only blood to be truly sprinkled. The burnt offering was then treated differently from all other sacrifices in that it was totally consumed by fire upon the Bronze Altar, with the exception that the

---

[11] Gayford, *Sacrifice and Priesthood*, 52.
[12] Isaiah 1:11,13b.
[13] Hebrews 10:26-29 is giving this kind of warning, as will be discussed in chapter eight.
[14] Leviticus 1:5,15. The altars in the temple had a red line around the outside wall of the altar. The blood of the burnt offering was dashed below this red line, and the remainder was "shed" at the altar's base. Differing from the burnt offering blood, sin offering blood was uniquely "shed". See Edersheim, *The Temple...*, 93f.

priests were allowed to keep the skin for themselves.[15]

As already noted in previous chapters, the standard order for sacrifice was first the sin (or guilt) offering, then the burnt offering, and finally the peace offering.[16] Edersheim explains concisely, "Where other sacrifices were brought, it [the burnt offering] followed the sin- but preceded the peace-offering."[17]

This order is observed in worship yet today. First, paralleling the sin offering, there is confession and absolution of sin. Second, paralleling the burnt offering, there is the worshiper's dedication expressed through praises and gifts to God. Third, paralleling the peace offering, there is the celebrative meal of the Holy Eucharist. These three elements have been and continue to be foundational parts of worship.

Holocaust and Communion Sacrifices

> "And he [Moses] sent young men of the sons of Israel, and they offered burnt offerings and sacrificed young bulls as peace offerings."
> Exodus 24:5

The two different categories of Jewish sacrifice have been called "holocaust" and "communion" sacrifices.[18] Such terminology is not based upon the *significance* of a sacrifice but upon what was *done* with a sacrifice.[19] The word "holocaust" literally means "completely burned," and the Greek

---

[15] Leviticus 7:8. One might also add that the 'sinew of the thigh' was neither eaten nor burned (Gen. 32:32). See Edersheim, *The Temple*, 94.
[16] Private sacrifices and the sacrifices at Israel's public feasts followed this order.
[17] Edersheim, *The Temple*, 93.
[18] Roland De Vaux, *Studies in Old Testament Sacrifice* (Wales: Cardiff University of Wales Press, 1964), 27ff.
[19] Others divide the sacrifices into their given *purposes*. E.g. *The Book of Concord*, ed. & trans. Tappert (Philadelphia: Fortress Press, 1959), 252, where the Jewish sacrifices are divided into two types, *propitiatory* and *eucharistic*. Such distinction is based on the *purpose* for sacrifice—forgiveness or thanksgiving.

word employed by the Jews for their burnt offering is literally the word *holocaust*.[20] A holocaust sacrifice was therefore any sacrifice or sacrificial portion that was *completely burned* on God's altar.

A *communion* sacrifice, on the other hand, has been defined as a sacrifice that involved some sort of eating on the part of the priest and/or the offerer.[21] The word *communion* can be understood to mean "sharing with" or "partaking with" or "participating with." Usually *communion*, in the sacrificial sense, was associated with the jointly-received food consumed in sacrificial feasting; this is the intended meaning when speaking of a *communion* sacrifice. However, there is also a kind of communion, as will be noted later in this chapter, that emphasizes the *location* of the meal rather than the food.[22] The term "communion" would be adopted in the Christian era to identify *the ultimate* sacrifice-related meal: Holy Communion. Communion involving food was quite common in the sacrificial process, and sacrifices beyond the burnt offering almost always involved the joint reception of a sacred meal.

Except for holocaust offerings, the priests were either privileged or obligated to eat of all other sacrifices.[23] When an OT text says that the priests may "have it" or that a sacrificial portion "belongs to" the priests, such wording indicated that these sacrificial portions were eaten. Leviticus 7 outlines this priestly communion:

> Every male among the priests may eat of it. It shall be eaten in a holy place; it is most holy. The guilt offering is like the sin offering, there is one law for them; the priest who makes atonement with it

---

[20] ολοκαυτωμα.
[21] De Vaux, *Studies*..., 39: "The term 'communion sacrifice', which we here retain, takes it origin from the rite which is peculiar to this sacrifice...the offerers eat the remainder [of the sacrifice] in a ritual meal." It should also be noted that the burnt offering was considered a "communion" with God as it connected man to the altar at which it was burned.
[22] As will be explained shortly, the children of Israel were in Communion with God at the Bronze Altar. The altar would thus stand as the point of OT communion.
[23] The burnt offering and the public sin offering we include in the category of *holocaust*, but these two kinds of sacrifice possessed very different significance.

shall have it. [...] Likewise every grain offering that is baked in the oven, and everything prepared in a pan or on a griddle, shall belong to the priest who presents it. And every grain offering mixed with oil, or dry, shall belong to all the sons of Aaron, to all alike. [...] [Of the peace offering:] And the priest shall offer up the fat in smoke on the altar; but the breast shall belong to Aaron and his sons. And you shall give the right thigh to the priest as a heave offering from the sacrifices of your peace offerings.[24]

The priests had a lot of eating to do, and yet it was not a casual action, nor was it simply eating dinner, but it was a highly sacred and important act of communion.[25] Such voluminous *General Sacramental Eating* wonderfully paved the way for understanding the *Specific Sacramental Eating* of the Lord's Supper, conveying to early Hebrew Christians an immediate and clear sense for The Lord's Supper.

In subsequent chapters such *communion* sacrifices will be shown to compare well with what Christianity calls "Holy Communion." The burnt offering, however, being by definition that sacrifice wholly burned on the altar, was the most common referent for the term *holocaust*.

God Ignited the Sacrificial Fire

> *"Then fire came out from before the Lord and consumed the burnt offering."*
> **Leviticus 9:24**

As revealed in this quote, God inaugurated the sacrificial system by

---

[24] Leviticus 7:6,7, 9,10, 31,32.
[25] Adolph Buchler, *Types of Jewish Palestinian Piety from 70 B.C.E. to 70 C.E.* (London: Jews' College, 1922),34,35, describes the priestly piety exhibited in sacred dining at the time of Christ. One priest, Joses b. Joezer, was so careful with his sacred eating that he even "guarded his ordinary food in ever higher purity, and was, for that observance, called a pious man among the priests."

personally consuming the burnt offering with His heavenly fire.[26] He then repeated this lighting of the altar-fire when Solomon's temple was dedicated for divine worship.[27] See also the accounts associated with Abraham and Elijah where God also personally "consumed" the sacrifice by sending fire.[28] As God sent the sacrificial fire it would no doubt remind His people that man's salvation and sanctification must be initiated and completed by Him. Since the tabernacle fire was also the icon of God's presence, such consuming fire also showed that God was personally consuming ("eating") these sacrifices.[29]

God commanded that the fire of the daily burnt offering was never to go out:

> This is the law for the burnt offering: the burnt offering itself shall remain on the hearth on the altar all night until the morning, and the fire on the altar is to be kept burning on it...Fire shall be kept burning continually on the altar; it is not to go out.[30]

Such perpetual stoking of the altar fire apparently implied that atonement and sanctification are continually needed, and God is their source. Moreover, the perpetual burning of the altar fire implied perpetual access to God. Of NT times, this perpetual fire associated with the daily burnt offering brilliantly portrayed Christ's perpetual offer of atonement, the Spirit's perpetual creation of sanctification, and the perpetual access that Christians now have to their heavenly Father through the Lord Jesus Christ.

---

[26] Evidently Moses and Aaron ignited the fire initially and the sacrificial portions were in the process of being burned upon the Bronze Altar, then God sent fire from heaven and instantly consumed all sacrificial portions, which consisted primarily, as verse 24 relates, of the burnt offering flesh.

[27] 2 Chronicles 7:1.

[28] Genesis 15:17; 1 Kings 18:38; also David's altar at Onan's threshing floor, 1 Chron. 21:26.

[29] Kleinig, *Leviticus*, 147. Though he disagrees with the actual eating performed by God, yet Kleinig agrees with the iconic nature of the fire, and with the fact that the Hebrew wording conveys the action of eating performed by the fire.

[30] Leviticus 6:9,13.

Public and Private Burnt Offerings

> *"Speak to the sons of Israel [not merely priests] and say to them, 'When any man of you brings an offering to the Lord, you shall bring your offering of animals from the herd or the flock."*
> Leviticus 1:2

Throughout this book the terms *public* and *private* will be employed to help the reader distinguish between two types of sacrificial ritual. Categorizing sacrifices as *public* or *private* will not only enable a better understanding of the burnt offering but of the other sacrifices as well. Generally speaking, a *public* sacrifice was offered for the entire nation or for a priest (especially the high priest), but a *private* sacrifice was offered for a layman (or several laymen). Consider now the categories of *public* and *private* as they apply to the burnt offering.

The *daily* burnt offerings had a *public* status to them; they were sacrificed for the entire nation. This was the most common public sacrifice. Only the priests were authorized to sacrifice these offerings twice a day on behalf of the *entire nation*. The priests also sacrificed additional *public* burnt offerings at the various national feasts. Again these were *public* sacrifices, offered for the entire nation, including the priests.[31]

On the other hand, Leviticus 1:2-4 explain that in addition to the various *public* burnt offerings, the laity were also to bring *private* burnt offerings:

> Speak to the sons of Israel [not merely priests] and say to them, 'When any man of you brings an offering to the Lord, you shall bring your offering of animals from the herd or the flock. If his offering is a *burnt offering* from the herd, he shall offer it a male without defect; he shall offer it at the doorway of the tent of meeting

---
[31] Numbers 28, 29.

that he may be accepted before the Lord. And he [the layman] shall lay his hand on the head of the *burnt offering*, that it may be accepted for him to make atonement on his behalf.' [italics and brackets added]

For a *private* sacrifice the layman, while laying his hands upon the creature's head, confessed aloud his and/or his family's sins.[32] Then he personally slew his creature while the priest caught the blood in an appropriate vessel, and then applied it to the altar. Such private burnt offerings, brought by the laity, would be sacrificed after their *private* sin or guilt offering had been sacrificed.

Whether *public* or *private*, the burnt offering signified dedication. Whereas the *public* burnt offering identified the dedication of the nation of Israel, the *private* burnt offering indicated the dedication of the individual bringing it. Such dedication on the part of the nation or on the part of individuals could only occur because God *had* delivered His people, a deliverance finding its basis in the crucifixion of Jesus.

Sacrificial Blood

> *"For it is the [sacrificial] blood by reason of the life that makes atonement."*
> Leviticus 17:11

Even though it may appear that the animal *body* burned upon the altar would offer atonement (forgiveness), it was especially the *blood* of the burnt offering (and of other sacrifices) that conveyed atonement. Though atonement was clearly associated with the burnt offering—by virtue of its

---

[32] This will be detailed in discussing the sin and guilt offerings in chapter five. Kleinig and others are convinced that such offerings were brought by both men and women: Kleinig, *Leviticus*, 44. Kleinig also maintains that the creature's head represented the whole animal, and simultaneously the person bringing it, 62.

blood applied to the altar—yet such blood-atonement was only a background concept for the burnt offering.[33] In our next chapter we will explain how forgiveness and atonement were the main feature of the sin and guilt offerings.

In OT sacrifices the blood was magnified more than any other element. Consequently, in OT worship one finds blood uniquely applied upon the Bronze Altar, upon the Altar of Incense, upon the Mercy Seat and upon certain people who were being ordained or cleansed.[34] The New Testament repeatedly directs Christians to the blood of Christ. Certain theologians maintain that the blood of Christ cannot be properly understood unless one is trained by the blood-teachings of the Old Testament.[35] Since sacrificial blood is so biblically and sacramentally important, consider at this point some of the concepts associated with it.

Consuming Blood Prohibited

In OT times God was vehemently opposed to anyone drinking blood. To the Jews He warned, "Any person who eats any blood, even that person shall be cut off [excommunicated] from his people."[36] This prohibition against consuming blood was in force long before the Jewish sacrificial system. Hundreds of years before Abraham, Noah was commanded, "You shall not

---

[33] W. W. Washburn, *The Import of Sacrifice in the Ancient Jewish Service*, (New York: Phillips & Hunt, 1883), 63: "The peace offering resembled the burnt offering in making the idea of atonement inconspicuous, though not unimportant."

[34] Thus it was placed upon the priests at their ordination and upon the leper when he was cleansed.

[35] John Leighton, *The Jewish Altar: An Inquiry into the Spirit and Intent of the Expiatory Offerings of the Mosaic Ritual* (New York: Funk and Wagnalls, 1886), 113: Leighton concludes that "any treatment of gospel facts which does violence to the impress made by the Mosaic ritual is false to the truth of God and damaging to the high interests of salvation. [...] But viewing the sacrifices of Moses as typical in the sense of containing and enforcing all the great principles underlying the gospel salvation, the record of those principles can never be safely left out of sight."

[36] Leviticus 7:27.

eat flesh with its life, that is, its blood."[37] Even as God had directed Noah, so He repeated the directive for His nation, Israel:

> For the life of the flesh is in the blood, and I have given it to you on the altar to make atonement for your souls; for it is the blood by reason of the life that makes atonement... For as for the life of all flesh, its blood is identified with its life.[38]

For the Jewish Apostles it must have seemed sacrilegious when Jesus offered them His blood to drink. The drinking of animal blood was considered evil and profane, how much more the drinking of human blood! Yet Jesus had avowed, even before the institution of the Lord's Supper, "My blood is true drink."[39]

In the minds of the Apostles who had seen Jesus perform numerous miracles, the sacramental invitation to drink His blood must also have been frightening. Surely these men, who had seen Jesus change water into wine, looked deeply into that Passover chalice and wondered if they would now *see* the blood that Christ declared to be present. They must have felt relief when they could neither see nor taste blood, only wine. But since their Lord had declared, "Drink from it...for this *is* my blood," they *must* believe it. His blood *must* be in the chalice, for He said it was; they had been schooled by Jesus to

---

[37] Genesis 9:4. Does this imply sacrificial participation with the *flesh* of animals? We think it does, as would be readily grasped by the Jews whose sacrificial system was officially in place as they heard this.

[38] Leviticus 7:11,14a. To have blood be the substance of life also made observational sense: All living tissue could bleed; when blood was drained, life ceased; a dead body would not bleed; all conscious life contains blood. Pagans also held that eating a creature's blood or fat endowed the diner with that creature's power and strength. Thus God forbade it. John Kleinig, *Leviticus*, 85ff.

[39] John 6:55. Certainly this text is debated. However when one realizes the common understanding in Jesus' day of sacrificial-eating, then one realizes that those hearing these words of Jesus would have understood them to refer to *sacrificial eating*.

always believe His word, even when it seemed to convey the impossible.[40] Now they were caught between God's restriction about blood and Christ's command to drink it. F. C. N. Hicks summarizes this Jewish conundrum: "To drink blood! That is to tamper with the Holy: that is either a supreme achievement or it is a blasphemous venture into the forbidden."[41] If Christ is the Son of God, then drinking His blood in the Lord's Supper is, undoubtedly, *a supreme achievement*!

Blood: Life

When Jesus instituted His Holy Supper, Matthew tells us that He said of the cup of wine, "Drink from it, all of you; *for* this is my blood..."[42] Only Matthew's account retains the little word *for*. Though Jesus' words can be understood correctly without the word *for*, yet through this little word Jesus identifies His *reason* why Christians should drink of the sacramental cup: "*for* this is my blood." God's people are not to hesitate or fear drinking Christ's blood from the sacramental chalice, but they are to drink it expressly *for* the very reason that it *is His blood!* It is apparent that God prohibited the drinking of blood in the OT for precisely the reason Christ invites the drinking of His blood in the NT: *Blood is life.*[43] God had consistently prohibited the drinking of blood as He repeatedly declared that a creature's life resides in its blood, and only He was eligible to receive such life-blood back to Himself when it was received at His altar. As will be discussed in later chapters, to eat what belongs to God is to commune with Him. Since OT sacrificial blood *only* belonged to God, to eat the blood of Christ is a sign of ultimate communion, a

---

[40] E.G.: They heard His command to fill the water pots with water, with the implication that it would then be wine. The fisherman had heard His word to let down the nets at the worst time to fish, into the deep water where abundant fish would not be found. They heard His word calling forth the dead, healing the sick and exorcizing the demonized—and His word never failed to accomplish what it was sent to do.
[41] F.C.N. Hicks, *The Fullness of Sacrifice* (London: S.P.C.K., 1956),246. Also Kleinig, 370.
[42] Matthew 26:27b,28a. Though some translations leave out the word *for*, it is undeniably present in the Greek.
[43] There are literally hundreds of OT texts that speak of the heart of man as the seat of his being. Since the ancients realized that the heart pumped the blood, this thinking made observational sense—because the heart pumped the life.

communion never even imagined in the OT!

Animal Blood?

The blood of animals is their life. It is certainly not as valuable as human life, but the parallels are clear. For instance, whether human or animal, once the life (blood) is taken, the life within the flesh ceases.

As a token of life for life, God received the blood of innocent animals at His altar, staving off the penalty of death by granting atonement to the believers who approached His altar with such blood. As surely as sin causes *death*, undefiled *life* (blood) is able to cancel sin. Life cancels death. For life to totally cancel death, it must destroy the root of death, sin. The sacrificial life-blood in the OT was the undefiled life of innocent animals.[44] This OT sacrificial blood was of course only a token. It was not able to *create* forgiveness but nevertheless able to *convey* it, much like the Lord's Supper in this respect. Through the blood of these innocent animals, God's OT people were prepared for the *real* atoning blood of Jesus. This life-blood of the undefiled Christ is so powerful that it can and indeed does reverse sin and death, for it is the blood of God (Acts 20:28)—and thus it is the *life* of God! Additionally Christ, unlike any OT sacrifice, would rise from the dead, thus enabling Him to invite what had been unthinkable: the drinking of undefiled

---

[44] The use of innocent animals made sense when one keeps one's eye on Christ. First, they were, like the One they portrayed, innocent. Second, man, having been created in God's image, was lord over all the animals. As such, the animals—though innocent—were cursed when man's world was cursed, and additionally man had the authority to place the animals in his stead, even as a king would command his foot-soldiers to die for the kingdom. In the OT God told man to take the innocent creatures—over which man was lord, cursed with his curse, of the same substance as he—to die in his place. The animals, however, could only stand as tokens of the ultimate sacrifice, for they were imperfect substitutes, being of lesser value than men. The animals, in a way, established a "stay of execution" for man. God is Lord over all men. He wants to free man by dying in man's place. God takes *the* innocent man Jesus, over whom He is Lord, and Jesus—who willingly bears man's curse—obeys and dies in *God's* stead. Jesus can stand in perfectly for man *and* God, because He is both! In Christ, *God dies* for man as man. But Christ is innocent, and thus Christ's life (His blood and His resurrection) truly frees man from his curse. Life truly cancelled death. When man is freed, the whole creation is freed, and this freedom will ultimately be totally revealed.

blood.[45] What Christians drink in Holy Communion is the blood of the Christ who died but is alive forevermore. To miraculously drink His blood is to drink life, and to drink life is to cancel sin and death. In the OT God was teaching about and preparing people for the blood of Christ.

Shedding Light on NT Texts

OT sacrificial blood was never burned or destroyed at God's Bronze Altar, but it was usually placed on the outside walls of, on the horns of, and, as a final application, at the base of this altar.[46] In relation to such blood-placement at the base of God's altar, the vision recorded in Revelation 6:9 conveys a profound meaning: "I saw underneath the altar the souls [lives] of those who had been slain because of the word of God." The base of the altar, the shed blood equaling the lives (souls) of the martyrs, God's exclusive authority to possess the shed blood/life—all of these come together here as one understands the meaning of blood and its sacred placement at the base of God's altar.[47] God used the OT sacrificial rites "to drill and prepare Israel for gospel times and gospel things."[48] Through God's training of the Jews via their OT sacrificial practices, all of the NT discussions about Jesus' blood (and martyr blood) made perfect sense.[49]

With God's declaration that blood is bonded with life, certain NT

---

[45] The Psalmist explains this negatively in Psalm 30:9: "What profit is there in my blood, if I go down to the pit?" Literally in the LXX the word for *pit* is *decay*, precisely the word used of Christ whose body would not decay in death. Christ's blood does not fail to profit; He would not decay, He would rise.

[46] The one exception to this is the sacrifice of the Red Heifer. Some of its blood was sacredly sprinkled, but then some of its blood was burned outside the camp (Numbers 19:4,5). Note, however, that this blood was not burned upon the Bronze Altar. This sacrifice was often considered the most intense sin offering. See Edersheim, *The Temple...*, 281. Sacrificial blood was placed on the horns of both of the altars.

[47] Daly, *Christian Sacrifice*, 302: "Rev. 6,9....this verse [is seen by some as] an allusion to the OT rite of pouring out the blood of the sacrificial victim at the foot of the altar."

[48] Leighton, *The Jewish Altar*, 20.

[49] Leighton, *The Jewish Altar*, 118: "It cannot well be denied that the frequent ascription of redemption to the blood of Christ is based squarely on this literal correspondence between the new covenant and the old, both being in the same way sealed with blood." How often does the NT reference the blood of Christ? Hicks, *The Fullness of Sacrifice*, 241: "It is Only St. James and St. Jude who do not touch it [blood] directly."

references take on a deeper meaning. References to Christ giving His life are parallel to His shedding His blood. For instance, consider Christ's self-avowed purpose that He came to "give His life a ransom for many."[50] Upon hearing such a statement a Jew would surely have related *both* "ransom" and "life" to blood! To "ransom" ("redeem") a person or other creature was to buy them back with something of great value.[51] What greater ransom than to give one's life? What greater life than the life of God's eternal Son! To give one's "life" was naturally connected to giving one's blood. So the thought of blood is doubly allied to what Jesus here asserts. The Hebrew mind would intuitively have understood that Jesus came to "give His *blood* a ransom for many." One's blood was one's life, and this was the cost of man's ransom: the blood/life of God's Son.[52] To offer up life was, in a sacrificial sense, to offer up blood.

Whereas talking about a creature's life often meant that you were talking about its blood, the reverse implied an even tighter link; to reference a creature's blood nearly always meant that you were referencing its life. For instance when Jesus offered His blood to drink, the Hebrew mind would have instantly considered this drinking to be the reception of Christ's life. St. Paul declared concerning the cup of the Lord's Supper, "Is not the cup of blessing which we bless a communion in the blood of Christ?"[53] Why would anyone want to commune Christ's blood? Because to do so is to commune His life! Commenting on this blood-life relationship, M. F. Sadler paraphrases St. Paul's rhetorical question by asking of the Cup of Blessing, "...is it not the common participation of all of us in the Blood of Christ, i.e., in the Life of

---

[50] Matthew 20:28.
[51] Often one was redeemed with silver, but certain creatures were redeemed by sacrificial blood. There were two types of redemption. One especially involved buying someone out of slavery. The other especially involved buying the firstborn back from God. It took money or life-blood to make the purchase.
[52] E.g. 1 Peter 1:18,19; Rev. 1:5; Eph. 1:7. Leighton, *The Jewish Altar...*, 119: "As 'the life is in the blood,' and as the blood of the Mosaic victim was shed before the Altar, so Jesus in this strict sense gave His life for the life of His people (Eph. 1:7; 2:13)."
[53] 1 Corinthians 10:16.

Christ (the life is in the blood)?"[54]

Blood: Resurrection

Since sacrificial blood was bound with life, it also makes sense that the Jews would relate it to the belief in resurrection. There was the Hebrew understanding that when the blood was placed upon the sides of and at the base of the altar but *never burned* on the altar, it *remained* the life of the sacrificial creature, even though the flesh was dead.   S. C. Gayford explains:

> There was a striking unanimity in this regard amongst races of all countries and ages. The blood is the seed of life; more than this, to the Semite [Jewish related people] it was the actual life itself. . . The Hebrews regarded the life-blood almost as a living thing inside the body which it quickened; and not only was it the vitalizing life while it pulsated within the body, *but it had an independent life of its own, even when taken from the body* [italics added].[55]

Probably most people today would consider the body *and* the blood of an OT sacrifice to foreshadow *only* Christ's death.[56] However the Hebrew mind would have seen the unburned OT blood to be a sign of *continued life*. Gayford explains: "'Blood' in a sacrificial sense always means a 'Risen' life, one that has passed through death, but is alive."[57] Such *risen life*, associated with OT sacrificial blood, would find its antitype not only in the shedding of Christ's life-blood upon the cross, but also in His resurrection. The One who

---

[54] M. F. Sadler, *The First and Second Epistles to the Corinthians* (London: George Bell and Sons, 1898), 155. Parentheses are in the text.
[55] Gayford, *Sacrifice and Priesthood*, 68.
[56] Gayford, *Sacrifice and Priesthood*, 68,69: "To us moderns blood...brings up the associations of death; to the Hebrews it meant life...We can hardly draw attention too emphatically to this radical difference between the modern western mind and the ancient Semitic associations of thought, running down, as they do, through the Hebrew and Jewish religion into Christianity..."
[57] Gayford, *Sacrifice and Priesthood*, 170.

had had his life drained, rose from the grave; life again courses through His risen body. This is the body and blood received in the Holy Supper, bringing us not only to the foot of the cross but also to the empty tomb.

Blood: Atonement

OT sacrificial blood was not only associated with life, but with atonement. The Hebrew word for *atonement* basically means "covering." To atone for sins is to cover them. To thus cover sins is not merely to blanket them with the possibility that they might become uncovered later, but atonement-covering is the permanent covering of sin, forever keeping such sins out of God's sight. By such covering, sins are obliterated!

Of the atonement associated with the OT sacrificial blood, God declared, "For it is the [sacrificial] blood by reason of the life that makes atonement [covering]."[58] From such a quote it is clear that not only *life* but also *atonement* was linked to sacrificial blood. Sacrificial blood conveyed the covering for sin. This made sense. Even as sin caused death, so atonement for sin was part of the formula for giving life. Obliterate sin and you obliterate death; only life remains. For all the types of animal sacrifices offered in the precinct of the tabernacle, the blood was the atoning figure. Whereas OT blood was *linked* to atonement, only Christ's blood *creates* it. Now Christ's blood, received by His people miraculously in the Lord's Supper, not only brings life but also atonement. It is a package deal, for where there is forgiveness of sins (atonement) there is also life and salvation.[59]

Concerning such life and atonement, the OT animal sacrifices had significance because they prefigured the coming Christ and because they drew from and were based upon His omnipotent sacrifice. In contrast to animal blood, the blood from His sacrifice is not a mere *token* (like the blood of animals), but it is the *real* atoning sacrificial life. The animal blood could

---

[58] Leviticus 17:11.
[59] See Luther's Small Catechism. In his instruction concerning the Sacrament of the Altar, he answers the question, "What is the benefit of such eating and drinking?" with such wording.

be *based upon* Christ's blood because the effects from Christ's shed blood reach back to the beginning of time. The Scriptures teach this time-leaping reality when they explain that Christ was slain from the foundation of the world.[60]

To summarize, the handling of OT blood uniquely combined the concepts of atonement, life and resurrection. Such a perception should also be present as one receives the blood of Jesus in the Lord's Supper; by partaking of *His* blood, His people are receiving atonement, life and the "infusion" of a bodily resurrection.

Man as Physical Being

> *"Touch Me and see, for a spirit does not have flesh and bones as you see that I have."*
> Luke 24:39

Modern religious belief splits a man into body and soul, associating life *only* with the *invisible* part of him, the soul.[61] Certainly the Scriptures express the reality of the soul, but today's thinking overemphasizes the value of the invisible, failing to realize that the *visible* part of a person deserves equal status relative to his/her life. Contrary to popular belief, the invisible soul is not what gives value to a human body.[62] Man's tangible, visible, physical nature has value in itself. Jews in Jesus' day grasped this value of the visible as they realized from their sacrificial rites that life was identified with one's visible, tangible blood, and that that life coursed through a visible,

---

[60] Revelation 13:8 (See the Greek); Ephesians 1:4; 1 Peter 1:19,20; John 17:24.
[61] Such a dualistic belief was totally foreign to Jewish thinking. F. Gavin, *The Jewish Antecedents of the Christian Sacraments*, (New York: The Macmillan Co., 1928), 14: "...so the Jew in his relentless if unconscious non-dualism would fail to recognize the antithesis always present to the mind of such present-day scholars.... [To the Jew] the whole of religion concerned the whole of man."
[62] Such confusion probably partly arises from the association of sin with the body, such as referring to the sinful nature as the "flesh" and the dying body as the "clay vessel".

tangible body. They then consistently considered eternal life simply as the resurrection of the body, not as a mere disembodied soul.[63] Christians must always bear in mind that this is one of the unique features of the Christian faith, that God wants His children to be *physical* creatures...even into eternity![64]

Though it is true that a person's "soul" departs his body at death, yet such a state is unnatural and incomplete.[65] The Scriptures, as they speak of the resurrection of the body, demonstrate that a person's body *and* soul are of ultimate value *together*. The body possesses such great value that God desires even to retrieve it from the grave. Truly to identify a human individual is to identify a unique body with blood (life) coursing through it.

The Lord's Supper emphasizes this importance of the body. First, the Holy Supper reminds the Christian of the physical realities of Christ's incarnation, His death and His resurrection. Second, if *I* wonder whether God really cares about *my* body, *my* consumption of the Lord's Supper answers with a resounding *yes*! God wants to infuse *me* through *my* personal, *physical* eating of Christ's sacred body *and blood*, thus declaring *my physical body and blood to be sacred and filled with life*! The Lord's Supper is fed to *me*. It is an *individualized, bodily* reception of life and salvation.

Concerning the "individualized" reception of the Supper, there is, we believe, the exception of the pregnant woman. What a word of encouragement and comfort for Christian women who have miscarried![66] The

---

[63] Gavin, *The Jewish Antecedents*, 10-11. Gavin (11) explains Jewish thinking: "Man is thus an indissoluble unity of body and soul, of which each part is essential. Man is neither one nor the other, but both." Thus when Jesus refuted the Sadducees' denial of the resurrection He pointed to God being the God of [the living] Abraham, Isaac and Jacob (Matt. 22:32). To the Jews, who did not divide body from soul, such life after death indeed meant *resurrection*—not disembodied souls. Today's orthodox Jews thus do not consider cremation a viable option, and they have much difficulty with organ donation.

[64] We don't know what resurrected bodies will be like. 1 Corinthians 15:35ff; 1 John 3:2; etc.

[65] There is theological uncertainty as to what the soul is "doing" after death, before the resurrection.

[66] We believe it is also correct to so encourage those Christian women who, in a time of youthful ignorance or arrogance, had an abortion. There is hope as the body and blood of Christ were encountered by the baby in the womb.

child, though indirectly, has surely received Christ's sacred body and blood while in the womb! Indeed this is a "physical" concept, but it is precisely a major point of the Lord's Supper: Our *bodies* eat salvation and drink life! Truly such children must "leap for joy" (Luke 1:44) as Christ's body and blood have come unto them through their faithful mothers.

God Eats!

> "Then the priest shall offer it up in smoke on the altar, as food..."
> Leviticus 3:11

Though no *people* ate of the burnt offering, nevertheless there was the understanding that eating occurred. The burnt offering creature and other sacrificial portions consumed by fire upon God's altar were understood to have been eaten *by God!*[67] Instead of merely saying that such sacrifices were "received" by God, frequently the biblical terminology and descriptions literally describe God *eating*. This is stated indirectly in such passages as Deuteronomy 32:38 where God sarcastically asks the people whether false gods were *really* eating the portions burned on *their* altar: "Who ate the fat of their sacrifices, and drank the wine of their libations [drink-offerings]. Let them [the "false gods"] rise up and help you. Let them be your hiding place." God here implies that He, the true God, was truly eating at *His* altar as surely as He could truly rise to help His people. But the false gods obviously were incapable of eating or helping, for there are no other gods. (However later it will be shown that there are indeed "demons" associated with eating sacrifices offered to other gods.)

This eating by God is perhaps more clearly revealed in Leviticus 21:6, wherein the priests who offered up the sacrifices in fire were warned to "be

---

[67] The burnt offering and the burned portions of the peace offering especially conveyed this understanding. Leviticus 1-3.

holy to their God and not profane the name of their God, for they present the offerings by fire to the Lord, the bread of their God; so they shall be holy."[68] Here the sacrifice consumed by fire is called "God's bread"; it is His "food." This line of thinking is also revealed in Leviticus 3:11: "Then the priest shall offer it up in smoke on the altar, as food, an offering by fire to the Lord." That which is burned on the altar is God's *food*.[69] Again hear of it in Numbers 28:2 where God says, "You shall be careful to present My offering, My food for My offerings by fire, of a soothing aroma to me, at their appointed time." The next verse explains such "offerings by fire" to be the daily burnt offering lambs. These were God's *food*.[70] Such burnt offerings were, as Hicks Biblically explains, "the bread of God; and the altar, on which He accepted them, was His table."[71]

The fire was a visible manifestation of God's presence in the tabernacle or temple. Even as God descended on Mount Sinai with fire and smoke, so the fire and smoke at His altar were visible expressions of His presence.[72] Consistent then with "bread of God" describing the portions on His altar, the Hebrew in several texts describes the fire as literally "eating" those portions.[73] Such wording signified that God participated by eating.

Directly paralleling these God-eaten sacrifices is the description of a "soothing aroma" or "fragrance" before God.[74] With such aroma-related descriptions, God is perceived to be "breathing in" the burned up sacrificial portions. This makes observational sense since the smoke of the burnt offering was truly the creature ascending heavenward. As an example, consider this priestly directive: "Then Aaron's sons shall offer it up in smoke

---

[68] J.B. Lightfoot, editor & translator, *The Apostolic Fathers Clement, Ignatius, and Polycarp*, vol. 2, (Grand Rapids: Baker Book House, 1981), "Epistle to the Romans," 561: Ignatius, who was martyred in 107AD, spoke of the Eucharist as "the bread of God, which is the flesh of Christ." "Bread of God" is OT sacrificial terminology, here linked to the Eucharist.
[69] The Hebrew uses the usual word for *bread*, which is frequently translated *food*.
[70] See also e.g. Ezekiel 44:7.
[71] Hicks, *The Fullness of Sacrifice*, 40.
[72] Kleinig, *Leviticus*, 147.
[73] E.g. Leviticus 6:10; 9:24.
[74] See Numbers 28:2 just quoted.

on the altar on the burnt offering, which is on the wood that is on the fire; it is an offering by fire of a *soothing aroma* to the Lord."[75] When God "smells" the *soothing aroma*, such a description is simply further explaining His eating. Thus God is teaching His people that eating is an integral part of worship, even on His part!

To some, God's eating or smelling seems to demean Him. Certainly God, as a spirit, need not nor could not "eat" as we do.[76] So there surely is a difference between His eating and ours. However, to say that God "smells" or "eats" a sacrifice should be no more strange or offensive than to say God "speaks" or "hears." God can only be understood if His actions are put into human terms, even though He surely does none of these things as we do them (until the incarnation!).

When God ate certain OT sacrifices, this was an example of General Sacramental Eating. Recall that General Sacramental Eating was any eating that possessed a miraculous element, and often in such supernatural dining the primary benefit to those eating was not in the food's nutrition. This was certainly true concerning God when He ate the burnt offering, for He needs no such nutrients or vitamins. God thus explained in Psalm 50 that He did not *need* to eat of the burnt offerings presented by the corrupted Israelites:

> I do not reprove you [Israelites] for your sacrifices, and your burnt offerings are continually before Me...If I were hungry, I would not tell you; for the world is Mine, and all it contains. Shall I eat the flesh of bulls, or drink the blood of male goats?[77]

God does not *need* to eat, but He does! Though no *man* ate of a burnt offering yet some theologians are convinced such a sacrifice still possessed a "communion" aspect, because God ate. W. W. Washburn

---

[75] Leviticus 3:5.
[76] Psalm 50:7-15. Of course God can eat as one of us after the Son's incarnation.
[77] Psalm 50:12,13.

represents this viewpoint as he explains, "The entire victim being food...is called the food of Jehovah, and shows the *communion between him and the worshiper* brought about by the sacrifice [emphasis added]."[78] In OT times God was "in communion" with His people through the burnt offering. However, this communion was not created through a common *meal* but through a common *table*, the Bronze Altar.[79] The burnt offering had a communion nature to it because such a sacrifice was understood to have been offered by man to God upon *His table*.

Such communion with God, though a non-edible communion on the part of the offerer, was nevertheless a very real fellowship relationship. Of this OT fellowship Saint Paul would write, "Look at the nation Israel, are not those who eat the sacrifices in communion *with the altar*?"[80] This fellowship *relationship* with the altar is magnified when one considers the peace offering, the offering that emphasized the communion meal drawn from the sacrifice which was eaten by the people of God. God ate of the *burnt offerings* and the people ate of the *peace offerings*, and the Bronze Altar served as the OT *place of communion*, and thus St. Paul would explain, as quoted above, that the Israelites were *in communion with the altar*. Because of this communion understanding, the burnt offering and the peace offering have at times been considered together. For example Alfred Edersheim connects the burnt offering to the peace offerings by explaining that *both* of these sacrifices communicated communion with God. He explains that Hebrew offerings were "either sacrifices of communion with God, or else intended to restore that communion...To the former class belong the burnt- and peace-offerings; to the latter, the sin- and the trespass-offerings."[81]

---

[78] Washburn, *The Import of Sacrifice...*, 64-65.
[79] 1 Corinthians 10:18 identifies this place of "communion."
[80] 1 Corinthians 10:18 (author's translation).
[81] Edersheim, *The Temple...*, 77.

The Burnt Offering, a Link to the Sacrament of the Altar

Why Would God Eat?

> *"...and walk in love, just as Christ also loved you, and gave Himself up for us, an offering and a sacrifice to God as a fragrant aroma."*
> *Ephesians 5:2*

God *communed* with His people in OT worship by eating (breathing in) the sacrifices burned upon His table. If God was not taking nutrition from His "meal" then why was He eating? In addition to receiving nutrition, one eats for at least two additional reasons: to receive *satisfaction* and/or to *commune* with someone else. It is apparent that both "satisfaction" and "communion" are what God wants to convey by His eating.

God participates in worship as He eats/smells of the sacrifices consumed on His altar. Thus the sacrifices are "internalized" by God, and He is *satisfied* as He *communes* with the offerer. By saying that He performs such human/earthy actions as eating or smelling, God communicates a clear picture of His down to earth participation in worship. Simply put, God demonstrates His love to His people by humbling Himself to commune with them. "Who is like the Lord our God, who is enthroned on high, who humbles Himself to behold the things that are in heaven and on the earth?"[82]

As God thus ate a holocaust sacrifice—finalized by breathing in its aromatic smoke—He indicated satisfaction derived from *faithful* sacrifices, with the ultimate result being His satisfaction with the giver of the sacrifice. God participates and is "soothed." The Jewish burnt offering represented the offerer giving himself to God. Andrew Jukes summarizes, "The offering, whatever it might be, stood for, and was looked upon as identical with the offerer."[83] It was the offerer's "gift" to God, because such a gift, being the very livelihood and the very food and sustenance of the giver, thus aptly

---

[82] Psalm 113:5,6. The humiliation of Christ has precedent as God condescended in OT times.
[83] Andrew Jukes, *The Law of the Offerings in Leviticus I. - VII Considered as the Appointed figure of the Various Aspects of the offering of the Body of Jesus Christ* (London: James Nisbet & Co., 13th ed., 1883), 38.

represented the giver giving himself.[84] The *sweet savor (or aroma)* of a burnt sacrifice implied that God was now pleased with the offerer.[85] This did not mean that God wanted to "eat" the offerer, but that such eating by God communicated in a down to earth way that He was pleased, and that He was in a type of communion/fellowship with the offerer. You willingly and joyfully eat with people when you are pleased with them. God and man could gather at the same table—an action indicating friendship or even family.

Of Christ's sacrifice St. Paul wrote in Ephesians 5:2, "... Christ also loved you, and gave himself up for us, an offering and a sacrifice to God as a fragrant aroma." Here, in the language of the burnt offering, God's complete satisfaction is conveyed by the sacrificial terminology of *fragrant aroma*.[86] Christ's crucifixion is truly *the* fragrant aroma, satisfying God completely. Christ did not offer an animal on behalf of Himself, but He actually offered Himself. Of course Christ was not burned up like the OT burnt offering, but certain aspects of the burnt offering portrayed Christ. God receives/accepts the sacrifice of his Son and is pleased, far more pleased than smelling the sweet aroma of the OT burnt offerings.[87] This is so because God's Son in the flesh is the only one with whom God was well pleased from the beginning. Through this ultimate sacrifice, God is both *satisfied* with and offers *communion* with mankind; God offers communion with this sacrifice uniquely in the Lord's Supper.

It is no coincidence that after the verse just cited (Eph. 5:2), the rest of the fifth chapter of Ephesians is devoted to God-pleasing Christian living. As noted earlier, the main emphasis of the burnt offering was sanctification, God's creation of holiness in the lives of his people, a holiness indicated by

---

[84] Gayford, *Sacrifice and Priesthood*, 15ff.
[85] Kleinig, *Leviticus*, 41ff. God is pleased not because men were meriting such pleasure, but because in God's ordained rituals He was always pleased with such gifts, given in faith.
[86] Hicks, *The Fullness of Sacrifice*, 233 identifies Ephesians 5:2 with the burnt offering. So also Alfred Cave, *The Scriptural Doctrine of Sacrifice and Atonement*, (Edinburgh: T & T Clark, 1890), 424.
[87] Kleinig, 66: "God's pleasure in the burnt offering foreshadows his delight in the sacrifice of his Son, about whom he declared, "With him I am well pleased" (Mt 3:17; 17:5)."

their loving *dedication* to Him. Christ is *the* dedicated one. He, in a far greater way than a mere animal sacrifice, fulfills the *purpose* of the burnt offering as His crucified body signifies the believer's sanctification.

Even as the burnt offerings in the OT were offered in the stead of the people bringing them, so in an infinitely greater way Christ's crucifixion stands in for His people. His sacrifice for us indicates our dedication to God. Thus the doctrine is rightly conveyed that apart from Christ's sacrifice, God is not pleased with man's good works. Only through Christ's sacrifice are the works of His people sanctified, as Jesus explained, "Apart from me you can do nothing."[88] God is pleased with what Christians do because He receives the "sweet aroma" of His Son's self-giving sacrifice. The Christian's works, like the OT burnt offering, become a "sweet aroma" to God, but only because they are conjoined to the sweet aroma of Christ's sacrifice.[89] Man's sanctification does not originate from self, but from Christ-crucified. Dedication was the primary meaning of the burnt offering. We cannot dedicate ourselves to God apart from Christ.

Because the sacrifice of Jesus creates such a "sweet aroma" to God, this sacrifice stands as both the foundation and the fulfillment of all OT burnt offerings. It is *foundational* to the OT burnt offerings because God's delight in the eating and smelling of the OT burnt offerings was founded upon the sweet aroma of Christ's crucifixion. Christ *fulfills* the burnt offering because the antitype of every burnt offering was the crucifixion of Jesus; His sacrifice fulfills every OT sacrificial aspect. Though the NT never states that God "eats" of the sacrifice of His Son, yet the eating-parallel of "smelling" the sweet aroma of Christ is set forth, as just noted. Such a reference is only grasped by understanding the OT offerings burned on God's altar. As God finds satisfaction in the "aroma" of Christ's sacrifice, He is pleased with Christ's people and with their holy works performed in His name.

---

[88] John 15:5b
[89] Other NT references to "fragrant aroma" (e.g. 2 Cor. 2:14; Phil. 4:18) then show a sanctification that begins with God.

Pagan Communion

> *"But I have a few things against you, because you...eat things sacrificed to idols..."*
> Revelation 2:14

Even as God was "eating" the OT sacrifices burned on His altar, consider now the parallel pagan belief that their gods were eating the sacrifices offered to them. Such pagan beliefs were no doubt blurred remnants of the actual reality that the true God desires to commune with His people. The common Greek technical term for *pagan feasting* was "koinonia." Though this word will be discussed further, relative to the peace offering, it is of value to realize how such pagan "koinonia" relates to the Jewish burnt offering. When a pagan "god" *ate* of a sacrifice burned upon his altar, and then when that god's people also ate of that *same* food, they were said to be in "koinonia." The word *koinonia* basically means "what is in common," and so it is often understood as a point of contact, sharing, fellowshipping, communing and the like. It is commonly translated *communion.*

Among pagans *koinonia* was a technical term for the *meal* whereby they communed with their god. In this communion, the people ate of the *same* sacrificial food that their god ate.[90] The *food* was, for pagans, the "point of contact" (*koinonia*) with their god. The flesh was taken from a single animal, part of which was burned on the pagan altar and the other part eaten by pagan worshipers. The pagan god first "ate" of the animal flesh when part of it was burned, and his people then ate of what was left of the *same*

---

[90] Friedrich Hauck, "κοινωνια," vol. III, *Theological Dictionary of the New Testament*, ed. Gerhard Kittel and Gerhard Friedrich, trans. Geoffrey W. Bromiley (Grand Rapids: Wm. B. Eerdmans Publishing Co., 1968), 797-809. 799: "On the level of popular polytheism the sacrificial meal then becomes a communion of the deity with men [...] Man and god are companions at table. Nor is this true only of the naïve primitive age. In the Hellenistic period, too, the gods arrange and conduct sacrificial meals. Men are invited as companions ......to the table of the gods."

sacrificial flesh. This was pagan communion (*koinonia*).

The Jews would never employ *koinonia* to describe their sacrificial communion with God. At first it may seem amazing that the Jews *never* used this word *koinonia* in their Greek translation of the OT to refer to a joint meal between humans and the true God.[91] Perhaps they avoided *koinonia* simply because the OT translators wanted to avoid describing *true* sacrificial eating with a word commonly used to portray *pagan* sacrificial eating. This is a possible explanation, but there appears to be a better one.

Unlike the pagans around them, God's OT people *never* ate of the *same sacrificial flesh* that God ate! For instance, the burnt offerings were *totally* eaten by God—consumed by fire—so the people ate *none* of this sacrifice. Similarly, when a human ate the *flesh* of the sin, guilt or peace offerings, such flesh was never burned on God's altar, and thus God *never* ate of the sacrificial flesh of these offerings. For sin, guilt and peace offerings *only God* could consume the fatty portions, and *only His people* could consume the flesh.[92] The blood, received on the outside of the altar, was never consumed by man. God had strictly forbidden the communing of fat or blood: "All fat is the Lord's...you shall not eat any fat or any blood."[93] Thus with the animal sacrifices in the Jewish sacrificial system, God was eating His portion and His people were eating theirs, but God and man were *never* communing the same meal, they were never "sharing" (*koinonia*) the same sacrificial elements. God strictly forbade eating His portion. In regard to sacrificial food, the word *koinonia* did not fit the OT animal sacrifices as it fit the pagan ones.[94] Roland De Vaux explains this thinking in relation to the

---

[91] Ibid., 801: "In the LXX ...we *never* find koinonia for the relation between God and man. This is a surprising fact, for there can be little doubt that in ancient Israel sacrifice, or the sacrificial meal, was widely regarded as a sacral fellowship between God and man....In respect of the close sharing and fellowship actualized in the sacrificial meal the word group 'Koinon-' *is avoided*." [emphasis added].

[92] Of course for a "public" sin offering, the creature was entirely consumed by God, except for the blood which was consumed by no one, but received by God "around" His altar.

[93] Leviticus 3:16,17; See also Leviticus 17:6,11.

[94] The apparent exception is the grain offering from which both God and the priests ate the identical substance. But this was not a blood sacrifice associated with forgiveness.

peace offering: "It is significant that in the communion sacrifice [peace offering] only the blood and the fat are offered to Yahweh, all flesh being excluded. It is not a meal which God shares with His faithful."[95]

In what seems to be an exception to this rule, in I Corinthians 10:18 St. Paul states that there *was* some sort of *koinonia* with the Jewish altar: "Look at the nation Israel; are not those who eat the sacrifices sharers [*koinonia*] in the altar?"[96] As explained earlier, this apparent exception is resolved as one realizes that the *altar* stood as the focal point, the "point of contact" (*koinonia*) between God and His people in OT times.[97] As the quote specifies, the Israelites and God were "sharers in *the altar*." Thus even before the construction of the tabernacle, God would, on several occasions, be in "communion" with His people at an *altar*.[98] Recall that this is what made the burnt offering a kind of communion sacrifice. The Bronze Altar was a *place* shared by God and man, but not a *food*. God and man were in *koinonia* when they both approached the same OT *altar,* as St. Paul verified. M. F. Sadler, observing this OT reality, explained that "the altar...was a means of communion between God and the worshippers."[99]

The Bronze Altar was so thoroughly associated with the burnt offering that frequently it was simply labeled the "altar for burnt offering."[100] Thus the burnt offering, and the altar upon which it was burned, were both associated with communion between God and man. Today it is no coincidence that the Lord's Supper has taken the name "Sacrament of the *Altar*." In the NT era, however, it is not at any specific physical *altar* where God and man now commune, but it is in sharing Christ's altar-related body and blood. Saint Paul

---

[95] De Vaux, *Studies in Old Testament Sacrifice*, 42.
[96] Literally the verse reads, "Look at the nation of Israel *after the flesh*..." Another understanding of the verse could be that St. Paul is describing Israel's apostasy, as referenced in verse 7, and that the "altar" spoken of was the altar of the golden calf, at which "Israel *after the flesh*" was in pagan communion.
[97] To a degree this was also the pagan understanding. Hicks, *The Fullness of Sacrifice*, 249: "The altar is the point of contact with the god."
[98] E.g. Genesis 35:1.
[99] M. F. Sadler, *The First and Second Epistles to the Corinthians* (London: George Bell and Sons, 1898), 160.
[100] E.g. Leviticus 4:7.

wrote of God's OT believers, "Look at the nation Israel; are not those who eat the sacrifices sharers [*koinonia*] in the altar?" Now God's people can say, "Look at the new Israel of God, are not they who *eat* of the Sacrament of the Altar in communion (*koinonia*) with God?"

Peculiar as it may seem, the pagan-related word, *koinonia*, is now fitting as a reference to the Lord's Supper! Just two verses before the one quoted above, the Apostle Paul wrote: "The cup of blessing which we bless, is it not a communion [*koinonia*] of the blood of Christ? The bread which we break, is it not a communion [*koinonia*] of the body of Christ?"[101] As a highly educated Jew, Paul was no doubt quite familiar with the Jewish avoidance of *koinonia* for describing their sacrificial *eating*, and yet here he uses *koinonia* to describe the Lord's Supper. An explanation consistent with the usual usage of *koinonia* is that Paul realized he could legitimately use koinonia, because uniquely in the Lord's Supper God and His people are truly in *communion* with one another; for here God and man both "receive" the elements of the utmost sacrifice—the body and blood of Christ. The Lord's Supper is a different sacrificial eating than that experienced by the OT Jews, for God and man now jointly participate (*koinonia*) in Christ's sacrifice, and both are satisfied. It is not that God "eats" His Son, as surely as Christ was not literally a cremated burnt offering; likewise our eating of Christ's body and blood is not like the eating of animal flesh and grain. Nonetheless God accepts the "sweet aroma" of the burnt offering of Christ, and we miraculously

---

[101] 1 Corinthians 10:16.

do eat of the once-sacrificed body and blood as well.[102] Thus Christ's body and blood take the place of the Bronze Altar as the point of contact (koinonia) between God and man. God is *there,* at the NT Communion Table, and our point of contact with Him is the body and blood of *the* sacrifice—the "food" of salvation that was given and shed once on the cross. God and man are thus doubly united at this Holy Meal, because *Christ is food* and because *God is uniquely satisfied* with Christ's sacrifice—the ultimate sweet aroma.

With their sacrifice-derived meals, pagans demonstrated that they believed their worship was the ultimate communion—a meal shared with their god. Israel's sacrificial meals fell short of this, as they disallowed a communion with that which satisfied God. Such meals inferred that the Jews were waiting for a fuller communion meal, waiting for a time when they could actually eat of the *food* that satisfied God, not merely eat at His *table.* In the Sacrament of the Altar the anticipation is fulfilled; God and man are in the most intimate communion (koinonia) this side of heaven.

It used to be that God's altar, the altar for burnt offering, was the point of contact between God and His people.[103] Now, the body and blood of Christ are the "point of contact" between God and man. Now the Sacrament of the Altar is appropriately called "Communion," *koinonia,* for there God and man meet. "There is one God and one mediator between God and men, the man [body and blood] Christ Jesus."[104]

---

[102] Ephesians 5:2 thus references Christ as "sweet aroma." It is possible that St. Paul is referring to the Eucharist in Ephesians 5, but he is appropriately doing so in the context of day-to-day Christian living. In 5:18 he gives the seemingly non-contextual warning not to be drunk with wine, the same warning given to the Corinthians concerning the Eucharist (1 Cor. 11:21,22). Immediately after such a warning, St. Paul then communicates the importance of worship, "speaking to one another in psalms and hymns and spiritual songs..." The very next verse follows, "always giving thanks for all things in the name of the Lord Jesus Christ to God, even the Father." *Giving thanks* is literally in the Greek, *Eucharist,* and *name of the Lord Jesus* is also worship language. Could it be that already the term *Eucharist* had begun to be used for the Lord's Supper? The following verses in Ephesians 5, which speak of the wife's submission to her husband, are also strikingly similar to St. Paul's worship admonition in 1 Timothy 2:11 and in 1 Corinthians 14:34,35 which speak of the worship setting.

[103] God communicated to Moses from the Mercy Seat. However God's point of contact with the Jewish laity was at the Bronze Altar.

[104] 1 Timothy 2:5.

The Burnt Offering: Love

> *"Walk in love, just as Christ also loved us, and gave Himself up for us, an offering and a sacrifice to God as a fragrant aroma."*
> *Ephesians 5:2*

Since the burnt offering was totally consumed on God's altar, it aptly illustrated Christ's total sacrifice of Himself.[105] Total self-sacrifice, as pictured by the total burning of the burnt offering, describes love.

Love is indeed the ultimate sanctification that God works within a Christian. Thus in Ephesians 5:2, St. Paul appropriately exhorts Christians to imitate Christ's love, speaking of His love in terms of the burnt offering: "Walk in love, just as Christ also loved us, and gave Himself up for us, an offering and a sacrifice to God as a fragrant aroma." Love finds its greatest expression in self-sacrifice, the total giving of one's life for God and man. Jesus' self-sacrifice at the cross becomes the Christian's definition of love. Of this, St. John likewise wrote, "We know love by this, that He laid down His life for us; and we ought to lay down our lives [show love!] for the brethren."[106]

Of course the sacrificial animals were unwilling victims, and thus theirs was no act of love. Nevertheless such burnt offerings showed the love of the people bringing them, because they were offered to God as valuable portions of their owner's livelihood. Once again one observes that the type falls far short of its antitype, for Christ does not merely present His livelihood but He gives His entire life to God. And unlike the animals that were brought unwillingly, Christ offered up Himself *willingly*.

In the burnt offering the animals *unwillingly* yet *totally* were offered up

---

[105] Jukes, *The Law of the offerings*..., 58: "His offering was not the surrender of one part......'He gave Himself,' in all His perfectness, and satisfied the heart of God."
[106] 1 John 3:16.

to God. It was the *total* cremation of the burnt offerings that typified Christ's *total* self-sacrifice, and this then is the ultimate statement of love. Even as the cremation of the burnt offering *flesh* pictured Christ's total self-sacrifice upon the cross, so likewise the complete shedding of sacrificial *blood* prefigured the total giving of Christ's life. Since complete self-sacrifice is a definition of the deepest form of love, the blood and the flesh of the burnt offering each vividly portrayed Christ's profound love. Christ totally yielded up His life, and this was foreshadowed both by the blood drained from OT sacrifices and by the burnt offering flesh that was totally consumed on the Bronze Altar.

Ignatius was an early Christian pastor who was martyred around 107AD. While imprisoned, just before his martyrdom, he frequently referenced the Eucharist in his writings. Of Christ's flesh, Ignatius exclaimed, "I desire the bread of God, which is the flesh of Christ who was of the seed of David." By calling it the *bread of God*, Ignatius spoke of Christ's flesh in terms of the burnt offering. Recall that the flesh burned upon God's altar was called the *bread of God*. Concerning Christ's blood, Ignatius continues in the same sentence, "And for a draught I desire His blood, which is love incorruptible."[107] This early Christian martyr referred to Christ's blood, received in the Eucharist, as love itself. Ignatius understood that no one has any greater *love* than to give his *life* for another.[108] Blood is life. Thus Christ's love is grasped as one realizes that His blood was willingly shed for man's salvation, and that He completely gave His body into death. This is *love*, total self-sacrifice.

Not only is Christ's sacrifice upon the cross the ultimate definition of love, but through that very body and blood Christians are now enabled to love. The author of the epistle to the Hebrews exhorts, "And let us consider how to stimulate one another to love and good deeds, not forsaking our own

---

[107] J.B. Lightfoot, editor & translator, *The Apostolic Fathers Clement, Ignatius, and Polycarp*, vol. 2, (Grand Rapids: Baker Book House, 1981), "Epistle to the Romans," 561. To the Trallians (556) Ignatius also wrote, "...recover yourselves in faith which is the flesh of the Lord, and in love which is the blood of Jesus Christ." To the Smyrnaeans (567): "....firmly grounded in love in the blood of Christ..."
[108] John 15:13.

assembling together."[109] This verse encourages the production of love through the *assembling together* in worship. Though it is true that Christians in a worship setting would encourage each other to "love and good deeds" by merely voicing such encouragement to one another, yet the *means* whereby such sanctification was and is created is the body and blood of Christ, the body and blood given and shed at the cross, the body and blood received in the Eucharist, the body and blood that infuses His people with love.[110] The early church *always* communed Christ's body and blood when they assembled for worship.[111] This is how God's people *stimulate one another to love and good deeds*—by the faithful joint-reception of the sacred body and blood of Christ. Not only does Christ feed His people with His body and blood in the Sacrament so they are infused with His strength to love and do good deeds, but additionally as His people truly consider the meaning of His body and blood received in the Sacrament, they will be stimulated to love and good deeds simply from contemplating the loftiest act of love—Christ's sacrifice.

Sanctification entails not only the love directed to one's neighbor but also the love directed toward God. Though loving one's neighbor is truly an essential way to love God, yet love toward God also finds expression in the sacrifices of praise and thanksgiving that Christians offer through Christ, and, in addition, through the very giving of their bodies, their time, and their treasures to God. Such sanctified living, as has been explained, is pictured by the sacrifice of the burnt offering. The Christian's NT sacrifices toward God become offerings that find a place of mediation between God and man,

---

[109] Hebrews 10:24,25a. To be explained in chapter eight, this section of Hebrews is almost certainly speaking specifically of the Lord's Supper.

[110] When we speak of Christ's body and blood "infusing" Christians we do not want the more adept theologians to think we are agreeing with the *gratia infusa* of Rome. Indeed Christians are infused with Christ and thus are empowered to love, but such love flowing from a Christian is not what saves him.

[111] Gayford, *Sacrifice and Priesthood*, 166: "If (as is of course true) in Heb. x. 19-25 the prime reason for the 'assembling of ourselves together' is the Breaking of Bread, we have in that passage also the same interchange of Earth and Heaven and the same interweaving of Communion and Sacrifice as in Heb. xiii. 10ff." Parenthetic comment is Gayford's.

and the celebration of the Eucharist has always been considered the foremost place of mediation, for Christ is uniquely there. Alan Stibbs explains that the Sacrament can be a vehicle for Christians to offer such sacrifices.[112] He then explains, "Indeed, the Eucharist is to be understood as an activity of Christian worshippers, who are united with Christ, or possessed by Him in the expression of such offering..."[113]

The Burnt Offering: Ascension

> *"For it came about when the flame went up from the altar toward heaven, that the angel of the Lord ascended in the flame of the altar....So Manoah said to his wife, 'We shall surely die, for we have seen God.'"*
> Judges 13:20,22

As the smoke of the burnt offering went upward, the burnt offering was understood to have ascended to God. Hicks explains:

> The Hebrew special term for the burnt-offering is 'olah'-probably = "that which goes up"; [...] the offering is not destroyed but transformed...so that it can ascend in smoke to the heaven above, the dwelling-place of God.[114]

This ascending smoke from the burnt offering not only explained the "sweet aroma" received by God but it also typified Christ's ascension into heaven. Hicks thus explains, "He has gone up, as did the burnt-offering [....] In Him mankind has begun its return to the presence of God."[115] The body and blood of a burnt offering typified the crucifixion of Christ, but then the

---

[112] Alan Stibbs, *Sacrament, Sacrifice and Eucharist* (London: Billing and Son LTD., 1961), 19.
[113] Ibid.
[114] Hicks, *The Fullness of Sacrifice*, 40.
[115] Hicks, *The Fullness of Sacrifice*, 337.

smoke ascending upward aptly portrayed His ascension.

The ascension of the Angel of the Lord in the presence of Manoah and his wife shows how the burnt offering is seen to typify the ascension of the Savior: "For it came about when the flame went up from the altar toward heaven, that the Angel of the Lord ascended in the flame of the altar...So Manoah said to his wife, 'We shall surely die, for we have seen God.'"[116] Recall that the "angel of the Lord" is usually identified as the Son of God, and thus this account aptly prefigures the ascension of Jesus by means of the ascending smoke of a burnt offering.

As the OT sacrifices stood in for the offerer, so too Christ's sacrifice stands in for His people, and the enduring results of His self-sacrifice now belong to them. Christians are thus already crucified, they are already raised from the grave, and they are already *ascended* in Christ Jesus! Saint Paul explains that even now God has "raised us up with Him and seated us with Him in the heavenly places, in Christ Jesus."[117] The OT burnt offering symbolized the offerer giving himself and then ascending as a pleasing aroma to God, because it stood in for that person. So too—but not merely symbolically—Christ's sacrifice and ascension stand in for us, indicating that His people truly *have* ascended to God. He is our burnt offering.

While Christians await their bodily death, resurrection and ascension, they are united with Christ through Baptism, in which the Christian trusts that these events are already accomplished. This union with Christ is often explained as marital oneness, and can be seen from two perspectives.[118] First, since the Church is Christ's body, she is even now united with Him. Supernaturally the bride of Christ is His body, and she has already ascended with Him into heaven, for the Church has become partaker of His divine nature.[119] A second way Christians can now "ascend" to God's presence is

---

[116] Judges 13:20,22.
[117] Ephesians 2:6.
[118] In explaining Christ's oneness with His bride, St. Paul brings in Baptism (Eph. 5:25,26).
[119] 2 Peter 1:3,4. Some early church fathers even saw the "partaking" in this text to be a reference to the Eucharist.

through the Eucharist, whereby they enter behind the heavenly veil here and now through the body and blood of Christ.[120] This ascension-understanding in the Eucharist is incorporated into many liturgies, and God's people express this "ascension" when they liturgically profess that they are joining "with angels and archangels and all the company of heaven" as they gather to eat the sacrament.[121]

These two themes, being united with Christ in heaven and being united with Him at his meal, are not exclusive of one another. The Church as Christ's bride has been united with Him in an inseparable marital oneness. Groom and bride are one no matter how far apart they may be, or seem to be. Consequently even though Christ has visibly departed, and His bride is unable to behold Him, yet they remain one. Of this marital oneness Paul wrote, "This mystery is great; but I am speaking with reference to Christ and the church."[122] They are also *one,* in unique fellowship with one another, as they dine together in the Eucharist. Dining with Christ now is a foretaste of heaven, a foretaste of that eon when the divine Bridegroom and Bride shall finally banquet together at a feast where sin and death will cease to be the table-talk.

The Burnt Offering: "Do this..."

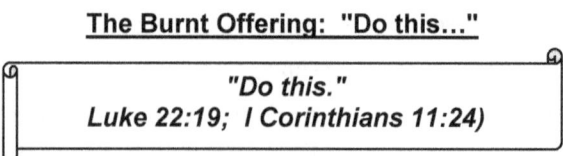

"Do this."
Luke 22:19; I Corinthians 11:24)

Some are convinced that Christ specifically caused His Apostles to consider the burnt offering when at the Last Supper He said, *"Do this* in remembrance of me." When the Jews officially translated the Hebrew OT into

---

[120] This concept of man "ascending" to God in the Eucharist is more prominent in Eastern Christianity. Thus F. C. N. Hicks, *The Fullness of Sacrifice*, 314: "...the definite tendency of the East has been....the lifting up of the worshippers to heaven [rather] than as [in the West] the bringing down of the Lord to earth..."
[121] *The Lutheran Hymnal* (St. Louis: Concordia Publishing House, 1941), 25.
[122] Ephesians 5:32.

Greek, the act of sacrifice was at times referred to simply as "doing."[123] Recall that this official Greek OT was called the *Septuagint*. Thus when the daily burnt offerings are referenced in Exodus 29:39, the translation from the Septuagint literally reads: "One lamb you shall *do* in the morning, and the second lamb you shall *do* in the evening." Along with "doing" each of these daily burnt offerings, a grain offering was burned upon them, and it was called God's "memorial portion."[124] Together, the burnt offering and the grain offering conveyed the concepts of "doing" and "memorial," paralleling the expression Jesus would make, "*Do* this in *memory* of me."

K. O. James identifies the fact that in second century Christian writings "the words 'do this in memory of Me' ...acquired a sacrificial interpretation." This interpretation was acquired, James continues, as the Greek word for *do* was "related to the morning and evening sacrifice in Judaism."[125] Such *morning and evening sacrifice* were of course the prescribed daily burnt offerings. Was Christ directing His people to the burnt offering by His Words of Institution? Certain second century Christians believed it was so.

Darwell Stone, also commenting on the Greek use of the word "do," says that if the "setting in which our Lord's words were spoken is thought to be sufficiently suggestive of sacrificial ideas, 'This do' may well be regarded as indicating...a sacrificial element in the rite instituted."[126]

What is that *sacrificial* element of which Darwell Stone speaks? Christ's self-sacrifice upon the cross is *the* sacrificial element in the sacrament. Thus to "do" the sacrament is simply to participate in Christ's sacrifice, and this participation occurs in the eating of His body and blood in

---

[123] This was true also of offerings beyond the burnt offering.
[124] e.g. Leviticus 2:2.
[125] K.O. James, *Sacrifice and Sacrament* (New York: Barnes and Noble, Inc., 1962), 207-208. James then footnotes: "Exodus xxix, 39; cf. Lev. ix, 7; xxiv,7; Num. x,10; Ps. lxvi, 15; Lock, Theology, 1923, vii, 284ff." James fails to mention that the word "do" was also associated in the LXX with keeping the Passover (e.g. Exodus 13:47-50).
[126] Darwell Stone, *A History of the Doctrine of the Holy Eucharist*, (London: Rivingtons, nd), 9.

the Sacrament. It must be understood, as made crystal clear in the epistle to the Hebrews, that Christ is not re-sacrificed when Christians celebrate the sacrament.[127] One must always bear in mind that "the term *sacrifice* does not apply to the consecrated elements or to what is done with them."[128]

Salting the Sacrifice

> *"...the priests shall throw salt on them, and they shall offer them up as a burnt offering to the Lord."*
> *Ezekiel 43:24*

Salt was routinely placed upon the sacrificial portions burned upon God's altar. God had directed, "With all your offerings you shall offer salt."[129] Such salt was particularly applied to the "bread" of the grain offerings that were burned upon both the burnt offerings and peace offerings. Since the burnt offering was the most significant holocaust offering, here consider the salt burned upon Jewish sacrifice.

A "covenant of salt" was considered a covenant that would endure, and this made sense because salt was the universal preservative; it made things endure. Thus Abijah declared concerning King David, "Do you not know that the Lord God of Israel gave the rule over Israel forever to David...by a covenant of salt."[130] David's reign was to endure, preserved as if by salt. Similarly, when God instituted the Jewish sacrificial rites He directed all sacrifices to be salted, and He referred to such salt as "the salt of the covenant."[131] God's covenant of forgiveness and blessing upon Israel would, from His side of the covenant, endure, as illustrated by the salt.

---

[127] When the epistle to the Hebrews is discussed in chapter eight, Christ's sacrifice will be shown to have been *once* and for all.
[128] Stone, *A History...*, 60.
[129] Leviticus 2:13. Such salting was emphasized with the burning of the grain offering.
[130] 2 Chronicles 13:5.
[131] Leviticus 2:13.

The Burnt Offering, a Link to the Sacrament of the Altar

When Jesus instituted the Lord's Supper, He also declared it to be covenantal when He said, "This is the blood of the covenant." This covenant would endure to the ultimate degree. How natural it was then for some in the early church to connect salt with the Lord's Supper! Oscar Cullmann explains that in certain early church texts one observes that "the Lord's Supper is celebrated with bread and salt, so much so that the expression 'to share the salt', has become the technical term for 'to celebrate the Lord's Supper.'"[132]

This practice was perhaps generated by the Lord Jesus Himself. In Acts 1:4, Luke writes literally, "And after *sharing the salt*, He commanded them not to leave Jerusalem..."[133] John Kleinig, relating this to the sacrificial rites, expounds, "Luke reports that Jesus "shared salt" with his disciples as a sign of his eternal covenant with them. ...Jesus, the great High Priest, joined with his fellow priests—his disciples—in a holy meal."[134]

Such a salt-related practice most likely arose because of the covenantal, sacrifice-related salting rites of the Jews, rites that were especially associated with the bread-related portions of the sacrifice. To the Jews, their sacrificial rites indicated that they were participating in God's enduring "salt of the covenant." To early Christians the covenant nature of the Lord's Supper was even more profoundly enduring; so for those familiar with OT sacrifice, it was natural to connect the Eucharist also to "salt of the covenant."[135] From such testimony one finds again that early Christians apparently associated the Lord's Supper with Jewish sacrificial rites.

---

[132] Oscar Cullmann and F. J. Leenhardt, *Essays on the Lord's Supper*, (London: Lutterworth Press, 1958), 12. Cullmann finds such reference in the Pseudo-Clementines. Scripturally, the application of salt to Jewish sacrifice appears especially to be associated with the grain offering (Lev. 2:13). Thus it was quite natural to add salt to the *bread* of the Eucharist, since such unleavened bread corresponded to the grain offering.

[133] This is the author's translation.

[134] Kleinig, *Leviticus*, 80.

[135] One wonders whether "having salt in yourselves" (Mark 9:50) is an indirect reference to the Eucharist.

Concluding Remarks

The feast of the Lord's Supper is truly important and central, for in it God and man actually commune, joining together at the meal of the Lord's Supper. Can this be found any place else? Man and God are both satisfied by the burnt offering of Christ given and shed at the cross, a sweet aroma and a sublime communion.

> "...in the place where the burnt offering is slain the sin offering shall be slain before the Lord; it is most holy. The priest who offers it for sin shall eat it. It shall be eaten in a holy place, in the court of the tent of meeting."
> Leviticus 6:25b,26

Chapter Five

SIN AND GUILT OFFERINGS, KEEN SHADOWS OF THE SACRAMENT

With God's glory brightly glowing behind the OT sacrifices, they cast a shadow in the shape of a cross. That shadow was so sharpened and focused by the sin and guilt offerings, that an OT believer was being trained to recognize—merely from the shadow—why Christ would die: He would die for sin and guilt. As taught by the OT shadow, every corpuscle of blood smeared upon Christ's cross and every drop flowing to the base of it cried out to God, "For sin and guilt." In addition to His blood, Christ's sacrificed, lifeless body loudly exclaimed, "For sin and guilt!" Because of the precise OT shadow cast by the sin and guilt offerings, first century Hebrew Christians quickly—even naturally—realized the cry of Christ's blood, and by faith they heard the exclamation of His sacrificed body. And when 1,500 years after Christ, Martin Luther summarized the Lord's Supper by the words, "Given and shed for you for the remission of sins," the depth of such a summary can only rightly be grasped because God in His infinite wisdom had instituted Israel's sin and guilt offerings some 1,500 years before Christ.[1]

We will treat the sin and guilt offerings together, because God

---

[1] Luther uses this condensed description of Christ's body and blood in the Lord's Supper three times in his explanation of the Lord's Supper in *The Small Catechism*.

established parallel regulations for their priestly consumption: "The guilt offering is like the sin offering, there is one law for them."[2] These sacrifices were offered when someone became aware of sinfulness or a specific sin.[3] J. H. Kurtz has identified the guilt offering as "a subordinate species of sin-offering."[4] With this understanding in mind, subsequent discussions of the sin offering will frequently encompass the guilt offering as well.[5]

The sin (and guilt) offering differed significantly from the burnt offering. Whereas the burnt offering was *totally* consumed by the fire on the altar, the sin offering had only non-fleshy, "fatty" portions burned upon God's altar.[6] Another marked difference from the burnt offering was that atonement was the *primary* focus of the sin offering, but not of the burnt offering. Though the sacrificial blood of every kind of animal sacrifice *involved* atonement, the blood of the sin offering *magnified* atonement.[7] Because of this, only sin and guilt offerings utilized the phrase, "And he shall be forgiven."[8] The sin offerings were again different from the burnt offering in that for both a *private* sin offering and for *every* guilt offering the priest was *required to eat* the flesh of the sacrifice. This eating uniquely foreshadowed the eating of the Lord's Supper. (*Private* and *public* sin offerings will be explained shortly.)

Consider the basic priestly liturgy for the sin offering. After listening to the confession of sins, the priestly responsibility continued with the capture of the creature's blood, to be appropriately applied within the tabernacle. That sacrificial blood, the ultimate token of atonement, was first—for a public sin

---

[2] Leviticus 7:7. This was only true of the *private* sin offering and the guilt offering.
[3] Leviticus 4-7. We agree that the guilt offering discussion does *not* begin with 5:1 but with 5:14. Roy Lee DeWitt, *Teaching from the Tabernacle*, (Grand Rapids: Baker Book House, 1988). John W. Kleinig, *Leviticus*, (St. Louis: Concordia Publishing House, 2003). J. H. Kurtz, *Offerings, Sacrifices and the Worship of the Old Testament*, trans. James Martin (Peabody, MA: Hendrickson Publishers, Inc., 1998), 208ff.
[4] Kurtz, *Offerings...*, 248.
[5] This is true especially in the discussion of private sin offerings.
[6] Only Leviticus 4:31 describes the fatty portions *from the sin offering* as a soothing aroma to God. All other *soothing aroma* references are connected to the other kinds of sacrifice.
[7] Kurtz, *Offerings...*, 175.
[8] Leviticus 4:20, 26, 31, 35; 5:10, 13; 5:16, 18; 6:7; 19:22; Numbers 15:25,28. See Kleinig, *Leviticus*, 104.

offering—sprinkled by a priest at God's designated sacred location.[9] The blood of all sin offerings was smeared upon the horns of one of the two altars: the Altar of Incense or the Bronze Altar. The remaining blood was finally poured at the base of the Bronze Altar. The fatty portions of the sin offering were then burned atop the Bronze Altar. Finally, for a *private* sin offering and for *every* guilt offering, the officiating priest was obligated to cook and eat the creature's flesh; the *public* sin offering flesh was not eaten but was burned outside the camp.

The bloodletting, the blood placement, the burning of fat and other portions, and the eating of the sin offering flesh were extremely solemn acts. "There was nothing joyous about it," Edersheim explains, "It represents a terrible necessity, for which God, in His wondrous grace, had made provision."[10] This solemn attitude should no doubt prevail in today's reception of Holy Communion, where there is a participation in the ultimate sin offering—the body and blood of Christ.

It is important to realize that the sin offering was God's unique institution for the nation of Israel. Pagans had no counterpart to this sacrifice, and the descendants of Abraham did not practice it until God instituted it through Moses. Kurtz summarizes: "And the first thing which strikes us is, that previous to the time of Moses we only read of *burnt-offerings* and *peace-offerings, never of sin- (and trespass-) offerings.*"[11] During the centuries before Moses, the people of God were familiar with both burnt and peace offerings, as attested by the Biblical witness; even pagans offered up these types of sacrifices—no doubt vestiges of the true worship of God. Though the blood of the burnt and peace offerings had been *associated* with forgiveness, both before and after the institution of the sin offering, yet forgiveness was not the sole goal of either of these types of sacrifice. Forgiveness is *the* reason for sin offerings. As the work of Christ unfolded, it became apparent that God

---

[9] The sprinkling of the blood was a unique practice for the public sin offering.
[10] Edersheim, *The Temple*..., 96, speaking especially of the sin offering.
[11] Kurtz, *Offerings*..., 177. Italics are in the text.

instituted the sin offering precisely because it specifically foreshadowed the ultimate work of Christ: *the* offering for mankind's sins. Only the people of Israel possessed such a sacrifice, and this was appropriate because the Christ would come, as promised, from the Israelites. There were no references in the Scriptures to the sacrifice of a sin offering until one was offered, as God directed, at the ordination of Aaron to the priesthood.[12] Roy DeWitt explains that no other sin offerings "are recorded before this. All of the other offerings were probably known before this time...The sin offering prefigured the atoning death of Christ."[13] When God instituted the sin offering, there began a privileged Jewish pilgrimage to the cross of Christ. Christ's crucifixion marked the arrival of the antitype. No more sin offerings were then needed.

Since the sin offering so aptly foreshadowed the death of Christ, it is fitting that the NT frequently either labels or explains Christ in sin offering terms. When John the Baptist pointed to Jesus and proclaimed, "Behold the lamb of God who takes away the sin of the world," he was portraying Jesus as a sin offering.[14] In Romans 8:2, the Apostle Paul uses sin offering terminology to explain that God exceeded the power of the law by "sending His own Son in the likeness of sinful flesh and as an offering for sin, He condemned sin in the flesh." Hebrews 10:12 says that Jesus, "having offered one sacrifice for sins, for all time, sat down at the right hand of God..." Jesus is the "sacrifice for sins"—the ultimate and final sin offering.

Though there are numerous other references in the New Testament

---

[12] Leviticus 8:14. God had explained this ordination sin offering in Exodus 29. Before this revelation to Moses on Sinai, the sacrifice of sin offerings had not been referenced in the Pentateuch. Since the Hebrew uses the same word for "sin" as for "sin offering" some have speculated that some pre-Mosaic references to sin may also be references to the sin offering. Still, there is no description of a sin offering *sacrifice* until Lev. 8:14. Even Moses' sacrifices on Mount Sinai (Ex. 24:5) consisted only of burnt and peace offerings.

[13] Roy Lee DeWitt, *Teaching from the Tabernacle* (Grand Rapids: Baker Book House, 1988 rep.), 131.

[14] John 1:29.

to Christ as sin offering,[15] the most significant reference—in view of our present study—is Jesus' declaration that His blood is "to be *shed* on behalf of many *for the forgiveness of sins.*"[16] Here Jesus describes His blood as that of a sin offering, and since this statement is within the words of institution, it *forces Christians to consider the Lord's Supper in terms of a sin offering.* Observe how Leviticus 4:25,26b clearly parallel Christ's words of institution, thus demonstrating Christ's deliberate description of Himself as the sin offering:

> Then the priest is to take some of the *blood of the sin offering*...and its *blood* he shall pour out *["shed"]* at the base of the altar of burnt offering....Thus the priest shall make atonement for him in regard to his sin, and he *shall be forgiven.* [italics added].

This reference indicates that OT sin offering blood was shed, and it was for the remission of sins. Only sin offering blood was commanded to be *shed* at the altar's base, and Jesus utilized the same Greek word for *shed* when instituting The Supper.[17] Christ's divinely selected wording in the Sacrament—*blood shed for the remission of sins*—connects His *blood* specifically to the OT sin offering. This was fitting because sin offering *blood,* more than any other sacrificial element, was tied to forgiveness of sins.

The sin offerings were the first in the "stages" of Jewish sacrifice.[18] This concept is worth repeating. When someone approached God there were

---

[15] Daniel 9:24 predicted the sin/guilt offering fulfillment in Christ. See then Gal. 3:13; Rom. 5:6-11; 2 Cor. 5:21; 1 John 1:7; 2:1f; 4:10. Many have failed to recognize περι αρμαρτιας and other semi-technical wording used for *sin offering.* See Robert J. Daly, *Christian Sacrifice,* (Washington, D.C.: The Catholic University Press, 1978) for an explanation of such texts.

[16] Matthew 26:28.

[17] Leviticus 4:7, 18,25, 30, 34; 5:9; 8:15; 9:9. See Kleinig, *Leviticus,* 102. Though other sacrificial blood, as it was dashed, ended up at the Bronze Altar's base, yet only the sin (or guilt) offering blood employed the same Greek word for *shed* in the LXX as Jesus would use in the words of institution: εκχεω.

[18] Kurtz, *Offerings...,* 175.

frequently three stages of sacrifice. First the sin offering was sacrificed, then the burnt offering, and finally the peace offering. The sin offerings were sacrificed first because they provided the first necessity, forgiveness. These OT sacrifices didn't earn forgiveness, but they conveyed forgiveness because of the retroactive sin payment of Jesus Christ upon the cross. After the sin offerings, the burnt offerings were sacrificed. As explained in the previous chapter, these indicated the dedication of the giver to God.[19] Dedicating one's self to God can only be God-pleasing because of the self-sacrifice of Christ to His Father. The third and final stage in the sacrificial process was the peace offering. Its main feature was the sacrificial feast, which created a statement of joy and peace. The Christian's great feast of the Lord's Supper *naturally* relates to this final stage of the sacrificial process—a feast celebrated in joy and peace. Not only relating to the festive eating of the peace offering, the Christian's sacramental consumption of Christ's body and blood also directly relates to the solemn meals drawn from OT sin offerings. Christ's sacrifice *and* His Supper are foreshadowed by all three kinds of sacrifice—sin, burnt and peace offerings.

Sin and Guilt Offerings Contrasted

> *"Now if a person sins and does any of the things which the Lord has commanded not to be done...He is then to bring to the priest a ram without defect...for a guilt offering."*
> Leviticus 5:17,18

Though the (private) sin offering and guilt offering had the same basic regulations, yet there were some noteworthy differences between them. Several theologians have concluded that the sin offering was more closely

---

[19] The sacrifices in this sense were symbolic. A "symbol" represents something that exists at the time of the symbol. A "type" is something which ultimately points to a greater reality yet to come. In pointing to Christ, these sacrifices were types, not symbols.

related to man's sinful nature or to sin in general, but the guilt offering was more closely related to a specific sin.[20] The specific sin that prompted a guilt offering was frequently identified as some form of robbery or fraud perpetrated either toward a fellow Jew or God.[21] Such robbery, Kurtz explains, was "not merely in material possessions and property which it would be possible to restore, but in rightful and obligatory services, based upon agreement or covenant."[22] From a different perspective, the sin offering concentrated on the *sinner* but the guilt offering dealt more with a particular *offense* or a specific *sense of guilt*.[23] These are generalities, and there was apparently some overlap between sin and guilt offerings.[24]

Some English translators call the *guilt offering* a "trespass offering" or a "reparation offering." Since the *guilt offering* was sacrificed in relation to sins that frequently incurred some sort of debt to God or to another person, if restitution could be made, this would be done first, and then the guilt offering would be slain by the offerer.[25] This guilt offering restoration statute resonates with Jesus' directive in the Sermon on the Mount: "If therefore you are presenting your offering at the altar, and there remember that your brother

---

[20] E.g. Edersheim, *The Temple...*, 94-95.
[21] Leviticus 6:1-7.
[22] Kurtz, *Offerings...*, 206.
[23] Edersheim, *The Temple...*, 94-95. Kurtz, *Offerings...*, 212: "Thus, from the very nature of the case, trespass-offerings could *only* be presented for *acknowledged* sins. Hence for sins which required trespass-offerings, but had not been acknowledged, it was necessary that sin-offerings be presented. [emphasis, Kurtz]"
[24] Kurtz, *Offerings...*, would consider our summary to be overly simplistic. Kurtz explains his analysis of the differences (189-213). He shows (212f) an overlap in the two sacrifices, "The expiation effected by the sin-offering might be regarded as comprehending that of the trespass-offering; but not vice versa." Kurtz (206) portrays the sin offering as related to "the sinful habitus of his (the offerer's) nature, which was thus brought to light." And the guilt (trespass) offering is sacrificed because of "a disturbance in the covenant relation towards Jehovah." The differences between sin and guilt offerings were debated even before Christ. Kurtz, e.g., disagrees with Philo and Josephus and with certain Rabbins of old (190). Some have held that the Decalogue was not specifically relevant to the sin and guilt offerings, but that these sacrifices only dealt with holiness and cleanness in relation to worship ordinances. We agree with Kurtz that the sin and guilt offerings also involved any violation of moral law (188).
[25] Leviticus 5:16; 6:1-5. In some cases such restitution could not be exacted (e.g. Lev. 14:12; 19:20-22).

has something against you, leave your offering there before the altar, and go your way; first be reconciled to your brother, and then come and present your offering."[26] These sacrifice-related words of Jesus have frequently been applied to the Lord's Supper, whereat God's people should make every effort to be reconciled with others before approaching the altar of Holy Communion.

By their sacrificial practices, certain pious Jews in Christ's day demonstrated their perception of the differences between guilt and sin offerings. Since the guilt offering dealt with a deep sense of guilt, certain particularly guilt-ridden Jews would bring frequent guilt offerings. At the time of Christ a very strict group of Jewish pious men—called *Hasidim*—were known to bring *daily* guilt offerings to the temple![27] R. Eliezer, who lived before the temple's destruction in 70AD, explained, "One may every day and at any time, whenever one likes, bring voluntarily [to the temple] a trespass [guilt] offering brought for a doubtful sin." There was then a record of a wealthy yet humble Jew who did just that: "It is said of Baba b. Buta that he voluntarily brought every day a guilt-offering for a doubtful sin, except on the day after the Day of Atonement."[28] Such men as Baba b. Buta were acutely aware that they daily sinned much, guilty of sins that they could not even specify; this is no doubt what is meant in the above quote by a "doubtful sin."[29] Recall that the Eucharist in early Christianity was celebrated daily,

---

[26] Matthew 5:23,24. Literally the "offering" mentioned here is the word "gift", a sacrificial word identifying especially that portion given to God to eat upon His altar. Jesus is not necessarily specifying the guilt offering. The Church has applied these words to the approach of the Eucharist. "Gift" ("Qorban") was often generally used for "sacrifice" (Mark 7:11).
[27] Edersheim, *The Temple...*, 98.
[28] Adolph Buchler, *Types of Jewish Palestinian Piety from 70 B.C.E. to 70 C.E.* (London: Jews' College, 1922), 73. Buchler explains the three distinct yet perhaps overlapping groups of pious men who lived between 70BC and 70AD: the Pharisees, the Essenes and the Hasidim. Within these groups there were the "saints", the "men of deed", and the "sin-fearers" who equated fearing God with fearing sin (28ff). Baba b. Buta was a Hasid. Baba was obviously quite wealthy, and he would have even brought a guilt offering on the day after the Day of Atonement if this had been allowed! Other pious men offered similar frequent guilt offerings as well, and thus they were called, "The guilt offerings of the pious" (74).
[29] Ibid., 74: "His was a conditional guilt offering, for a sin of which he was not sure at all." See Psalm 19:12,13.

reflecting also this hunger for daily forgiveness.[30]

Though the sin offering emphasized the sinner and not so much the sin, yet when an *individual* brought a sin offering, as identified in first century practice, he was expected to specify the sin for which this private offering was to be sacrificed. For this reason those Jewish "Hasidim"—who daily sacrificed guilt offerings in the temple—did not offer daily sin offerings, because this would necessitate the confession of a specific sin; they were convinced that almost never did such "confessable" sins arise in their lives. Still, to make sure all their sins were covered, certain pious men—some of whom did not bring daily guilt offerings—deeply desired to bring a sin offering to God's temple, but they desired a sin offering that would be only *generally* associated with atonement, because they did not want to specify any particular sin. To get around this obstacle some of the pious Jews would at times take the vow of a Nazarite, a vow that could be fulfilled in as short a time as one month. At the end of that month, these Israelites could then legitimately sacrifice the required Nazarite *sin offering*, thus establishing a monthly "atonement" for themselves before God.[31] From these sacrificial practices one realizes that at the time of Christ very real differences were perceived between the sin and guilt offerings.

Another difference between sin and guilt offerings was the prescribed sacrificial creature. Unlike the guilt offering, the emphasis set forth in a sin

---

[30] We should not think that such pious men were completely opposed to Jesus. Many of Jesus' admonitions were already practiced by such Jewish pious men; e.g. giving alms privately (Buchler, *Types...*, 29). These pious men did not agree on the differences and use of the sin and guilt offerings.

[31] Buchler, *Types...*, 76f: "While Baba B. Buta in the same anxiety resorted to a daily guilt-offering for a doubtful sin, the pious men either knew nothing of its admissibility or disapproved of it, or did not consider such a sacrifice of sufficient force for their need of atonement. The sin-offering prescribed in Num. 6.14 for the Nazirite at the conclusion of his temporary vow was not brought for any definite breach of the law, but for an unknown, yet possible levitical defilement and for other offences against the rules of the vow, and could therefore include in its atonement other trespasses of the same uncertainty. As the temporary vow of the Nazirite extended only over thirty days, the pious men could repeat the vow as often as they liked, bring the sin-offering every month, and thus satisfy their desire for regular atonement."

offering was upon the person (or nation) rather than upon the sin itself. Apparently, with the sin offering emphasizing the *person*, such a sacrifice would be based upon what that person could afford. The very poorest could even bring flour as a sin offering.[32] On the other hand, since the *offense* was being emphasized in the guilt offering—and all guilt is equally condemnatory in God's eyes—it made sense that every guilt offering was the same for all; both the rich and the poor brought a ram as their guilt offering.[33] Thus the sin offering could involve several different sacrificial creatures, but the regular guilt offering was always a ram.[34] Of this guilt offering ram, after its blood and fatty portions were properly presented to God, the flesh was cooked and eaten by the officiating priest. The officiating priest, and only a priest, *always ate* the guilt offering ram's flesh.[35] God commanded, "It shall be eaten in a holy place; it is most holy."[36] This most holy meal, drawn from every guilt offering, was certainly a profound shadow of the eating of the Lord's Supper—a most holy eating still performed solely by priests.[37]

In contrast to sin offerings, which could be offered for the entire nation, guilt offerings were always of a "private" nature; they were never offered for the nation but only for personal offenses. Since sin offerings could be offered for the entire nation, they thus frequently—as will be explained

---

[32] Leviticus 5:11ff. There could be no atoning blood with a sin offering of flour. It is apparent such atonement would have been provided only through the *eating* of the flour by the officiating priest (5:13).

[33] Leviticus 4,5. Kurtz, 214f: "Fraud in connection with the property of another bore precisely the same character,...so that the ethical compensation which accompanied it, and was estimated according to it, was also the same for all in the case of the trespass-offering."

[34] Leviticus 5:18; 6:6; etc. Some cite Lev. 14:12 and Numb. 6:12 wherein the guilt offering for a defiled Nazarite or a leper was a *male lamb*. There is little difference between a male lamb and a ram. Edersheim, *The Temple...*, 99, notes that leprosy and the defilement of a Nazarite were considered trespasses either against God or against the congregation of Israel, leprosy being "symbolic" of wronging the congregation as a whole.

[35] There are no directives in Scripture for a priestly guilt offering. Most likely it was eaten by another officiating priest. If it was considered a public sin offering and burned outside the gate, then its blood should have been brought into the Holy Place, and guilt offering blood was never brought into the Holy Place.

[36] Leviticus 7:6.

[37] All Christians are priests, as we will further explain in this and later chapters.

shortly—could possess a "public" status.

As cited, there is record of certain pious men who—while the temple stood at the time of Christ—observed clearly defined differences between sin and guilt offerings. While making every effort not to compromise these differences, they strove to maximize their sin and guilt offerings. In defense of their apparently extreme practices, observe that these men—as they earnestly desired to sacrifice sin or guilt offerings—had the noble attitude of hungering and thirsting for righteousness. One can only imagine how distraught those pious men were when the temple was destroyed in 70AD. That is unless they followed Christ, in which case they would have been privileged to participate regularly in *the* sin/guilt offering whenever they partook of the Sacrament of the Altar. Their hunger and thirst for righteousness would then have been satisfied by the body and blood of the crowning sin/guilt offering—Christ crucified.

Public and Private Sin Offerings

> *"Now if the whole congregation of Israel commits error...then the assembly shall offer a bull of the herd for a sin offering [...] Now if anyone of the common people sins unintentionally...he shall bring ...a goat, a female without defect...And he shall lay his hand on the head of the sin offering."*
> Leviticus 4:13,14,27-29

Whereas all guilt offerings were only of a *private* nature, the sin offerings (like the burnt offerings and peace offerings) could be considered either *private* or *public* sacrifices.[38] There were vast differences between *public* and *private* sin offerings.

Consider the *public* sin offering. Strangely, a *public* sin offering

---
[38] Edersheim, *The Temple...*, 95.

emphasized one person, the high priest; when the high priest needed atonement, a *public* sin offering was sacrificed.[39] Usually such sacrifices were offered for the entire nation, which included the high priest. They were appropriately called *public*, because they were almost always offered for the nation. Such a *public* sacrifice, whether for the nation or specifically for the high priest, was prescribed to be a male creature slain by the high priest.

The blood of a *public* sin offering was to be brought into the *Holy Place* and ceremonially *sprinkled* against the veil that covered the entrance into the *Most Holy Place*. Only public sin offering blood was thus *sprinkled*, and only such blood required application in the Holy Place. While the high priest was still in the Holy Place—again unique to the *public* sin offering—he daubed some of the blood on the horns of the *Altar of Incense*, and he then carried the remaining blood to the Outer Court where he *shed* it at the base of the *Bronze Altar*. The fatty portions were then burned atop the Bronze Altar, and finally the remainder of the animal—once again exclusive to the *public* sin offering—was totally burned outside the camp.[40] God had a similar prescription for the *public* sin offering sacrificed on the Day of Atonement. The highlight of this unique public sin offering was that its most sacred atoning blood, unlike any other, was brought not merely into the *Holy Place* but into the *Most Holy Place*—the heart of the tabernacle—and there it was *sprinkled* upon the Mercy Seat which covered the Ark of the Covenant. The remaining liturgy for the Day of Atonement sin offering was identical to other *public* sin offerings: Blood was daubed on the horns of the *Altar of Incense*, with the remainder shed at the base of the *Bronze Altar*, the fat was then burned on the *Bronze Altar*, and finally the remainder of the creature was burned outside the camp.[41]

---

[39] Leviticus 4:1-3, 13-21. The high priest's sin offering would seem to be a *private* one, but it was the very definition of a *public* sin offering. Any sin offering that included him was *public* (Lev. 4:3-12). The high priest in Leviticus 4 is called "the anointed priest."
[40] Leviticus 4:1-21; 6:30.
[41] Leviticus 16. The ceremony of the scapegoat was also important on the Day of Atonement.

Since the flesh of every *public* sin offering was totally burned outside the camp—including that sacrificed on the Day of Atonement—it was thus impossible for any worshipper to eat of a *public* sin offering. When the *public* sin offerings for the nation or for the high priest were totally consumed by God outside the camp, these then became another form of "holocaust" sacrifice, totally burned up. The blood of a public sin offering was thus uniquely associated both with *sprinkling* and with the *Altar of Incense* in the Holy Place; the blood of the loftiest public sin offering also exclusively connected the *Ark of the Covenant*—specifically the *Mercy Seat*—with the sin offering liturgy.

In contrast to the *public* sin offering, consider now the *private* sin offering liturgy. *Private* sin offerings (including guilt offerings) were for laymen.[42] If a sin offering were for a single layman, then he would be the one slaying it. If it were for the nation of laymen (all Israel excluding the priests), then the high priest would slay it.[43] For all *private* sin offerings, no blood was brought into the Holy Place or into the Most Holy Place, and thus no *private* sin offering blood was ever placed upon the Altar of Incense or on the Ark of the Covenant. All of the sacrificial activity for a *private* sin offering occurred in the Outer Court. The blood of the *private* sin offering, unlike that of the *public* sin offering, was never truly *sprinkled*.[44] *Private* sin offering blood was first "smeared" upon the horns of the Bronze Altar, corresponding to the *public* sin offering blood smeared upon the horns of the Altar of Incense. Like the *public* sin offering, the fat of the *private* sin offering was burned atop the Bronze Altar and the remaining blood was *shed* at its base. Diametrically opposed to

---

[42] We assume from Scripture that the sins of priests were borne by the high priest, and thus a public sin offering was ultimately required for these.

[43] For individuals other than the king, a *private* sin offering would be a female creature. For a king or for the entire nation (excluding the high priest), the creature would be male: Leviticus 5:6. When a high priest offered a sin offering for "the congregation," excluding himself, this too would be a male. Since the high priest was not the sinner, it was a private sin offering, and the officiating priest was obligated to eat of it. Leviticus 4:27ff.

[44] Kurtz, *Offerings...*, 215.

the *public* sin offering, which no one could eat, a *private* sin offering *had to be eaten* by the priests. Thus the final rubric for every *private* sin offering was that its flesh be cooked and eaten by priests. Such a directive certainly stood once again as a type of the priestly eating of the Lord's Supper. Note well this important difference: *Public* sin offering flesh was to be burned outside the camp, but *private* sin offering flesh was a most holy food for priestly consumption.

When the sin offering blood was "smeared" or "daubed" upon the horns of one of the two altars, it was recognized as highly sacred; when it was placed on these high points of an altar, this blood was considered to have been brought close to God.[45] With very little blood sprinkled or daubed on the horns of either altar, the majority of the blood from sin offerings was solemnly poured ("shed") at the base of the Bronze Altar.[46]

The Sprinkled Blood Now Internalized

> *"But you have come...to Jesus, the mediator of a new covenant, and to the sprinkled blood..."*
> Hebrews 12:24

The blood was the atoning element for both the sin and guilt offerings, as was the case for the burnt and peace offerings. According to Jewish rabbis, however, the sin offering blood was more sacred than any other sacrificial blood. The Rabbis would rank the holiness of the ten most sacred sacrificial elements, and the very highest degree of holiness belonged to the

---

[45] Leviticus 4:7,18,25,30,34. Kurtz, *Offerings*..., 215. Kleinig, *Leviticus,* 102: "They [the altar horns] were the place where the sacred realm of God intersected with the common realm of humanity."
[46] Leviticus 4,5,6,7. We disagree with Kurtz who maintains (217) that such blood at the base of the Bronze Altar "was nothing more than a fitting arrangement by which the blood was disposed." We believe there was significance with the base of the altar even as with the horns of the altar. The altar was founded, so to speak, upon sacrificial blood (Lev. 8:15).

blood of the sin offering.[47] No wonder Jesus would speak of His blood in sin offering terms when He instituted the Lord's Supper! With this degree of holiness, all sin offering blood was to be treated with utmost reverence.

Of all the blood from the four blood-related sacrifices, only that of the public sin offering was truly *sprinkled*.[48] Burnt offering and peace offering blood was "strewn" or "dashed" upon the sides of the altar, and *private* sin offering blood was neither sprinkled nor dashed, but it was daubed on the horns of the Bronze Altar, with the remainder poured (shed) at its base.[49] *Sprinkling* of blood was reserved solely for the blood of the *public* sin offering.[50] Recall that the public sin offering blood was *sprinkled* either toward the inner veil or upon the Mercy Seat. This ritual *sprinkling* elevated the public sin offering blood above all other sacrificial blood. *Sprinkling*, the first rubric for public sin offering blood, was unique to this offering; the final rubric for the blood of both public and private sin offerings was also unique: *shedding* the blood at the base of the Bronze Altar.[51]

Since Christ describes His blood in the chalice of the Lord's Supper as blood *shed for the remission of sins*, such blood is indeed sin offering blood. It should then come as no surprise that references to "sprinkled blood" in the NT have appropriately been cited as references to the blood of the Lord's Supper. Some are convinced that the sprinkling of the OT sacrificial blood was at times viewed by the early church as typical of the blood

---

[47] Edersheim, *The Temple*..., 80. The blood of the sin offering is number one, the burnt offering is number two, the sin offering itself is number three and the guilt offering is number four in this Rabbinic ranking.
[48] Edersheim, *The Temple*..., 83-84. Some have misunderstood and thus mistranslated the "strewn" blood from other sacrifices, believing it too was sprinkled.
[49] Leviticus 4:25, 30, 34.
[50] The cleansing from the ashes of the Red Heifer also involved sprinkling as did the cleansing involving ceremonial washings. Note that such sprinkling therefore was always associated with cleansing of sins/uncleanness.
[51] Both public and private sin offering blood were thus *shed*.

consumed in the Eucharist.[52] In the Lord's Supper Christ's blood is of course not sprinkled, but it is internalized by drinking. Even as OT blood from public sin offerings found a unique application in sprinkling, so now the unique application of Christ's blood is in drinking. Consider Hebrews 12:24 as it explains that Christians may now come to "Jesus, the mediator of a new covenant, and to the sprinkled blood." How does one approach Christ's *sprinkled blood*? This Hebrews 12:24 passage is likely Eucharistic, not only because it uses the rare wording that Jesus used when He declared the chalice of His blood to be the "new covenant," but because it speaks of approaching the "sprinkled blood." John Field comments on this text:

> The thought conveyed by the sprinkling no doubt is that the reception of the Eucharistic cup is a spiritual sprinkling of the heart with the Blood of Christ to fit it for the worship of God, just as the old ritual sprinklings removed the various kinds of legal defilement.[53]

In another reference to sprinkled blood, St. Peter introduces his first epistle by explaining that he was truly "an apostle of Jesus Christ." This fisherman, ordained by Christ to feed His sheep, then exhorts God's chosen people to continue to "obey Jesus Christ and be sprinkled with His blood." (1 Peter 1:2) How are Christians continually *sprinkled with His blood*? This they

---

[52] Tibor Horbath, *The Sacrificial Interpretation of Jesus' Achievement in the New Testament*, (New York: Philosophical Library, 1979), 73: "The sprinkling of the blood of Jesus may have some relation with the Last Supper, as it is witnessed in the early tradition." In chapter eight the use of sprinkled blood will be further considered.

[53] John Edward Field, *The Apostolic Liturgy and the Epistle to the Hebrews* (Waterloo Place, London: Rivingtons, 1882), 380. Kleinig, *Leviticus*, 371: "By giving his blood to drink, he sprinkles their hearts, their consciences (Heb 9:13-14; 10:22; 12:24; 1 Pet 1:2). ...In the light of all this, it comes as no surprise that the description of the Divine Service in Heb 12:22-24 culminates in 'the blood for the sprinkling.' Our involvement in the heavenly liturgy is only possible through the blood of Jesus. Through his blood the risen Lord Jesus gives God's holy people access to the heavenly city here on earth."

do by obeying Jesus Christ when He says of the Lord's Supper, "Do this."[54] Tibor Horbath explains:

> I Peter 1,2 indicates an interesting purpose for the apostolic calling. The writer feels that he had been chosen and destined...for the sprinkling with the blood of Christ [...]. The sprinkling of the blood of Jesus may have some relation with the Last Supper, as it is witnessed in the early tradition.[55]

Sprinkling of Unique Peace Offering Blood

We have mentioned how *public* sin offering blood was the only blood *sprinkled* in the tabernacle liturgy. However, before the tabernacle was built and before the sin offering was instituted, Moses *sprinkled* the blood of the *peace offering* toward the people saying, "Behold the blood of the covenant."[56] Observe that Moses sprinkled this unique peace offering blood *before* sin offerings had been introduced into the sacrificial system. Perhaps the "sprinkling" of *this* peace offering blood was related to the blood of the sin offering yet to be instituted. Sprinkling of *peace offering* blood is only found in this account of Moses' institution of the covenant; no other *peace offering* blood—before or after Moses—was *sprinkled* in this way.[57] This inauguration of the Old Covenant at Mt. Sinai has often been compared to Christ's

---

[54] Might the several NT references to "obeying" Christ's Gospel be speaking of the obedience found in "doing" the Lord's Supper?
[55] Horbath, *The Sacrificial Interpretation*..., 73.
[56] Exodus 24:8. This blood was blood from the peace offering (the covenant sacrifice) because the sin offering had not yet been instituted. However, this "sprinkling" of the people with the sacrificial blood (Exodus 24) was viewed as quite peculiar and not at all in accord with any ritual heretofore associated with sacrifice.
[57] An exception may be in the rite of ordination to the priesthood. In Lev. 8:30, the blood from the altar was mixed with oil, and then Aaron and his son were *sprinkled* with it. This ceremony again demonstrated the uniqueness and holiness of the priesthood. The blood was from the altar, probably especially the blood from the ordination sacrifice (a form of peace offering), but perhaps also some of the blood from the sin offering shed at the base of the altar. The source of the blood is not specified, other than it was from the altar. Contact with the altar made the blood holy, and thus this blood sanctified Aaron and his sons.

inauguration of the New Covenant wherein He similarly declared, "This is my blood of the covenant."[58] The Old and New Covenants were both inaugurated with unique reference to and application of *the blood of the covenant*. In the first covenant the blood was personally applied by *sprinkling*, but in the second covenant it is by *drinking*. Hicks thus explains of Christ that

> ...His Blood itself, the very Life of the sacrifice, too holy in the old days ever to be received, and never imparted to any offerer, priest, or layman, more closely than by an external sprinkling, is given to every Christian worshipper to drink.[59]

Eating the Public Sin Offering Today

> *"Take, eat; this is My body, which is given for you [as a sacrifice] [...] Drink from it, all of you; for this is My blood of the covenant, which is to be shed [as sin offering blood] on behalf of many for the forgiveness of sins."*
> *Matthew 26:26-28; Luke 22:19*

Like any other *public* sin offering, the sacrificial flesh on the Day of Atonement was burned outside the camp, never eaten.[60] The loftiest of sin offerings was this once-a-year sacrifice performed on the Day of Atonement.[61] A priest could never eat of this public sin offering, not only because it was totally burned but because he was guilty and in need of atonement himself.

---

[58] Matthew 26:28. This reference to Moses' application of peace offering blood will be further explored in future chapters.
[59] F.C.N. Hicks, *The Fullness of Sacrifice*, (First Published by Macmillan & Co., 1946, Reprinted London: S.P.C.K., 1953), 237. See also 245.
[60] Leviticus 16.
[61] Some however consider the sacrifice of the Red Heifer to be *the* most sacred sin offering, *entirely* burned outside the gate. Edershiem, *The Temple...*, 281 calls it "the most intense of sin-offerings."

As such he could not absolve himself.⁶² Of the public sin offering, God directed, "But no sin offering of which any of the blood is brought into the tent of meeting to make atonement in the holy place shall be eaten; it shall be burned with fire [outside the camp]."⁶³ God was obviously consuming this entire sin offering; the regular fatty portions He consumed at the Bronze Altar, and the rest He consumed outside the camp. By his sins or by the sins he carried, the high priest was profaning God's tabernacle, and thus such a sacrifice could not be consumed there; it had to go beyond the tabernacle, it had to be handled by God beyond the "priestly" system.⁶⁴

Christ's sacrifice was likewise too holy to be handled by the Jewish priestly system. Though He was fittingly sentenced to die by the high priest, yet He would not be sacrificed in the precincts of the temple nor even within the city of Jerusalem.⁶⁵ Like the most-sacred sin offerings of old, His flesh—and even much of His blood—would be "offered" outside the gate.⁶⁶ Appropriately the New Testament explains that the *public* sin offering is fulfilled in Christ's death, as testified in the epistle to the Hebrews:

> We [Christians] have an altar, from which those who serve the tabernacle [O.T. priests] have no right to eat. For the bodies of those animals whose blood is brought into the Holy Place by the high priest as an offering for sin, are burned outside the camp. Therefore Jesus also, that He might sanctify the people through His own blood,

---

⁶² Kurtz, *Offerings*, 237, presents such a description, and he adds, "…the law itself…always enforces the necessity for the burning outside the camp…that the flesh of these sin-offerings was holier than that of others, and too holy even for the priests to eat."
⁶³ Leviticus 6:30.
⁶⁴ Edersheim, *The Temple…*, 98. This was God's method for sanctifying the high priest and, as will be explained, for sanctifying the entire nation—for the high priest bore the nation's sins.
⁶⁵ Matthew 26:26. The high priest, Caiaphas, in condemning Jesus offered the ultimate *Yom Kippur* (Day of Atonement) sacrifice.
⁶⁶ Hebrews 13:12. Note that much of His blood was shed at the temple—by the flogging, the crown of thorns, etc. With not only His *body* offered outside the camp but also much of His *blood* shed outside the camp, Christ then is also antitypical of the sacrifice of the Red Heifer (Numbers 19:1ff). This most intense of sin offerings is also used to explain Christ in the epistle to the Hebrews (9:13).

suffered outside the gate.[67]

These verses clearly describe the public sin offering as they identify the sacrificial blood *brought into the Holy Place*, and as they explain how such sacrifices were *burned outside the camp*. Jesus, who here is described as the one who *suffered outside the gate*, is as such the antitype of the public sin offering. These verses also then correctly identify the Jewish regulation that the OT priests had no right to *eat* of a sacrifice that was to be burned *outside the camp*. Such a sacrifice was a *public* sin offering and, recall, not even the high priest could eat of such a sacrifice. On the other hand these verses imply that we Christians *have an altar* from which we may *eat*. The obvious implication is that now Christians *may eat* of the most sacred *public* sin offering, and *that* sin offering is indeed Christ-crucified—and the sacrificial meal is the Sacrament of the Altar.[68] Christians eat of a *public* sin offering—but that's impossible, isn't it? With God all things are possible.

Concerning such super-priestly privileges given to Christ's people, briefly contemplate Hebrews 10:19-22. Note particularly in these verses the references to Christ's flesh and blood, and to the priestly rights now allotted to all Christians. Bracketed comments help to explain the text:

> Since therefore, brethren [fellow Christians], we have confidence to enter the [Most] Holy Place by the blood of Jesus, by a new and living way which He inaugurated for us through the veil, that is, His flesh, and since we have a great priest [Jesus] over the house of God, let us draw near with a sincere heart in full assurance of faith, having our hearts sprinkled clean from an evil conscience and our bodies washed with pure water.[69]

---

[67] Hebrews 13:10-12.
[68] Some spiritualize this text and deny its connection with the Eucharist.
[69] Hebrews 10:19-22.

As it explains the high priestly duty of bringing the sin offering blood behind the veil to the Mercy Seat located in the heart of the Most Holy Place, this text is describing the OT liturgy for the Day of Atonement. Observe the water-cleansing in the text. The high priest could enter the Most Holy Place only after he had ceremonially *washed with pure water.*[70] This priestly washing on the Day of Atonement foreshadowed NT baptism, as purposely implied in this text. The blood-and-water-related entrance behind the veil was performed in the OT solely by the high priest on one day a year—on the Day of Atonement. The text, however, explains the astounding fact that now Christ has established a *new and living way* so that all Christians may thus enter God's throne room: "Brethren, we have confidence to enter the Most Holy Place."[71] Recall that when Christ's body and blood were given and shed at the cross, the veil covering the entrance into the Most Holy Place was torn in two, indicating that Christ's sacrificed body and blood opened the Holy of Holies to more than just the earthly high priest. After his death, Jesus—who is both the heavenly high priest and the final atoning sacrifice—once and for all presented His blood to His Father at the heavenly Mercy Seat, and He then created access for all Christians to this heavenly place.[72]

Observe in the Hebrews text just quoted that Christ's *new and living way* involves His *blood* and His *flesh*, by which all Christians may *draw near* to God: "We have confidence to enter the Most Holy Place by the *blood* of Jesus, by a new and living way which He inaugurated for us through the veil, that is, His *flesh*... let us *draw near* with a sincere heart in full assurance of

---

[70] Edersheim, *The Temple*..., 246. The high priest bathed his whole body 5 times that day, and washed his hands/feet 10 times. See e.g. Lev. 16:24. The high priest had to be baptized repeatedly. Now we have one sacrifice, one High Priest, one Lord, one faith, one baptism.
[71] Hebrews 10:19.
[72] Hebrews 9:12,24. The Jews often related their understanding of a "heavenly tabernacle" after which the earthly was patterned. Jewish writings outside of the Bible often demonstrated such an understanding of a "heavenly pattern" for the earthly tabernacle. James L. Kugel, *The Bible As It Was* (London: Belknap Press, 1997), 420.

faith."[73] To *draw near* was a technical term describing the approach to God in worship, and the term was consistently used in the OT to describe the *priestly* privilege of *drawing near*.[74] When Hebrews 10:19ff combines these priestly and sacrificial themes, the text then explains how these lofty high priestly privileges are now granted to all Christians—the "brethren". Now not merely the OT high priest but all Christian brethren, having *full assurance of faith* and having been *washed with pure water* of Baptism, may *draw near* to the Holiest Place, God's holy presence. They may enter behind the heavenly veil via Christ's *blood* and *flesh*.[75]

Where does such drawing near take place? Though this Hebrews text does not specify eating or drinking, yet when those early Hebrew Christians heard that their approach to God occurs through Christ's flesh and blood, they would have immediately nodded their heads and expressed a smile of acknowledgment as they realized that this happens in the Eucharist. Their NT priestly activity had already—for decades before this epistle—found its loftiest liturgical expression in the weekly reception of Christ's *flesh* and *blood*, and so a Eucharistic understanding was no doubt intended by the author of the epistle and then naturally grasped by those Jews who first heard it. If during the very worship service where the reception of Christ's flesh and blood is highly magnified, worshippers hear that they can approach the Most Holy place by the flesh and blood of Christ, these listeners would have needed no explanation that the Lord's Supper was being referenced. For those who had been catechized, this text from Hebrews—and indeed the entire epistle as it was read aloud in a worship service— would have been effortlessly received as instruction pertaining to the reception of the Lord's Supper.

Hebrews 10:19ff is then quite instructive concerning the Lord's

---

[73] Hebrews 10:19,20. We have added to the NASB translation the word *Most,* which is the intent of the text, and which is reflected in numerous English translations.
[74] Jon Scholer, *Proleptic Priests, Priesthood in the Epistle to the Hebrews* (Sheffield: Sheffield Academic Press, 1991), 91-149.
[75] These verses from Hebrews will be further explored in chapter eight.

Supper. As today's Christians consider this text from the epistle to the Hebrews, they should realize from it that when they consume the body and blood of the most sacred sin offering, they now have a priestly privilege that far transcends OT practice. Christ has now opened to all Christians the priestly right to eat of *the* public sin offering! All Christians are, in a new way, priests—now interceding not for a single nation, but interceding for the Church and, in certain respects, for the entire world.

How blessed Christians are to have an *altar*, from which God has given the privilege to sacramentally eat! Such sacred dining is a "communion" with a holocaust offering. This was unheard of among the OT Jews, and was in fact impossible because by definition a holocaust offering was totally burned. Brooke Westcott explains the Christian's seemingly impossible privilege:

> In respect of this, our privilege is greater than that of priest or high-priest under the Levitical system. Our great sin-offering, consumed in one sense outside the gate, is given to us as our food. The Christian therefore who can partake of Christ, offered for sins, is admitted to a privilege unknown under the old Covenant.[76]

Holy and Most Holy Meals

> "This is the law of the [private] sin offering: ....it is most holy. The priest who offers it for sin shall eat it. It shall be eaten in a holy place."
> **Leviticus 6:25,26**

Though the OT priests *could not eat* of a *public* sin offering,

---

[76] Brooke Westcott, *The Epistle to the Hebrews*, (Grand Rapids: Wm. B. Erdmans Publishing Co., 1973.), 439.

nevertheless when a layperson in the OT came to present either a *private* sin offering or a guilt offering, the priest *had to eat* of these. Recall that for both the private sin offering and the guilt offering, the only things burned upon the Bronze Altar were the fat portions.[77] After the blood was appropriately daubed on the horns of the Bronze Altar, the priest who officiated such *private* sin offerings *had to eat* of the flesh.[78] God commanded Moses: "...in the place where the burnt offering is slain the sin offering shall be slain before the Lord; it is most holy. The priest who offers it for sin *shall eat it*. It *shall be eaten* in a holy place, in the court of the tent of meeting. [italics added]"[79] This was a highly sacred meal—far from merely eating the leftovers, it was *most holy*.

The extreme holiness of the priestly eating of the sin offering is brought out, interestingly, by a mistake made by Aaron's sons. When God set the sacrificial system into motion, Aaron's sons failed to eat the sin offering.[80] This was a grave mistake, as shown by Moses' anger vented precisely over the fact that they had failed to eat it:

> But Moses searched carefully for the goat of the sin offering, and behold, it had been burned up! So he was angry with Aaron's surviving sons Eleazar and Ithamar, saying, *"Why did you not eat the sin offering at the holy place?* For it is most holy, and He gave it to you to bear away the guilt of the congregation, to make atonement for them before the Lord."[81]

Eleazar and Ithamar had been solemnly enjoined to eat the sin

---

[77] Leviticus 4:8-10, 19-20, 26, 31,35; 5:3-5.
[78] Leviticus 6:26,29; (of flour, 5:13; 7:10); 7:6. The priest was also "guilty" when the whole nation sinned.
[79] Leviticus 6:25b,26.
[80] Though this sin offering was not for an individual, yet it possessed a *private* nature because it was not for the high priest, and thus the blood had not been brought into the Holy Place.
[81] Leviticus 10:16,17. Italics added.

offering flesh, but they failed to do so. This was no small matter, especially since they had just witnessed their two brothers struck dead by God after they had profaned His sanctuary by presuming to do their own liturgy.[82] Moses is now angry with Eleazar and Ithamar, the remaining sons of Aaron, not only because they too had apparently broken God's sacred liturgy, but because such a most holy meal is essential in the atonement process.

Distinguishing Holy and Most Holy Food

The priestly eating of the sin offering, as described in the above text and elsewhere, is identified as a *most holy* meal. The guilt offering was likewise *most holy*: "The guilt offering like the sin offering, belongs to the priest [to eat]; it is *most holy*."[83] The peace offering on the other hand, along with its derived feast, was simply called *holy*.[84] It is valuable to understand that certain eating performed by Hebrew priests was identified as *most holy*, while other eating was simply labeled *holy*.[85]

When sacrifices were identified as *holy* or *most holy* it showed that the food drawn from these had a "sacramental" nature to it, by which we mean that both the *holy* and the *most holy* meals were indeed sacred, and thus they differed from ordinary meals; they possessed a God-related nature. The holiness of these meals was derived from God's holiness, having been consecrated in His holy dwelling place. Both the *holy* and *most holy* food were sanctified particularly by their association with the Bronze Altar.[86]

Being sacred, the *holy* and *most holy* food had strict regulations. While the *holy* meals were eaten by the priests, their families, and at times

---

[82] Leviticus 10:1ff.
[83] Leviticus 14:13.
[84] See chapter six.
[85] Not merely the eating of a sacrifice was deemed *holy* or *most holy*, but the actual sacrifice itself was thus labeled.
[86] Kleinig, *Leviticus*, 11. Kleinig here has an excellent summary of the holy and most holy foods. See Matthew 23:18,19 for the sanctifying power of the altar. An apparent exception to this, as will be cited in the next chapter, is the leavened grain offering associated with the thank offering.

qualified laity, the *most holy* meals could only be consumed by the priests.[87] The *holy* meals given by God to the priests were a major source of sustenance for the priests' families.[88] Even though the priests shared their *holy* food with their families, the laity were prohibited from eating it. The laity's portion of food from the peace offering would nonetheless be deemed a *holy* food as well, but it would remain separate from the *holy* food of the priests.

Sin and Guilt Offerings: Most Holy

Eating of the sin/guilt offerings was *most holy*, which meant, among other things, that the flesh of these offerings could only be consumed by priests. The priests were uniquely connected to God's holiness. Kleinig explains, "God used this most holy food to communicate his holiness with the priests through its physical consumption."[89] Still today God *communicates his holiness* to those who eat of the most holy sin offering of Christ's body and blood, but the antitype far exceeds its type.

The *most holy* description of sin/guilt offerings was appropriate because of the most holy *feature* of forgiveness and because of the most holy *location* of the eating. Concerning the *location* of the priestly eating, Leviticus 7:6 sets forth the regulation that the guilt offering "shall be eaten in the holy place; it is most holy." This *holy place* was the location for eating both sin and guilt offerings. Since the sin and guilt offering food was called *most holy*, one might expect that these *most holy* offerings would be eaten in the Most Holy Place, behind the veil. But in the OT no one could eat there, thus these sacrificial portions were eaten in the holy place of the tabernacle court. God had directed, "The priest who offers it [sin offering] for sin shall eat it. It shall be eaten in a holy place, in the court of the tent of meeting."[90] Now however,

---

[87] E.g. Leviticus 7 and 22. An uncertified priest could not eat of the most holy food (e.g. Ezra 2:62,63). The laity's portion of the peace offering will be explored in the next chapter.
[88] Kleinig, *Leviticus*, 181.
[89] Kleinig, *Leviticus*, 11.
[90] Leviticus 6:26.

in the Christian era, God's priestly people may eat of their most holy sin offering by supernaturally entering the *heavenly Most Holy Place*! The author of the epistle to the Hebrews explained how Christ's flesh and blood are our means whereby we may enter the Most Holy Place: "We have confidence to enter the Most Holy Place by the *blood* of Jesus...through the veil, that is, His *flesh*." So the *heavenly* Holy of Holies is now—in NT times—the most holy *location* for the most holy sin offering meal, and it is accessible through the body and blood of Jesus.

The most holy *feature* of a private sin offering was that it conveyed forgiveness. Concerning this most holy *feature* of the sin offering, recall that when Eleazar and Ithamar failed to eat the sin offering, such an omission was extremely troubling to Moses because it was associated with the *most holy* concept of forgiveness (atonement, bearing away guilt). "Why did you not eat the sin offering at the holy place," Moses asked, "For it is *most holy*, and He gave it to you *to bear away the guilt* of the congregation, to *make atonement* for them before the Lord?"[91] Though the blood of the sin offering was the chief element associated with forgiveness, yet this description by Moses shows that the sin offering fleshly *eating* also possessed an absolving character.[92] Thus, in addition to the priestly application of the sacrificial blood, there was the priestly eating of the sacrificial flesh; through these OT applications of flesh and blood there was, in a sense, a double-dose of forgiveness.

Eating the Sin Offerings—Bearing Sin

Many are convinced that by *eating* the sin offering flesh the priest in

---

[91] Leviticus 10:17

[92] This understanding is not unanimous; in fact we are probably in the minority. For agreement see Angel Manuel Rodriguez, *Substitution in the Hebrew Cultus*, Andrews University Doctoral Dissertation Series 3 (Berrien Springs, MI: Andrews University Press, 1979), 130-136. Kurtz, *Offering...*, 240ff claims the priestly eating was merely "official eating" and not a "priestly act." Why was Moses so angry if it was merely "official eating"?

effect "internalized" the sin that had been placed upon the animal.[93] It was as if a priest—ultimately the high priest—became God's "holy vessel" for sin, bearing in his body the sins of God's people as he ate the *private* sin offerings and guilt offerings.[94] Through the holiness endowed by God upon the priestly office, and through *public* sin offerings offered in the future, such sin would ultimately be removed from the high priest and all would be sanctified.[95] In the NT this personal bearing of sin is accomplished by Christ alone, because Christ is the one and only heavenly high priest. As high priest, Christ has borne the sins of the whole world. In addition to His priestly bearing of sin, Christ's singular sacrifice carried and canceled all sin and guilt for all time. Saint Peter wrote, "He Himself bore our sins in His body on the cross."[96] Pastors no longer need to be priests, *bearing away* the sins of the people in their bodies, and pastors need not offer up sacrifices to atone for sins. Christ finished this process both by His high priestly intercession and by His all-encompassing sin offering at the cross. The sins that *this* high priest bore were not communicated to a sacrificial beast as a sin offering, but He directly became the sin offering. Christ's dual status as priest and victim is captured in an anonymous seventh century communion hymn:

> Draw nigh and take the body of the Lord
> And drink the holy blood for you out-poured.

---

[93] Though the blood was the primary sacrificial element associated with forgiveness, yet the non-bloody sin offering portions must also have been associated with forgiveness, else why would flour be permitted as a sin offering for the poor? As already noted in footnote 32, such flour was partially eaten by the priests, thus absolving the sinner, even though it was a bloodless sacrifice.

[94] Such "bearing iniquity" is found in Exodus 28:38; Numbers 18:1.

[95] C. F. Keil and F. Delitzsch, *Commentary on the Old Testament in Ten Volumes, Vol. I, The Pentateuch*, trans. James Martin (Grand Rapids: Wm B. Eerdmans Publishing Company, 1978), 355. Keil ascribes the removal of such priestly borne sin to be from "the holiness and sanctifying power belonging to their office." Kleinig, *Leviticus*, does not agree that the priests bore the iniquity when they ate of the sin offering, but he agrees that the priests did indeed bear the sins of the people as they applied the atonement blood to God's altar; and on the Day of Atonement the sins borne by the high priest were removed and all was sanctified (235f).

[96] 1 Peter 2:24.

> Offered was He for greatest and for least,
> Himself the Victim and Himself the Priest.[97]

The primary feature of the Holy Eucharist, similar to the private sin offering of old, is the most holy and grand gift of forgiveness associated with sacramental eating. Even as the priests were to eat the sin offering and thus convey forgiveness, so now all of God's people are invited to eat the sin offering—and have forgiveness conveyed to them. How sad it is when God's people—without excuse—fail to eat the sin offering when they avoid the Sacrament of the Altar.[98] When these NT priests fail to receive this most noble and holy meal, should not fellow Christians, like Moses, ask, "Why did you not eat the sin offering at the holy place, for it is most holy?"

Absolution

> ***"So it shall be when he becomes guilty...that he shall confess that in which he has sinned."***
> ***Leviticus 5:5***

Absolution is forgiveness that is bestowed on God's behalf. The account of Eleazar and Ithamar shows that the priestly eating of the sin offering was associated with absolution—"bearing the guilt" and "making atonement" for the guilty ones.[99] An ancient Jewish writing explains the atoning forgiveness that was conveyed by *eating* the sin offering: "The priests

---

[97] *The Lutheran Hymnal* (St. Louis: Concordia Publishing House, 1941), hymn 307, v. 1.
[98] Leviticus 10:19. It appears that Aaron's explanation is that the two living sons had become ineligible to eat because of the death of their brothers (10:1ff). Such deaths apparently created a state of uncleanness. There are of course valid reasons not to receive the Lord's Supper (e.g., one's health, or one has become incapable of eating such food).
[99] See also e.g. Numbers 18:1.

eat, and for the masters (who provide the sacrifice) atonement is made."[100] Such consumption of the sin offering also explains why a sin offering for the poor could simply be flour. The sin offering flour obviously had no atoning blood; nonetheless when the priest ate of this most holy bread, he bore the iniquity of those poor folk who brought it. Thus God's people were "absolved" (forgiven before God) by the liturgy of the OT sin offering.

The OT priests became a picture of *the* high priest, the man Christ Jesus, who literally bears all sin and guilt. They also, as men, typified the incarnation of the Son of God, for he truly became a fully approved *flesh and blood* priest. But perhaps the clearest implication is that an OT priest, as he would *bear away guilt*, stood as an OT type of the exercise of the NT Office of the Keys. The NT *Office of the Keys* now stands as the antitype of the bearing of sins performed by the OT priests.

In the Christian era the word "keys" is employed because this is the word used by Christ, and because it refers to "locking" and "unlocking" sins. Christ established this NT antitype, authorizing His church to "forgive and retain sins."[101] NT pastors hold the *office* to officially handle the *keys* which Christ bestowed upon His church, but one must realize that—as is the case for all types and antitypes—the nature of the antitype far exceeds its type.

In Matthew 16:19, the Son of God explains His peculiar gift to be given to His church: "I will give you the keys of the kingdom of heaven; and whatever you shall bind on earth shall have been bound in heaven, and whatever you shall loose on earth shall have been loosed in heaven." The authority to forgive and retain sins is here referred to as "loosing" or "binding."[102] These words, Gavin has found, "are represented by exact parallels in Rabbinic Hebrew."[103] These Jewish terms were used in Christ's

---

[100] Joachim Jeremias, *New Testament Theology* (New York: Charles Scribner's Sons, 1971), 236.
[101] John 20:21-23.
[102] Matthew 18:18; John 20:21-23 are further Christian application of this Jewish concept.
[103] F. Gavin, *The Jewish Antecedents of the Christian Sacraments* (New York: The Macmillan Col.: 1928), 107-108. Gavin refers to Josephus.

day to describe the authority to teach and apparently also to lift or impose the sentence of excommunication. Rabbis not only possessed such authority relative to the local churches (synagogues), but clearly the priests in relation to the temple sin offerings were thus authorized to absolve as they were called upon to eat the sacrifice.

Though the temple and its practices are now in the remote past, yet it is striking that a record still exists explaining why a priest would refuse to eat a guilt offering. A Jewish priest, Simeon the Just, "stated that he had never eaten of the guilt-offering of the defiled Nazarite..."[104] A "defiled Nazarite" was one who had broken one of God's OT laws, usually a law connected to his vow as a Nazarite. When a priest thus refused to eat, it was in effect the "binding" of the sin upon an unrepentant offerer, but eating the offering would have been the "loosing" of the sin.

As surely as a priest *would not eat* the sin/guilt offering of a defiled, unrepentant sinner, so too if a priest himself were defiled he *could not eat* of a sin or guilt offering, nor even of a peace offering brought to him. A priest who was thus ceremonially defiled could "not eat the holy gifts, unless he has bathed his body in water."[105] Such ceremonial bathing was again typical of NT Baptism.[106] Christians do not have to be re-baptized, but they are privileged to return to their baptism by contrition and repentance, and upon such contrition and repentance they realize that God's absolution again cleanses them.[107] Upon being absolved, the forgiven sinner is given God's permission to eat again of His holy gifts, for—like his OT priestly counterpart—such a sinner has been "washed" with the pure water connected

---

[104] Daly, *Christian Sacrifice*, 82, footnote.
[105] Leviticus 22:6.
[106] See the discussion above on Hebrews 10:19ff. Verse 22 connects such priestly washing to Christian Baptism. Also Titus 3:5 and Ephesians 5:26 connect the *Laver* to Baptism.
[107] We are baptized but once (Eph. 4:5), yet the continual death of the "old man" and the continual rising of the "new man" occurs by continual repentance (E.g. Col. 3:5-10, referring back to the baptism reference in Col. 2:12).

with God's Holy Name.[108]

The OT priests, by such eating of the sin offering, were in a real sense eating on behalf of God! We agree with those theologians who maintain that through the priestly eating of the sin offering, guilt was removed. This is a very "earthy" concept, that guilt is removed by human eating. Yet God certainly must be active in the process, since He is *the only* source of forgiveness, and only He can authorize a man—based upon *the* Man who carried the guilt of the world—to remove another man's guilt,.

Private/Specific Confession of Sins

While laying his hand(s) upon the head of the soon-to-be sacrificed animal, the penitent layman who presented a sin or guilt offering was, if possible, to *confess specific sins* in the presence of the priest.[109] Such confession of sins is described in Leviticus 5:5: "So it shall be when he becomes guilty in one of these, that he shall confess that in which he has sinned."[110] For each type of animal sacrifice one finds the directive to "lay hands" upon the head of the sacrificial beast. This laying-on-of-hands—as will be explained below—inferred a simultaneous audible confession. Of the burnt offering, Leviticus 1:4 directs: "And he shall *lay his hand on the head* of the burnt offering." Of the peace offering, Leviticus 3:2 directs: "And he shall *lay his hand on the head* of his offering and slay it at the doorway of the tent of meeting."[111] Of the sin offering, Leviticus 4:24 explains: "And he shall *lay*

---

[108] Recall that the name of God was connected to the place of worship. E.g. Deut. 12:5.

[109] Edersheim, *The Temple...*, 81. Edersheim explains how the *men* were to bring the sacrifices as they represented their families. Some are convinced that only one hand was thus pressed upon the creature's head.

[110] See also e.g. Numbers 5:7. Kurtz, *Offerings*, 82ff. Though he agrees that such laying on of hands conveyed the sin/guilt of the offerer, Kurtz does not agree that a verbal confession was made over the sacrifice, and he does not believe the above references indicate this. Kurtz believes such laying on of hands involved a strong pushing upon the animal head "with all the powers of the body." (83). There is also justification in believing that only one hand was laid upon the creature.

[111] As will be explained in our discussion of the peace offering (chapter six), a confession of praise rather than a confession of sins was likely pronounced over the head of a peace offering.

Sin and Guilt Offerings, Keen Shadows of the Sacrament

his hand on the head of the male goat...it is a sin offering."[112]

In the middle ages there was a Jewish scholar named Maimonides (b. 1135 AD). His writings have been recognized by both Jewish and Christian scholars to carry tremendous authority. Maimonides recorded specific sacrifice-related instructions for the Jewish temple liturgy, thus shedding light on certain Biblical texts.[113] He wrote that the following was the confession spoken at the temple when a layman laid hands on the head of a sin offering, guilt offering or burnt offering:

> I entreat, O Jehovah: I have sinned, I have done perversely, I have rebelled, I have committed (naming the sin, trespass, or, in the case of a burnt-offering, the breach of positive or negative command); but I return in repentance, and let this be for my atonement (covering).[114]

In the OT sacrificial liturgy, before a worshiper would slay his sin/guilt offering he would lay his hands upon the creature's head. While in this posture—as explained by Maimonides—the worshiper would *privately* confess his sins in the presence of the officiating priest. Sins were specified, out loud. This was a *private* confession.

Even as Jewish worship at times involved this practice of *private* confession of specific sins, so too Christianity has maintained a liturgy of *private* confession and absolution, especially as a preparation for reception of the Lord's Supper. Stretching from early Christianity to the present, Christians have prepared to partake of the Sacrament of the Altar by *privately* confessing specific sins in the presence of a pastor. They then heard the absolution (forgiveness from God), spoken by that pastor. The Lutheran

---

[112] Buchler, *Types of Jewish...*, 74: Baba b. Buta opined that certain Jews "were wrong in prohibiting on the festival the laying of the hands upon a private sacrifice."
[113] Not everyone agrees with Maimonides statements. Kurtz *Offerings*, 83, footnote 1. Here Kurtz concedes that this audible confession of sins was the "unanimous tradition of the Jews."
[114] Edersheim, *The Temple...*, 82. Parenthetic comments are in the text.

Church—though currently not always consistent with her confession—has maintained this practice of private confession: "It is taught among us that private absolution should be retained and not allowed to fall into disuse." [115] Such a practice flowed naturally both from Jesus' directive to "bind" or "loose" sin, and from the Jewish practice of confessing specific sins to the priest when presenting a blood sacrifice.

Public/General Confession of Sins

The Jews also practiced a more general, or *public* confession of sins. Such a confession of sins for the whole nation of Israel was spoken particularly over the public sin offering on the Day of Atonement. This confession, spoken by the high priest, was related not to private confession of *specific* sins, but to a *public* more *general* confession of sins.[116] On the Day of Atonement, the high priest alone laid hands upon the sin offering.[117] During this act the high priest would *generally* confess his sins, the sins of his household, and the sins of all priests.[118] In another part of the Day of Atonement liturgy, the high priest, as representative of the people, spoke a "confession of sin with prayer for forgiveness, closing with the words, '*Praise be to Thee, O Lord, Who in Thy mercy forgivest the sins of Thy people Israel.*'"[119] It was during this liturgy for the yearly Day of Atonement, some

---

[115] *The Book of Concord*, ed. Tappert, 34.
[116] Edersheim, *The Temple...*, 95. Edersheim thus distinguishes between the "private" and "public" sin offerings.
[117] Public sin offerings that were not sacrificed on the Day of Atonement often involved the laying on of hands by the "elders" of the congregation. See Leviticus 4:15. Thus whether by priest or by elders, a "public" confession of sins is encountered.
[118] Edersheim, *The Temple...*, 247, apparently referencing Maimonides: "He [the High Priest] then laid both his hands upon the head of the bullock, and confessed as follows: 'Ah, Jehovah! I have committed iniquity; I have transgressed; I have sinned---I and my house. Oh, then, Jehovah, I entreat Thee, cover over...the iniquities, the transgressions, and the sins which I have committed, transgressed, and sinned before Thee, I and my house---even as it is written in the law of Moses, Thy servant: 'For, on that day will He cover over (atone) for you to make you clean; from all your transgressions before Jehovah ye shall be cleansed.'" 249: "The seed of Aaron, Thy holy people," is included in the general confession of the High Priest.
[119] Edersheim, *The Temple...*, 259f. Textual emphasis is Edersheim's.

contend, that God totally removed the "basketful" of sins bodily borne by the high priest—the temporary, and imperfect bearer of sins for OT Israel.[120]

This priestly confession for the nation of Israel is an example of a general, *public* confession of sin. This OT practice of *public* confession of sin also finds its counterpart today in Christian worship. In Christian churches one will, in various denominations, observe a *public*, general confession of sin preceding the reception of Holy Communion in the worship service.[121] No sins are specified in such a *public* confession of sin, they are only *generally* confessed—even as the high priest only *generally* confessed the sins of the nation of Israel. Such a Christian practice can readily be seen to flow naturally from the OT Jewish liturgy.

The ancient document called the *Didache (Teaching of the Twelve Apostles)*—likely dating from Apostolic times—states: "On the Lord's own day, assemble in common to break bread [celebrate Communion] and offer thanks; but first confess your sins..."[122] Whether such confession of sins was *public* or *private* is debated. We believe it was public. Nonetheless such a statement shows that, within mere decades after Christ, confession of sins before receiving Communion was a Christian practice.

Confession of sins before the Lord's Supper was consistent with and flowed from Jewish practice. "The mould is Jewish, if the thought be Christian. It is a more subtle process than direct copying or borrowing," explains Gavin. He further explains, "Jewish precedents, usages, and ideas determined its [the Lord's Supper's] form."[123]

Some think there should be absolute and direct parallels between OT worship and NT worship, as if the Old is simply a miniature of the New. They want to view the OT *types* to be like miniature footprints, completely

---

[120] Keil and Delitzsch, *Commentary...*, 355. See Ex. 28:38, Numbers 18:1; and consider the implication of Num. 35:25,28, where the death of the high priest implied atonement!
[121] See e.g. *The Lutheran Hymnal*, 15ff.
[122] Johannes Quasten & Joseph C Plumpe, ed.; James E Kleist, trans. and annotator, *Ancient Christian Writers*, No. 6 (New York: Paulist Press, nd, copyright 1948), 23.
[123] Gavin, *The Jewish Antecedents...*, 80, 96.

correlating with the bigger footprints of Christ. It is perhaps helpful to consider the OT *types*—here consisting of the confession of sins and the sin offering meal—to be instead like mere hoof prints formed by the sin offering beasts. The NT *antitypes* of these, which are Absolution and Holy Communion, are to be seen as the divine footprints of the Savior. Both NT footprints and OT hoof prints lead to a sacrifice for sin. However, the footprints of the incarnate God—though foreshadowed by the OT hoof prints—are obviously infinitely superior to and clearly *different from* the hoof prints of beasts. For instance the OT priests absolved OT believers by applying the blood and eating of the sin offering; today absolution is *spoken* (usually by a pastor), and the NT priesthood of believers eat of the sin offering for their own forgiveness. Additionally, the OT high priest became himself a sin-bearer, but today's pastors do not perform this function; Christ is the ultimate sin-bearer.

Isaac Watts, in his hymn *Not All the Blood of Beasts,* has captured poetically the relationship between OT sin offering, Christ's sacrifice, and Christian confession of sins:

> My faith would lay her hand
> On that dear head of Thine
> While like a penitent I stand
> And there confess my sin.[124]

In certain Christian traditions, sins are confessed and absolved both *publicly* and *privately*. Absolution is the forgiveness from God expressed in the OT by the priestly eating, and in the NT by the pastor speaking on God's behalf. Both OT and NT absolution—bestowed either privately or publicly—is

---

[124] *The Lutheran Hymnal*, hymn 156.

validated and empowered by the sacrifice of Jesus. The Jewish liturgy for the sin or guilt offerings prefigured the NT liturgy of confession. The audible confession of sins in the liturgy preceding the Christian Eucharist is readily recognized as a continuation of Jewish worship practices.[125]

Christ's Supper and Isaiah 53

> *"But the Lord was pleased to crush Him, putting Him to grief; If He would render Himself as a guilt offering, He will see His offspring, He will prolong His days...."*
> Isaiah 53:10

As one relates Hebrew sacrifice to Christ, it can be argued that Isaiah 53:10 is the *only* OT prediction that *specifically* describes the coming Savior in terms of the Jewish sacrificial system.[126] This verse predicts, "But the Lord was pleased to crush Him, putting Him to grief. If He would render Himself as a *guilt offering*, He will see His offspring, He will prolong His days." This magnificent prediction describes Christ's crucifixion in terms of a *guilt offering*, and it foretells His resurrection by predicting that He would see His offspring and have His days prolonged. As the Holy Spirit through Isaiah 53 unfolded the work of the Christ, many Jews must have come to realize that their guilt offerings typified the coming Messiah.[127]

---

[125] Concerning eating Christ's sacrifice, an appropriate observation might be that, similar to the OT priests, when the priesthood of believers in the Christian era *eat* of *the* sin offering they are non-verbally pronouncing an absolution upon fellow Christians who come forward in repentance. As such, they perform a role similar to the OT priests who *by eating* would "bear away the guilt" of a penitent. Christians do not "bear" the sins of fellow communers, but as priests there is perhaps an absolution-inference to their participation. Such thinking further explains why all Christians must lovingly prevent an unrepentant person from approaching the Eucharist; to absolve the impenitent is to condone their sin and thus mock Christ's crucifixion.

[126] Daniel 9:24 may also be a specific prediction of Christ as sin/guilt offering.

[127] Edersheim, *The Temple*..., 92: "....such early works as *Targum Jonathan* and the *Jerusalem Targum* frankly adopt the Messianic interpretation of these prophecies." Edersheim then sadly reports the attempted Jewish "cover-up" of such an interpretation.

The original Hebrew wording of this verse predicts Christ as a *guilt offering*, but the Septuagint—the official Jewish Greek translation—describes Him here by using *sin offering* terminology.[128] Perhaps the only reason for the change is the similarity between the sin and guilt offerings. On the other hand, it seems likely that the Greek translators tried to make sense of Isaiah's strange guilt offering. It was a strange guilt offering because it described a "public" sort of sacrifice, a sacrifice for the "many"; however, as already explained, guilt offerings were never viewed as *public* sacrifices. Moreover, guilt offerings were always to be eaten by priests, but public sin offerings were never eaten by anyone.

Could it be that the text is indeed describing a public sin offering, but in order to endow such a sacrifice with the privilege of eating, the Holy Spirit called it a guilt offering? It appears as though the original Hebrew text of Isaiah 53 is describing a kind of hybrid sacrifice, a public sin offering yet officially a private sort of guilt offering, from which priests were to sacredly dine. The solution is found in Christ's sacrifice, a public sacrifice from which the ultimate priestly meal—the Eucharist—is derived, at which NT communers are the priests.

The main point to be considered here, however, is that the coming Savior was predicted in Isaiah 53 to be a sin/guilt offering. Since He is the antitype of both types of sacrifice, and since these two kinds of sacrifice were clearly related, it matters little which sacrifice is the intended one in Isaiah 53:10.

Isaiah 53 shows Christ to be the antitype of the sin offering of the Jews. How then does Isaiah 53 relate to the Lord's Supper? One observes a strong rope, woven of many cords, tying the Eucharist to Isaiah 53. Certainly one cord of that rope binding the Lord's Supper to Isaiah 53 is simply the fact that Christ is deemed a sin offering, and certain sin offerings were *eaten* by

---

[128] The Hebrew is indeed the technical term for guilt offering. The LXX Greek is περι αμαρτιας, a technical term for sin offering.

Sin and Guilt Offerings, Keen Shadows of the Sacrament

priests, and the Lord's Supper is clearly a priestly meal drawn from a sin (guilt) offering. However Christ Himself created additional cords binding Isaiah 53 both to His self-sacrifice and to the Last Supper.

Another binding-cord is the word "many." Jesus instituted the Eucharist by saying, "This is my blood of the covenant, which is to be shed on behalf of *many* for the forgiveness of sins."[129] Merely the Last Supper reference to *forgiveness of sins* is enough to connect Christ and His meal generally to the sin offering of Isaiah 53, but Christ's use of *many* creates another cord tying the Lord's Supper to Isaiah 53. Concerning the word "many", Joachim Jeremias explains, "Whereas it [the word "many"] occurs relatively rarely in the Old Testament, it appears no less than five times in Isaiah 53; it is virtually the link word of this chapter." Then Jeremias almost seems to exaggerate when he concludes, "Without Isaiah 53 the eucharist words remain incomprehensible.[!]"[130]

Robert J. Daly similarly maintains that "the words of institution themselves carry unmistakable references to it [Isaiah 53]."[131] Though there are additional words connecting the Lord's Supper with Isaiah 53, yet Jeremias, Daly and others agree that the primary link-word is "many." Christ magnified this link when He said in the Words of Institution that His blood "is shed on behalf of *many* for the forgiveness of sins."[132]

Another cord binding Christ's Supper to Isaiah 53 is Christ's use of the word "shed." Recall that in the Last Supper Jesus spoke of His blood as "shed." Jeremias explains that such a word "is taken from the language of sacrifice. It is linked with... Isaiah 53:12, 'because he poured out [shed] his

---

[129] Matthew 26:28.
[130] Jeremias, *New Testament Theology*, 291. Actually it is not in Isaiah 53 alone, but from Isaiah 52:13-53:12 the word "many" is used five times. See also Daniel 9:27 as explained in Andrew E. Steinmann, *Daniel*, (St. Louis: Concordia Publishing House, 2008), 449.
[131] Daly, *Christian Sacrifice*, 222.
[132] Matthew 26:28; Mark 14:24.

Sin and Guilt Offerings, Keen Shadows of the Sacrament

life to death...'"[133] As explained in chapter four, blood and life were practically interchangeable in ancient thinking, and thus when Isaiah 53:12 predicted that the coming Christ would *pour out his life*, it was equivalent to saying that He would *pour out (shed) his blood*. Recall that only sin offering blood was thus shed.

In relation to such shed blood, Isaiah 52:15 introduces Isaiah 53 by predicting that the coming Christ "will sprinkle many nations." To speak of "sprinkling" especially brought to mind the blood of the public sin offering, a blood that, as explained earlier, was uniquely sprinkled in the sacrificial process.[134] Such blood, according to Isaiah 52 and 53, bespeaks international atonement since it predicts the sprinkling of "many nations."[135] Recall also that such "sprinkling" has been connected to the drinking of Christ's blood in the Sacrament. So again Christ and His Supper are uniquely bound by a strong cord to the sin offering of Isaiah 53.[136]

With these several cords of Christ binding His Last Supper to Isaiah 53, the knowledgeable Jew would have needed no prompting to recognize at least a couple of these connections. Such a realization would have caused knowledgeable Jews to combine Christ, the Lord's Supper, and the guilt/sin offering into a unified concept—a concept foreseen by the prophet Isaiah. Isaiah 53 thus not only foresaw the sin offering of the Savior, but the sin offering meal of the Lord's Supper as well.

---

[133] Jeremias, *The Eucharistic Words...*, 226. Also Darwell Stone, *A History of the Doctrine of the Holy Eucharist* (London: Rivingtons, 1909), 11-12: "...the word ["shed"] suggests the pouring out of the blood of the slain victim at the base of the altar in the Jewish sacrifices, rather than the shedding of the blood in death."

[134] This word for sprinkling is indeed the same word used for the sprinkling of the sin offerings. This reference also brings to mind the time when Moses sprinkled the people with the blood of the covenant sacrifice.

[135] Kleinig, *Leviticus*, 120, speaking of the "sprinkling" of the public sin offering blood: "In Isaiah 52:15 the verse is used of the Suffering Servant: 'He shall sprinkle many peoples,' meaning that the blood of Jesus Christ will atone for the sins of all people."

[136] Daly, *Christian Sacrifice*, 222ff, shows how others have noted that Christ's *memorial* command, His use of *covenant* and other factors connect the Words of Institution to the "Servant songs" of Isaiah. Additionally it is of value to realize that the Aramaic word for "servant" is the identical word for "lamb" (Daly, 301, citing Jeremias and others).

Special Occasion Sin Offerings

> *"As for the leper...he shall cover his mustache and cry, 'unclean! unclean!'"... "For the guilt offering [for lepers] like the sin offering, belongs to the priest; it is most holy."*
> **Leviticus 13:45; 14:13**

God's ordinances caused OT Jews to recognize the condition of uncleanness. When someone was *unclean* they could not participate in the OT sacrificial rites; most particularly they were banned from eating the sacrificial flesh.[137] Contact with a dead body, either with a human corpse or non-sacrificial animal corpse, caused uncleanness.[138] Certain things that related to sexual intercourse, both normal activity and abnormal conditions, established uncleanness.[139] Leprosy or contact with a leper created uncleanness.[140] As a final example, certain worship-oriented duties—particularly those associated with the sacrifice of the Red Heifer and with the release of the Scapegoat on the Day of Atonement—rendered a person unclean.[141]

In order for an *unclean* Israelite to be recognized as *clean*, he had to ceremonially bathe or offer the sacrifice of a sin offering, or a combination of these. As such, uncleanness was a sin-issue. With sin and guilt offerings uniquely sacrificed when someone was rendered *unclean*, such special-occasion sin or guilt offerings taught the Israelites many truths about man's sinful condition. They still teach God's people today.

Several theologians have noted that it was normal or even noble

---

[137] Leviticus 7:19-21; this certainly relates to closed Communion in NT times.
[138] E.g. Leviticus 11.
[139] E.g. Leviticus 12, 15.
[140] E.g. Leviticus 13, 14.
[141] E.g. Leviticus 16:26; Leviticus 10:9,10 appears to ascribe uncleanness for wine consumption in the sacred courts;   Numbers 19:7.

activities that made a person unclean. What is nobler than to minister to the dying and to properly care for the body of a deceased relative, yet such actions would have made a person unclean. Certainly motherhood and childbearing are most noble, yet uncleanness was associated with this. People became lepers by no fault of their own, so why should a leper be singled out as unclean? And probably the strangest pronouncement of uncleanness occurred in relation to certain official worship activities—activities commanded by God!

Yet, on the other hand, uncleanness illustrated a very important reality: The world is fallen.[142] Eve was cursed in relation to childbearing, and babies are born sinners, thus it made sense that that which was associated with reproduction rendered one unclean. The dead and the lepers were unclean because Adam received the curse of death, and consequently the curse of disease. Leprosy—a kind of representative disease—is an obvious result of the corruption of this world. Additionally, the sacrificial system, which would not have been in existence had the world not fallen into sin, at times brought uncleanness via certain God-ordained rituals, because such rituals were to purify man's putrid condition.[143]

All such uncleanness was associated with sin, and thus sin or guilt offerings were often prescribed to "reverse" a person's uncleanness.[144] What is God teaching by all of this? W. Washburn summarizes nicely:

> The law of 'uncleanness,' then, could not fail to call to the mind of the reflective worshiper the woeful event of the Fall, and the entailment of sin upon Adam and all his posterity... In its sad isolation and

---

[142] W. W. Washburn, *The Import of Sacrifice in the Ancient Jewish Service*, (New York: Phillips & Hunt, 1883), 85.

[143] It is this author's contention that unclean animals, being recognized as such even before the flood, were deemed unclean by virtue of the fact that they were markedly changed after God's curse. Note how the clean and unclean animals are basically divided between herbivores and carrion eaters. Man fits the latter category. In addition to being sinful, man is an unclean carrion eater, drastically changed from the fall.

[144] E.g. Leviticus 12:6,7; 14:12,13, 19; 15:15,30.

exclusion it told the mournful tale of man's unavoidable, innate unfitness to approach a holy God. It was the pathetic and impressive declaration of the doctrine of man's natural depravity; it was the Mosaic form of the dogma of original sin.[145]

So complete is Christ's sin/guilt offering, that now Christians—and indeed the entire creation—are *declared* clean, and such "cleanness" will be fully realized and observed when the sons of God are revealed.[146] Thanks be to God who gives His people the victory through the Lord Jesus Christ! So thoroughly cleansed are God's people even now by faith in Christ, they may enter into the Most Holy Place of God and there dine with Him, as priests consuming *the* sacrifice given and shed for their uncleanness. Instead of Christ being offended by a believer's sinful nature, He is pleased to have His holiness internalized by His people because their sinful nature has been declared clean. Christians now anxiously await the time when the banquet with God will be face to face.

Some Closing Thoughts

Obviously The Lord's Supper has characteristics typified by the sin and guilt offerings. It is a marvelous meal. However, the warning must again be sounded—especially when relating Holy Communion to the sin offering—that God's people not revere or honor the Sacrament as if it somehow *makes* satisfaction for their sins. It does not. The *Book of Concord* explains:

> Surely the Lord's Supper was instituted for the sake of forgiving guilt. For it offers the forgiveness of sins, which necessarily implies real guilt. Nevertheless, it does not make satisfaction for guilt; otherwise, the Mass [Lord's Supper] would be on a par with the death of

---

[145] Washburn, *The Import of Sacrifice...*, 85-86.
[146] Romans 8:19.

Christ.[147]

As a final point, consider the solemnity associated with the liturgy surrounding the sin offerings. There could be no frivolity or jesting associated with such OT worship. The OT sin offering meal, though eaten in the peace of God's gracious mercy, was nevertheless a solemn meal as it called to mind the necessity of death to bring forgiveness. Shall not the Lord's Supper be at least equally solemn? It was the *death of the Son of God* that procured man's eternal forgiveness and created the most holy sin offering meal. It is true that the NT Eucharist is a *peace offering* meal that exudes joy and celebration, as will be further explained in the next chapter, but such attitudes must be tempered with the solemn realization that the body and blood which Christians miraculously eat was given and shed *for the remission of sins*. The Sacrament of the Altar is a solemn *sin offering meal*, to be consumed by priests who, with humble awe, encounter the heavenly Holy of Holies.

---

[147] *The Book of Concord*, ed. Tappert, 266.

> *"Now when you offer a sacrifice of peace offerings to the Lord... It shall be eaten the same day you offer it, and the next day; but what remains until the third day shall be burned with fire."*
> *Leviticus 19:5,6*

Chapter Six

THE PEACE OFFERING, PORTRAYER OF THE EUCHARIST

Many believe that of all the OT sacrifices the peace offering presented the clearest connection to the Lord's Supper. W. W. Washburn summarizes the relationship: "The peace offering of the old dispensation, telling in expressive symbol the sweet and hallowed story of divine communion, so far, had the same significance as the eucharist in the new."[1] The OT peace offering, like the Eucharist that it typified, was indeed *the story of divine communion*, a communion realized in the joyous, worship-related eating of a sacrificial meal. As this chapter unfolds there will likely be surprise at the many kinds of and occasions for peace offerings in the OT. Then there will probably be amazement at the many intimations of the Lord's Supper created by the OT peace offering.

God's OT people would joyously eat peace offerings on many occasions. Imagine, for the moment, that instead of festive food for the mouth the peace offering presented music for the ear. The OT peace offerings would then be comparable to a symphonic orchestra playing magnificent background music—music designed to embrace a melody and song yet to be revealed. Imagine the *thank offerings* sounding forth as brass instruments,

---

[1] W. W. Washburn, *The Import of Sacrifice in the Ancient Jewish Service* (New York: Phillips & Hunt, 1883), 64-65.

majestically trumpeting a priest's ordination, a king's coronation, the temple's dedication, the close of a great national feast, or simply a public confession of God's goodness expressed by a layman. The *votive offerings* and *free-will offerings* cried to God as stringed instruments, expressing tearful appreciation to God for some great deliverance. The woodwind section sounded forth the harmonious chords of the *covenant sacrifices*, as God and man joined in communal agreement. The drums, cymbals and bells rang out the consistent rhythm of *salvation and peace*, the cadence to which all of the peace offerings confidently kept time.

Altogether it was harmonious and beautiful to listen to, and from it one could *almost* make out the melody, yet alas this OT music was only the setting. Though the melody and song had been composed from the dawn of time, yet the melody and song would not be revealed until the Christ had reached His goal. The melody was softly played when Christ Jesus instituted the Holy Eucharist, and then it was played vivaciously at His crucifixion. It was the melody of salvation in the body and blood of the Lamb, and the lyrics were those of a new creation. The song was first sung in heaven when the Lamb that was slain rose again from the dead. What a melody and song they were! They fit perfectly the OT peace offering setting. The world had never heard such a composition for it was a new song, the song of the living Lamb that had been slain. Yet there was an air of familiarity to it; it was a song and a melody that fit so perfectly into the OT setting that those listening could draw no other conclusion than that this was the Composer's intent. And seeking the source of all this superlative music one could peer into the orchestra pit and find that all, even the OT peace offering setting, was emanating from the cross.

Sacrifice of the Peace Offering

> *"You shall build the altar of the Lord your God....and you shall sacrifice peace offerings and eat there, and you shall rejoice before the Lord your God."*
> *Deuteronomy 27:6,7*

All of the animal-related peace offerings followed the same basic procedure.[2] First the *blood* of this offering, like that of the burnt offering, was reverently dashed on the outer walls of the Bronze Altar, much of it running to the base of the altar.[3] The *fatty portions* of the peace offering—treated identically to that of the sin offering—were subsequently burned upon the Bronze Altar, and thus they were consumed by God as His holy portion. Next, the priest received two portions from the *flesh* of the peace offering— the breast and the right thigh. These were called the "wave offering" and the "heave offering," and they were to be prepared and *eaten* as a holy meal by the priests and their families.[4] Finally, the layman who brought the peace offering was privileged to cook and eat the remaining peace offering *flesh*. This too was a holy meal. Both the priestly meal and the meal eaten by laymen were figures of the Sacrament of the Altar.

Some have misunderstood the peace offering, believing that it was offered to God to *make* peace. Such a belief is not correct. "These were not sacrifices to obtain peace," William Moenkemoeller explains, "but offerings made in grateful acknowledgement of the peace, i.e. of the blessings,

---

[2] The tithe as a kind of peace offering did not necessarily involve an animal sacrifice.
[3] The blood of the animal sacrifices frequently ended up at the base of the Bronze Altar.
[4] Leviticus 7:28-34; Numbers 18:11. Some have suggested that the "waving" and "heaving" of the priestly portion was an action making the sign of the cross. This suggestion was first heard by this author from Rev. Prof. John Saleska in a class lecture. It is apparent that such waving and heaving were movements that indicated the giving of the flesh to God, and His giving it back to His priests.

received from God."[5] Peace offerings were sacrificed and eaten by an offerer *because* he realized that peace with God was an already established reality.

The peace offering had two general characteristics whereby the participants demonstrated that peace from God was a realized fact. First, there was simply the location of the peace offering in the Jewish sacrificial process.[6] Recall that in this process the three main categories of sacrifice could be perceived as stages. The first stage in the process was the sin offering.[7] This offering signified and conveyed the forgiveness of sins, thus *bringing* spiritual peace.[8] The second sacrifice in the stages of sacrifice was the burnt offering, which signified the self-surrender of the offerer who, realizing he was at peace with God, was willing to have this highly valued creature wholly burned upon God's altar.[9] The final sacrifice in the stages of sacrifice was the peace offering,[10] and this final sacrifice was particularly associated with a meal eaten with thanksgiving and praise. Having received forgiveness in the sin offering, the peace offering was obviously sacrificed *after* peace with God was an already recognized reality. Of course all peace with God finds its origin in the sacrifice of Jesus Christ on the cross, and because the arms of His sacrifice reach back to the beginning and forward to the end of time, both OT and NT believers could realize peace from God.

A second way the peace offering demonstrated that it was subsequent to an already established peace with God was in its final activity.

---

[5] William Moenkemoeller, *The Festivals and Sacrifices of Israel Compiled from the Mosaic Regulations* (Saint Louis: Concordia, 1932), 32. He continues: "They were thanksgiving sacrifices, but thanksgiving sacrifices of an especially joyful character."
[6] This was discussed in previous chapters.
[7] The private sin offering and guilt offering are here considered together. The stages of sacrifice can be seen in references like Lev. 9:1-4.
[8] The blood of every animal sacrifice was associated with atonement, but this was the primary emphasis of the sin offering.
[9] All was burned with the exception of the blood and the hide. The blood was placed around the altar and at its base, and the skin of the burnt offering belonged to the priests.
[10] F.C.N. Hicks, *The Fullness of Sacrifice* (London: S.P.C.K., 1956), 341: "The third stage in the Sacrifice, once more for Christ and for us, is the sharing of the Life that has been set free in the surrender of the Cross, and offered, accepted, and transformed. It is the stage of the Communion-meal."

The culmination of the peace offering liturgy occurred when the layman who brought the sacrifice prepared and ate most of the peace offering flesh, often inviting friends and relatives to this joyful meal.[11] The shedding of the blood and the burning of the peace offering fat upon the altar were essential to such a sacrifice, but these were not the primary activities. The joyful eating of the peace offering meal was integral to this sacrifice, and indeed such eating was considered the primary activity. Eating was part of the act of sacrifice; the sacrifice was not accomplished until there was eating.[12] Even though this eating was sacred, it was marked with great joy and celebration, and as such it vividly demonstrated the realization that there *was* peace with God. One does not eat and celebrate if there is no peace, and one does not eat and celebrate to create peace, but one eats and celebrates because there *is* peace.

Eating and *rejoicing* are in fact the two emphases of the peace offering. Deuteronomy 27:7 summarizes this: "You shall build the altar of the Lord your God...and you shall sacrifice peace offerings and *eat* there, and you shall *rejoice* before the Lord your God." This eating united with godly celebration identified the climax in the stages of sacrifice. Of the *rejoicing* surrounding the peace offering, Hicks goes so far as to say, "And it is probable that, not only the actual phrase 'sacrifices of thanksgiving' but all outbursts of rejoicing and thankfulness in Psalms that have anything to do with the Temple should be referred to it [the peace offering]."[13] Concerning the significance of *eating* the peace offering, Alfred Edersheim summarizes,

---

[11] S. C. Gayford, *Sacrifice and Priesthood*, (London: Methuen & Co. LTD., 1953), 38: "The rest of the flesh [of the peace offering] was then eaten by the sacrificer and his friends. It was a meritorious act to invite guests and especially the poor to share in this banquet with its associations of sacred and social festivity (.....cf. Ps. xxii.26)."

[12] In this respect, one can say that the Lord's Supper is a peace offering sacrifice—for it is still the meal which is part of the peace offering sacrifice of Christ.

[13] Hicks, *The Fullness*..., 93. The Psalms are full of such peace offering references, especially as one realizes the abundant terms and phrases used to refer to peace offerings.

"In peace-offerings the sacrificial meal was the point of main importance."[14]

In summary, the *meal* and *thankful rejoicing* were the two primary activities surrounding every peace offering, with the meal being the most important act. What a fitting type of the Lord's Supper!

The Peace Offerings

> *"Now as for the flesh of the sacrifice of his thanksgiving peace offering, it shall be eaten on the day of his offering...But if the sacrifice of his offering is a votive or a freewill offering, it shall be eaten on the day that he offers his sacrifice; and on the next day what is left of it may be eaten..."*
> Leviticus 7:15, 16

A variety of terminology was used for the peace offering, often reflecting the occasion for such a sacrifice. This terminology included *thank offering, votive offering, free-will offering, sacrifice of praise, salvation sacrifice, confession sacrifice, covenant sacrifice, ordination sacrifice, coronation sacrifice* and *ending (completion) sacrifice*. Additionally the *tithe* and sacrifice of the *first-born* have been considered forms of peace offerings. These will be explored throughout this chapter.

Though there was an abundance of terms and occasions standing under the umbrella of the peace offering, yet there were basically only three types of "private" peace offerings. These are introduced in Leviticus 7:15,16. Italics identify the three types:

> Now as for the flesh of the sacrifice of his *thanksgiving* peace offering, it shall be eaten on the day of his offering...But if the sacrifice of his offering is a *votive* or a *freewill* offering, it shall be eaten on the day that he offers his sacrifice; and on the next day what

---

[14] Alfred Edersheim, *The Temple, Its Ministry and Services* (Peabody, MS: Hendrickson Publishers, updated edition 1994), 99.

is left of it may be eaten.

As observed in this reference, the three types of peace offerings were commonly called the *thank (or "thanksgiving") offering*, the *votive (or "vow") offering*, and the *freewill (or "free-will") offering*.[15] These three sacrifices were appropriately called *peace* offerings because the person bringing such sacrifices knew he was at peace with God. God would accept a person's thanks in a *thank offering*, his vow in a *votive offering* and his donation to God in a *free-will offering*, because God through Christ was retroactively at peace with His OT people. Though each of these three types of peace offering could be considered distinct from the others, yet there was some overlap in understanding them.

The regulations for all three types of peace offering were nearly identical, with basically the following exception. The *thank offering* had to be eaten before the morning after the sacrifice, but the *votive* and *free-will offerings* could be eaten up to the morning of the *third day*, and after the third day the eating of such offerings was strictly forbidden.[16] Some theologians have noted that the "third day" strikes a familiar chord in the orchestration of God's work of salvation—the ultimate third-day event being Christ's resurrection.[17] Andrew Jukes is convinced that these peace offering restrictions pointed directly to Christ's resurrection: "Now the 'morning' and the 'third day' [in relation to the peace offering] are sufficiently common types, and are both constantly used, I believe, to denote the resurrection."[18]

---

[15] A "private" peace offering was one brought by laity.

[16] Leviticus 7:15,16. Such "morning after" instructions were reminiscent of the Passover.

[17] Robert J. Daly, *Christian Sacrifice* (Washington, D.C.: The Catholic University of America Press, 1978), 184, shows how the many references to "the third day" in the Old Testament correspond with God's acts of deliverance. "The enigmatic 'in accordance with the scriptures' of 1 Cor. 15,4, therefore, refers directly not to the resurrection but to the theologically laden technical term 'on the third day'..." For this technical use of 'on the third day,' see e.g. the accounts of Abraham's sacrifice of Isaac and the giving of the Decalogue.

[18] Andrew Jukes, *The Law of the Offerings in Leviticus I. - VII Considered as the Appointed figure of the Various Aspects of the offering of the Body of Jesus Christ* (London: James Nisbet & Co., 13th ed., 1883), 126.

It is reasonable to think that God prohibited the eating of the votive and free-will offerings simply because of the putrefaction of the sacrificial flesh beyond the third day. The Lord's Supper is a peace offering meal that never reaches putrefaction, because the sacrifice rose from the dead as the third day dawned! The sacrifice of Christ, unlike the OT peace offerings, would never undergo decay[19], and in fact the Lord's Supper would never be celebrated with a dead sacrifice. The Apostles ate not a dead Christ, but ate His body and blood with Him visibly present. Similarly, Christians began to celebrate the Eucharist not while Jesus was dead but while He was physically alive, after His resurrection.[20] God's people are now not limited to three days in which they must eat the peace offering of Christ's body and blood; they eat it until He returns! The antitype is far superior to its type. There is no "third day" restriction for the peace offering meal of the Lord's Supper, for this "sacrificial" meal remains eternally viable and valid. Of course Christians do not tear off and eat pieces of Christ's flesh, as if they were cannibals; it is a miraculous sacrifice-related meal. Christ Jesus is a real flesh and blood human being who actually died—but He also rose from the dead. Christians continually partake of this Lamb that was slain but is alive forevermore!

The Priestly Meal

> *"The offering of their gift, even all the wave offerings [from the peace offerings] of the sons of Israel; I have given them to you and to your sons and daughters with you...Everyone of your household who is clean may eat it."*
> **Numbers 18:11**

Concerning the meal aspect of the peace offering, first consider the

---

[19] Acts 2:27.
[20] This was of course true while Christ visibly walked the earth for forty days after His resurrection (perhaps the reference in Acts 10:41), but it is also true today; we eat the body and blood of the crucified yet very-present *living* Christ.

priestly eating. After God's portions (fatty portions, blood) were placed on or around the altar, the priest and his family were to eat what were called the *heave offering* and *wave offering*. This is summarized in Leviticus 7:30-32:

> His own hands shall bring the offering made by fire to the Lord. The fat with the breast he shall bring, that the breast may be waved as a *wave offering* before the Lord. And the priest shall burn the fat on the altar but the breast shall be Aaron's and his sons. Also the right thigh you shall give to the priest as a *heave offering* from the sacrifice of your peace offerings.[21]

There appears to be justification in understanding the "heaving" and "waving" of such sacrificial portions to be their dedication to God, and then His gifting them back to the priest's families.[22] God was thus sharing His food with the priests and their families.[23]

The peace offering flesh was called a *holy thing*, and the peace offering meal that a priest shared with his family was a *holy* meal. Other kinds of sacrifices generated *most holy* meals for the priests. Recall that from the sin and guilt offerings—as well as from the grain offerings yet to be investigated—the officiating priest was required to eat certain *most holy* portions. No laity could eat of these offerings; not even a priest's family could eat of the *most holy* offerings. As such, the meals drawn from these were identified as *most holy* meals. The peace offering, however, was the least

---

[21] *The Holy Bible, NKJV* (Atlanta: Thomas Nelson Publishers, 1994). Italics added.
[22] See e.g. J. H. Kurtz, *Offerings, Sacrifices and the Worship of the Old Testament*, trans. James Martin (Peabody, MA: Hendrickson Publishers, Inc., 1998), 268.
[23] John W. Kleinig, *Leviticus*, (St. Louis: Concordia Publishing House, 2003), 180: "The breast that had been elevated before the Lord was assigned to all the priests (7:31), while the thigh was assigned to the officiating priest (7:32,33). They were God's gift to them, their endowment from him."

holy of the Hebrew sacrifices, and thus it was simply *holy* and not *most holy*.[24] Concerning these two degrees of holiness, God declared that a priest "may eat the bread of his God; both of the *most holy* and of the *holy*."[25] The less holy nature of the peace offering meal permitted *this* priestly food to be shared with the priest's family. God directed, "Those who are born in his house may eat of his [holy peace offering] food...but no layman shall eat of it."[26] John Kleinig explains that the *most holy* food actually conveyed holiness, but the *holy* meals did not; nonetheless the *holy* foods conveyed communion with God—a communion with holiness.[27] Even though a priest could share his holy peace offering food with the laity in his family, he could not share this food with other laity.

Jesus used peace offering terminology when He said, "Do not give what is holy [literally, *holy thing*] to dogs."[28] Such *holy things* are often translated into English as "holy gifts." The *holy things* (holy gifts) recorded in the OT are often references to the priestly peace offering food.[29] As an example of this peace offering usage, God prohibited leprous priests from eating the *holy things*: "No man, of the descendants of Aaron, who is a leper...may eat of the holy gifts [*holy things*] until he is clean."[30] In a moment we will further explore such *holy thing* terminology as it relates to Holy Communion.

---

[24] Certain exceptional peace offerings attained the status of *most holy*, thus generating food only for the priests. A unique peace offering on Pentecost was pronounced *most holy*. The leavened thank offering bread was also *most holy*. The peace offering bread at a priest's ordination was *most holy*. See Edersheim, *The Temple*..., 100.
[25] Leviticus 21:22. Italics added in the quote.
[26] Leviticus 22:11,13.
[27] Kleinig, *Leviticus*, 11.
[28] Matthew 7:6.
[29] This also included the priestly eating of the first-born and the tithe.
[30] Leviticus 22:4.

Holy Things Eaten by Laity

> *"It shall be eaten."*
> *Leviticus 7:15, 16; 19:6; 22:30; etc.*

With few exceptions, everyone got to eat a portion of the peace offering. God ate His part (the fatty portions[31]), and the priests and their families ate their *holy things* (the heave and wave portions). Then, if a layman had brought the peace offering, he and his family were privileged to *eat the rest* of the flesh from this holy sacrifice. Observe that though the priests and their families consumed their *holy* portions from the peace offering—the portions waved and heaved—theirs was not the only *holy* food. The remaining peace offering flesh constituted the only *holy* meal that God offered to the laity. This eating done by the laity is summarized in Leviticus 19:5-8:

> Now when you offer a sacrifice of peace offerings to the Lord, you shall offer it so that you may be accepted. *It shall be eaten* the same day you offer it, and the next day; but what remains until the third day shall be burned with fire. So if it is eaten at all on the third day, it is an offense; it will not be accepted. And everyone who eats it will bear his iniquity, for he has profaned the *holy thing* of the Lord; and that person shall be cut off from his people. [italics added]

From this divine directive one realizes that even the laity's portion of the peace offering was considered a *holy thing*, something not to be profaned. Obviously it was thus designated because this meal for the laity, like that eaten by the priests, was a worship-related meal. Kleinig generally explains the *holy things* that God gave to his people: "Thus God communicated his holiness physically with his people through the holy things. By their access to

---

[31] Leviticus 3:1-4.

the holy things the people shared in God's holiness."³² The peace offering feast—though connected with joy and celebration—was still not a picnic, for through it God's people indeed shared in God's holiness. Kleinig explains how important this was for the laity:

> The main kind of holy food was the meat from the peace offering (Lev 19:8). It was the most important item of holy food that was available to the lay Israelites, their way of sharing in God's holiness. Their sacred banquets therefore revolved around the eating of that holy meat. Through it they enjoyed holy communion with God.³³

Indeed, through the holy things eaten by God's OT people they participated in holy communion with God. It must be noted that this was not a holy communion equivalent to the Holy Communion of the body and blood of Christ; nonetheless it was an OT version of holy communion, a communing of holy things.

As this *holy thing* terminology referred to both priestly and lay eating of the peace offering sacrifice, it presented an historical connection between the peace offering and the Lord's Supper. Ancient Christian liturgies employed the expression "holy things" as a liturgical designation for the sacred food of the Eucharist.³⁴ These technical words are central in the common liturgical phrase, "Holy things for Holy persons." This phrase is found in certain ancient Communion liturgies apparently from the very inception of Christianity! J. M. Neale has even concluded, "These words are no doubt of Apostolic origin and are quoted over and over again by the

---

³² Kleinig, *Leviticus*, 11.
³³ Kleinig, *Letivicus*, 11.
³⁴ Herman Sasse, *This is My Body* (Augsburg Publishing House, 1959; revised edition, Adelaide: Lutheran Publishing House, 1977), 320ff. Sasse shows the antiquity of the terminology and how it applies to the creedal phrase, "Communion of *saints (holy things)*."

Eastern Fathers."[35] As *holy things for holy persons* would be spoken (or chanted) in the Divine Service, the priest would then lift up the host, the "embreaded" body of Christ.[36] Is this elevation of the host also reminiscent of the heaving or waving of the peace offering before it is presented to the priests?

The peace offering connection to Eastern liturgies is enhanced as one finds repeated references to peace, and even some liturgical expressions specifically identifying the presence of the peace offering.[37] One reference to the peace offering is in a Deacon's response to the Bishop: "*Deacon*: Let us stand with piety; let us stand with the fear of God and compunction of heart; let us attend to the holy Anaphora, to offer peace [i.e. a peace-offering] to God."[38] We believe Neale and Littledale are correct with *their* bracketed comment in this translation, that the *peace offering* is being referenced in this liturgical text. The holy *Anaphora*—an unusual word contained in the preceding text—was also a Jewish technical term used as a verb for the lifting up of sacrifices, at times specifying the peace offerings (Lev. 17:5).[39] The people responded to the Deacon in the above liturgical phrase with the following: "The mercy of peace, the *sacrifice of praise*."[40] As will be discussed shortly, *sacrifice of praise* was also a technical term for the peace offering. Thus one encounters peace offering references in certain ancient Eastern liturgies, and from such evidence one observes that the early Eastern

---

[35] J. M. Neale and R. F. Littledale, translators, *The Liturgies of SS. Mark, James, Clement, Chrysostom, and Basil, and of the Church of Malabar* (London: Griffith Farran & Co., 2nd ed. 1869, nd for 7th ed.), 119: In Chrysostom's Liturgy the phrase occurs just as the Supper is to be distributed: *"And the Priest, elevating the holy Bread, exclaims,* 'Holy things for holy persons.'" 27: This phrase is "the famous exclamation which makes a part of all Eastern Liturgies, and is accompanied with the Elevation of the Host." (footnoted)
[36] Ibid.
[37] The Eastern Church also uses leavened bread, a bread associated with the thank offering.
[38] Neale and Littledale, *The Liturgies*..., 47.
[39] See Walter Bauer, William F. Arndt, Wilbur Gingrich, *A Greek-English Lexicon of the New Testament and other Christian Literature* (Chicago: University of Chicago Press, 1979, 2nd ed.), 63, where *anaphora* is called "a t. t. of the sacrificial system." *Anaphora* as a noun is rarely used in the LXX, found in Psalm 51:19 (50:19, LXX) likely of the peace offering.
[40] Neale and Littledale, translators, *The Liturgies*, 47.

Church clearly connected the Lord's Supper to the OT peace offering.

Fortifying this belief, certain other liturgical acts demonstrate that the liturgical form of the Eastern Church was, to an extent, shaped by OT rites. Thus, for instance, within the *Liturgy of Chrysostom* there is a time when the priestly garments are donned to parallel those of *OT priests*. Gordon Wakefield explains that in the Eastern Church the ceremonial vesting of the priests for a Communion Service "is a service of vesting which relates each priestly garment to a relevant text, *mostly from the Old Testament* and not to the items of Christ's Passion as in the medieval West."[41]

With such adoption from the OT it is no wonder that the terminology *holy things*—employed to refer to OT peace offering meals—would be adopted in the east to identify the food of the Lord's Supper.

Though peace offering terminology and OT practices influenced especially the liturgical practices of the East, the use of peace offering terminology is not absent from Western liturgies. Kleinig explains: "The traditional Western liturgy for the Lord's Supper quite explicitly confesses Jesus as our peace offering in the Pax and in the Agnus Dei."[42] In the *Pax* the pastor says, "The peace of the Lord be with you always." In the *Agnus Dei* the congregation requests of Christ, the Lamb of God, that He would grant them peace. With both of these liturgical phrases directly preceding the reception of the Lord's Supper, they are reminders to the communicants that peace with God has been established in Christ's sacrifice, and communicants are then ready to eat of Christ's peace offering sacrifice—the holy things.

---

[41] Gordon S. Wakefield, *An Outline of Christian Worship* (Edinburgh: T & T Clark, 1998), 49. Italics added.
[42] Kleinig, *Leviticus*, 96.

The Peace Offering, Portrayer of the Eucharist

God Communes with His People

> *"[The peace offering fat] is an offering by fire of a soothing aroma to the Lord. [...] Then the priest shall offer it up in smoke on the altar, as food, an offering by fire to the Lord."*
> *Leviticus 3:5,11*

Of the peace offering, as just explained, both the priests and the laity ate holy portions. Recall also that God "ate" His portion of the peace offering as well, for the fat of the peace offering burned upon God's altar was considered His food. Andrew Jukes explains: "The altar is the 'table of the Lord:' whatever was put upon it was 'the food of God.'"[43] The fatty portions of the peace offering burned upon God's altar were thus described in Scripture as "food, an offering by fire to the Lord."[44]

Since the fatty portions of a creature belonged exclusively to God, it is apparent from Scripture that Jewish families would reserve a fattened calf for an occasion of special thanksgiving—an occasion to offer a thanksgiving peace offering to the Lord. Through the prophet Amos, God explained how he was disappointed when such peace offerings were presented to Him hypocritically: "And I will not even look at the peace offerings of your fatlings."[45] The fat of such "fatlings" was indeed reserved for God, but He did not want it if it were given insincerely.

A family that possessed such a "fatling" could not simply butcher it and leave God out of the process, for God had directed that *any* livestock to be killed for a personal feast had to be sacrificed as a peace offering.[46] God was to be given credit for every blessing, and thus He was to be "invited" to

---

[43] Andrew Jukes, *The Law of Offerings...*, 49.
[44] Leviticus 3:11.
[45] Amos 5:22b. Verse 23 describes how God would also then be displeased with hypocritical songs of celebration that went with such peace offering sacrifices.
[46] Kleinig, *Leviticus*, 12f: "They were therefore bound to observe a basic level of ritual purity even in their common life apart from the sanctuary. In fact, the meals in their homes were related to their meals at the sanctuary." The liturgy, of necessity, reached beyond the temple. We will later explain this relative to the peace offering.

every OT feast of thanksgiving. Consequently, in the earliest history of the Jews when a layman wanted to create a family feast from his livestock, the fatling's blood and fat had to be officially presented and burned at God's altar, its heave and wave portions had to be given to the priests, and *then* the family could join in their feast of thanksgiving. God had directed:

> Any man who slaughters an ox, or a lamb, or a goat in the camp or who slaughters it outside the camp...[shall] bring them in to the Lord at the doorway of the tent of meeting to the priest, and sacrifice them as sacrifices of peace offerings to the Lord. And the priest shall sprinkle the blood on the altar of the Lord at the doorway of the tent of meeting, and offer up the fat in smoke as a soothing aroma to the Lord.[47]

God later modified this procedure. When He fulfilled His promise and expanded the borders of Israel, God allowed the personal slaughter of livestock: "If the place which the Lord your God chooses to put His name [the temple] is too far from you, then you may slaughter of your herd and flock..."[48] This slaughter of livestock too remote for the temple, still possessed a peace offering status.[49] Such a directive infers that if a peace offering be led to the slaughter within range of the temple, that creature was yet to be sacrificed as an official peace offering at the temple, as God had originally commanded.

In the parable of the prodigal son, Jesus explained the celebration—caused by the returning son—in terms of a celebrative peace offering. The father in the parable excitedly exclaims, "Let us bring the fattened calf, kill it, and let us eat and be merry." This is a custom-made peace offering turn of words. The word for "kill" is actually the most common Greek word used for

---

[47] Leviticus 17:3,5,6.
[48] Deuteronomy 12:21. Though here referencing the tabernacle, yet the place of God's name would later be the temple, and the same directive applied.
[49] This was probably one of the legitimate uses of the sacrificial locations called "high places."

"sacrifice."⁵⁰ The pious Jewish father in this parable had reserved the fat of this *fattened calf* for God, for the fat was to be burned upon God's altar and thus "eaten" by Him, as was the case for all peace offerings slain near the temple. And the references to *eating* and being *merry* are indeed designations of the two core activities of every peace offering. Note also that the reason for such a peace offering was the *thanksgiving* generated by the return of the prodigal.⁵¹

In this parable Jesus is referencing a *thank offering*, and, interestingly, the Jews at this time would have labeled such a sacrifice a *eucharist!*⁵² *Eucharist* was the official Greek word employed by the Jews for their thank offering, and within a century after Christ's resurrection, *Eucharist* became the most common technical term for the Lord's Supper. Shall not Christians now join at the Eucharist of the Savior, eating of *the* peace offering and being merry at every prodigal who returns to the Lord? At every Eucharist, God and man join in thankful communion.

Let us summarize. Via the peace offering process, all of God's OT people—both laity and priest—were in communion with Him *at the altar* where such sacrifices were presented. Consequently, like no other OT sacrificial rite, the peace offering communicated an all-inclusive form of communion between God and man. God "ate" the fatty portions burned on the Bronze Altar, the priests and their families ate their holy *wave* and *heave* portions, and the laity joyfully ate their holy portion as well. S. C. Gayford explains the application to the Lord's Supper:

> The spiritual order is the same as in the Old Covenant, and again,

---

⁵⁰ See Johannes Behm, "θυω, θυσια, θυσιαστηριον," vol. III, *Theological Dictionary of the New Testament*, ed. Gerhard Kittel and Gerhard Friedrich, trans. Geoffrey W. Bromiley (Grand Rapids: Wm. B. Eerdmans Publishing Co., 1968), 180ff.
⁵¹ The father in the parable represents God the Father. What peace offering did the heavenly Father offer up in acceptance of prodigal man?! Yes, Jesus is the sin offering, but He is also the peace offering through which the heavenly Father expresses celebration!
⁵² This will be explained shortly.

as of old, the response to sin and burnt offering comes in the peace offering with the call to fellowship with God, with the Priest and with one another in Christ Jesus. He it is who offers the peace-offering and bids God and man to join with Him in the Feast.[53]

Connecting Holy Communion to the Peace Offering

> "The cup of blessing which we bless, is it not the communion of the blood of Christ? The bread which we break, is it not the communion of the body of Christ?"
> I Corinthians 10:16

Some might question whether it is legitimate to connect the Lord's Supper to the peace offering. To do so is simply to follow the example of the Apostle Paul who linked the peace offering to the celebration of the Lord's Supper. Undeniably 1 Corinthians 10:16,17 are key references to Holy Communion:

> The cup of blessing which we bless, is it not the communion of the blood of Christ? The bread which we break, is it not the communion of the body of Christ? For we, being many, are one bread and one body; for we all partake of that one bread.[54]

These verses are found in a peace offering context. Immediately before these Eucharistic verses, St. Paul cites the Jewish eating of the abominable golden-calf *peace offering*. He explains that the Jews committed idolatry when "the people sat down to eat and drink" of the peace offering

---

[53] Gayford, *Sacrifice and Priesthood*, 133.
[54] NKJV.

The Peace Offering, Portrayer of the Eucharist

sacrificed to the golden-calf.[55] In the same Eucharistic context, Paul then warns the Corinthians about the danger of eating any pagan *peace offering* by admonishing them not to "become communers with demons." Then again, continuing this *peace offering* theme, the Apostle goes on to warn, "You cannot drink the cup of the Lord and the cup of demons; you cannot partake of the table of the Lord and the table of demons."[56] Such peace offering descriptions and warnings—though thus far only referencing pagan peace offerings—show that the learned Apostle considered Holy Communion to be definitely related to the sacrifice of peace offerings.

In our study of the burnt offering, we explained how I Corinthians 10:16 (quoted above) is, strange as it may seem, a description of Holy Communion couched in pagan peace offering terminology. Recall from this discussion that the Greek word used by St. Paul for *communion*—"koinonia"—is the technical word used by pagans for their communion sacrifices, sacrifices that combined burnt and peace offering concepts. Demonstrating that OT peace offerings—not just pagan ones—are typical of the Lord's Supper, St. Paul cites *Jewish* communion meals in the verse immediately following the I Corinthians 10:16,17 Eucharistic reference: "Look at the nation Israel, are not those who *eat the sacrifices* sharers [peace offering *communers*] in the altar?"[57] When the Jews ate the sacrifices, this eating was especially associated with the peace offering. With pagan *and* Jewish peace offering meals being compared to communing the body and blood of Christ, there can be no doubt that St. Paul perceived the Lord's Supper to be a peace offering meal.[58] Hicks explains St. Paul's argument in I Corinthians 10:

---

[55] 1 Corinthians 10:7. Exodus 32 specifies that this was indeed the golden calf peace offering.
[56] 1 Corinthians 10:21.
[57] 1 Corinthians 10:18. It is possible this is referring to the eating of the peace offering sacrificed to the golden calf, as referenced in verse 7. It is usually understood to refer to any and all sacred eating done by the priests, or to the eating done by the laity as they consumed the peace offering. Or it could be all of the above.
[58] As will be demonstrated in the next chapter, the grain offering fits the concept of Hebrew Communion as well.

The Christian act of communion therefore is assumed to stand to the whole Christian sacrifice in the same relation as the eating by *pagans* stands to *pagan sacrifice; and the peace-offering of Israel is given as an analogy to both* which will explain the argument to those among the Corinthians who are familiar with, and were perhaps, like St. Paul, brought up upon, the Jewish worship. Here we have the one passage—and it is therefore of supreme importance—where *the Eucharist is definitely brought by St. Paul into its place in the Christian conception of sacrifice.*[59]

One of the foremost Lutheran experts on the Sacrament of the Altar, Hermann Sasse, concluded that I Corinthians 10:18-21 is *the* section of Scripture that presents "the understanding of the Sacrament of the Altar as a sacrificial meal..."[60]

From a Jewish perspective it made sense to connect the Lord's Supper to the peace offering because, as Hicks explains, "Jewish tradition taught that the one sacrifice that should continue in the Messianic age would be the peace-offering."[61] From such a prediction, it is apparent that certain Rabbis were convinced that the burnt offering, sin offering, guilt offering and grain offering would cease. But the peace offering—the one sacrifice uniquely associated with a praise-oriented meal—would continue into the era of the Christ. Of course Christians now know that the peace offering meal *will* continue to the end, in the celebration of the Holy Eucharist.

---

[59] Hicks, *The Fullness...*, 235. Italics added.
[60] Sasse, *This is My Body*, 16.
[61] Hicks, *The Fullness...*, 237. See also Kleinig, *Leviticus*, 173.

Other Peace Offering Connections

> "....having made peace through the blood of His cross;...He has now reconciled you in His fleshly body through death...."
> Colossians 1:20,22

When NT texts divide Christ into *body and blood*—or describe His work by referencing only His *blood*—the purpose of these descriptions is to present Him as a sacrifice.[62] Robert Daly explains that such NT references to body and blood "presupposed the slaughtering which separates the sacrificial elements of flesh and blood."[63] Those texts that draw attention simply to the blood of Christ, and not to His flesh or body, are also magnifying Christ as sacrifice.[64] When hearing or reading such NT descriptions, the early church would have in this way been reminded immediately of the cross, the place of sacrifice, the place of salvation. Additionally, since the Eucharist was from the very beginning central to worship, one can be certain that such references to Christ's sacrifice would have triggered Eucharistic thinking among early Christians as well.

As an example, consider Colossians 1:20-22 where St. Paul, though referencing neither any OT sacrifice nor the Eucharist, nevertheless clearly presents the sacrifice of Christ:

> [God was working] through Him [Jesus] to reconcile all things to Himself, having made peace through the *blood* of His cross; through

---

[62] At times Christ is described as "flesh and blood" to designate His humanity (e.g. Heb. 2:14); yet even this may be obliquely referencing His sacrifice.. What we are referencing are those passages that purposely divide Christ into flesh (body) and blood, or simply discuss His work of salvation by only referencing His blood.

[63] Daly, *Christian Sacrifice*, 223.

[64] E.g. texts dividing Christ into body and blood: John 6:53-56; Ephesians 2:13-15; Colossians 1:20-22; Hebrews 9:16ff (blood); 10:1-12 (body); Hebrews 10:19,20; Hebrews 13:11,12. In several texts the sacrificial blood is only mentioned, but the flesh of Christ is implicit, usually implied by His resurrection (e.g. 1 Peter 1:2,3; Revelation 1:5; Hebrews 13:20).

Him, I say, whether things on earth or things in heaven. And although you were formerly alienated and hostile in mind, engaged in evil deeds, yet He has now reconciled you in His *fleshly body* through death, in order to present you before Him holy and blameless and beyond reproach. [italics added]

Paul here describes both the *blood* and the *fleshly body* of Christ as the peace-makers with God. They are the peacemakers, because as the ultimate sin offering they bring forgiveness and reconciliation with the heavenly Father. However *blood* and *body* are general sacrificial terms, and all of the various OT offerings blend together in such a quote. This blending of the various sacrifices would have been natural for Jews, for when two or three types of OT sacrifice "were offered together, as was frequently the case," Kurtz explains, "there was a...crowding together of the individual features."[65] At Christ's cross all the different Jewish sacrificial features *crowded together* like never before, and like they never will again! Christ-crucified is the peace-making sin/guilt offering. But then He is also the offering of sanctification (burnt offering), and He is the celebrative peace offering. Relative to the peace offering, those who realize the completeness of His blood-bought peace may eat of Him as they join with thankful hearts in the peace offering meal. Jesus is not re-sacrificed to separately fulfill each of the OT sacrifices, nor is He re-sacrificed at every celebration of the Lord's Supper, but He has established the Lord's Supper to be the ongoing sacrifice-related meal—a meal related to every kind of OT sacrifice. When His people eat and drink of His body and blood, they eat of *the* peace offering—that which is eaten *because* they are at peace with God.

When the NT Scriptures speak of Christ as sacrifice—at times accomplishing this by "dividing" Christ into body and blood and at other times

---

[65] Kurtz, *Offerings*...., 181.

simply by referencing His blood—such language should arouse the minds of today's Christians to consider not merely Christ's sacrifice in general, but to consider each aspect of His sacrifice. All the sacrificial descriptions of Christ in the NT should generate reminders of the many OT sacrificial activities, *including the peace offering meal*. Consequently every sacrificial reference to Christ in the NT should bring to mind the Lord's Supper. This meal is the Christian's unique means enabling participation in the sacrifice of Christ. In the OT, the meal was an integral part of the sacrificial process, and a peace offering sacrifice was not finished until the meal was eaten. So too now, the sacrifice of Christ is not "complete" without the meal being eaten by His thankful people, and they will eat it until the end of time. A holy meal is now the only remaining sacrifice-related activity whereby God's people today can directly, physically participate in the once-sacrificed Christ.[66]

Public and Private Peace Offerings

> "And Solomon offered for the sacrifice of peace offerings, which he offered to the Lord, 22,000 oxen and 120,000 sheep."
> I Kings 8:63

Thus far only *private* peace offerings have been considered; these are primarily the thank offering, the votive offering and the free will offering. Consider now the fact that—similar to the sin and burnt offerings—there were both private *and public* peace offerings. *Public* peace offerings were offered on behalf of the nation, but *private* peace offerings were offered for individuals (or families).

Peace offerings—sometimes called *communion sacrifices*—were

---

[66] One could perhaps argue that Baptism is also a direct participation in Christ's sacrifice, prefigured by the many sacred washings surrounding OT sacrifice.

extremely common in OT worship. Concerning their presence in the OT historical books, Roland De Vaux makes the following calculation as he counts only the *public* peace offering references.

> In ancient times the communion sacrifice was the most frequent, and it is mentioned forty-seven times in the historical books, from Joshua to Kings. It is offered on the great feasts, on the occasion of a pilgrimage to the sanctuary (I Sam. i.21, ii19), and as a sacrifice of the clan (I Sam. xx.6, 29, &c).[67]

Though *forty-seven* is a considerable amount of references to communion sacrifices, yet De Vaux here considers only the *public* peace offerings, those offered at official national feasts and pilgrimages. Also observe that his calculation is computed solely from the historical books of the Bible. De Vaux does not take into account the plentiful *private* peace offering references, nor does he take into account the many references to peace offerings beyond the historical books. The very common *private* peace offerings—consisting primarily of thank offerings, votive offerings and free-will offerings—are not even counted by De Vaux. There are, however, abundant references to these *private* peace offerings throughout the Scriptures, and thus the number of references and allusions to peace offerings scattered throughout the OT far exceeds the forty-seven calculated by De Vaux. As the reader now encounters peace offerings in the OT, whether *public* or *private* ones, it should be understood that the people, in conclusion to these sacrifices, joyfully ate and drank in their worship of God.

Thus, for instance, when Solomon dedicated the temple, there was a voluminous presentation of *public* peace offerings. Solomon's sacrifice of peace offerings indicated there was a gigantic *public feast* and celebration in

---

[67] Roland De Vaux, *Studies in Old Testament Sacrifice* (Wales: Cardiff University of Wales Press, 1964), 34-35.

God's presence:

> Now the king and all Israel with him offered sacrifice before the Lord. And Solomon offered for the sacrifice of peace offerings, which he offered to the Lord, 22,000 oxen and 120,000 sheep. So the king and all the sons of Israel dedicated the house of the Lord.[68]

Even though this text does not explain that there was a feast, yet there had to have been a tremendous public feast, because Solomon sacrificed *peace offerings*, and eating was the *main activity* associated with the peace offering. It is hard to imagine 22,000 oxen and 120,000 sheep. What a colossal communion meal enjoyed by the people as they ate the peace offerings sacrificed at the temple's dedication! One also observes in this account the exceptional procedure of a *public* peace offering: Someone else—in this case Solomon—could present a peace offering *for* the people. The laity did not bring the sacrifices on that lofty day of celebration, but they could and did eat of them.[69] Christ presented the greatest peace offering on the cross, offering Himself as *the* public peace offering; the people brought nothing. Now everyone in His kingdom may celebrate at a feast that is even more abundant than Solomon's—for an even greater Temple has been raised up, and One greater than Solomon has arrived.[70]

As explained in the chapter dealing with the burnt offering, there were two "categories" of sacrifice: *holocaust* and *communion*. God's OT people perceived their peace offerings to be the primary representative of the *communion* sacrifice. In the peace offerings, whether public or private, they communed with God by eating.

An important example of this OT "communion" was when Moses—

---

[68] 1 Kings 8:62,63.
[69] Though the laity did not bring the thousands of sacrificial animals for peace offerings, yet no doubt Solomon had received these creatures from them, probably as tax payments.
[70] John 2:19-22; Luke 11:31.

actually at the very inception of the Jewish sacrificial system—built an altar and "sent young men of the sons of Israel, and they offered burnt offerings and sacrificed young bulls as *peace offerings* to the Lord." (Ex. 24:5) The intervening verses are important and will be related shortly to the Lord's Supper, but verse 11 continues: "...and they beheld God, and they *ate and drank*." What were they eating? The public peace offering! They were communing with God!

What were they *drinking*? Were they drinking blood? No, this was prohibited, as already explained. They very likely drank wine, as will be explained in our next chapter.

Sacrificial Meals and John 6

> "He who eats my flesh and drinks my blood has eternal life; and I will raise him on the last day. For my flesh is true food, and my blood is true drink."
> John 6:54,55

From the evidence presented thus far, there is no doubt that the practice of sacrifice-related eating was universally realized by Jews in Jesus' day. Even pagans clearly grasped sacrifice-related eating as well. When and where Christ walked the earth, it was nearly universally understood that sacrifice-related eating was *a* (if not *the*) most important act of worship. Because of this sharpened awareness of sacrifice-related eating, when Jesus instituted the Lord's Supper the disciples must have immediately considered Christ's invitation to eat and drink His body and blood to be a clear *worship directive* connected to sacrifice-related eating. Darwell Stone explains what was obvious to a first century Jew:

> His words [of Institution] were of such a kind as to suggest a

connection between the rite which He was instituting and the sacrificial feasts in which the worshippers partook of the sacrifice and thereby received the blessing associated with it.[71]

Eating of sacrifices was understood by the Apostles as central to worship, and present day Christians must cultivate this apostolic mindset, thus obtaining an enhanced perception of the Supper—a perception of Christian worship.

In relation to sacrificial eating, there is a text in the NT that has generated much debate as to whether it is a reference to the Lord's Supper. We believe the answer is yes *and* no. The text is John 6, especially verses 53-56:

> Jesus therefore said to them, 'Truly, truly, I say to you, unless you eat the flesh of the Son of Man, and drink His blood, you have no life in yourselves. He who eats My flesh and drinks My blood has eternal life; and I will raise him on the last day. For My flesh is true food, and My blood is true drink. He who eats My flesh and drinks My blood abides in me, and I in him.'

When Jesus here repeatedly spoke of eating His flesh and drinking His blood, He was speaking of Himself as a sacrifice—separating flesh and blood. He was, however, not referencing the Lord's Supper, for it would be yet another year before He would speak the words instituting His Holy Meal. Nonetheless the Lord's Supper makes possible the sacrifice-related eating described by Christ in this sixth chapter of John. From the common understanding of sacrificial eating in Jesus' day, almost certainly those who heard these words of Jesus immediately realized that He was speaking of

---

[71] Darwell Stone, *A History of the Doctrine of the Holy Eucharist*, (London: Rivingtons, nd), 8. Sasse, *This is My Body*, 16: "[One should understand] the Sacrament of the Altar as a sacrificial meal in which we receive that which has been sacrificed at Calvary once for all."

sacrificial feasting upon his flesh and blood.[72] Moreover these words of Jesus recorded in John 6 would have purposely prepared the Apostles to hear His Words of Institution which created the Lord's Supper exactly one year later. Hicks believes that without these words in John 6, "it is difficult otherwise to account for the apparent ease with which the disciples a year afterwards could receive His words about His Blood at the Last Supper."[73] We agree with John Stephenson who maintains that "in John 6:51-58, our Lord spoke prophetically of His upcoming institution of the Holy Supper..."[74] The Apostles must have recalled these words of Jesus when almost exactly one year later He instituted the Supper in which He invited them to truly eat His body and drink His blood.

Both the account in John 6 and the institution of the Lord's Supper took place at the yearly Passover celebration, a time of concentrated sacrificial feasting. In the Eucharist, Christ's flesh was to be realized as true food and His blood as true drink, even as He had thus mysteriously declared one year earlier—as recorded for us in John 6.

A person seeking Christian truth might ask how it is possible that Christ could, in Holy Communion, sacrificially feed the millions of Christians throughout the centuries with His "finite" body and blood. Anticipating this question, Jesus, as recorded in John 6, fed the 5,000 men with five loaves and two fish—with more left after the meal than when the meal began. Including women and children, the number that Jesus fed likely exceeded 15,000! It is apparently not a coincidence that on the heels of this occasion Jesus chose to refer to eating His body and drinking His blood. Christ truly and miraculously fed around 15,000 people with merely a handful of bread and fish. If Christ can feed 15,000 with the truly finite elements of fish and bread, can He not feed millions with His body in which the fullness of deity

---

[72] It was precisely this understanding of literally eating Christ's flesh and drinking His blood that caused such offense and perhaps disgust. John 6:60.
[73] Hicks, *The Fullness*..., 244.
[74] John R. Stephenson, *The Lord's Supper* (St. Louis: The Luther Academy, 2003), 40.

dwells?[75] In the Lord's Supper Christ is not consumed or used up; the body and blood of Christ will not run out, something taught by the continually-flowing bread in this miraculous feeding of the 15,000.

The wording in the Gospels indicates that the Apostles ultimately understood this miraculous feeding event to be instructive concerning the Lord's Supper. Hicks observes, "The feeding of the multitude was a sign of something beyond itself."[76] The feeding of the 15,000 was an event that really transpired, yet through it Christ taught lessons beyond the actual event itself.[77] Concerning the bread that Jesus multiplied, Matthew, Mark and Luke infer the Eucharist by using the familiar sacramental terminology, *breaking bread*. Matthew writes, "He blessed the food, and *breaking the loaves* He gave them to the disciples and the disciples gave to the multitudes."[78] The *breaking of bread* (loaves) had, in Christian history, *immediately* become a technical referent for the Lord's Supper. "Is not the bread which we break," writes St. Paul, "a sharing in the body of Christ?"[79] Because the Gospels were written and distributed after Holy Communion had already been faithfully observed for decades, such wording in the Gospels would purposely have reminded listeners of the *Breaking of Bread* they had been celebrating.[80] Observe also in the feeding of the 15,000 that Jesus gave *to the disciples*

---

[75] Colossians 2:9.
[76] Hicks, *The Fullness...*, 244.
[77] We believe there are numerous "living parables" in the NT. In Matthew 16:9,10, Jesus identifies the feeding of the 4,000 and the 5,000 as events that were instructive, for example, in the number of baskets taken up. We believe many other of Jesus' acts were instructive beyond the actual externals (e.g. changing water to wine; healing the man born blind; washing the disciples' feet; revealing Himself to the Emmaus disciples), and there are hints or outright statements reflecting this in the texts.
[78] Matthew 14:19. See also Luke 9:16 and Mark 6:41.
[79] 1 Corinthians 10:16b; see also e.g. Acts 2:48.
[80] Many have also suggested that the Gospels were shaped by the Communion liturgy already in place. Certainly the accounts themselves are accurate historical records, but the wording divinely chosen to convey those accounts appears to purposely convey sacramental emphases.

(Apostles), and they then gave to the multitudes.[81] This would be the chain of distribution for the Lord's Supper: Jesus, to the Apostles, to the Church.

In John's Gospel, instead of stating that Jesus *broke the bread*, John simply records that Jesus "gave thanks."[82] This verb is the Greek word *eucharist*, a word which had been used by Luke and Paul to record Christ's Words of Institution.[83] As a noun, *eucharist* would within the first century of Christianity become *the* technical term for the Lord's Supper. Though *breaking bread* and *giving thanks* were common practices before every Jewish meal, yet early Christians came to associate this terminology especially with the holiest of meals, the Lord's Supper. It becomes even more plausible that Jesus is teaching something about the Lord's Supper in the feeding of the 15,000, when in the discussion immediately following this miraculous feeding Jesus declared that His flesh is true food and His blood is true drink. Thus there is a contextual link between the feeding of the 15,000 and the feasting upon Christ's flesh and blood. The *General Sacramental Eating* in the feeding of the 15,000 helps Christ's followers understand the *Specific Sacramental Eating* of the Lord's Supper.

The bread, as set forth in the feeding of the 15,000, is an obvious ingredient of the Sacrament. It takes little effort to recognize the sacramental hints conveyed in this account simply by considering the broken *bread*. However the fish in the account also conveyed a sacramental flavor to early Christians as well, for the fish was not only an early symbol for Christianity but *specifically* for the Lord's Supper. Oscar Cullmann explains, "Early Christian art frequently represents the Lord's Supper under the form of a meal of fish."[84]

---

[81] *The Book of Concord*, ed. & trans. T. Tappert (Philadelphia: Fortress Press, 1959), 237: "They [Rome] quote passages that mention bread, like Luke 24:35, which says that the disciples recognized Christ in the breaking of the bread. They quote other passages that talk about the breaking of the bread. We do not seriously object if someone takes these passages as referring to the Sacrament."
[82] John 6:11. Reemphasized in 6:23.
[83] Luke 22:19; 1 Corinthians 11:23ff.
[84] Oscar Cullmann and F. J. Leenhardt, *Essays on the Lord's Supper*, (London: Lutterworth Press, 1958), First Essay: "The Breaking of Bread and the Resurrection Appearances," 10.

From such evidence, certain people in the early church must have perceived sacramental instruction from the times Christ participated in *General Sacramental Eating* involving fish.[85]

Christ explained in John 6 that by eating His flesh and drinking His blood, a person possesses eternal life! His audience would have connected this dining invitation to the sacrifice-related meals performed in temple worship. Christ's crucifixion became the antitype of every OT sacrifice; but where is the meal?

Some have misunderstood John 6:51ff by maintaining that it only refers to the *spiritual eating* Christ's body and blood.[86] *Spiritual eating* is simply faith in Christ; to believe in Christ is to spiritually eat of his flesh and blood. Certainly *spiritual eating* is critical, for people cannot rightly eat of Christ in the Lord's Supper unless they first *spiritually eat* of Him. Christ first and foremost desires His people to participate in such *spiritual eating*, consuming His body and blood spiritually—by believing in Him. However He also desires that they eat and drink His body and blood sacramentally—by *physically* participating in His sacrifice through *bodily eating* the Sacrament of the Altar. This is called *sacramental eating*. By speaking of His body and blood as *true food* and *true drink*, Christ is obviously going beyond spiritual eating. Spiritual eating does not involve *true food*, but Jesus says, "My flesh is *true food* and my blood is *true drink*." (John 6:55). By describing His flesh and blood as real food and drink, Jesus is not referring to *spiritual eating*, but He is speaking of *sacramental eating*.

In the Christian faith the human body is of the utmost importance; it will rise from the grave. Sacramental eating thus makes sense. Even as OT believers physically participated in sacrifice-related eating, so now NT believers physically participate in sacrifice-related eating. Christ's people bodily participate in His sacrifice as they eat of Him with their mouths. Jesus

---

[85] See especially John 21:9-13, where bread and fish are linked in a special meal with Christ.
[86] The distinction between spiritual eating and sacramental eating is discussed in the "Formula of Concord." *The Book of Concord*, Tappert, 579.

promised that by eating and drinking His flesh and blood—first *spiritually* and then when eligible *physically* communing His sacrifice—His people indeed have eternal life, which includes the resurrection of the body![87]

Eating the Peace Offering with Joy!

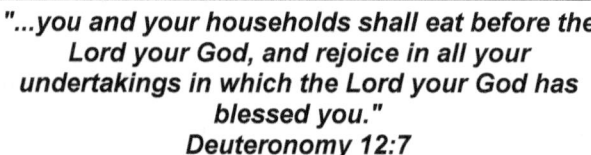

"...you and your households shall eat before the Lord your God, and rejoice in all your undertakings in which the Lord your God has blessed you."
Deuteronomy 12:7

To one degree or another, rejoicing and celebration were associated with every peace offering.[88] A peace offering was eaten with "gladness", as set forth in I Chronicles 29:22: "So they ate and drank that day before the Lord with great gladness." This joyful eating is again described in Deuteronomy 12:5,7, wherein the joyful eating of the peace offering is connected to the *place* God had chosen, the tabernacle [Italics added]:

> But you shall seek the Lord at the place which the Lord your God shall choose from all your tribes to establish His name there for His dwelling, and there you shall come...There also you and your households *shall eat* before the Lord your God, and *rejoice in all your undertakings* in which the Lord your God has blessed you.

---

[87] This resurrection theme is woven into Jesus discussion in John 6, verses 39, 40, 54.
[88] We believe the Psalms that speak of "dance" might be referencing an informal peace offering celebration. (e.g. Psalm 150:4). Such celebration can be compared to today's wedding receptions: The wedding itself is the worship service, but an informal celebration—with dancing and with a band—continues at the reception. A parallel practice surrounded the peace offering. It too first consisted of temple-related worship, but then it often culminated in a vivacious celebration, praising God in an informal gathering associated more with home than with the temple. Another comparison would be the family that attends worship on Easter, then goes home to celebrate with a multi-course meal, and then an Easter egg hunt for the children. It is all part of the celebration, but not all of the celebration is directly related to worship.

Verse 18 continues in the same vein:

> But *you shall eat* them before the Lord your God in the place which the Lord your God will choose, you and your son and daughter, and your male and female servants, and the Levite who is within your gates; and you shall *rejoice* before the Lord your God in all your undertakings.

NT believers should learn from this godly, rejoicing spirit connected to OT sacrificial participation. As God's OT people ate the peace offering with a *rejoicing spirit,* so also NT believers, for even greater reasons, should rejoice in the celebration of the Lord's Supper. Unfortunately today's culture has difficulty differentiating fun and joy. There is nothing wrong with clean fun and entertainment, but the Lord's Supper was never intended to be fun or entertaining. The food of the Lord's Supper is admittedly not very tasty compared to the delectable feasts that a chef could prepare; in fact many people rightly consider the bread and wine of the Lord's Supper to be quite bland. But the Lord Supper's joy comes neither from its flavor nor from its fun, but from receiving the results of Christ's cross and empty tomb. *This* joy can exist even in the midst of turmoil, misery and pain. With such joy, a Christian can rejoice always, especially in relation to the meal that brings the ingredients of such joy to the fore.

As they consider the meals drawn from the *sin and guilt offerings*, God's people—as NT priests—all approach to eat the Lord's Supper with solemnity. Nonetheless, as they consider the meal drawn from the *peace offering*, shall not Christians also partake of the Supper with rejoicing and thanksgiving—having consumed the wine of forgiveness that makes glad the hearts of men? Christians have peace with God, and it is finished; they will naturally *rejoice in* the peace offering banquet of His body and blood!

The Special Passover Peace Offering

> "They led Jesus therefore from Caiaphas into the Praetorium; and it was early; and they themselves did not enter into the Praetorium in order that they might not be defiled, but might eat the Passover."
> John 18:28

With the anticipation of celebrative feasting, God's OT people anxiously awaited the peace offerings, especially those peace offerings which were required finales for certain Jewish festivals. One such finale always occurred at Passover. Recall that at the time of Christ—as commanded by God—the actual sacrifice of the Passover lambs was done in the temple, with the slaying of the lambs being a very solemn act of worship. On that evening, the 14th of Nissan, the meal of the Passover lamb was eaten with one's family, limiting the number in attendance to between ten and twenty people. On the next day, the 15th of Nissan, the sacrifices culminated in a unique offering called the "chagigah." ('khagigah")[89] The chagigah was none other than a climactic *peace offering* that God's people were to eat while expressing joy and celebration! When Judas left the Last Supper, his fellow Apostles thought he was on his way to give something to the poor.[90] Edersheim maintains that the Apostles thought Judas was "applying some of the common stock of money in helping to provide 'peace-offering' for the poor."[91] This *chagigah* peace offering was deemed so wonderful and important that

---

[89] Edersheim, *The Temple*..., 170-171. Such Chagigah were also sacrificed on the actual Passover, especially if the group joining in the Passover celebration needed more than one lamb to eat. When Psalm 118:27 refers to binding the sacrifice to the altar, this may be a unique reference to this special peace offering. If this is so, it could be an intriguing prediction of Christ as sacrifice.
[90] John 13:29.
[91] Edersheim, *The Temple*..., 195.

it—like the Passover lamb eaten the day before—was also referred to as "eating the Passover"![92]

If a Jew entered a pagan building, it would render him unclean and thus unfit to eat of a communion sacrifice. When Jesus was being led on the 15th of Nissan into the gentile judgment hall called the Praetorium, the Jewish leaders would not enter the hall because they did not want to become ceremonially defiled and then have to miss eating the celebrative peace offering—the *chagigah*. This is recorded in John 18:28: "They led Jesus therefore from Caiaphas into the Praetorium; and it was early; and they themselves did not enter into the Praetorium in order that they might not be defiled, but might eat the Passover." This reference has confused some. If the Passover had already been eaten, then how could the Jewish leaders be concerned about missing the Passover feast? In this text, however, to *eat the Passover* almost surely does not refer to the family-related Passover lamb, but to the *chagigah*—the climactic peace offering meal eaten the day after the regular Passover meal.

As the Jewish people joyfully ate their *chagigah* at the end of that Holy Week, Christ was being crucified. The followers of Christ surely could not bring themselves on this sad occasion to celebrate the *chagigah*—but then came Easter! Now Christ our Passover has been sacrificed for us, *now* let us celebrate the feast, *now* let us eat the Passover peace offering!

Eating of a sacrifice was a vivid, commonly perceived reality in the minds of the Apostles of Christ, and thus even before He gave them the Lord's Supper they were quite familiar with the activities surrounding peace offerings. To worship by *eating* of Christ's sacrifice made perfect sense, if only there were a way to do it. Christ supplied the way to miraculously eat of His sacrifice when He instituted The Eucharist. M. F. Sadler explains: "If, then, the offering of Christ be a true Sacrifice, there must be means ordained

---

[92] Edersheim, *The Temple...* 200. Making the same point is Alfred Cave, *The Scriptural Doctrine of Sacrifice and Atonement*, (Edinburgh: T & T Clark, 1890), 465.

whereby it is to be partaken of; and so there are. Christians have by Christ's own ordinance a means by which they may perpetually partake of Him..."[93]

The Thank Offering: "Eucharist"

> "Now as for the flesh of the sacrifice of his thanksgiving peace offerings, it shall be eaten on the day of his offering."
> Leviticus 7:15

Of the three types of peace offerings, the *thank offering* (or *thanksgiving offering*) is by reference the most common type of peace offering, and it is at times used as a synonym for *peace offering*.

A popular Greek term for the thank offering was *eucharist*. At the time of Christ *eucharist* was a common technical term for the Jewish thank offering. To speak of *eucharist* was to speak of the thank offering, its meal, and the giving of thanks surrounding such sacrifice. Philo (30 BC to 50 AD) and Josephus (37 AD to 100 AD), two Jewish historians from the time of Christ, indeed employed *eucharist* to refer to the Jewish thank offering.[94] Shortly after the time of Christ, a Jew named Aquila translated the Hebrew OT into Greek (This is not the Septuagint).[95] Where the "thank offering" was introduced in Leviticus 7:12, Aquila employed *eucharist* to translate the Hebrew word for "thank offering." Aquila did this consistently for other OT

---

[93] M. F. Sadler, *The First and Second Epistles to the Corinthians* (London: George Bell and Sons, 1898), 79-80. "So the Lord's table in our churches is.....an altar...[...] Christ our Passover has been slain,...and there at our altars we keep the feast." (160).

[94] Hans Conzelmann, "ευχαριστεω," vol. IX, *Theological Dictionary of the New Testament*, ed. Gerhard Kittel and Gerhard Friedrich, trans. Geoffrey W. Bromiley (Grand Rapids: Wm. B. Eerdmans Publishing Co., 1968), 415: Josephus, speaking of the Jewish "thank offering," writes it in the Greek as *Eucharist*. Philo uses the word *Eucharist* so frequently (often using it to refer to the sincere thanksgiving of the heart which was to accompany the thank offering) that Conzelmann concludes: "In the 2nd and 3rd century and under Philo's influence theologians came to use "eucharist" almost exclusively for the sacrifice of "eucharist.""

[95] E.g. Hicks, *The Fullness...*, 20: "In fact, in Philo and in Aquila the word "eucharist" is frequently used to describe it [thank offering with praise/thanksgiving]."

thank offering references as well.[96]

There is ample evidence that Jews in the first and second centuries used *eucharist* as a technical term for their *thank offering*. After the temple was destroyed in 70AD, the Jews could no longer sacrifice or eat their *eucharist* (thank offering). When the dust had settled after the temple's destruction, there sat a perfectly good technical term—*eucharist*—but it was homeless. Christianity quite naturally adopted *Eucharist* as a name for the Lord's Supper. One can readily imagine the unintended jealousy created as Christians claimed to be eating a *thank offering* (Eucharist), while non-Christian Jews were—because of the temple's destruction—unable to do so.

Eucharist was precisely *the* word most commonly used for the Lord's Supper in the first century after Christ. When Christ inaugurated the Lord's Supper, all the texts record that He "gave thanks," and the Greek word for this is eucharist. Jesus was here using a *verb* possessing the same root as the *noun* employed to translate the thank offering. Such giving of thanks was appropriate for any meal. However, as just pointed out, the noun *eucharist* was *commonly* used as a technical term for the Jewish *thank offering*. So when the early Christian Church adopted *Eucharist* as a technical term for the Lord's Supper, it makes the most sense that this happened because of the *noun* usage (thank offering) rather than from the *verb* usage (give thanks). Naming the Lord's Supper *Eucharist* is noun usage, not verb. Thus referring to the Lord's Supper as *Eucharist* probably resulted more from the Jewish *thank offering* than from Jesus' *giving of thanks* at the Last Supper. Hicks explains this adoption of the Jewish terminology:

> A [Jewish] communion-feast is a Eucharist. The *thing* is in the New Testament: the *name*, not expressly applied to the [Christian] communion feast, is there; and the earliest literature (Clement,

---

[96] E.g. Psalm 50:14; 69:31; 107:22; 146:7; Amos 4:5. Aquila was quite mechanical in his translation, thus consistently using a certain Greek word for a certain Hebrew word.

Ignatius, etc.)... does no more than make the inevitable connection [of making *Eucharist* refer to the Lord's Supper]. [97]

Eucharist may not be so common today as a technical term for the Lord's Supper, yet in second century Christian writings it had become the standard word for the Lord's Supper. As an example of this consider Ignatius who, shortly after the Apostles, repeatedly referred to the Lord's Supper as *Eucharist*. Ignatius was a child when Christ died and rose again, and Ignatius personally knew the Apostle John and perhaps other Apostles as well! Moreover Ignatius was in his prime when the Jewish temple was leveled in 70AD, and thus it is almost certain that he was aware of the technical Jewish usage of *eucharist* for thank offering. Ignatius, as an imprisoned elderly pastor, referenced the Eucharist in several letters near the time of his martyrdom around the year 107AD. Parenthetic comments are in his text; we have added bracketed comments:

> Be ye careful therefore to observe one Eucharist (for there is one flesh of our Lord Jesus Christ and one cup unto union in His blood; there is one altar...)[from the letter to the Philadelphians]. They abstain from Eucharist (thanksgiving) and prayer, because they allow not that the Eucharist is the flesh of our Savior Jesus Christ, which flesh suffered for our sins, and which the Father of His goodness raised up... Let that be held a valid Eucharist which is under the bishop or one to whom he shall have committed it...[from

---

[97] Hicks, *The Fullness*...,272: "The Jewish tradition, which they [Christians] inherited, knew the sacrificial meal as the sacrifice of praise or of thanksgiving. It is at this point that the New Testament breaks off, and the post-New Testament literature begins. The link between the two is the word ευχαριστια, Eucharist." The above quote continues this; emphasis Hicks.

the letter to the Smyrnaeans].[98]

Hicks explains, "In the second century, from Ignatius onwards, 'Eucharist' becomes the characteristic name for what the New Testament calls 'the breaking of the bread'."[99] Why had Ignatius and others in the early church adopted the term *Eucharist* for the Lord's Supper? Most likely Ignatius and others, living at the time when many Christians were familiar with the sacrifice *and the eating* of thank offerings in the temple, realized that no longer shall Christians eat of *animal* flesh in a thank offering ("eucharist"). Now they may miraculously *eat of Christ's* flesh as they partake of the Lord's Supper—the Eucharist. With this understanding of the word *Eucharist*, the Lord's Supper was perceived to be the participation in a *thanksgiving peace offering.*

Since Ignatius emphasized that Christianity is the proper continuation of Judaism, it seems quite likely that he and others appropriately culled "eucharist" from the Jewish worship vocabulary. In his letter to the Magnesians, Ignatius shows his concern about Jewish traditions and rites: "It is monstrous to talk of Jesus Christ and to practise Judaism. For Christianity did not believe in Judaism, but Judaism in Christianity."[100] Indeed the Jewish practice was *designed* to embrace the Christian, and undeniably the many early Christians who were Jews would rightly appropriate OT terminology when it applied to Christ.[101] On mankind's behalf Christ's death is truly *the* thank offering from which His people are now invited to eat—with thanksgiving—in the sacrament He established. Christians miraculously, yet truly, *eat the Eucharist*—the flesh of the thank offering. It is obvious that

---

[98] J.B. Lightfoot, editor & translator, *The Apostolic Fathers Clement, Ignatius, and Polycarp*, vol. 2 (Grand Rapids: Baker Book House, 1981), 564, 569.
[99] Hicks, *The Fullness...*, 272.
[100] Lightfoot, *The Apostolic Fathers...*, 553.
[101] Brooke Westcott, *The Epistle to the Hebrews* (Grand Rapids: Eerdmanns Publishing Co., 1973), 458: "The writings of Cyprian mark a new stage in the development of ecclesiastical thought and language. In them the phraseology of the Levitical Law is transferred to Christian institutions." (Cyprian, born c. 200).

Christ's death and His institution of the Lord's Supper are the appropriate fulfillment and "continuation" of the OT *eucharist* (thank offering).

Could it then be possible that the many references to "eucharist" in the Greek of the New Testament are frequently oblique references to the thanks offered at the celebration of the Lord's Supper? As St. Paul began most of his epistles with such eucharistic references—though these are usually verb uses of the word—could he be purposely calling to mind the Eucharistic feast?[102] If this is the case then already *Eucharist* in these NT texts had become a semi-technical term for the Lord's Supper. We do not think this is improbable, especially with the almost immediate adoption of *Eucharist* as a technical term for the Lord's Supper in early Christian jargon.

A Unique Thank Offering Bread

> **"With the sacrifice of his peace offerings for thanksgiving, he shall present his offering with cakes of leavened bread."**
> **Leviticus 7:13**

As the thank offering (*eucharist*) was introduced in Leviticus 7:12, the very next verse described a unique "sacramental" food exclusively associated with the thank offering: "With the sacrifice of his peace offerings for thanksgiving [thank offering], he shall present his offering with *cakes of leavened bread.*"[103] Since this bread was *leavened*, no portion of it could be offered upon God's altar, and yet this *leavened* bread was considered a *most holy* food to be eaten solely by the priests. As such, it could not have been a donation to feed the priests' families. Nor could it have been a *holy* peace

---

[102] Rom. 1:8; 1 Cor. 1:4; 2 Cor. 1:11; Eph.5:20; Phil 1:3; Col.1:12; 1 Thess. 1:2; 2 Thess. 1:3.
[103] Leviticus 7:13. The specifics of this leavened bread are explained in relation to the Jewish festivals in Leviticus 23:17ff. Edersheim, *The Temple....*, 210, explains that these loaves were directly associated with the thanksgiving for daily bread, very much related to "the truth which our Lord embodied in the prayer, 'Give us this day our daily bread.'" The Orthodox have considered this phrase of the Lord's Prayer to have Eucharistic overtones as well.

offering, but it was an exclusive "sacramental" food associated with a *most holy* priest-related thanks to God.

Such *leavened* bread in the regular worship rites of the Jews is only found in the context of the thank offering. It is interesting that the Eastern branch of Christianity ("Orthodox"), the branch that apparently draws much from the OT in its liturgical practices, has insisted from the beginning that *leavened* bread be used in the Eucharist. Could this practice be partly founded upon this OT *leavened* bread which was eaten by the OT priests while they simultaneously ate the thank offering flesh?[104]

The Eastern Church was so adamant in its use of *leavened* bread that ultimately the issue of whether to use *leavened* or *unleavened* bread became a major point of contention dividing the Eastern and Western branches of Christianity. While the East insisted on using *leavened* bread, the Western branch ("Rome") insisted upon the use of *unleavened* bread in the Eucharist—no doubt because Jesus used unleavened bread when He instituted His Supper on that Passover night.

Rendering Thanks Today in the Eucharist

> *"Therefore by Him let us continually offer the sacrifice of praise to God, that is the fruit of our lips, giving thanks to His name. But also do not forget to do good and to share, for with such sacrifices God is well pleased."*
> **Hebrews 13:15,16**

Christ has already fulfilled all thanksgiving of man to God by His sacrifice upon the cross.[105] From His cross, Christ now enables our

---

[104] The Eastern Church appears to have no strong reason why they maintain *leavened* bread as a chief ingredient of the Eucharist, except that this was the way it was done from the beginning. Some have expressed the argument that the *leavened* bread symbolized life and thus had to be used because Christ rose from the dead. See p. 342 for other leavened bread rituals.

[105] See Alan M. Stibbs, *Sacrament, Sacrifice and Eucharist* (London: Billing and Son LTD., 1961), 59.

thanksgiving to be pleasing to the heavenly Father, as the author of the epistle to the Hebrews explains: "*By Him* let us continually offer the sacrifice of praise to God, that is the fruit of our lips, giving thanks to His name."[106] This text declares that through Jesus ("by Him") we may offer thanks. How do Christians express such Christ-mediated thanksgiving? Alan Stibbs explains that there are three basic ways to express thanksgiving to God.[107] These three expressions of thanksgiving are *words* of thanks, *self-sacrifice* to God and *eating* of the Lord's Supper. Each of these should occur in the worship setting.[108] No doubt the same three expressions of thanksgiving (words, giving of self, eating) would have been linked by the Jews to their OT thank offering as well.

Consider the first expression of thanks: the *words* of praise and thanksgiving. These *words*, at times set to music, have always been identified as sacrifices offered to God.[109] The prayers of thanks should to this day be considered an integral part of the Eucharistic sacrifice in the worship service. The *Book of Concord* explains that when the early church "Fathers call the Mass a sacrifice...They make it clear that they are talking about [verbal] thanksgiving; hence they call it 'eucharist'"[110] These Lutheran Confessions further explain that the Lord's Supper "can be called an offering, as it is called a eucharist, because prayers, thanksgivings, and the whole worship are offered there."[111] Verbal thanksgiving is here being magnified.

The second expression of thanks—the *self-sacrifice* of a worshiper's physical, bodily possessions—has consistently been recognized as a "living sacrifice" to God.[112] As will be discussed later, the self-sacrificial act of giving

---

[106] Hebrews 13:15. Chapter eight will show how this text relates to Holy Communion.
[107] Under the category of *self sacrifice* one can include any number of activities and donations that can glorify God. As such, they render Him thanks.
[108] Stibbs, *Sacrament, Sacrifice...*, 59.
[109] Psalm 141:2.
[110] *The Book of Concord* (Tappert), 261.
[111] *The Book of Concord* (Tappert), 265. This quote appears to understand *eucharist* as a reference to the thank offering.
[112] Romans 12:1.

to the poor was an extremely important expression of thanksgiving associated with the eucharistic feasts in both Old and New Testament times.

The third expression of thanksgiving—*eating* of the Eucharist—is a foreign concept for most people today. It seems strange to think that *eating* the Lord's Supper could be a way of giving thanks, but this was the understanding of the Early Church. Hicks explains that shortly after Christ, "the general idea of Christian thanksgiving is concentrated in the Eucharist, which is the *food received*, as well as the action of giving thanks."[113] By publicly *eating* the sacrament there is a public confession and proclamation that God is the giver of all good things through Christ. Because a public proclamation of God's faithfulness is really the essence of rendering thanks to Him, the public confession declared by *eating* the Eucharist was and remains a powerful expression of giving thanks! Alan Stibbs summarizes, "The very act of receiving [eating] can, almost paradoxically, be described as the most appropriate form of thank-offering."[114] The *eating* of the thank offering was and remains its core activity. Such activity communicates, among other things, a thanksgiving to God.

A Word of caution must be heeded, however, a word of caution pertaining to sacramental hypocrisy. To eat of the Eucharist and to be devoid of the other two expressions of thanks (words and giving of self) is to become ritualistic, artificial, and to lose the meaning of love conveyed at the cross. This would be comparable to preaching the Gospel to the poor but letting them starve and go naked. One cannot rightly give thanks by simply eating the Eucharist, and then ignore the other aspects of giving thanks—especially the thanks expressed by giving to the poor.

As realized in the early church, the unique presence of Christ's body

---

[113] Hicks, *The Fullness...*, 274, drawn from the *Didache*, Ignatius and Clement. Italics added.
[114] Stibbs, *Sacrament, Sacrifice...*, 58, footnoting also Psalm 116:12,13. See also *The Book of Concord* (Tappert), "Apology", (33), 256: "...the reception of the Lord's Supper itself can be praise or thanksgiving." Also (74), 263: "...it [the cleansed conscience] uses the ceremony itself as praise to God."

and blood in the Eucharist is *the* avenue by which all three expressions of thanksgiving find their way to God. Gayford explains, "But there is no offering of ourselves apart from Him and His offering; and in this way the Eucharist is bound up with Calvary."[115] Christ as mediator is uniquely present, both as food and as host, at every Communion Service. To come to the Service of Holy Communion was and is to come to the place where God's people meet to give thanks. Here, in Holy Communion, Christians truly participate in Christ's sacrifice as He is seen to be the fulfillment of the kind of peace offering called the *thank offering*, and through such participation, thanksgiving to God is rendered.

The Votive Peace Offering

> "Only your holy things which you may have and your votive offerings, you shall take and go to the place which the Lord chooses."
> Deuteronomy 12:26

Consider now a second type of private peace offering, the *votive offering*. Probably most people today rarely use or understand the word *votive*. The word *votive* simply means that which is dedicated to God by a vow. When an Israelite fulfilled a special vow to God, he would also bring a votive offering. The votive offering process was set in motion when a person vowed something to God. This vow was based upon the condition that *if* God would grant deliverance out of some peril or pain, *then* the person making the vow would "pay" their vow. This payment culminated with the sacrifice of a votive offering, an official peace offering sacrificed at God's House.

As was the case for all peace offerings, when the time came for the votive offering to be sacrificed, first the priest ceremonially applied the blood

---

[115] Gayford, *Sacrifice...*, 175.

to the Bronze Altar, the fatty portions were then sacredly burned, the priest would next receive his holy food, and finally the sacrificer would joyfully gather his family and friends to feast upon the remaining holy portions of the peace offering flesh. Obviously the *votive offering* was in this respect a form of *thank offering*, thanking God for deliverance from peril or pain. If the vow had not been formally made and there was no specific vow or creature vowed to be sacrificed, such an offering might be labeled a *free-will offering*. From such understanding one can grasp the overlap—and at times the interchange of terminology—for the three basic types of private peace offerings (*thanks, votive, free-will*).

There are numerous references to votive offerings in the OT, especially when one realizes that often they are merely cited as "paying vows" to God. When God's Word then enjoins a believer to "pay his vows," what is meant is that God has performed His act of deliverance, and the man who made the vow needed to fulfill his promise to God and, after slaying his votive sacrifice, share the resulting peace offering meal with friends and relatives. Hicks explains how many have failed to grasp the abundant votive offering references in the OT:

> Again this shows how little some commentators grasp the constant sacrificial meaning of words apparently untechnical. Dt. 23:23 fixes the meaning of a vow: "That which is gone out of thy lips thou shalt observe and do; according as thou has vowed unto the Lord thy God, a freewill offering, which thou hast promised with thy mouth."[116]

So, the votive offering begins with the mouth, with a vow to God. As an example, consider Hannah who so deeply desired a son that she promised to commit him to service in the Temple. The text simply relates, "She made a

---

[116] Hicks, *The Fullness*, 97-98. See also e.g. Nahum 1:15.

vow."[117] This statement indicates not merely her vow to commit Samuel to temple service, but it indicates the beginning of the votive offering process. Hannah's vow was the first step in the votive offering, and, according to God's regulation the head of the household had to approve all such vows.[118] After God blessed her with a baby boy, whom she named Samuel, then Hannah's husband (Elkanah) went up to Jerusalem "with all his household to offer to the Lord the yearly sacrifice *and pay his vow.*"[119] The head of the household, after realizing God had fulfilled His act of deliverance, was bound to *pay his vow*, making the appropriate votive sacrifice. The family then joined in the celebrative feast. Even though no feast is specified in this account, yet it is certain a feast was celebrated because this was the final act for the votive offering.[120] Thus to pay one's vow meant to offer to God a votive offering, and to offer a votive offering ultimately meant to join in a festive meal.

Christ's Eucharist in Psalm 22

> *"My praise is of thee in the great congregation: I will pay my vows before them that fear him. The poor shall eat and be satisfied; and they shall praise the Lord that seek him: their heart shall live forever"*
> Psalm 22:25,26

Psalm 22 presents a votive offering that is of profound interest. This Psalm, which starkly portrays the Savior's death, is also very likely *specifically*

---

[117] 1 Samuel 1:11. Of course Hannah was vowing to give her yet-to-be conceived son to temple service. However, such a vow would also bind her to the giving of the votive sacrifice.
[118] Numbers 30.
[119] 1 Samuel 1:21. Part of Hannah's vow was the sacred dedication of her son, Samuel, but this is not what the text is here referring to since it would still be several years before Samuel would be dedicated.
[120] Interestingly, Hannah decided to stay home with little Samuel. She obviously did not eat of the votive sacrifice.

predicting the Lord's Supper in terms of the votive offering.[121]

The richness of the first half of the Psalm is in its startlingly vivid description of Christ's death, but the richness of the second half of Psalm 22 is in its comforting descriptions of Holy Communion. John Edward Field summarizes Psalm 22 by dividing it into two parts. He maintains that the first portion of the Psalm refers "to the Passion, and the later portion to the Eucharistic commemoration of it which our Lord appointed and by which He announced the Name of God unto His brethren."[122]

Summarizing the Psalm's predictions of Christ's agonizing death, the first half of Psalm 22 predicts Christ's passion by stating that He is given over to "dogs" (Gentiles), and His hands and feet are pierced. He experiences taunting while hanging on the cross, and lots are cast for His outer garment. His joints are stretched to dislocation and He endures tremendous thirst—common experiences endured by crucified people—and finally He expires. These predictions vividly describe Christ's crucifixion.

In Psalm 22:24 Christ explains why He would offer a votive offering: "For he [the Father] has not despised nor been angry at the supplication of the poor; nor turned away his face from me; but when I cried to him, he heard me."[123] Recall that the votive offering was sacrificed after God delivered a person from calamity. The author of the epistle to the Hebrews explains that Christ prayed for deliverance with "loud crying and tears to the One able to save Him from death, and He was heard because of His piety."[124] Christ's deliverance is not a deliverance from sufferings and death upon the cross, but deliverance from the grave. He rises from the dead. Thus, as explained in the verses from Psalm 22 just cited, the impoverished Christ cried to God, and He was heard. We too realize the same reality in our lives; God does not

---

[121] Kleinig, *Leviticus*, 95. Kleinig also sees in Psalm 22 the messianic king whose hands and feet were pierced, hosting the Eucharistic banquet.

[122] Field, *The Apostolic Liturgy. . .*, (London: Rivingtons, 1882), 69.

[123] The LXX puts the description in the first person, "...When *I* cried to Him, He heard *me*." Thus Christ is the "first" of the poor and afflicted whom God hears.

[124] Hebrews 5:7.

despise the supplication of the poor. Jesus was so certain of His Father's deliverance, that His sacrifice upon the cross stands then as His votive offering, the sacrifice fulfilling His vow.[125]

Christ then invites all God's people to join in His votive meal. He says to His Father, "My praise is of thee in the great congregation: I will pay my vows before them that fear him." (v. 25). Remember that to pay one's vows was ultimately to invite others to the celebration meal—a meal drawn from a peace offering sacrifice. The Septuagint identifies *the great congregation* in the above verse—the location of Christ's praise—literally as *the great church*.[126] Thus already in Psalm 22:22 Christ speaks of the *church*, a word He would use in the NT to describe that vast assembly of believers over which the gates of hell could not prevail.[127] In this *great church*—the holy church throughout all the world, the church through the centuries, the church in heaven and upon earth—Christ offers praise as He invites those that fear God to join in the votive offering meal! So Christ invites the largest crowd ever, those that fear God, to the Holy Supper of His body and blood. J. M. Neale briefly states that in this verse Christ "plainly hints at the Blessed Eucharist."[128]

After "plainly hinting" at the blessed Eucharist, Christ goes on to clearly present it in Psalm 22:26: "The poor shall eat and be satisfied; and they shall praise the Lord that seek him: their heart shall live forever." Delitzsch, first considering this verse in application to King David, comments:

> Being rescued he will bring...the thank-offerings, which he vowed to God when in the extremist peril. When the sprinkling with blood...and the laying of the fat pieces upon the altar...were completed, the remaining flesh of the shelamim [peace offering] was

---

[125] Jonah's vow (2:9,10) and deliverance seem to typify this (Matt. 12:39-41; 16:4).
[126] εκκλησια μεγαλη.
[127] Matthew 16:18ff.
[128] Neale and Littledale, *A Commentary...*, 301.

used by the offerer to make a joyous meal.[129]

After further discussion, Delitzsch breaks forth, "How natural, then, is the thought of the sacramental eucharist, in which the second David, like to the first, having attained to the throne through the suffering of death, makes us partakers of the fruits of His suffering!"[130] Of this verse in Psalm 22, Neale states that concerning primitive and medieval commentators, "None ever commented on this verse without referring it to the Holy Eucharist."[131]

The description first informs us of Christ: He is risen from the dead, and thus He is able to offer this feast of victory. "If we take the words in their more natural sense, there is no doubt a reference to the connection between the reception of the Blessed Eucharist and the Resurrection," Neale summarizes. He then adds the historical dimension: "Hence, the Second Council of Nicaea calls that Sacrament the symbol of the Resurrection."[132]

But the verse under consideration also describes Christ's people as the "poor," who are in this respect like Him (v. 24), as they too are afflicted and cast down. Such poor folk are all those who would be physically and/or spiritually poor.[133] But now they are invited to this feast before Almighty God; the result of faithfully receiving this blessed sacrament is summarized simply by the word *satisfied*. With the reception of forgiveness, God's love, God's saving presence and eternal life can anyone not be satisfied?[134] I shall not want; the Good Shepherd has prepared a table before me![135] No wonder the

---

[129] F. Delitzsch, *Commentary on the Old Testament, Psalms*, vol. V, trans. Francis Bolton (Grand Rapids: Eerdmans Publishing Co., reprinted 1978), 323.
[130] Ibid., 324.
[131] Neale and Littledale, *A Commentary....*, 301.
[132] Ibid., 302.
[133] Delitzsch, *Psalms*, 324.
[134] Elwood Sylvester Beri, *Commentary on the Psalms*, (New York: Benziger Brothers, 1915), 178, commenting on this verse of Psalm 22: "The sacrificial banquets of the Old Law prefigured the Eucharistic Banquet of the new, in which Christ is the victim of the sacrifice and the spiritual food of those who partake of the banquet. Those who eat of this spiritual food shall be refreshed with eternal newness of life."
[135] From Psalm 23, also understood in the early church to have Eucharistic overtones.

next phrase further explains that these poor who sought the Lord now— upon feasting with Him—offer their praise to Him. Their hearts have become so uplifted that they mount up with wings like eagles, and thus the Lord declares, "Their heart shall live forever." Delitzsch summarizes the blessing offered by the meal and its promises: "May this meal impart to you ever enduring refreshment."[136]

Such spiritual refreshment and worship is for the entire world. The next verses of the Psalm explain the global character of such worship: "All the ends of the earth shall remember and turn to the Lord: and all the kindreds of the nations shall worship before him. For the kingdom is the Lord's; and he is the governor of the nations."(vv. 27,28). Jesus said of the Lord's Supper that it would be done *in remembrance* of Him. The Psalm agrees, for "all the ends of the earth shall *remember.*"[137] This remembering is not a mere recalling, but a faith in the Lord, an act of repentance, for the Psalmist explains that those who remember will *turn to the Lord.* Note once again in these verses the international participation in the Eucharist as "*all the ends of the earth* shall remember" and "*all the kindreds of the nations* shall worship" because Christ is "governor of *the nations.*" These verses were not describing localized Hebrew worship at the temple, but something far greater—an international votive meal!

As the Gospel is preached throughout the world, it is truly a wonder in the making, but how unfortunate that the nations are sometimes taught of Christ and left hanging as to their worship and their Eucharistic nourishment. The portion of Psalm 22 herein under study speaks of the right worship—the godly celebration of the Holy Eucharist—to which the crucified and risen Christ invites His people. The *kingdom is the Lord's,* as these verses state,

---

[136] Delitzsch, *Psalms*, 324.
[137] Neale and Littledale, *A Commentary...*, 303: "KS. Albertus ingeniously connects this with the prophecy in the preceding verse, of the Blessed Eucharist, by reminding us of our Lord's injunction, 'This do in remembrance of me.'" Concerning "ends of the earth," Neale reports that "Hugh of S. Victor would refer this to the Blessed Eucharist, because to those who receive it worthily, all earthly things have an end, and heaven is already begun." (303).

and He invites those of *all the nations* to His feast.[138] The Lamb that was slain is truly governor of all, King of kings and Lord of lords!

Even the earthly rich, those wealthy and fat from the abundance of this present life, are invited to Christ's feast. The Psalmist thus continues, "All the fat ones of the earth have eaten and worshipped: all that go down to the earth [dust] shall fall down before him: my soul also lives to him." (v. 29) Delitzsch explains:

> So magnificent shall be the feast that all...those who stand out prominently before the world and before their own countrymen by reason of abundance of their temporal possessions,...choose it before this abundance, in which they might revel, and, on account of the grace and glory which the celebration includes within itself, they bow down and worship.[139]

Similarly A. F. Kirkpatrick remarks: "The Psalmist sees homage already paid to Jehovah even by the haughty nobles of the earth. They abandon their proud self-sufficiency, and join in the eucharistic meal with the meek (v. 26), whom once they despised and persecuted."[140] Neale relates a different Eucharistic viewpoint: "Others take it to mean that they who were once poor, shall, by feeding on this blessed Sacrament, become fat upon earth: that is, have an antepast of heaven, even here."[141] Either view is consistent with the theology and mission of the church. The poor become rich in the Gospel, and the rich become poor in their humility—and all fall down

---

[138] This dovetails with the descriptions heretofore mentioned concerning the participation of the nations in the peace offerings predicted in the OT.
[139] Delitzsch, *Psalms*, 325,326.
[140] A. F. Kirkpatrick, ed., *The Book of Psalms* (Cambridge: University Press, 1957), 123.
[141] Neale and Littledale, *A Commentary...*, 304. If such an "antepast" is understood as earthly riches, we would disagree, for this is a theology of glory. But if the "antepast" is understood as the riches of the cross, then this could be a viable exegesis of the passage.

before Him.[142] This is worship.[143] Connecting the sacred votive offering meal with those who bow down, Kirkpatrick summarizes wonderfully:

> Those who were on the edge of the grave, ready to die from want and misery and trouble, come as guests and gain new life. Rich and poor, strong and weak, alike partake of the feast: for it the rich desert their wealth; in it the poor receive the compensation for their privations; and those who were ready to die find life.[144]

In Holy Communion, Christians *eat* of the votive offering *of* Christ and *with* Christ. As His self-sacrifice is the antitype of the Hebrew votive offering, He is not only the *host*—inviting His friends to the votive offering meal—but *He is the votive offering meal* of which His brethren partake! The resurrected Christ, who is never re-sacrificed, shares and hosts the meal of peace and deliverance with His people. Christ, seeking deliverance before His crucifixion, vowed to join His brethren in a meal when His deliverance would be realized.[145] Having been delivered by resurrection, He now invites His brethren to share in the celebrative *votive offering* meal, drawing those who eat to recall and participate in His sacrifice. The Lord's Supper is the finale of all sacrifice. It is not a re-sacrifice or a re-presentation of Christ's sacrifice, but a true votive feast of victory, a feast upon the body and blood of the once

---

[142] Beri, *Commentary on the Psalms*, 178-179, speaking of these verses of Psalm 22: "Not only all nations but even all classes and conditions of men shall worship God. The rich and the poor, the high and the low, Jew and Gentile, shall partake of the Eucharistic Banquet and adore the one true God of all."

[143] Bruce Cameron, *Luther's Summary of the Psalms (1531)--a Model for Contemporary Psalm Interpretation*, STM, 1991, Concordia, St. Louis, 69: (translation of what Luther says of this Psalm) "It is indeed one of the chief psalms. It belongs in the first commandment, for it promises a new worship of God." This is Eucharistic talk.

[144] Kirkpatrick, *The Book of Psalms*, 123.

[145] E.g. Luke 22:30.

crucified *and risen* Christ.[146]

Malachi and the Lord's Supper

> *"But cursed be the swindler who has a male in his flock, and vows it, but sacrifices a blemished animal, for I am a great King."*
> *Malachi 1:14*

In view of the Lord's Supper, Malachi 1:14 is an interesting votive offering reference. Before this verse is treated, first consider Malachi 1:11, which the early church consistently regarded as a prediction of the Lord's Supper. This verse predicts:

> "*From the rising of the sun, even to its setting*, My name will be great *among the nations*, and every place *incense is going to be offered* to my name, and a *grain offering that is pure*; for My name will be great *among the nations*," says the Lord. [italics added][147]

Incense was burned particularly with the grain offerings, and the reference here to a *grain offering* may be a general reference to sacrifice or it may be specifying the grain offering that was burned with every burnt offering and peace offering.[148] Though this verse has been treated as a prediction—as it predicts true worship practiced *from the rising of the sun, even to its*

---

[146] Washburn, *The Import of Sacrifice*..., 65: "The peace offering of the old dispensation, telling in expressive symbol the sweet and hallowed story of divine communion, so far, had the same significance as the eucharist in the new. It was the reception by Jehovah of his covenant children, who, having their sins covered by atoning blood, now sit down at his feast of love."
[147] Malachi 1:11.
[148] The Hebrew term "minchah," found in Malachi 1:11, was usually used for the grain offering, but occasionally it was used for sacrifice in general. Malachi 1:13, speaking of sacrificial flesh, uses "minchah" to reference a non-grain offering sacrifice, so one is justified in understanding it as such in verse 11.

setting—nevertheless it also includes directives for the Jews in Malachi's day. Malachi's directive, both to the Jews who first heard it and for those in the Christian era, is that there be a "pure" offering. Of course Christ is the fulfillment and antitype of *every Jewish* sacrifice, however this verse goes beyond the circle of the Jews as it specifies *the nations* participating in a genuine sacrificial worship setting.

Various first and second century Christian documents, such as *The Didache* (perhaps written partly by the Apostles themselves), the writings of Justin Martyr (born 100 AD), and the writings of Irenaeus (born 115 AD) all agree that Malachi 1:11 was a specific prediction of the Lord's Supper. Concerning *The Didache*, Irenaeus and Justin Martyr, Darwell Stone writes: "They regard it [Mal. 1:11] as a prophecy of Christian worship, and *in particular of the Eucharist.*"[149] Where else but in the Lord's Supper could Malachi's prediction of sacrificial participation be fulfilled?

Malachi 1:12 continues, "But you are profaning it [God's Name], in that you say, 'The table of the Lord is defiled, and as for its fruit, its food is to be despised.'" The "table of the Lord" was understood to be the bronze altar, the table from which God consumed His portions in the altar's fire, and the table from which God shared holy food with His faithful people. St. Paul employs this *table of the Lord* terminology to describe Holy Communion in 1 Corinthians 10 where he directs, "You cannot partake of the *table of the Lord* and the table of demons." Westcott explains: "When the offering is regarded as the material of a feast, the 'altar' becomes a 'table.'"[150] When Malachi talks of the table of the Lord, he is speaking of a peace offering *meal*. As this verse describes God's people *despising* the *food* from *the table of the Lord*, the despised food is the *communion food* they were privileged to eat. As will be observed in Malachi's following verses, the Jews of Malachi's day were despising the communion food that was derived from a votive peace offering.

---

[149] Stone, *A History...*, 49. Italics added.
[150] Westcott, *The Epistle to the Hebrews*, 454.

In verse 13 Malachi continues to describe God's displeasure with His OT worshippers in that they had begun to "disdainfully sniff" at the peace offering meal:

> "You also say, 'My, how tiresome it is!' And you *disdainfully sniff at it*," says the Lord of hosts, "and you bring what was taken by robbery, and what is lame or sick; so you bring the offering! Should I receive that from your hand?" says the Lord. [italics added]"

One can readily visualize the "sniffing" at the sacrificial meal, refusing to eat of it—like a spoiled child sniffing at but refusing to eat his lima beans. Likely these hypocritical Jews "sniffed" at the sacrifice because *they* knew it had been sickly and *they* didn't want to eat it! Certainly God would be even more displeased today when someone "disdainfully sniffs" at and refuses to eat the Supper instituted by Christ.

Verse 14 specifically connects the theme of Malachi 1:11-13 to the communion sacrifice of the *votive offering*: "'But cursed be the swindler who has a male in his flock, and *vows it*, but sacrifices a blemished animal to the Lord, for I am a great King,' says the Lord of hosts, 'and My name is feared among the nations.'" Note the votive offering referent, that the offerer had *vowed* a quality sacrificial creature. This verse is connected to the previous one via the theme of inferior sacrificial animals. Those Jews presenting their votive offerings were bringing sickly and blemished creatures instead of the quality ones that they should have sacrificed as votive offerings. Malachi's entire prediction, as it was understood to be a prediction by the early church, is couched in the terminology and practice of Hebrew sacrifice—particularly the votive offering.

That which made Malachi 1:11 appealing as a reference to the Eucharist was its description of a sacrifice that would be not merely for the Jews but for *the nations*. In verse 14 the votive offering—referred to as the *vowing* of one's flock—is again related to *God's name* which is feared *among the nations*. Thus verses 11 and 14 not only have proximity and thus contextual attachments, but they have connecting concepts as well. They both talk about a sacrifice (verse 14 specifying the *votive offering*) and they both relate the international flavor of such sacrifice. Verses 12 and 13 each hint at a peace offering meal, with verse 14 then clearly confirming the peace offering nature of the prophecy as it specifies the votive offering. Thus the sacrifice emphasized in Malachi's prediction was particularly the peace offering, the sacrifice that uniquely highlighted the sacred meal. How else *could* Malachi predict the Lord's Supper except by utilizing the sacrificial terminology of his day? No wonder the early church considered Malachi 1:11 to be a specific prediction of the greatest peace offering meal, the Holy Eucharist.

When first penned, the first chapter of Malachi stood on its own as a condemnation of the Jews who in some way reneged on their votive offering. Concerning the future, God is simply relating here in Malachi that in some way sacrificial participation is going to be opened for *all nations*. The church has rightly realized that the global sacrificial participation predicted in Malachi is fulfilled in the *entire* act of worship performed by God's NT people.[151] Also legitimate is the recognition of the communion nature of the *votive offering*—spoken of here in Malachi—as that which typified the Christian celebration of Holy Communion.

---

[151] *The Book of Concord* (Tappert), 256: "Malachi is talking about all the worship of the New Testament, not only about the Lord's Supper."

Was Isaiah Predicting the Eucharist?

> *"And nations will come to your light, and kings to the brightness of your rising...They will go up with acceptance on my altar."*
> Isaiah 60:3,7b.

As just noted, the early church consistently perceived the first chapter of Malachi to be predicting the Eucharist. Rome then used this first chapter of Malachi to defend the validity of the "bloodless sacrifice" of the Mass. Such a bloodless sacrifice was understood to be a bloodless re-sacrifice of Christ.[152] Because the Roman church used Malachi 1:11 to support this faulty doctrine—that Christ is re-sacrificed in the Lord's Supper—many who argued against such re-sacrifice of Christ did not apprehend the sacramental value of Malachi's prediction. The early church's use of Malachi 1:11 demonstrated that these ancient theologians had such a strong sense for the Lord's Supper, that they effortlessly perceived it in their reading of the OT. Gavin explains, "Justin Martyr, Irenaeus, and others in the early church *found in the eucharist the fulfillment of O.T. prophecy and the term of the O.T. sacrificial system.* [italics added]"[153]

The early church perceived the Eucharist in their reading of Malachi 1:11. If Gavin is correct—that the early church *found in the eucharist the fulfillment of O.T. prophecy*—then other OT predictions of *gentiles* participating in sacrifices should certainly be considered eucharistic predictions as well. Would not such OT predictions *have to be* predictions of NT worship in which Christians truly eat of *the* sacrifice (*not* re-sacrifice

---

[152] Daly, *Christian Sacrifice,* 333-372: Justin Martyr, Irenaeus, Hippolytus and others used Malachi 1 to discuss the Lord's Supper. At the time of the Reformation this passage was used by Rome to "prove" the sacrifice of the mass. The Lutheran Confessions emphatically deny that such a passage predicts the "re-sacrifice" of the Mass. *The Book of Concord* (Tappert), 255: "Even if this [Malachi 1] were a reference to the Mass, it would not follow that the Mass justifies ex opere operato."

[153] F. Gavin, *The Jewish Antecedents of the Christian Sacraments* (New York: The Macmillan Col.: 1928), 92.

Christ), and in which they offer their sacrifices in word and deed?

Now consider some predictions of genuine gentile worship penned through the prophet Isaiah, and realize that Isaiah, like Malachi, could only couch his inspired predictions in the sacrificial terminology of his day. The concept of sacrifice is often summarized simply by referring to an *altar*. Italics are added to highlight this and other connections between gentiles and sacrifice; Isaiah 19:19, 21b: "In that day there will be *an altar to the Lord* in the midst of the *land of Egypt*...They will even worship with *sacrifice and offering*, and will *make a vow* to the Lord and perform it." Isaiah 56:6a,7a: "Also the *foreigners* who join themselves to the Lord...Even those I will bring to My holy mountain, and make them joyful [peace offering concept] *in my house of prayer.* Their *burnt offerings* and their *sacrifices* will be acceptable *on my altar.*" Isaiah 60:3,7b: "And *nations* will come to your light, and kings to the brightness of your rising...They will go up with acceptance *on My altar.*"

It makes sense that an OT prophet would predict NT worship in terms of the sacrificial practice at the time of his prediction; he utilized his worship vocabulary. If one makes the connection between the OT sacrificial system and the NT sacrifice of Christ, and then if one also makes the connection between eating OT sacrificial portions and eating the NT Eucharist—then these passages from Isaiah are precisely predicting both Christ's crucifixion *and* the Sacrament of the Altar to be celebrated by non-Jewish people.

By their *words, self-giving* and Eucharistic *eating*, even gentiles could and would offer thank-sacrifices to God through the sacrifice of Christ Jesus. The body and blood of Christ are the heavenly elements enabling sacrificial participation on the part of God's people throughout the world. The Christian's sacrificial participation, as inferred in the above predictions made by Isaiah, is not only to eat, but to offer prayers, alms and even vows before God.

The sacrifice at the cross, being *the* sacrifice of the Son of God, never ceases to be able to be provided to and to provide for God's people. Through the miraculous sacrificial eating of the Lord's Supper, God's people of *all nations* now have immediate contact with the Savior. God's NT people do not need to make a pilgrimage to the temple and its altars, for now His people in all nations find proximity to the cross of Christ at the Sacrament of the Altar.

The Free-will Offering

> *"But if the sacrifice of his offering is a votive or a freewill offering it shall be eaten on the day that he offers his sacrifice; and on the next day what is left of it may be eaten."*
> **Leviticus 7:16**

The third type of private peace offering was the free-will offering. The Scriptures do not thoroughly explain the free-will offering, probably because it—like the thank offering—was self-explanatory by its very name, being an offering made of one's own *free will*. Such a sacrifice freely expressed thanks to God for His abundant blessings. Deuteronomy 16:10 conveys the basic meaning of the free-will offering, explaining that this type of sacrifice is "a freewill offering of your hand, which you shall give just as the Lord your God blesses you." Such descriptions present the free-will offering as a kind of votive offering, even though no preliminary vow had been made to God. Though a free-will offering did not obligate people by a vow to bring sacrifices, yet when God's OT believers realized a blessing or deliverance from God, they brought such a sacrifice to God anyway—of their own *free will*. Consistent with this, the Biblical descriptions and regulations for votive offerings and free-will offerings are identical.

Since there is such scant reference to the *free-will offering*, the reader is simply reminded that it was a *peace offering*, and again "the central and distinctive idea of the peace offering, a fellowship with God, was expressed by its peculiar ceremonial feature—the common meal."[154] Christ gave the

---

[154] Gayford, *Sacrifice and Priesthood*, 37.

ultimate free will offering as he willingly went to the cross. We now celebrate—with all whom Christ has invited—by eating the meal drawn from that free will offering.

The Covenant (Testament) Sacrifice

> *"Drink from it, all of you; for this is my blood of the covenant."*
> *Matthew 26:27,28*

The peace offering was the sacrifice that sealed a covenant, and thus at times it was simply called a "covenant" sacrifice.[155] De Vaux states succinctly, "The 'selamim' [peace offering] might then be called a covenant sacrifice."[156] And thus—because a covenant sacrifice was a peace offering—Brooke Westcott explains, "The Covenant sacrifice became the groundwork of a feast."[157]

When Jesus instituted Holy Communion, He did so by speaking of it in *covenant* terms. He said, "This cup is the new *covenant* in My blood." Darwell Stone grasps how Christ's wording created a connection to the *covenant meals* of the OT: "His words were of such a kind as to suggest a connection between the rite which He was instituting and the sacrificial feasts in which the worshippers partook of the sacrifice and thereby received the blessing associated with it."[158]

As Jesus specified the Eucharist to be a covenant-related meal, it would have been natural for a Jew to associate the Lord's Supper with the

---

[155] Daly, *Christian Sacrifice*, 22: (describing particularly Genesis 31,54) "The zebah [often a type of peace offering] is a covenant-sealing festive sacrificial meal..." Daly maintains (90,93) that "selamim," another word for peace offering, is really best described as "covenant sacrifice."

[156] De Vaux, *Studies*..., 38. He continues: "In support of this one might point to the part played by the meal (Gen. xxvi.30, xxxi.54; Joshua ix.14) and by the blood (Exod. xxiv.8) in the sealing of a covenant."

[157] Westcott, *Epistle to the Hebrews*, 440.

[158] Stone, *The Doctrine*...., 8.

peace offering. William L. Lane explains the reason for the covenant-making peace offering meal:

> Covenant ratification necessarily involves a peace offering to signify the acceptance of the covenant by the participants [...] The fellowship meal, which was the characteristic feature of the peace offering, displayed the peaceful relationship of the participants.[159]

As God's OT people joined together in eating a covenant sacrifice, the gathering to eat such a peace offering meal, Lane explains, "became an occasion for the public recital of God's Covenant faithfulness."[160] Today such a *public recital* occurs at every celebration of the Lord's Supper, for Christ's meal brings together those who unitedly *confess* peace in the blood of His cross. St. Paul associates this covenant-related public recital of God's faithfulness with the Lord's Supper: "As often as you eat this bread and drink this cup you *show forth [proclaim]* the Lord's death until He comes."[161] Such a proclamation of Christ's death is the essence of the Gospel, and it is the core of God's covenant faithfulness. The eating of the covenant meal, along with the preaching and the liturgy surrounding it, are now the public recital of God's covenant faithfulness.

Psalm 50 gives some insights concerning the covenant meal of the peace offering.[162] In verse 5 God commands, "Gather My godly ones to Me, those who have made a covenant with Me by sacrifice."[163] This is describing

---

[159] William L. Lane, *A Call to Commitment* (Peabody: Hendrickson Publishers, 1985), 139.

[160] William L. Lane, *Hebrews 9-13*, Word Biblical Commentary, vol. 47b (Dallas: Word Books, 1991) 139-140. Lane also points to the covenant "recitals" of God's faithfulness as recorded in Psalms 26:4-7; 116:12-19.

[161] Recall that this was directly related to the Passover proclamation. There were, as already explained, clear parallels between the Passover and the peace offering.

[162] Psalm 50:5,14,16,23 are verses that speak of or infer the peace offering. Verses 7-13 speak of God's displeasure over the insincere, formalistic attitude toward sacrifice in general.

[163] Delitzsch, *Psalms*, 120: Delitzsch translates the Hebrew: "Gather My saints together unto Me, who make a covenant with me over sacrifice." It is *over* God's sacrifice that they enter into His covenant.

God's people "covenanting" with Him through sacrifice; the covenant sacrifice was particularly the peace offering. In verse 16 the Psalmist informs us that God's communion is to be closed to the wicked: "But to the wicked God says, 'What right have you to tell of My statutes, and to take My covenant in your mouth?'"[164] The wicked have no right to proclaim God's gracious covenant acts, nor do they have the right to take God's covenant in their mouth—that is, to eat of it. They may want to flagrantly participate in evil and then commune with God, but they have no right to do so!

As Jesus instituted His sacred meal He indicated it to be a *covenant* meal by declaring that the cup is His *blood of the Covenant*.[165] What Christ was abbreviating is that the sacramental cup contains the blood of the covenant sacrifice, and *He is the covenant sacrifice*.[166] From Christ's words one might be led to conclude that He was only identifying His *blood* in covenant terms, but the early church realized that His entire sacrifice—both blood and body—identified the covenant sacrifice. Consequently in certain early liturgies not only the blood but also appropriately the body of Christ received in the Lord's Supper was recognized as part of the covenant meal.[167]

---

[164] Delitzsch, *Psalms*, 121. Delitzsch translates this verse: "But to the evil-doer Elohim saith: How dost though dare to tell my statutes, and that thou takest My covenant into thy mouth…?!'" Many translators miss this message about divine communion, and translate this verse as if it is expressing the fact that the wicked have no right to *speak* of God's covenant. Interestingly this prohibition is also true, for it also fits the attitude that should be associated with the covenant sacrifice. Translating literally from the LXX this verse reads, "And to the sinner God has said, 'Why do you declare my statutes, and take up my covenant through your mouth?" How does one take the covenant *through* the mouth? By eating!

[165] Hicks, *The Fullness…*, 209: "…this is the language of sacrifice. …no Jew ever thought of a covenant apart from sacrifice." 325: "No covenant-meal was other than sacrificial.....To Jewish Christians, as to us, feeding upon the body and the blood would have been so abhorrent as to be impossible unless it had been from the first understood by them as the spiritual appropriation of the living Christ, slain and offered for them first as a Covenant Victim."

[166] Hicks, *The Fullness…*, 22: "It must be realized that when a Jew thought of a covenant he thought of a sacrifice."

[167] Gordon S. Wakefield, *An Outline of Christian Worship* (Edinburgh: T & T Clark, 1998), 29, quoting from the *Apostolic Constitutions of Clement* (c. 375): "For in the night in which he was betrayed, he took bread in his holy and undefiled hands and looking up to you his God and Father, he broke [it], and gave [it] to his disciples, saying: This is the mystery of the New Covenant, take of it, [and] eat, this is my body [which is] broken for man, for the remission of sins…"

In the Lord's Supper the flesh of the covenant sacrifice is eaten, and the blood of the covenant sacrifice is consumed as well. Other than consuming the blood, the Lord's Supper has the marks of a covenant meal—a *peace offering* meal drawn from the ultimate sacrifice, Christ Himself.

Covenant Inauguration by Moses and Jesus

> **Moses: "Behold the blood of the covenant."**
> **Exodus 24:8**
> **Jesus: "This is My blood of the covenant."**
> **Matthew 26:28**

Why did Christ emphasize His blood when He spoke of *covenant* in His Words of Institution? Almost certainly He did this because blood was the key ingredient employed at the installation of God's "first" covenant at Sinai. God's OT covenant with the nation of Israel was inaugurated through Moses and Israel's elders on Mount Sinai.[168] At this inauguration Moses simply said, "Behold the blood of the covenant." Compare this to what Jesus said, "This is My blood of the covenant."[169] Christ's Words of Institution are no doubt directing God's people to that lofty occasion when Moses reverently handled covenantal blood. Alfred Cave explains this relationship:

> The words of Christ Himself, therefore, at the first celebration of the great Christian sacrament, immediately recall that scene in the desert, when, in ratification of the first covenant, the great lawgiver

---

[168] There were covenants with Noah, Abraham, etc.; but the covenant instituted pertaining to God's people and to sacrifice was through Moses. The epistle to the Hebrews sets forth the primacy of the Mosaic covenant inauguration, calling it the *first* covenant: "Therefore even the *first covenant* was not inaugurated without blood." (Hebrews 9:18). Daniel 9:27 also likely predicts Messiah's confirming of a new covenant. See Andrew E. Steinmann, *Daniel*, (St. Louis: Concordia Publishing House, 2008), 475f.

[169] As will be explained in chapter eight, the author of Hebrews (Hebrews 9:20) conforms Moses' wording to fit Christ's.

[Moses] sprinkled the blood of the sacrifices.[170]

Exodus 24 explains that Moses had called for the sacrifice of covenant-related peace offerings: "And they...sacrificed young bulls as *peace offerings* to the Lord." (v. 5). Drawn from these peace offerings, blood was sacredly sprinkled upon the people with the declaration, "Behold the blood of the covenant, which the Lord has made with you..." (v. 8).[171] The covenant meal is then described in verse 11, "They beheld God, and they ate and drank." Jeremias explains the meaning of this meal consumed by Moses and the elders of Israel: "In these last words the thought is of a covenant meal: the fact that God grants to the envoys the fellowship of his table is the pledge of the covenant."[172] As the Israelites later would regularly commune by eating the peace offerings sacrificed in God's House, they were in effect continuing their participation in God's covenant inaugurated through Moses at Sinai.[173] Of this Mosaic covenant, the author of Hebrews reminds his readers that "the first covenant had regulations of divine worship."[174] Christ, as He instituted the New Covenant meal, was also creating *regulations of divine worship*.

Christ inaugurated His covenant meal as He instituted the Lord's Supper with Moses-like words, "This is the blood of the covenant." Now instead of applying the covenant blood by *sprinkling*—as Moses had—Christ applies it by *drinking*. This correlates also with the sprinkled blood of the sin offering, as noted in our previous chapter, which also finds its NT expression

---

[170] Cave, *The Scriptural Doctrine*...., 280. Daly, *Christian Sacrifice*, 221: "The Markan and Matthaean words over the chalice.....are an obvious reference to the institution of the covenant sacrifice in Exod. 24,4-8."

[171] Such "sprinkling" of the peace offering blood was unique. Ritual sprinkling of blood, toward the altar and not upon the people, would later be reserved only for the sin offerings.

[172] Jeremias, *The Eucharistic Words of Jesus*, 235.

[173] Covenant participation was not limited, however, to the peace offering. All of the Hebrew sacrifices involved covenant participation—but the peace offering, being itself the "covenant sacrifice," especially called to mind participation in God's covenant. Sin and guilt offerings could be said to "maintain" the covenant.

[174] Hebrews 9:1.

in the drinking of Christ's blood.

The covenant blood is indeed now the blood of the Living One; greater than the OT sprinkled blood, it is to be consumed! Though Christ is the Living One, yet it is at His crucifixion where the power of such blood is unleashed, for there it was shed for man's salvation. After His resurrection, God's people—like the Jews of old—join in divine worship to celebrate the renewed application of God's covenant to His people, and here they regularly receive of the Lord's Supper—the grandest of covenant meals.

Feasting Implications of Jeremiah's Covenant Prediction

> *"Behold the days are coming," declares the Lord, "when I will make a new covenant with the house of Israel and with the house of Judah..."*
> *Jeremiah 31:31*

Through the prophet Jeremiah, God had predicted that He would institute a *New Covenant*:

> "Behold the days are coming," declares the Lord, "when I will make a *new covenant* with the house of Israel and with the house of Judah...But this is the covenant which I will make with the house of Israel after those days," declares the Lord, "I will put My law within them, and on their heart I will write it; and I will be their God, and they shall be My people. And they shall not teach again, each man his neighbor and each man his brother, saying, 'Know the Lord,' for they shall all know Me, from the least of them to the greatest of them." declares the Lord, "for I will *forgive their iniquity*, and *their sin I will remember no more.* [italics added]"[175]

---

[175] Jeremiah 31:31,33,34.

God had established His first blood covenant through Moses at Mt. Sinai. Jeremiah here predicts that God would establish a new covenant, which infers a new covenant sacrifice and a new covenant meal.

As has been repeated, Christ is *the* covenant sacrifice. However, the *only* time that Christ identifies Himself in covenant terms is in His institution of Holy Communion. Christ was undoubtedly referencing Jeremiah's prediction by highlighting both "covenant" and "forgiveness of sins" in His Words of Institution: "For this is my *blood of the covenant*, which is to be shed on behalf of many *for the forgiveness of sins*."[176] Jeremiah had prophesied, as just quoted, that in God's *new covenant* He would *forgive their iniquity* and their sin He would remember no more. By His Words of Institution, Jesus is showing that His sacrificial blood fulfills this prophecy of Jeremiah.

In their records of the Last Supper, Matthew and Mark do not put the word "new" in front of the word "covenant." From these more abbreviated records one might wonder if indeed Christ was referencing Jeremiah's prediction. However, in the records of both Luke and Paul, Christ promised, "This cup is the *new covenant* in My blood." Along with certain other theologians, Darwell Stone maintains that Christ's *new covenant* wording, as recorded by Luke and Paul, would have *intentionally* called to mind "the promise of a 'new covenant' in the prophecies of Jeremiah."[177]

It is significant that Jeremiah's prediction interconnects two important kinds of Jewish sacrifice which are emphasized in the Eucharist: the peace offering and the sin offering. Consider first the peace offering. As Jeremiah predicted a *new covenant* he implied a peace offering. Not only because covenants were routinely ratified by a peace offering, but because the original covenant was ratified by a peace offering, the Jews would have realized that the new covenant predicted by Jeremiah would be ratified by a peace offering

---

[176] Matthew 26:28.
[177] Stone, *A History of the Doctrine*....,8. Daly, *Christian Sacrifice*, 221: "The Lukan-Pauline formulation....also includes reference to the familiar 'new covenant' passage in Jer. 31, 31-34."

as well. Christ's sacrifice on the cross is indeed that sacrifice of the new covenant. The final seal of covenant ratification was the peace offering meal. The peace offering meal—inferred in Jeremiah's prediction of a new covenant—directs God's people to Christ's institution of the Lord's Supper. Christians now participate in God's new covenant through *eating* the covenant sacrifice in the Sacrament of the Altar.

Jeremiah implied the presence of a sin offering when he predicted that when God would look at His people He would forgive their iniquity and cease to remember their sins. An OT Jew would have likely associated such a prediction of forgiveness with a sin offering (See Heb. 10:17,18). Christ's sacrifice at the altar of the cross is the ultimate sin offering. Recall that the sin offering (if it was not for the high priest) was prescribed to be eaten by the OT priests. Thus Jeremiah's prophecy—as it spoke of forgiveness—created a connection between the OT sin offering meal and the NT meal of the Holy Eucharist. The Sacrament of the Altar, like an OT sin offering meal, is drawn from a sin offering, and it is to be eaten by priests. As with an OT sin offering, all NT priests may and should eat of Christ's sin offering, for it was not sacrificed for the High Priest's sins (Jesus!). Who are such priests? All catechized and penitent Christians are now eligible priests, required and privileged to eat of *the* sin offering flesh.

Both the *sin offering* and the *peace offering* implied by Jeremiah's prediction are subsumed under Christ's words, "This cup is the *new covenant* in my blood, *shed for the remission of sins.*"[178] Jeremiah is thus observed to be—at least indirectly— predicting the *peace offering* meal Christ would institute to confirm the blessings of His new covenant. Similarly Jeremiah also indirectly identifies the future *sin offering* meal to be distributed to Christ's priestly band; a meal linked to the forgiveness that radiates from His sin offering sacrifice.[179]

---

[178] This wording combines Matthew 26:28 and 1 Corinthians 11:25.
[179] Jeremiah 31:31-34 is quoted in Hebrews 9:8-12.

The Death of the Testator

> *"For where a covenant [testament] is, there must of necessity be the death of the one who made it."*
> *Hebrews 9:16*

The words *covenant* and *testament* are often used interchangeably to translate a single Hebrew word or a single Greek word. Some contend that *covenant* should be the English word used when a "deal" is struck between two parties, and *testament* should be used when there is essentially a one-way "contract" from one party to another. Such a one-way contract is frequently considered a person's *will*—often called a *last will and testament*. Those receiving a person's will and *testament* certainly have obligations, and yet a testament is not a deal between "equals", but it is more of a regulated gift conveyed from a giver to a receiver. From this understanding, God—as the initiator and giver—should be identified as the *testator*, and His one way "contract" should be recognized as His *testament*. God presented such a "will and testament" twice—once through Moses at Sinai, and a second time through His Son at the Last Supper.[180]

When and how would such testaments be put into force? Hebrews 9:16f explains: "For where there is a testament, there must also of necessity be the death of the testator. For a testament is in force after men are dead, since it has no power at all while the testator lives."[181] This understanding of *testament* was emphasized by Martin Luther and others of his time. Luther said, "A testament, as everyone knows, is a promise made by one about to

---

[180] Hebrews 9:16-20 show that God's testament through Moses was indeed the "first" such testament. In both presentations of His testament one finds reference to "blood of the testament." Such testamental blood indicated a testament sealed by death, the giving of a life.
[181] NKJV

die, in which he designates his bequest and appoints his heirs."[182] Thus, even concerning the OT references to *testament*, Luther would write:

> Hence the words "covenant" and "testament of the Lord" occur so frequently in the Scriptures, which words signified that God would one day die [...] Now God made a testament: therefore it was necessary that He should die. But God could not die unless He became a man. Thus both the incarnation and the death of Christ are briefly comprehended in this one word "testament."[183]

The testamental nature of the Lord's Supper is obvious, for in this testamental meal the body and blood of the Son of God are bequeathed to His people—and what an inheritance this is! The inheritance possessed and consumed by Christ's people consists of the most valuable elements in the universe—the body and blood of the eternal Son of God. Though offered under the simple food of bread and wine, yet what is more precious than the body and blood of the incarnate Creator? Christ has willed His body and blood to His people, and this testament was officially activated when He, the testator, died. When He rose from the dead, His testament was verified to the utmost.

As one considers the Lord's Supper and its ingredients, one should realize that Christ's *will and testament* is to be treated as precise and irrevocable. Even as one would never consider modifying a mere human's will and testament, neither should one consider tampering with the words or elements of the Son of God's testament.[184]

---

[182] *Works of Martin Luther*, vol. 2, "The Babylonian Captivity," trans. A. T. W. Steinhaeuser (Philadelphia: Muhlenberg Press, 1915, renewed 1943), 196. Luther references Romans 4; Galatians 3,4; Hebrews 9 for this understanding of testament.
[183] Ibid., 197.
[184] An example of such tampering would be a change of ingredients.

The Sacrifice of Completion

> *"When Jesus therefore had received the sour wine, He said, 'It is finished,' and He bowed His head, and gave up His spirit."*
> *John 19:30*

The idea of "completion" was frequently associated with the peace offering. As already indicated, the peace offering was the finale in the sacrificial process. Alfred Edersheim explains that the peace offering "might be rendered, the offering of completion."[185] Since the peace offering was the finale in the stages of sacrifice, it was at times simply labeled the *sacrifice of the end*. From such a viewpoint, the Septuagint translator of Judges at times chose the Greek word for "the end (finish)" to translate the Hebrew for *peace offering*.[186]

The peace offering was sometimes simply called the "final" sacrifice, because the celebrative meal drawn from it stood as the final activity in the sacrificial process. One has to wonder if Christ's last words from the cross, "It is finished," indicate in a semi-technical way the completion of the sacrificial process. Christ's word for "finished" is a cognate of the word used for the peace offering, the final sacrifice in the sacrificial process. The final stage in the sacrificial process—the peace offering, the "finishing" sacrifice—has truly been offered. And now, after Christ's death, the only sacrificial activity remaining is the joy-related meal!

Many today fail to grasp the fact that OT sacrifice was directly connected to eating. Eating was part of the act of sacrifice. When Hicks explains that the concept of "sacrifice" is certainly "applicable to the act of eating with which the complete sacrificial action ended," one begins to understand why many in the early church perceived the Eucharist to be a

---

[185] Edersheim, *The Temple*..., 99.
[186] Judges 20:26, 21:4 use τελειας. 2 Chron. 29:31-35 speaks of the peace offering by using three different Greek terms: Τελειωσεως, σωτηριον, αινεσεως.

sacrificial activity, and thus it was often labeled as *sacrifice*.[187]

The "Salvation" Sacrifice

> *"This is the law of the salvation sacrifice, which they are to bring to the Lord."*
> **Leviticus 7:11**
> *(author's translation from the Septuagint)*

The Jews of Jesus' day were especially familiar with their official Greek translation of the OT, called the *Septuagint*. As they read and frequently listened to readings from the *Septuagint*, certain words must have created specific associations and mental pictures for such Jews.

As one relates the peace offering to the NT, an important communion connection is realized by a distinctive Greek word that created a unique image in the minds of the Jewish people. This Greek word was occasionally used for *salvation*, but more often it was used for the *peace offering*. One observes that the word was used infrequently, *except* to translate the Hebrew for *peace offering*. The Septuagint more often than not utilized this otherwise uncommon Greek word to translate the Hebrew word for the peace offering.[188] The Septuagint translators were so fond of this word for the peace offering, that out of the 86 times the Hebrew OT specified *peace offering*, 72 times this unique Greek word for *salvation* is used to translate it![189] This Greek word was thus a highly familiar technical term among the Jews of Jesus' day.

---

[187] Hicks, *The Fullness...*, 311. Hicks would concede to calling the Eucharist a sacrifice in so far as the peace offering meal is very much a part of the sacrificial process.

[188] It makes sense that the peace offering would be called a "salvation" sacrifice since the ultimate peace from God *is salvation*, centering in Christ's sacrifice on the cross.

[189] Georg Fohrer, σωτηριον in the LXX, vol. vii, *Theological Dictionary of the New Testament*, ed. Gerhard Kittel and Gerhard Friedrich, trans. Geoffrey W. Bromiley (Grand Rapids: Wm. B. Eerdmans Puiblishing Co., 1968), 1022-1023. This is *not* the common Greek for salvation, σωτηρια. The two words are similar, but σωτηριον is a substantive. Though used to translate *salvation* yet by far it is most frequently used in the LXX for *peace offering*.

Consequently when the Greek-speaking Jews used this special Greek word for *salvation*, they would have automatically thought of their *peace offering*.[190]

The statement of Simeon in Luke 2 becomes quite profound when one realizes the use of this word. God had promised Simeon he wouldn't die until he had seen the Christ. To fulfill God's regulations, the infant Jesus was brought to the temple by his parents. When the trio entered the temple, aged Simeon took the child in his arms and professed, "Lord, now You are letting Your servant depart in peace, according to Your word; for my eyes have seen Your *salvation* which You have prepared before the face of all peoples..."[191] Where the word *salvation* is found in this quote, Luke was inspired to use *not* the normal word for salvation, but the Greek technical term for *peace offering*. Simeon, the man speaking, is a Hebrew, and to him the peace offering was as common as Sunday dinner. Moreover he is speaking these words within the courts of the temple, *the* place associated with peace offerings. Furthermore, the first statement of Simeon is that he is ready to depart *in peace*. For these reasons it seems nearly certain that Simeon was intentionally referring to the Christ child as his *peace offering!*[192] Thus Simeon is saying, "Lord, now You are letting Your servant depart in peace, according to Your word; for my eyes have seen Your *peace offering*, which You have prepared before the face of all peoples..." Even the word *prepared* was a sacrificial term, describing how a creature was made ready for

---

[190] The NT texts where σωτηριος is found are: Luke 2:30; 3:6; Acts 28:28; Ephesians 6:17; Titus 2:11. Some believe that the substantivized σωτηριον should be separated from σωτηριος, and thus Titus 2:11 stands apart from the other four. See for example Robert Young, *Young's Ananlytical Concordance to the Bible* (Nashville: Thomas Nelson Publishers, 1980), 832.
[191] Luke 2:29-31. NKJV, Thomas Nelson Publishers.
[192] Cave, *The Scriptural Doctrine...*, 425: "Christ is the true peace offering: As Simeon said, 'Mine eyes have seen thy peace offering.'" Others who have seen this connection: Field, *The Apostolic Liturgy...*, 656; Kleinig, *Leviticus*, 95.

The Peace Offering, Portrayer of the Eucharist

sacrifice.[193] Simeon says that God Himself had *prepared* this peace offering not just for the Jews, but before the face of all people!

Since the Greek word employed by Luke in this account had been chosen 72 out of 86 times in the Septuagint to translate the Hebrew for *peace offering*, then Luke's record is almost certainly showing that Simeon—who probably spoke Aramaic—was referring to the baby Jesus as a *peace offering*.[194] Simeon actually understood that he held the peace offering, the baby Jesus. By identifying Jesus as such, Simeon was acknowledging Christ to be the finishing sacrifice—the sacrifice identifying the existence of peace with God, and the sacrifice that would ultimately be joyfully consumed. Salvation was a certainty even when Christ was an infant, as demonstrated by the angelic message to the Shepherds, "Glory to God in the highest and on earth *peace*, good will to men."[195] Thus Simeon could speak of Jesus as a peace offering, the offering that recognizes a peace from God already in place.

It is then perhaps no coincidence that certain liturgies have inserted these words of Simeon immediately following the Lord's Supper, for indeed God's people are able to depart *in peace* as they, like Simeon, recognize Christ as the *peace offering*.[196] Simeon could only hold the peace offering in his arms, but now in the Lord's Supper God's people literally do what had been done with peace offerings for millennia—they *eat* it!

---

[193] Walter Grundmann, ετοιμαζω, vol. II, *Theological Dictionary of the New Testament*, ed. Gerhard Kittel and Gerhard Friedrich, trans. Geoffrey W. Bromiley (Grand Rapids: Wm B. Eerdmans Publishing Co., 1968), 704ff, footnote 2, 704: "ετοιμαζειν is worth noting in connection with the sacrificial cultus: [...] cf. In the LXX 2 Ch. 35:12 (ολοκαυτωσις), 16 (λειτουργια κυριου)."

[194] Though it is nearly certain Simeon spoke Hebrew or Aramaic, yet Luke's inspired rendition must reflect Simeon's words, and what better Greek word for peace offering than the one used most frequently in the LXX?

[195] Luke 2:14.

[196] E.g. *The Lutheran Hymnal* 29-30. It is entirely possible that the liturgical placement of this canticle after Holy Communion is mere coincidence. However, its placement makes perfect sense in relation to the peace offering, for indeed God's people in the Eucharist have, like Simeon, experienced a physical encounter with *the* peace offering, Jesus.

The Sacrifice of Praise

> *"And let them offer to him the sacrifice of praise, and proclaim his works with exultation."*
> *Psalm 107:22 (Septuagint)*

The peace offering was a celebration sacrifice,[197] and as such it was directly related to praising God. Consequently, as John Field observes, it "was frequently called, the Sacrifice of Praise."[198] This terminology, *sacrifice of praise*, was employed in the Septuagint, to reflect the fact that temple-related praise—which even employed hired singers—was directly linked to the sacrifice of thank offerings.[199] The general Hebrew word for *peace offering* was usually translated into Greek with that special *salvation* word just discussed. However, the Hebrew word for *thank offering* would at times be translated into Greek by words that literally mean *sacrifice of praise*. Brooke Westcott explains that the phrase *sacrifice of praise* recorded in Leviticus 7:12 refers to "the highest form of peace-offering."[200] When good things happened to God's OT people, they would thank God with both audible praise and with a sacrifice of praise (a peace offering). Some have read in the Scriptures the phrase s*acrifice of praise*, and only considered it to be verbal praise. It is true that preaching, prayer, confession and all good works are *sacrifices of praise* as they flow from Christ.[201] In the OT, however, the thanksgiving peace offering itself was called a *sacrifice of praise*, and in the immolation of such a sacrifice, a person or family would praise God both by *giving* the sacrifice and by *eating* the holy meal drawn from it.

---

[197] Hicks, *The Fullness...*, 93, "That it [peace offering] remained the most joyful of the sacrifices is beyond doubt, if only from the constant expression of this in Deuteronomy..."
[198] Field, *The Apostolic Liturgy...*, 92.
[199] Kleinig, *Leviticus,* 160.
[200] Westcott, *The Epistle...*, 443. θυσιαν αινεσεος, is the Greek. Hicks, *The Fullness...*, 294: "The 'sacrifice of praise' was the peace-offering."
[201] *The Book of Concord* (Tappert), 253.

The Peace Offering, Portrayer of the Eucharist

Several Psalms utilized this thank offering terminology. The following Psalm portions from the Septuagint speak of the peace offering (thank offering) as *sacrifice of praise*. At times they refer to spoken praise as *sacrifice of praise*, but they do this in a peace offering context. Italicized portions and bracketed comments further explain the peace offering connotations:

> Offer to God the *sacrifice of praise*;[202] and *pay thy vows* [peace offering reference] to the Most High. [...] The *sacrifice of praise* will glorify me: and that is the way wherein I will show to him the *salvation* [peace offering term] of God. (Psalm 50:14,23)[203]

> And let them offer to him the *sacrifice of praise*, and proclaim his works with *exultation*. [Exultation is fitting for the peace offering.] (Psalm 107:22)

> I will offer to thee the *sacrifice of praise*, and will call upon the *name*[204] of the Lord. I will *pay my vows* [peace offering reference] unto the Lord, in the presence of all his people, *in the courts of the Lord's house*, in the midst of thee, Jerusalem. [The reference to this *sacrifice of praise* being accomplished in God's house shows that peace offerings are being spoken of.] (Psalm 116:17,18)[205]

Christ is now the actual sacrifice of praise; His praise is *the* praise.

---

[202] The Greek here, θυσιαν αινεσεως, is a translation of the Hebrew word for thank offering. This is the case for each of these Psalm references.

[203] All Psalms quoted from here on are from the LXX, yet we maintain the English numbering of the Psalms.

[204] Frequently praise and prayer have as their object, "His Name." In the worship setting God's Name was the place of the altar. See e. g. Deut. 12:5-7; Ex. 20:24.

[205] Concerning the Eucharistic nature of Psalm 116, see Neale and Littledale, *A Commentary...*, 504: "This Psalm, from verse 10 to the end, is one of those appointed to be recited by Priests of the Western Church before saying Mass."

The church's preaching, prayers, confessions and all good works flow from His sacrifice, and of His sacrifice the church may now eat—praising God as she eats of the *sacrifice of praise*!

The Confession Sacrifice

> *"For the inward thought of man shall give "confession" to thee: and the memorial of his inward thought shall keep a feast to thee."*
> *Psalm 76:10 (Septuagint)*

In the Septuagint, the Jewish "official" Greek translation of the OT, the peace offering was also occasionally called a *confession sacrifice*.[206] There is good evidence that when an offerer approached God's altar to sacrifice a peace offering he would lay his hands upon the sacrifice and then—instead of confessing *his sins* as with the burnt, sin and guilt offerings—he would speak a *confession* of *praise*.

Information pertaining to such temple-related practices comes to us through that scholarly Jew of the middle ages, Maimonides. "According to Maimonides, in peace-offerings a record [confession] of God's praise, rather than a confession of sins, was spoken."[207] John Field specifically connects such "confession" sacrifices to the Lord's Supper: "Now the peace-offering, which this word *Confession* represents, is the form of sacrifice under the Mosaic Law which corresponds most closely with the Christian Eucharist."[208] Shall not Christians confess the highest praise as they come to the Eucharist?

---

[206] Otto Michel, ομολεγεω [and cognates], vol. V, *Theological Dictionary of the New Testament*, ed. Gerhard Kittel and Gerhard Friedrich, trans. Geoffrey W. Bromiley (Grand Rapids: Wm. B. Eerdmans Publishing Co., 1968), 202. Field, *The Apostolic Liturgy...*, 93: "And accordingly, this word *Confession*, like the word *Eucharist* or *Thanksgiving*, was one of the terms in the Jewish Church for the Peace-offering."
[207] Edersheim, *The Temple..*, 82.
[208] Field, *The Apostolic Liturgy...*, 95.

The Peace Offering, Portrayer of the Eucharist

In the Psalms, the Greek word used to translate *peace offering* is at times that word which often means *confession*. In English it is frequently translated *thanksgiving*. In several Psalms this Greek word for *confession (thanksgiving)*—even when it is not used specifically to identify a sacrifice—is we believe a flag identifying the presence of the peace offering in the context of a given Psalm. Frequently such Psalms reference the temple, tabernacle or simply God's altar—thus implying a sacrifice. Italics and footnotes identify peace offering markers in the following Psalm portions. When we place *confession* in brackets, it indicates that the previous word is that special Greek word[209] used for the peace offering; very often the word indicates also the verbal confession of praise connected to the peace offering:

> ...I will go to the place of thy *wondrous tabernacle*, even to the *house of God*, with a voice of *exultation* and *thanksgiving* ["confession"] and of the sound of those who keep *festival* [peace offering feast]. [...] Hope in God; for I will *give thanks* ["confession"] to him; he is the *salvation*[210] of my countenance. (Psalm 42:4, 5b)

> And I will go to the *altar of God*, to God who gladdens my youth: I will *give thanks* ["confession"] to thee on the harp[211], O God, my God. [...] Hope in God; for I will *give thanks* ["confession"] to him, who is the *health*[212] of my countenance, and my God. (Psalm 43:4,5b)

> For the inward thought of man shall *give thanks* ["confession"] to thee: and the *memorial* of his inward thought shall *keep a feast* to

---

[209] ομολεγεω and its cognates are the words under study here.
[210] The Greek word is σωτηριον (not σωτηρια), *the* technical term for the peace offering in the LXX translation of the Pentateuch. This is one of the rare instances when this word is not used specifically for the peace offering; how appropriate, though, for a peace offering context!
[211] To say that the Psalmist gives thanks on the harp or with song or even in dance does not lessen the likelihood that peace offerings are being referred to. Quite the contrary, such actions were part of the resultant godly celebration associated with the peace offering.
[212] σωτηριον. See footnote 210.

thee. *Vow and pay your vows* [votive offering] *to the Lord your God; all that are round about him shall bring gifts*[213]... (Psalm 76:10,11)

Let us come before *his presence* [at the temple] with *thanksgiving* ["confession"[214]], *and make a joyful noise unto him with Psalms.* (Psalm 95:2)

Enter into his gates with *thanksgiving* ["confession"], and his courts with hymns; *give thanks* ["confession"] to him, *praise* his *name*. (Psalm 100:4)[215]

I will *give thanks* ["confession"], O Lord, with my whole heart; I will sing psalms to thee *before the angels* [worship language[216]]; for thou hast heard all the words of my mouth. I will *worship toward thy holy temple*, and *give thanks* ["confession"] to *thy name*, on account of thy mercy and thy truth. (Psalm 138:1,2a)[217]

---

[213] δωρα is frequently a sacrificial term. Jesus uses this term in the NT when He speaks of bringing your "gift" to the altar (Mt. 5:23f) Also throughout Matthew this word is used for sacrifice. The church has rightly applied Mt. 5:23f to the Lord's Supper. "Gift" often was equated with "Qorban", which often was a general word for sacrifice (Mark 7:11).

[214] This use of εξομολογησει is a translation of the Hebrew technical word for thank offering.

[215] Neale and Littledale, *A Commentary...*, 269: "The Rabbinical interpretation of this verse is that, in the days of Messiah, all the sacrifices of the Law will be done away save the thank-offering of flour or bread, so that the coarse rites of slaughter of animal victims, suggestive of pollution and sin, shall have no place under the New Covenant. How precisely this accords... with the prophecy of Malachi..."

[216] The Scriptures describe angels as joining us in worship. Communion liturgies yet today retain reference to the presence of angels as we gather to worship. E.g. in *The Lutheran Hymnal*, 25: "Therefore with angels and archangels and all the company of heaven..."

[217] So many other Psalms could also be considered in relation to the peace offering. See e.g. Hicks, pp. 95,96: "...the peace offering is definitely a eucharstic meal: [See] Psalm 22:25f...as it is in Psalms 26:6-8,12 and 27:1,4-6...So too the Psalms 42 and 43...I need not add quotations; but they could be supplied from such Psalms as 54:6; 56:12f, 81:10, 87:7; 92 (The Sabbath Psalm), 95:2,7, 100:esp. 3, 107:9,17-22; 116; 118. Even Psalm 119 [e.g. verses 103, 108] ...In Psalm 103:3-5 He forgives--heals--redeems--crowneth thee with lovingkindness and tender mercies,...satisfieth thy mouth with good things; and in Psalm 111...Who hath given meat unto them that fear Him, (verse 5), Who will ever be mindful of His covenant (verse 5)--God to whom the memorial, the 'Azkarah', is not made in vain."

Eating of the Tithe and the First-born

> *"And there [at God's dwelling] you shall bring...your tithes...and the first-born of your herd and of your flock...There also you and your households shall eat before the Lord your God..."*
> *Deuteronomy 12:6,7*

Both the *tithe* and the sacrifice of the *first-born* were classified as peace offerings.[218] In Deuteronomy 12:17,18 Moses explains the communion nature of these sacrifices while listing them with other peace offerings. By listing *tithes* and the sacrifice of the *first-born* together with peace offerings, Moses thus inferred their peace offering status:

> You are not allowed *to eat* within your gates *the tithe* of your grain, or new wine, or oil, or the *first-born* of your herd or flock, or any of your votive offerings which you vow, or your freewill offerings, or the contribution [heave offering] of your hand. But *you shall eat them* before the Lord your God in the place which the Lord your God will choose... [italics added][219]

Observe that part of the tithe and sacrifice of the first-born were *eaten before the Lord*. This identifies them with the central peace offering rubric.

As shown in previous chapters, several sacrificial practices directly related to the Passover. The sacrifice of first-born animals demonstrated yet another connection between the sacrificial system and the Passover. The Passover event had magnified the concept of first-born, because in the Passover the sparing of the first-born children established God's ownership of

---

[218] Kurtz, *Offerings, Sacrifices* . . ., 441ff. Kurtz maintains the first-born (and tithe?) are not ordinary thank offerings, but perhaps better seen as totally "owned" by the priests who would then offer portions of them as thank offerings. We agree with Keil, summarized by Kurtz on 441, that the first-born livestock are indeed thank offerings, eaten regularly by the laity as such.
[219] See also Deuteronomy 12:5-7.

them. Since God had spared the first-born, He then desired the first-born of man and livestock be dedicated to Him, and such dedication was incorporated into the regulations for the Jewish sacrificial system. Robert Daly maintains that "the dedication etc. of the first-born (and therefore concerning also the ransom-redemption and the substitution ideas) are associated without exception with the Paschal [Passover] feast."[220] None will argue that the Eucharist is also *associated without exception with the Paschal feast.* The Lord's Supper is then connected to the sacrifice of first-born creatures simply because of the Passover association. Additionally, Christ *the* first-born is typified by the sacrifice of first-born creatures. As God's OT people could commune with Him through their first-born animals, how much more profoundly do God's people today commune with God through *the One* who is *the* first-born from the dead![221]

The *General Sacramental Eating* associated with the eating of first-born creatures enables Christians to better sense the *Specific Sacramental Eating* of Holy Communion. This is also true of the tithe.

Giving to the poor was an important act associated with the tithe offerings. This fit the pattern of the peace offering, because those sacrifices more commonly identified as peace offerings also involved the giving of alms. Charitable giving, as will be explained shortly, was also connected to the celebration of the Lord's Supper in the early church.

---

[220] Daly, *Christian Sacrifice*, 205. Daly makes the same connection with *first-fruits*.
[221] Colossians 1:18.

The Consecration Sacrifice

> *"And Aaron and his sons shall eat the flesh of the ram, and the bread that is in the basket, at the doorway of the tent of meeting."*
> *Exodus 29:32*

Especially at the ordination of priests, the peace offering functioned as a *consecration* or *ordination* sacrifice. When Aaron and his sons were consecrated, Kurtz explains that "the true consecration-offering was neither the sin-offering nor the burnt-offering which followed it, but simply and solely the peace-offering, which concluded the whole ceremony..."[222] The following is the pertinent excerpt from the account of the ordination of Aaron and his sons:

> Then Moses said to Aaron and to his sons, "Boil the flesh at the doorway of the tent of meeting, *and eat it there together with the bread* which is in the basket of the ordination offering, just as I commanded, saying, 'Aaron and his sons *shall eat it.* [italics added]'"[223]

This unique peace offering, which Moses emphatically commanded be eaten, sealed the *high priesthood* upon Aaron and the *priesthood* upon Aaron's sons. Unlike other peace offerings that were only considered *holy*, the priestly ordination peace offering was *most holy*, and consequently only Aaron and his sons could eat of it. In the verses just cited, one observes that an ordination offering forthrightly connected *bread* with the sacrificial *flesh*—these were to be eaten together. Of this special peace offering *flesh* God

---

[222] Kurtz, *Offerings...*, 332.
[223] Leviticus 8:31.

commanded, "Eat it there together with the bread."[224] Such bread and flesh conjoined in a sacred meal stand as an earthy picture of the bread and flesh conjoined in the heavenly feast of the Lord's Supper. This ceremony and meal for Aaron and his sons continued for seven successive days, and "on the eighth day the persons initiated entered upon the independent discharge of their priestly functions..."[225]

As one considers the priestly nature of all NT believers, such OT sacrificial eating wonderfully prefigures the Lord's Supper. As abundantly attested in the epistle to the Hebrews, Christ is the great High Priest, and, as attested in Hebrews and elsewhere, all Christians are priests.[226] Christ is of course the antitype of every sacrifice, so again He is perceived to be the *consecration peace offering*. Christ's once-sacrificed body and blood consecrate Him and all of His people as priests.[227] As Christ and his people now eat of the meal He instituted, He is recognized as the ultimate High Priest, and His people are recognized as priests under Him. Christians, the priesthood of believers, miraculously eat of Christ's flesh *together with the bread*, even as flesh and bread were united in the consecration meal of the OT priests. When one receives his first Communion, he is embarking upon the loftiest priestly privileges he will ever encounter in the worship setting.[228]

Sacrifices for ordination into the priesthood, like all other OT sacrifices, were performed until Christ came. His sacrifice is the final ordination sacrifice. Now, once again, all that is left is the meal.

Not only were *priests* consecrated by a special peace offering, but many have noted a similar practice for the coronation of *kings*. E. J. Young

---

[224] Perhaps this was the special *leavened* bread associated with the peace offering.

[225] Kurtz, *Offerings*..., 340. The early church appropriated the symbolic significance of the eighth day for circumcision. Kurtz is convinced that there is sufficient biblical evidence that every time a new High Priest was ordained, the same procedure was used.

[226] E.g. Hebrews 4:14 for Christ's High Priesthood; 1 Peter 2:4-10 for our priesthood.

[227] As noted already, some theologians have maintained that Christ's priestly work really did not begin until after the resurrection/ascension.

[228] We are not here saying that a Christian becomes a priest at this point. Priestly privileges were conferred at his/her baptism.

explains that "it was customary after a coronation to sacrifice and to celebrate a sacrificial meal."[229] Thus when Saul was consecrated as Israel's first king, the Holy Spirit informs us, "There they also offered sacrifices of peace offerings before the Lord; and there Saul and all the men of Israel rejoiced greatly."[230] These peace offerings indicated a sacred feast. When Samuel was on his way to Bethlehem to anoint David as the next king, the Lord told him, "Take a heifer with you, and say, 'I have come to sacrifice to the Lord.' And you shall invite Jesse to the sacrifice...and you shall anoint for Me the one whom I designate to you."[231] Again coronation peace offerings were sacrificed when certain leaders tried to establish Adonijah as king over Israel: "And he has sacrificed oxen and fatlings and sheep in abundance, and has invited all the sons of the king [to the meal]... "[232]

Who then is the King of kings and the Lord of lords? Young is convinced that the coronation banquet of Christ is predicted in Isaiah's 25th chapter.[233] Isaiah 24:23 briefly yet wonderfully describes Christ's coronation: "For the Lord of hosts will reign on Mount Zion and in Jerusalem." Isaiah 25:6 then presents the banquet: "And the Lord of hosts shall make a feast for all the nations: on this mount they shall drink gladness, they shall drink wine: they shall anoint themselves with ointment in this mountain...."[234] Such a prediction indicates celebrative eating at the coronation of the Great King. Truly Christians shall join in this coronation banquet in heaven, but are they not already joining in His royal coronation banquet as they eat the Eucharist here and now?[235]

---

[229] E. J. Young, *The Book of Isaiah* vol. II, (Grand Rapids: Wm. B. Eerdmans Publishing Co., 1969), 191.
[230] 1 Samuel 11:15.
[231] 1 Samuel 16:2,3. Verse 5 identifies the peace offering nature: "In peace I have come to sacrifice..."
[232] 1 Kings 1:19. See also verses 9,25.
[233] Young, *The Book of Isaiah*, 191.
[234] Translation from *The Septuagint Version of the Old Testament with an English Translation* (Grand Rapids: Zondervan, 1970).
[235] 1 Kings 19:21 shows a prophet's ordination connected with a peace offering feast.

Christians are all priests. However, Christ's people are not only declared to be priests, but kings as well! Christians receive their anointing as priests and kings in Holy Baptism. The Lord's Supper can then be seen to connote the coronation banquet identifying not only the King of kings, but identifying the *royal* priesthood of believers as well: "To Him who loved us, and washed us from our sins by His blood, and has *made us kings and priests* to His God and Father; to Him be the glory and the dominion forever and ever. Amen."[236]

Pagans and Peace Offering Meals

> *"For they invited the people to the sacrifices of their gods, and the people ate and bowed down to their gods."*
> **Numbers 25:2**

Before leaving the discussion of the peace offering, it is helpful to consider the negative practices related to it.

The major attraction of paganism is that it is fun and upbeat, celebrating especially the earth and her glory. Many forms of paganism have existed, but they all seem to return to a worship and celebration of the earthy, and the worship of self. Within such pagan celebrations, even before the Jewish sacrificial system, sacrifice was quite common.[237] Pagan sacrifices were mere corruptions of the *true* peace and burnt offerings offered to God. Thus sacrificial eating was illegitimately yet commonly practiced in pagan worship.

Carousing and partying are often basic elements of pagan religion, with an attitude of self-indulgence. It is no wonder then that when a peace offering was offered before a pagan god, it incited the people not to true,

---
[236] Revelation 1:5,6; NKJV. The blood reference here brings in Christ's sacrifice. We are called the *royal* priesthood in 1 Peter 2:9.
[237] E.g. Genesis 31:54.

godly rejoicing, but to "eating and drinking and *rising up to play*."[238] The "peace offerings" sacrificed to pagan gods thus became "legitimized" occasions for godless partying and acts of immorality.

An example of this occurred when Moses tarried on Mount Sinai and the children of Israel fashioned a golden calf as an idol. The biblical record relates their worship of this idol: "So the next day they rose early and offered burnt offerings, and brought *peace offerings*; and the people sat down to eat and to drink and rose up to play."[239] When the text explains that they began to "eat and to drink and rose up to play," it is simply reporting the activity that surrounded the peace offering that had just been offered to this idol. They *ate* and they *celebrated* (rose to play), only this *worship* was wholly pagan—a worship of the golden calf.[240]

Recall how St. Paul, in 1 Corinthians 10, introduced a discussion about the Lord's Supper by speaking of this pagan sacrificial eating performed by the Jews at Sinai: "And do not be idolaters, as some of them were; as it is written, 'The people sat down to eat and drink, and stood up to play.'"[241] One would have difficulty realizing why St. Paul speaks of *idolatry* as *eating* and *playing* unless one understood that the eating and partying was directly connected to the pagan peace offering offered to the golden calf. As such, it constituted a *worship* of the golden calf; by this eating and drinking, the children of Israel were in idolatrous communion with the golden calf.

Shortly after this quote the Apostle Paul introduced the *true* Communion, namely the Lord's Supper: "The cup of blessing which we bless, is it not the communion of the blood of Christ? The bread which we break, is it not the communion of the body of Christ?"[242]   By bringing the Lord's

---

[238] Exodus 32:6.
[239] Exodus 32:6.
[240] Observe also in Exodus 32 how Aaron and the people tried to justify this peace offering by saying that it was to the LORD. The insidiousness of syncretism is that it names the worship of the true God but mixes it with the worship of other gods. Such worship is a grave evil.
[241] 1 Corinthians 10:7.
[242] 1 Corinthians 10:16, NKJV.

Supper into the discussion, the learned apostle directed his hearers to *the true* peace offering, whereby they are truly blessed through communing with the true God, celebrating in a godly manner. Christ's sacrifice is *the* peace offering; Holy Communion is *the* peace offering meal.

Since many of the Corinthians most likely came from pagan backgrounds, they had questions about pagan communion and about eating the meat that had been sacrificed to idols. In verses 19-21, the Apostle Paul then addresses such questions pertaining to pagan "communion":

> What do I mean then? That a thing sacrificed to idols is anything, or that an idol is anything? No, but I say that the things which the Gentiles sacrifice, they sacrifice to demons, and not to God; and I do not want you to become sharers ["koinonia"] in demons. You cannot drink the cup of the Lord [Holy Communion] and the cup of demons [pagan communion]; you cannot partake of the table of the Lord [Holy Communion] and the table of demons [pagan communion].

Are idols anything? No, but to commune with them is to commune with demons! Paul is not expressing this theology for the first time. God had already said it in Deuteronomy 32:17: "They sacrificed to demons, not God." This then is also the danger yet today should a missionary attend a pagan sacrifice and eat.[243]

This kind of warning for God's people comes up again and again. Returning to the OT, shortly after the golden calf incident God informed His people:

> ...you shall not worship any other god, for the Lord, whose name is Jealous, is a jealous God—lest you make a covenant with the

---

[243] 1 Corinthians 8:10 shows how there *could be* Christian liberty to dine in the public hall of a pagan deity, but in the text referenced above Paul gives a very strong warning.

inhabitants of the land and they play the harlot with their gods, and sacrifice to their gods, and someone invite you *to eat of his sacrifice.* [italics added]"[244]

Recall that a *covenant sacrifice* was a *peace offering.* Here God warns His people not to enter into a covenant with another god and subsequently worship *by eating* of the covenant sacrifice.

Another example demonstrates again the sacramental understanding of "joining together" with a false god by the act of sacrificial eating: "For they [the Moabites] invited the [Jewish] people to the sacrifices of their gods, and *the people ate* and bowed down to their gods. So Israel joined themselves to Baal of Peor, and the Lord was angry against Israel."[245] They *ate* of sacrifices offered to Baal, and by this act they were joined to—in communion with—this false deity.

The Children of Israel also sacrificially ate and drank at locations called the "high places." Sometimes such eating was associated with a worship of the true God, but more often it was done in the worship of false gods.[246]

Warnings about sacrificial eating in relation to false gods are observed in various NT texts. Some of these warnings are found in the last book of the Bible, where, for instance, Christ admonishes the Christians at Pergamum: "But I have a few things against you, because you have there some who hold the teaching of Balaam, who kept teaching Balak to put a stumbling block before the sons of Israel, *to eat things sacrificed to idols*, and to commit acts of immorality."[247] Again in the book of Revelation, Christ chides the church at Thyatira, "But I have this against you, that you tolerate the woman Jezebel, who calls herself a prophetess, and she teaches and

---

[244] Exodus 34:14,15.
[245] Numbers 25:2,3.
[246] Of the true God see 1 Samuel 9:12,13. Of false gods see 1 Kings 12:32,33.
[247] Revelation 2:14.

leads My bondservants astray, so that they commit acts of immorality and *eat things sacrificed to idols.*"[248] Such warnings against eating sacrifices offered to other gods infer that there is a true sacrificial eating practiced by God's people: the Lord's Supper! Satan has his counterfeits.

Lest someone think the book of Revelation is "too cryptic," consider that a similar admonition was appended to James' highly regarded church council letter. In this letter, the Jerusalem council warned that Christians throughout Christendom should "abstain from [eating] things sacrificed to idols..."[249] This was a general letter of instruction for all of Christendom, attempting to create unity between Jew and Gentile. In this short conciliatory letter the church council felt obligated to warn about pagan *sacrificial eating*. By including such a directive in this brief exhortation, the Apostles indicated that sacrificial eating was not an insignificant matter.

How do these warnings apply to God's people in these later centuries? First, it is inconsistent to eat the Lord's Supper and simultaneously to eat food directly connected with pagan worship. Are there pagan sacrifices today? Certainly! And perhaps Christians will see more of this as the world appears to be moving increasingly toward pagan religious practices. Second, *worship involved eating*, and *what* a person eats and *with whom* he eats, even in today's worship, are not trivial matters.

If indeed the eating of pagan sacrifices is a real communing with demons, how much more shall Christ's people desire the true Communion, eating and drinking of the once-sacrificed body and blood of the Son of God, entering into a communion with the living God! Satan almost always has counterfeits of God's truths; shall Christians not avert his communion counterfeits by regularly eating and drinking of the *true* sacrificial meal, the Lord's Supper? Christ's people have the real thing; may they dine with and upon the true God regularly!

---

[248] Revelation 2:20.

[249] Acts 15:29. Acts 21:25 shows how this related to eating. We believe the prohibitions in the Jerusalem Council letter especially addressed pagan worship.

Sharing a Meal with the Poor

> *"And the Levite, because he has no portion or inheritance among you, and the alien, the orphan and the widow who are in your town shall come and eat [the tithe] and be satisfied..."*
> Deuteronomy 14:29

God needs nothing from us. He desires our thanks, however, and repeatedly He explains that by helping the poor we can render thanks and honor to Him. "He who oppresses the poor reproaches his Maker, but he who is gracious to the needy honors Him."[250] It should then come as no surprise that helping the needy has frequently been recognized as an important part of worship.

Recall that the Jewish tithe was considered a form of thank offering, from which the giver was to eat, and from which he was to *donate* to the Levites and the needy. The tithe, the major part of which was collected every third year, was a return to God that amounted to 10% of a person's earnings. An example of the tithe-meal to be given to the poor is recorded in Deuteronomy 14:22,23,28,29:

> You shall surely tithe all the produce from what you sow, which comes out of the field every year. And you shall eat in the presence of the Lord your God, at the place where He chooses to establish His name, the tithe of your grain, your new wine, your oil, and the first-born of your herd and your flock.[...] At the end of every third year you shall bring out all the tithe of your produce in that year, and shall deposit it in your town. And the *Levite*, because he has no portion or inheritance among you, and the *alien, the orphan and the widow* who are in your town shall come and eat and be satisfied... [italics added]

---

[250] Proverbs 14:31.

The tithe was a means through which thanksgiving was offered to God by returning a portion to Him, and some of this portion returned to God was a *meal shared with the alien, the orphan and the widow.* What better way to offer thanks to God than by sharing with those in need?

Besides the tithe, peace offerings in general were also shared with the poor. Gayford explains that in eating the peace offering, "it was a meritorious act to invite guests and *especially the poor* to share in this banquet."[251] Concerning the special peace offerings sacrificed at festivals such as Pentecost, "the poor and the Levite were bidden as the Lord's welcome guests."[252]

It should be borne in mind that none of the OT sacred meals were equivalent to partaking of the Lord's Supper. Though these OT meals presented a generic communion with God, they did not offer any literal communion in the body and blood of Christ, and again, in contrast to the mere sampling of bread and wine in Lord's Supper, these OT sacrifices presented an occasion for a full nutritional meal. The major purpose behind inviting the poor to such peace offerings was simply to give them a good meal. Nevertheless, the poor who ate of the peace offering flesh had to be ceremonially clean, thus again demonstrating that these meals were still worship-oriented.[253] Probably then the wisest direct comparison between the peace offering and the Lord's Supper should be in the *priestly* consumption of this holy meal. Only the priest and his family were to eat of their peace offering food, and thus they were not even to share it with the poor; yet the priests found other ways to give to the poor. Christians are the priesthood of believers, and only the priests are to eat of Christ's sacred peace offering; nonetheless, Christ's people are never exempt from giving to the poor.

NT believers, like the OT partakers of the eucharist (thank offering),

---

[251] Gayford, *Sacrifice...*, 38. Italics added.
[252] Edersheim, *The Temple...*, 211.
[253] Leviticus 7:19-21

realize it is appropriate to eat of the NT Eucharist with a view toward thanking God, and one of the supreme ways to thank God is by sharing with the needy. The early church viewed an outward expression of Eucharistic thanks to be not only their prayers but also their distribution of food and clothing to the needy. Christians have always responded to Christ's sacrifice by returning a portion of their physical blessings both to God's work and to those in need. God's people are "a holy priesthood, to offer up spiritual sacrifices acceptable to God through Jesus Christ."[254]

As noted already, the Jewish Passover was seen to be linked to the peace offering. Consistent then with the usual peace offering practice, the Jews maintained an intensified almsgiving during the week of the Passover. This practice is described in the *Book of Concord:*

> Individuals coming to the celebration of the Passover had to bring some gift as a contribution. Originally the Christians kept this practice. The apostolic canons show that when they gathered they brought bread, wine, and other things. Part of this was taken to be consecrated, the rest was distributed to the poor.[255]

The early Christian church conscientiously maintained this Jewish practice of "eucharist charity" in relation to the Lord's Supper. Though they did not share the actual Lord's Supper with the non-catechized needy, yet the "agape meal" (love feast), which preceded the Lord's Supper, was a meal shared with the poor. Apparently such love feasts were regularly eaten before joining in the Lord's Supper.[256] Abuses associated with this pre-communion charitable meal caused St. Paul to write to the Corinthians:

> Therefore when you meet together, it is not to eat the Lord's

---

[254] 1 Peter 2:5.
[255] *The Book of Concord* (Tappert), 265.
[256] See Jude 12; 2 Peter 2:13.

Supper, for in your eating [the love feast] each one takes his own supper first; and one is *hungry* and another is drunk. What! Do you not have houses in which to eat and drink? Or do you despise the church of God, and shame *those who have nothing*? [italics added][257]

A Christian's gift to the hungry should not shame them through a haughty, condescending attitude. The body and blood of Christ not only motivate His people to help the needy, but Christ's body and blood become the Christian's avenue by which such actions redound as a thanksgiving to God. Christ became the peace offering when He died on the cross, now His people can offer God a sacrifice of thanksgiving as they share their wealth with the poor.

Concluding Remarks

John Kleinig summarizes superbly: "The Lord's Supper is therefore the ultimate and definitive peace offering—not a new or ongoing sacrifice, but the Meal in which the communicant receives the offering provided by God the Father through the once-for-all sacrifice of His Son."[258] The peace offering truly stood as an impressive type of the Lord's Supper. All who were ceremonially clean could eat of the peace offering, and simultaneous with such eating they rejoiced in God's peace. How much more shall God's NT people now anxiously desire to eat and rejoice as they partake of that Peace Offering which confirms and proclaims the peace that surpasses understanding!

---

[257] 1 Corinthians 11:20-22.
[258] Kleinig, *Leviticus*, 95f.

> *"And the one who presents his offering shall present to the Lord a grain offering...and you shall prepare wine for the libation..."*
> **Numbers 15:4,5**

Chapter Seven

THE GRAIN OFFERING, FOOD OF HOLY COMMUNION

Bread and wine are common foods, and they have frequently come to the fore in God's dealings with man. The first baker was the first man, fallen Adam, who was told he would eat bread until he returned to dust.[1] The first vintager was the secondary first man, Noah, who was shamefully exposed because of his winebibbing.[2] Melchizedek, while presenting bread and wine, blessed Abraham.[3] Bread and wine were also the basic elements of the Jewish grain offering, the topic of this chapter. Now Christ, who is the new Adam and the antitype of priestly Melchizedek, has sanctified these grain offering ingredients to be the vehicles of His flesh and blood, so that the world, inherited from Adam and Noah, can truly be refreshed.

There is an uninterrupted rhythm as one steps from OT worship into NT worship. That rhythm is not only observed as it flows from the animal sacrifices, but also as it flows from the grain offering. The divine ritual surrounding the grain offering, like that of the animal sacrifices, has certain counterparts in Holy Communion. Consider the following grain offering traits to be explored in this chapter. The grain offering was basically *unleavened*

---

[1] Genesis 3:19.
[2] Genesis 9:20ff.
[3] Genesis 14:18-20. See also Psalm 110 and Hebrews 5 & 7.

bread, a portion of which was frequently eaten *with the flesh* of certain sacrifices.[4] Upon entrance into the Holy Land, the *unleavened bread* of the grain offering was always to be offered with *grape wine*. Of all the sacrificial portions, the grain offering was the kind most closely associated with a *remembrance (memorial)* before God. Finally, the grain offering stood as the only sacrificial substance in the Jewish sacrificial system from which both God and man *ate the identical food*.

Grain Offering Directives

> **"The priest then shall take up from the grain offering its memorial portion, and shall offer it up in smoke on the altar as an offering by fire of a soothing aroma to the Lord. And the remainder of the grain offering belongs to Aaron and his sons; a thing most holy, of the offerings to the Lord by fire."**
> **Leviticus 2:9,10**

The *grain offering* has been translated as *meal offering, cereal offering, food offering,* and in the old English of the KJV it was called a *meat offering*. Referring to it as a *meat offering* has generated much confusion among those who read the KJV, because "meat" in modern English means "flesh," but the *grain offering (meat offering)* was never the sacrifice of flesh.

Consider the main rubrics surrounding the grain offering. It was basically presented as unleavened bread, with literally a handful of it burned as a memorial upon the Bronze Altar, and the remainder eaten by the priests.[5]

---

[4] It is unknown whether the grain offerings were *always* eaten with sacrificial flesh.
[5] Brooke Westcott, *The Epistle to the Hebrews* (Grand Rapids: Eerdmans Publishing Company, 1973), 292: "The unbloody offerings [grain offerings] of the people except the part burnt as a 'memorial' ....were eaten by the priests alone in the court of the sanctuary: Lev. vii.9f; x.12ff."

The Grain Offering, Food of Holy Communion

After the Israelites entered the Promised Land, God specified that a wine-offering was to be offered with every grain offering.[6] A liquid offering such as wine was called a *libation*. This sacrifice-related wine was entirely poured at the base of the Bronze Altar[7]—at the same place where the sin offering blood was poured. Even though the priests were *commanded to eat* the bread of the grain offering, they were absolutely *forbidden to drink* wine in God's courts.[8]

The grain offering was offered in conjunction with both the burnt offering and the peace offering, but it was not offered directly with the sin or guilt offerings.[9] However, even though it was not offered with the sin or guilt offerings, the priestly eating of the grain offering was related to the sin and guilt offerings in that the meal drawn from it had the same high degree of sacredness; the grain offering food was considered a *most holy* meal, just like the meals drawn from the sin and guilt offerings.

Grain offerings—though later in Jewish history accompanied by wine—consisted mainly of unleavened bread.[10] The second chapter of Leviticus describes the three varieties of unleavened bread that made up the grain offering. These varieties were *fine flour with oil*, unleavened *grits*, and *cakes* (or *wafers*).[11] The cakes (wafers) were recognized as various forms of unleavened bread (griddled, baked, or fried), and the fine flour and the grits were the raw ingredients of unleavened bread "cooked" upon the altar.

---

[6] "When you enter the land where you are to live,….you shall prepare wine for the libation..." (Numbers 15:2,5). See J. H. Kurtz, *offerings, Sacrifices and the Worship of the Old Testament*, trans. James Martin (Peabody, MA: Hendrickson Publishers, Inc., 1998), 300.

[7] Kurtz, *Offerings...*, 301ff, disagrees with the location of the wine-placement, though he, self-admittedly, is one of only a handful who thus disagree.

[8] Leviticus 10:9.

[9] There was a "flour offering" which was in itself a sin offering offered by the poor. This should not be confused with the grain offering.

[10] E.g. Alfred Cave, *The Scriptural Doctrine of Sacrifice and Atonement*, (Edinburgh: T & T Clark, 1890), 466: "Unleavened bread and wine formed the common material of the *minchah*; and as far as the ...unleavened bread is concerned...its connection for the Jew was with the rites of sacrifice."

[11] Leviticus 2:2,4,14. John W. Kleinig, *Leviticus*, (St. Louis: Concordia Publishing House, 2003), 74: "Each category of grain offering [was designated]…a "gift to the Lord"."

The Grain Offering, Food of Holy Communion

Though the priests could and did eat *leavened* bread, God would not allow it upon His altar. "No grain offering," God directed, "which you bring to the Lord, shall be made with leaven."[12] Leaven was often a symbol for evil, and this is likely why God would not allow it to profane His altar.[13] The unleavened grain offering, as will be explained, has significance in relation to the unleavened bread of the Lord's Supper. As he likely references the Lord's Supper, St. Paul mixes the physical reality of feasting with the symbolism of leaven: "Let us therefore celebrate the feast, not with the old leaven, nor with the leaven of malice and wickedness but with the unleavened bread of sincerity and truth."[14]

Certain grain offerings were baked in an oven (Lev. 2:4) to create unleavened wafers, but before they were presented to God they were first anointed with oil. Because they were christened with oil, these unleavened wafers had a messianic character to them—simply by virtue of their anointing. Recall that "Christ" (or "messiah") means "anointed". Those sacred things and people which were anointed have been perceived to possess a connection to the coming Anointed One.[15] What makes this anointing of the wafers even more intriguing is that the rabbis taught that each wafer was to be anointed in the form of the Greek letter *chi*, which was considered the mark of a cross![16] Of course this may be just a fascinating coincidence, for we can't say with certainty that such anointing was a shadow of Jesus Christ because the Scriptures—other than being expressly about Christ—do not specify that this foreshadowed Him. Nonetheless, when crosses are now imprinted or impressed upon the wafers of Holy Communion, the reader will

---

[12] Leviticus 2:11.
[13] Luke 12:1; 1 Corinthians 5:8. Honey was considered the liquid equivalent of leaven so it too was disallowed on God's altar. Honey mixed with any number of liquids quickly turned into wine ("mead").
[14] 1 Corinthians 5:8. This is a Passover referent, but the grain offering paralleled it.
[15] Recall the references and explanation in chapter three, which dealt with the tabernacle, its furnishings and the priests—all of these being anointed with the holy anointing oil. These were anointed with a special holy oil recipe; the oil on the wafer was, apparently, just olive oil.
[16] Kleinig, *Leviticus*, 72.

The Grain Offering, Food of Holy Communion

realize that there is a precedent for this in the OT grain offerings!

The grain offering was more important than many realize.[17] At the beginning of Leviticus, where God introduced the directives for the various sacrifices, recall that the daily burnt offering was the initial sacrifice delineated by God, and indeed the Jews believed it to be the basic sacrifice. Recall also that the lambs of this twice-daily sacrifice were reminiscent of the Passover lambs. Immediately after explaining the burnt offering, God introduced the grain offering and, as just noted, this sacrifice consisted primarily of unleavened bread. Combining the burnt offering with the grain offering, as was God's statute, these sacrifices called to mind the feast of Passover where both lamb and unleavened bread were the foundational ingredients. When one adds the fact that wine also became an essential ingredient of both the grain offering and the Passover meal, one realizes the likelihood that the unified burnt and grain offerings would have been daily reminders of God's Passover deliverance. The grain offering did not exceed the blood-offerings in importance, yet by its proximity to and combination with the burnt offering it is apparent that God emphasized it to remind His people of the Passover.

If indeed the unified sacrifice of the grain offering with the daily burnt offering is rooted in the Passover, then in this respect the combined grain and burnt offerings have an indirect connection to the Lord's Supper, as it too has its roots in the Passover.

The grain offering, which later in Israel's history always included wine (libation), was commonly called *minchah* ("minka").[18] The *minchah* thus consisted of unleavened bread and grape wine. Gayford is one who believes there is a correlation between the ingredients of the Last Supper and the materials of the *minchah*: "He took Bread and Wine, the materials of the

---

[17] E.g. it was emphasized by Joel (1:9, 13. 2:14...God gives the minchah ingredients.)

[18] *Minchah* was at times used, like so many other sacrificial terms, in a more general sense. Malachi 1:11, a text that has long been considered Eucharistic, uses this Hebrew word. It is apparently being used in Malachi 1:11 in a general sense, not specifying the grain offering. For a discussion of Minchah as grain offering, see Kurtz, *Offerings...*, 281ff. Kurtz also includes the oil and incense as part of the *minchah*.

minchah; He spoke of them in terms of Body and Blood, the objects of the offering of animal sacrifices..."[19] Christ used the ingredients of the *minchah*—bread and wine—but He spoke of Himself as *flesh and blood*, the two key foundational elements of the other Hebrew sacrifices. In so doing, Christ neatly laced together all of the sacrificial ingredients into one sacrificial statement about Himself; and all of the sacrificial meals He divinely condensed into one repeatable meal. As the various sacrifices find their fulfillment in Christ, it must be remembered that Christ is not re-sacrificed, for He was sacrificed *once* at the cross. However, the sacred meal drawn from and associated with this sacrifice will be celebrated until He returns.

The *minchah* was offered with both the burnt offering and the peace offering, but not with the sin or guilt offerings.[20] There is a ring of consistency here. The burnt and peace offerings have frequently been considered together because neither of them focused primarily on the concept of forgiveness.[21] As such, the grain offering fit the picture of the burnt and peace offerings because it too was not directly associated with forgiveness. Similarly, the burnt and peace offerings commonly stood together in that they were both associated with communion.[22] This was also a focus of the grain offering, because from it the priests communed with God by consuming the unleavened bread. Thus the grain offering had an affinity to the burnt and peace offerings.

The grain offering, on the other hand, was associated with the sin and guilt offerings. Though the grain offering was not offered with the sin or guilt offerings, yet it had an affinity to these offerings by virtue of its *most holy* meal. As such it was not to be eaten by laity or even by the priest's family

---

[19] S. C. Gayford, *Sacrifice and Priesthood*, (London: Methuen & Co. LTD., 1953), 161.

[20] There is some debate concerning this. See Kurtz, 303. Kurtz is convinced that the grain offering was never offered alone, but *only* with the burnt and peace offerings.

[21] W. W. Washburn, *The Import of Sacrifice in the Ancient Jewish Service* (New York: Phillips & Hunt, 1883), 63: "The peace offering resembled the burnt offering in making the idea of atonement inconspicuous, though not unimportant."

[22] Recall that the communion associated with the burnt offering was a relationship-communion, while the communion associated with the peace offering was a meal-communion.

members—but solely by the priests. In this respect it stood separate from the burnt offering and peace offering because neither of these had such a *most holy* status. In Leviticus 6:7 God set forth the *most holy* nature of the grain offering, specifically comparing it to the sin and guilt offerings. Of the grain offering He directed, "I have given it as their [priestly] share [to eat] from my offerings by fire; it is *most holy, like the sin offering and the guilt offering.*"[23]

OT *minchah* (bread and wine) thus created a bridge connecting the four blood-related sacrifices—the burnt, peace, sin and guilt offerings. John Kleinig explains, "The grain offerings gain their ritual function from their combination with the animal offerings."[24] The grain offering bridge rested on the shore of the burnt and peace offerings because it was not only sacrificed with these but, like these sacrifices it was especially associated with communion. As it spanned the river of God's mercy it also rested on the shore of the sin and guilt offerings, for it embraced the liturgy of these offerings in that it was treated as *most holy*, with a most holy meal derived from it. As a bridge-like sacrifice, the bread and wine of the *minchah* communicated the connectedness of all the OT sacrifices and sacrificial meals. How appropriate then that Christ Jesus would employ bread and wine to be the visible ingredients of the Lord's Supper, and that these ingredients would once again be associated with, and actually convey, the flesh and blood of the ultimate sin, guilt, burnt and peace offering—Christ crucified.

The Feast of First-fruits

> **"You shall bring in the sheaf of the first fruits of your harvest to the priest."**
> **Leviticus 23:10**

Along with the *Passover*, there was embedded within the *Feast of*

---

[23] Leviticus 6:17.
[24] Kleinig, *Leviticus*, 40.

Unleavened Bread a "mini-feast" called the *Feast of First-fruits*. Though "first-fruits" could refer to the first-harvested portion of any crop, yet for this feast it had a unique meaning.[25] The first-fruits in the *Feast of First-fruits* consisted of barley, a grain that grew through the winter and was harvested in the spring. The first sheaf of this harvest—identified as the *first-fruits*—had to be dedicated to the Lord, and this was done by the priests on the "third day of Passover."[26] This sheaf of barley grain was first rendered into fine flour, and then—as with other grain offerings—a portion of it was burned upon God's altar, and what remained was a most holy food for the priests. In any given year, no new grain could be eaten by the Jews until the barley first-fruits had been offered to God by the priests.[27]

Of tremendous importance is the fact that Christ rose from the dead on the exact day when the *first-fruits* were presented to God! As this grain was the first to rise from the earth each year, so Paul describes Christ as the "first-fruits" from the dead: "But now Christ has been raised from the dead, the first fruits of those who are asleep."[28] This then amplifies why Christ would describe His resurrection in terms of seed entering the ground and then sprouting: "Truly, truly I say to you, unless a grain of wheat falls into the earth and dies, it remains by itself alone; but if it dies, it bears much fruit."[29]

Now God is satisfied with the sprouting "grain" of His Son's resurrection, and the priesthood of believers is privileged to eat of the "first-fruits", eating that "grain" that was first to rise from the earth. That "first-fruit grain" is none other than our Lord Jesus Christ; let us celebrate His resurrection by joining in that most holy first-fruits meal which He instituted.

---

[25] First-fruits were the "harvest" version of the first-born of livestock.

[26] Kevin Howard and Marvin Rosenthal, *The Feasts of the Lord*, (Printed in the United States, no printer specified, 1997), 75ff. See Leviticus 23:9-23. *First-fruits* would also be used to describe that first grain harvested in the fall, brought to the Lord on the Jewish *Feast of Pentecost* (Lev. 23:15-21; Num. 28:26).

[27] Leviticus 23:14.

[28] 1 Corinthians 15:20.

[29] John 12:24. The Greek word here translated "wheat" also means "grain". Jesus spoke these words less than a week before the *Feast of First-fruits*. See also 1 Corinthians 15:36

Priestly Eating of the Grain Offering

> "And what is left of it [grain offering] Aaron and his sons are to eat. It shall be eaten as unleavened cakes in a holy place; they are to eat it in the court of the tent of meeting."
> **Leviticus 6:16**

Because the grain offering was a "bloodless sacrifice," and because it was eaten solely by the OT priests, it has been commonly related to the Lord's Supper. The Roman Catholic Church has maintained that its NT priests (*not* the priesthood of believers) do indeed repeatedly perform a *minchah*-like bloodless sacrifice in the celebration of the Eucharist. This re-sacrifice of Christ, they maintain, atones for actual sins.[30] Many Protestants (and Catholics!) consider such a notion to be inconsistent with the facts surrounding both Christ's death and His Supper; they see it as inconsistent with the Biblical witness.[31] Protestants have consequently been hesitant to consider the *minchah* as a type of the Lord's Supper. Kurtz speaks from this point of view: "The view defended with such zeal by Roman Catholic theologians, that the bloodless sacrifice [the *minchah*] was a type of the Lord's Supper, we cannot possibly admit." Kurtz then explains that for those who want the *minchah* to be a type of the Eucharist, "The fact that the Old Testament Minchah was allotted exclusively to the priests...and therefore was taken entirely away from the people, is sufficient proof to the contrary."[32]

Though we agree that the grain offering does not typify a "bloodless" re-sacrifice of Christ, yet how unfortunate that Kurtz and others stumble at the

---

[30] *The Book of Concord*, ed. & trans. T. Tappert (Philadelphia: Fortress Press, 1959), 58: "At the same time the abominable error was condemned according to which it was taught that our Lord Christ had by his death made satisfaction only of original sin, and had instituted the Mass as a sacrifice for other sins."
[31] The epistle to the Hebrews emphasizes the fact that Christ was sacrificed but once.
[32] Kurtz, *Offerings...*, 285, footnote 1.

priestly eating of the grain offering (and the sin/guilt offerings). From Luther's very biblical understanding of the priesthood of all believers, all the offerings that were eaten by the OT priests obtain an updated reality as Christians now may eat of the antitype of these *most holy* offerings, by virtue of the fact that *all* are priests. Indeed Kurtz—in the same paragraph where he rejects the grain offering as a type of the Lord's Supper—states, "No doubt the sacrificial worship of the Old Testament does present a type of the Lord's Supper; but this is sought for, not in the eating of the Minchah by the priests alone, but simply in the sacrificial meal."[33] We heartily agree that the Lord's Supper is typified *in the sacrificial meal*, but why prohibit the *minchah* meal or any other priestly sacrificial meal from typifying the priestly consumption of the Lord's Supper? Christ made all of His people to be priests: "To Him who loves us, and released us from our sins by His blood, and He has made us to be a kingdom, priests to His God and Father; to Him be the glory and the dominion forever and ever. Amen."[34] As emphasized in the Scriptures, Christians have been given a priestly "washing with pure water" in their Baptism, and thus God's NT people are each, by virtue of their Baptism, priests—having rights even exceeding OT priests.[35] Now, like the priests who serviced the OT temple sacrifices, God's people may today eat of the *most holy* sin, guilt *and grain offerings* as they partake of the Lord's Supper; Christ's people have each been given priestly privileges only foreshadowed in the OT.

The grain offering, unlike any other Jewish sacrifice, was a true *communion (koinonia)* between God and the Jewish priests—but alas it was only a bloodless sacrifice, and thus there was no atonement to be found in this communion. As explained when the burnt offering was discussed, *communion (koinonia)* was a technical term used especially to describe the identical food eaten by pagans and their gods. Among pagans such

---

[33] Ibid.
[34] Revelation 1:6.
[35] Hebrews 10:22. Also in Ephesians 5:26 and Titus 3:5 the word often translated as "washing" is really the Greek word for the Jewish Laver, the sacred basin for priestly washing.

communion food was particularly the *flesh* of a sacrificed animal. Recall, however, that the Jews had no atoning animal sacrifice from which both God and man ate the same flesh. Nevertheless from the Jewish grain offering God *and* man did eat of the *identical* substance, and though the Hebrew priests were not communing in an *atonement meal*, yet God and his OT priests did jointly eat the grain offering. When the priests burned a handful of the grain offering upon the Bronze Altar, God was "eating" this portion of the grain offering, and the remainder of it was then consumed by priests in the outer court.[36] Together with the burnt and peace offerings, God described His portion of the grain offering burned upon the Bronze Altar as "My offering, My food for My offerings by fire, of a soothing aroma to Me."[37] By means of the grain offering, God and a limited number of men were in genuine communion (*koinonia*) in OT times as they ate of the same substance. This prefigured the Lord's Supper, as Kleinig explains in his section describing the grain offering: "Like the sacred meals eaten by the priests at the temple, this meal [Lord's Supper] is an integral part of the Divine Service."[38]

In his first epistle to the Corinthians St. Paul asked rhetorically, "Are not those [Jews] who eat the sacrifices sharers (*koinonia*) in the altar?"[39] Many have only gone so far as to admit the *peace offering* meals to such a reference, but the most fitting type of sacrifice—if the emphasis is placed upon eating instead of upon the Bronze Altar—is clearly the *grain offering*. It was *only* through eating the unleavened bread of the OT grain offering that God and man were truly communing (*koinonia*), truly eating the identical substance.[40] Thus the grain offering becomes a most wonderful type of the Lord's Supper, standing as an unbloody figure of the body and blood of

---

[36] Kurtz, *Offerings...*, 299: "According to the more minute directions in Lev. vii.9,10, ...the *Minchah* of cake was to be eaten by the officiating priest alone, whilst the *Minchah* of meal and groats was to be eaten by all the sons of Aaron..."
[37] Numbers 28:2.
[38] Kleinig, *Leviticus*, 80.
[39] 1 Corinthians 10:18.
[40] Whereas the Bronze Altar was the *place* of communion between God and man, the grain offering—for only the priests—presented a communion *food*.

Christ. For even as the OT priests communed with God via the grain offering, so today all NT priests commune with God via the body and blood of Christ, as they consume the grain offering ingredients of unleavened bread and wine. The same body and blood of Christ received by God as a grain offering-like "sweet aroma" has now become the Christian's priestly food.[41] Through Christ's Holy Supper God and the priesthood of believers are in the loftiest communion this side of heaven.

In contrast to the OT grain offering, in Holy Communion Christians are not merely eating unleavened bread, but through eating such bread they are, as Christ promised, eating His body. Indeed all of the OT sacrifices find their antitype in Christ's crucifixion, and all of the sacrificial meals find their antitype in the Lord's Supper. The grain offering thus stands as only one of the many sacrificial puzzle pieces that, once fit together with the other OT pieces, powerfully portrays Christ's Holy Supper. Combine the pure communion nature of the grain offering with the solemnity of the priests in eating the flesh of the sin offering with the celebration and thankfulness of all of God's people as they feasted on the peace offering flesh—and then an enhanced OT picture of the Lord's Supper emerges.

The grain offering not only stands as an unbloody figure ("type") of Holy Communion, but additionally the only eaten ingredient of the grain offering—unleavened bread—is an essential ingredient to be consumed in Christ's Supper. Unleavened bread was and is critical in both Old and New Testament worship. St. Paul certainly did not hesitate to convey the necessary presence of bread in the Eucharist. "Is not *the bread* which we break," he rhetorically asked, "a communion in the body of Christ?"[42] When speaking here of the reality of bread in The Sacrament, the learned Apostle is careful to include the loftier reality—that Christ's people really commune His body. Again St. Paul speaks of the bread of the Supper when he warns,

---

[41] Ephesians 5:1,2.
[42] 1 Corinthians 10:16.

"Therefore whoever *eats the bread* or drinks the cup of the Lord in an unworthy manner, shall be guilty of the body and blood of the Lord." [43] Though here warning of the real possibility of profaning Christ's body and blood—because they are truly present—St. Paul does not hesitate to refer to the fact that we are truly eating bread. He continues: "But let a man examine himself, and so let him *eat of the bread* and drink of the cup."[44] We examine ourselves because we are eating the body and blood of Christ, but Paul had no problem referencing Christ's Supper by saying we *eat of the bread*.

Paul also highlighted the symbolic nature of the unleavened bread as he instructed, "Let us therefore celebrate the feast, not with the old leaven, nor with the leaven of malice and wickedness, but with the unleavened bread of sincerity and truth."[45] Leaven was often perceived as a symbol of evil. The unleavened nature of the Communion bread—paralleling the unleavened nature of the grain offering—symbolizes the removal of wickedness in the lives of those who commune.

Yes, bread is an essential element of the Lord's Supper. We taste it and we eat it, and while doing so we reverently trust—as promised—that we are miraculously consuming the body of Christ.

Public and Private Grain Offerings

> *"So every grain offering of the priests shall be burned entirely. It shall not be eaten."*
> Leviticus 6:23

Even as the priests were prohibited from eating the public sin offering, so too they were forbidden to eat of one special grain offering. There was a "public" status to the grain offering that was presented to God on the day of

---

[43] 1 Corinthians 11:27.
[44] 1 Corinthians 11:28.
[45] 1 Corinthians 5:8.

the high priest's ordination, and only on this unique occasion were the priests forbidden to eat of the grain offering.[46] This public grain offering parallels the public sin offering, for they both were sacrificed especially for the high priest. Another parallel is that both the public sin offering and public grain offering were totally burned up—instead of being eaten by the priests. The public sin offering was burned outside the camp, but the public grain offering was baked into unleavened bread and then entirely burned upon the Bronze Altar. God directed, "So every grain offering of the priests shall be burned entirely. It shall not be eaten."[47] From such a practice God was apparently indicating the fact that He alone could ordain the high priest, and that this office was thus not of human origin. God's command to burn the entire grain offering emphasized the uniqueness of the high priest's ordination.

The special ordination bread that the priests were allowed to eat also magnified the importance of this event. The bread that was eaten by the priests on this special occasion was the *leavened* bread associated with the ordination sacrifice. Recall that this consecration sacrifice was a peace offering, and the leavened bread was eaten by the priests together with the consecration peace offering flesh.

In OT worship there were three occasions when leavened bread was considered a most sacred food, consumed only by the priests. The leavened bread at the high priest's ordination, the leavened bread brought to God's house on Pentecost, and the most holy leavened bread consumed by the priests in connection with a thank offering are the OT sacred breads that included leaven.[48] We believe it is this OT eating of leavened bread that lends credence to the practice of the Orthodox Church, which mandates eating leavened bread in the celebration of the Eucharist. Though leaven itself is often symbolic of evil, leavened *bread*, the Orthodox Church has

---

[46] Leviticus 6:19ff. Kleinig believes this was a daily public sacrifice; Kleinig, *Leviticus*, 154ff.
[47] Leviticus 6:23.
[48] Of *Pentecost* see Leviticus 23:17. No doubt this was also a most holy priestly meal. The thank offering bread, also a most holy food of priests, was discussed in chapter six.

maintained, is symbolic of Christ's resurrection.

Sacrificial Flesh and Bread Eaten Together

> *"Then Moses spoke to Aaron and to his sons Eleazar and Ithamar, 'Take the grain offering that is left over from the Lord's offerings by fire and eat it unleavened beside the [Bronze] altar, for it is most holy."*
> **Leviticus 10:12**

A miracle of the Lord's Supper is that the body of Christ is actually eaten when communicants partake of the consecrated bread. This is true because Christ said so. We here use "flesh" and "body" interchangeably, justifying such usage by the fact that Christ referred to both eating his flesh (John 6:51ff) and eating His body (Matthew 26:26). The early church would often speak of the Eucharist as a sacred meal upon the *flesh* of Christ.[49] The use of the word *flesh* rather than *body* seems to emphasize the reality of participation in a sacrifice. The difficulty with using "flesh" when speaking of the Eucharist, is that it perhaps gives the impression that the communicants are tearing off bits and pieces of Christ; this is of course not so, for each communicant consumes the body (entirely) of Christ, and this is a miraculous occurrence found in every valid celebration of Holy Communion.

In OT worship, flesh and bread were often consumed together. Only God and the priests could eat the bread of the altar, especially the unleavened bread of the grain offering. Simultaneous with such bread consumption, the priests often ate sacrificial flesh apportioned to them, especially the flesh from the sin and peace offerings.

Consider first the sin offering. Certain OT texts reveal that the priestly eating of the *flesh* of the sin offering was consumed in conjunction with the

---

[49] Recall the quotes from Ignatius (d. 107) in the previous chapter.

eating of the grain offering *bread*. This makes sense because they were both *most holy* meals. The priests would congregate in the holy court, and there they would likely gather together all the most holy portions involved in recent sacrifices—flesh and bread—and consume them in one most holy meal.

Again relative to the sin offering, recall the account of Eleazar and Ithamar. Immediately before Moses questioned why they had failed to eat the *sin offering flesh*, he reminded Aaron and his sons: "Take the grain offering...and eat it unleavened beside the altar, for it is most holy. You shall eat it...it is your due."[50] In these back-to-back directives, Moses speaks of eating the grain offering *bread* and sin offering *flesh*. If not eaten together, this flesh and bread must have been eaten in immediate succession. In Leviticus 6:16 God explained the regulation for the priestly eating of the *grain offering* by comparing it to the eating of the *sin/guilt offerings*: "It shall be eaten as unleavened cakes in a holy place...it is most holy, like the sin offering and the guilt offering."[51] From such records, we believe, the attentive Jew—especially the priests—would likely have perceived a worship-oriented continuity when Jesus offered His *sin offering flesh* to eat with the familiar worship element of unleavened *bread*. The *bread* of the grain offering and the *flesh* of the sin offering are now again consumed "together" by Christ's NT priests, only in a much loftier way than any OT priestly meal.

Now under the same association of bread and flesh, consider the burnt offering. As explained in previous chapters, a grain offering was to be sacrificed with a burnt offering. When God directed that the burnt offering and the grain offering be sacrificed together, the burning of the grain offering *bread* and the burning of the burnt offering *flesh* on God's altar indicated that God was eating these portions—*flesh* and unleavened *bread*—together.

Consider the peace offering flesh consumed with bread. When God directed the grain offering to be offered with the peace offering, the priests

---

[50] Leviticus 10:12.
[51] Leviticus 6:16,17.

The Grain Offering, Food of Holy Communion

alone were privileged to eat the unleavened *bread* from the grain offering along with their holy portion of *flesh* from the peace offering. *Flesh* and *bread* were eaten together. At the sacrifice of a thanksgiving peace offering, the priests were given a unique most holy *leavened bread* to eat with their heave and wave portions of the *flesh* from the thank offering. Once again bread and flesh were eaten together, only in this case it was *leavened bread* and flesh.

Finally, recall how *bread* was eaten together with the *flesh* of the consecration peace offering during the priest's ordination ceremony. God directed, "And Aaron and his sons shall eat the *flesh* of the ram and the *bread* that is in the basket, at the doorway of the tent of meeting."[52] Though not a grain offering bread, yet again we observe *bread* eaten with the ram's *flesh* in this peace offering ordination ritual. So again the *flesh* of a sacrifice was perceived to be connected to the sacred eating of *bread*.

In OT worship, sacrificial *bread* and sacrificial *flesh* were quite likely perceived to be united—a sacred combination of bread and flesh in a sacred meal. From such OT shadows, NT believers can better perceive God's worship continuity as they realize that now again in the Lord's Supper *flesh and bread* are inseparably and uniquely bound together in the most sacred meal this side of heaven. Obviously the Lord's Supper is on a much higher plane inasmuch as Christ's sacrifice is infinitely more glorious than any animal sacrifice. Moreover the flesh of the Lord's Supper is beyond what is seen with the eyes or tasted with the mouth, for it is the transcendent flesh of the Son of God. Nonetheless, in the Holy Eucharist the mouths of communicants truly eat Christ's body, as surely as their mouths eat the bread of The Supper— and as surely as the mouths of the OT priests repeatedly ate sacrifice-related *bread* together with sacrifice-related *flesh*.

---

[52] Exodus 29:32. Since Leviticus 6:23 prohibits the eating of grain offering bread at the high priest's ordination, it is apparent that this bread was not grain offering bread. It perhaps was the leavened bread associated with the priestly consumption of the thank offering flesh.

The Grain Offering, Food of Holy Communion

The "Minchah" (Bread and Wine) of the Inner Court

> *"And you shall make a table of acacia wood.....And you shall make its dishes and its pans and its jars and its bowls, with which to pour libations [wine offerings]...And you shall set the bread of the Presence on the table before Me at all times."*
> *Exodus 24:23a,29,30*

Recall that *minchah* ("minka") consisted primarily of unleavened bread and wine. We have only thus far considered the minchah of the *Outer Court*: A memorial portion of unleavened bread from each grain offering was burned at the Bronze Altar, with the remainder eaten by the priests as a most holy meal. The wine was then poured at the base of the altar.

Moving then from the Outer Court to the Holy Place (also called the *Inner Court*) many have noted that the Holy Place also had its unique *minchah* of bread and wine.[53] Upon the Table of Showbread, which was against the north wall of the Holy Place, there rested primarily bread and wine.[54] This bread was called "bread of the presence" or "showbread." Even as the main ingredient of the minchah of the Outer Court was bread, so too the main ingredient for this Inner Court minchah was bread, and—as with the Outer Court—there was also wine with the bread. An additional parallel between the minchah of the Outer Court and the minchah of the Inner Court, is that, like the grain offering wafers, the bread of the presence was anointed with oil in the form of a cross![55] Coincidence? Consider now this *minchah* of bread and wine perpetually present within the Holy Place of the tabernacle.

---

[53] Kurtz, 315ff. Alfred Edersheim, *The Temple: Its Ministry and Services*, (Peabody, Mass.: Hendrickson Publishers, Inc., 1994), 77, explains that the term *Minchah* also encompassed the first sheaf at the Passover and the two loaves at Pentecost.

[54] Additionally frankincense was setting on the Table of Showbread. Such incense is not even mentioned in Exodus 25:23-30. Leviticus 24:1-9 includes it. The frankincense, as will be explained later, relates to the memorial nature of the Lord's Supper.

[55] Edersheim, *The Temple*, 143.

Eating the Bread of the Presence

> *"Then you shall take fine flour and bake twelve cakes with it...And it shall be for Aaron and his sons, and they shall eat it in a holy place; for it is most holy to him..."*
> **Leviticus 24:5,9**

The bread of the Inner Court was a singular bread that was not directly associated with the altar but was nevertheless related to the sacrificial rites. This bread was often called "showbread" (old English, "shewbread"), but its literal translation is "bread of the face," for it rested in the very "face" or presence of God. Consequently many translators render it as "bread of the presence." This bread is first encountered in Exodus 25:30 where God directed the priests, "You shall set the bread of the presence on the table before Me at all times." As with the *minchah* bread of the Outer Court (the grain offering), this *minchah* bread of the Inner Court (showbread) was to be eaten solely by the priests, uniquely in the presence of God.[56] In Leviticus 24:9 God says of this showbread, "And it shall be for Aaron and his sons, and they shall eat it in a holy place; for it is most holy to him from the Lord's offerings by fire, his portion forever." This bread was designated as a *most holy* meal because it—like the sin, guilt and grain offerings—involved a superlative, worship-oriented meal that only priests were to consume. This bread of the inner court paralleled the unleavened bread of the grain offering that was consumed in the outer court; thus they were both called *minchah*.

The priests were commanded to eat this most holy "showbread" every Sabbath Day.[57] From this *weekly* eating of the showbread, some believe the pattern was set for the *weekly* eating of the Lord's Supper. Edersheim

---

[56] Interestingly King David was allowed to eat of the showbread when he and his men were famished. 1 Samuel 21:3ff; Matthew 12:3ff.
[57] Leviticus 24:5-9. There appears to be scholarly agreement that the showbread was—some say it had to be—unleavened, though there is no Scriptural directive.

summarizes, "The apostolic practice of partaking the Lord's Supper every Lord's Day may have been in imitation of the priests eating the shewbread every Sabbath."[58]

Edersheim explains how both Old and New Testament believers considered the bread of the presence to point to Christ: "Ancient symbolism, both Jewish and Christian, regarded 'the bread of the Presence' as an emblem of the Messiah."[59] In addition to this connection with the Messiah, if one realizes the identity of "angel of God's *presence*" to be the Son of God, the connection between the bread of the *presence* and the Messiah becomes two-fold.

Consider the angel of God's presence. Isaiah spoke of Him: "And the angel of His presence saved them."[60] Though the word "angel" often identified a *created* spirit-being, yet it frequently signified a spirit-being who had not been created, and this is the Son of God himself. The word *angel* is used in Scripture to mean *heavenly-messenger*, and the definitive heavenly-messenger is indeed the Son of God. We already spoke of this "angel" in chapter three, how he was at times called "The Word of God." This unique uncreated "angel" possessed God's Name (Ex. 23:21), is called God (Ex. 3:2,4,14), and is thus identified as very God of very God. Yet somehow this "angel" is different from God, for God sends Him to be a special messenger to represent Him. To the Christian it is obvious that the Sender and the "Angel of the Lord" are the Father and the Son, two of the three persons in the Holy Trinity.[61] A curious identification of this God-angel is the "angel of God's presence." When this angel is present, God is present. Edersheim thus writes concerning the "bread of the presence":

---

[58] Edersheim, *The Temple...*, 145.
[59] Ibid., 144.
[60] Isaiah 63:9.
[61] Justin Martyr, in the century after Christ, explained Christ's deity to Trypho the Jew by identifying the deity of the Angel of the Lord in the OT. Gal. 4:14 may be identifying Christ as this "angel of God." See Charles "Gieschen, *Angelomorphic Christology*, (Leiden: Brill, 1998).

The scriptural name is 'Bread of the Face' (Exod. 25:30; 35:13; 39:36); that is, 'of the presence of God,' just as the similar expression, 'Angel of the Face' (Isaiah 63:9), means the 'Angel of His Presence.'[62]

The name of this bread of the Inner Court—*bread of the presence*—surely signifies God's unique presence relative to His tabernacle, but some theologians are convinced it also relates to the *angel of God's presence*. Edersheim states what he believes is an obvious conclusion:

That this 'Presence' [with the bread of the presence] meant the special manifestation of God, is afterwards fully vouchsafed in Christ, 'the angel of His Presence,' it is scarcely necessary to explain at length in this place.[63]

Even as God chose to speak of Himself in terms of the Angel of His Presence, so too He chose to speak of His presence in relation to this unique bread of the presence in the Inner Court. Not coincidentally, bread has again been chosen by the Lord to be the element associated with His presence in today's worship. Concerning the bread of the Lord's Supper, Christ has simply declared, "This is my body." God the Son is bodily present in the bread; it is bread of His presence! Now, unlike the OT bread of the presence, which was restricted to a relatively small group of priests, NT believers are given the priestly privilege of eating a far superior bread of the presence as they partake of the Lord's Supper, eating bread *in* and *of* the very presence of God—perhaps done weekly because this precedent was set by their OT priestly counterparts.

---

[62] Edersheim, *The Temple...*, 140.
[63] Ibid., 145.

Wine Next to the Bread of the Presence

> *"And you shall make.....its bowls, with which to pour libations....And you shall set the bread of the Presence on the table before Me at all times."*
> *Exodus 25:29,30*

Resting alongside the bread of the presence were gold flagons of wine to be used for libations.[64] A libation was a drink offering poured at the base of the Bronze Altar.[65] Evidently only a small amount of this wine would be drawn for certain drink offerings to be poured at the foot of God's altar.[66] The point here is that bread and wine rested side by side on this holy, sacrifice-related table, and likewise bread and wine stand side by side in the Lord's Supper. Thus Darwell Stone writes in *A History of the Doctrine of the Holy Eucharist*, "In the first century of the Christian Era bread and wine would naturally suggest the idea of sacrifice."[67] The earliest Christians, most of whom were Jews, must surely have perceived a special meaning in the Lord's Supper simply from Jesus' use of bread and wine.

Amplifying this connection, some theologians believe the *minchah* of bread and wine suggested not merely the idea of sacrifice, but they believe these elements were ordained to directly correspond to sacrificial *flesh* and *blood*; the sacrificial bread was intended to correspond to sacrificial flesh, and the sacrificial wine was intended to correspond to sacrificial blood. Bahr is

---

[64] Edersheim, *The Temple...*, 142: tells of the traditional understanding that "...the 'covers,' or rather 'flagons,' and the 'bowls' [were on the table of shewbread] for the wine of the drink-offering." However, Edersheim is doubtful of this tradition, and wonders if drink offerings were ever brought into the Holy Place.

[65] E.g. Exodus 25:29.

[66] It is obvious that such wine on the Table of Showbread was not the sole source for libations. Numbers 28 and 29 direct that larger amounts of wine be poured with various sacrifices, especially during special festivals.

[67] Darwell Stone, *A History of the Doctrine of the Holy Eucharist*, (London: Rivingtons, 1909), 12.

The Grain Offering, Food of Holy Communion

one who holds such an opinion: "The bread (meal, corn) corresponded to the body of the animal,...and the wine to the blood, which was likewise poured upon [the base of] the altar."[68] If the Jews of Jesus' day also recognized in their worship rites this correlation—between bread and body, and between wine and blood—then the Last Supper connections between *bread and body*, and again between *wine and blood* would have been readily recognized.

The Wine with the Blood

> *"Then the libation with it shall be a fourth of a hin for each lamb, in the holy place you shall pour out the libation of strong drink to the Lord."*
> **Numbers 28:7**

After the children of Israel entered the Promised Land—when of course they ceased to wander the desert and they were able to become vinedressers—God expected that wine be offered with every grain offering.[69] As this wine was offered to God it was called a *libation* or a *drink offering*. God explained, "When you enter the land where you are to live, which I am giving you...you shall prepare wine for the libation..."[70] Hebrew libations were often not mere thimbles of wine, but they consisted of a fairly significant amount of wine, as exemplified in the following directives for the Jewish "New Moon" festival. In such a quote, realize that a "hin" of wine was approximately a gallon and that the following sacrifice is only a fraction of the total sacrifices offered in a given month:

And their libations shall be half a hin of wine for a bull and a third of a

---

[68] Kurtz, *Offerings...*, 286, who references and explains Bahr. Kurtz basically disagrees with such an understanding, especially when Bahr correlates also the holy oil with the animal fat.
[69] Numbers 15:2ff.
[70] Numbers 15:2,5. Numbers 28,29 detail the libations of the yearly feasts.

hin for the ram and a fourth of a hin for a lamb; this is the burnt offering of each month throughout the months of the year.[71]

Strangely, there were no specific Scriptural directives for the application of the libation-wine. Though wine was usually made to be consumed by people, yet if a priest drank wine in the Holy Courts he was under the penalty of death![72] It is also apparent that the laity were not to drink of the *minchah* libation-wine, since the entire *minchah* of bread and wine belonged to God, with a portion of His bread and none of His wine going to His priests.[73] Though there were no specific directives for applying the various libations, yet there is evidence that at least part if not all of the libation-wine was poured out. God directed, "...in the holy place you shall pour out the libation of strong drink to the Lord."[74] It is possible that part of the wine was also burned upon the altar, but ancient Jewish records only speak of it being entirely poured at the base of the Bronze Altar.[75]

From extra-biblical Jewish writings and from the Bible as well, a picture emerges in which the libation-wine is seen to mingle with the sacrificial blood. Kurtz explains that the opinion of most historians "is that the wine was poured out at the foot of the altar of burnt-offering, like the blood of the sin-offering..."[76] Kurtz himself rejects this viewpoint because, he believes, "the wine had nothing in common with the blood of expiation."[77] We respectfully believe that Kurtz is here wrong. The wine in Jewish worship had much in

---

[71] Numbers 28:12-14. Numbers 28 gives directives for the spring festivals, and Numbers 29 for the fall festivals. Numbers 15 discusses libations offered with certain private sacrifices such as votive offerings.
[72] Leviticus 10:9.
[73] Leviticus 6:16,23; 10:12,13. As will be explained shortly, wine related to peace offerings was consumed by the laity.
[74] Numbers 28:7.
[75] Numbers 28:8 seems to indicate some of the libation was burned with the burnt offering. However it is apparent that the Jews understood the directive in this verse and others like it to mean the sacrificial lamb was burned, and not the wine.
[76] Kurtz, *Offerings*..., 302.
[77] Ibid.

The Grain Offering, Food of Holy Communion

common with the sacrificial blood—especially now that wine and sin offering blood are observed to be uniquely bound in the Eucharist. The OT *type*—wine poured at the same place as sin offering blood—made little sense until the arrival of its NT *antitype*. The wine of the Eucharist is the antitype; it is at the same place as the blood of Christ, and now it is no longer poured out at the base of an altar, but it is drunk. And when the wine is thus consumed, the blood of Christ is simultaneously consumed.

Several Jewish practices and descriptions demonstrate the connection between libation wine and sacrificial blood. First, as Kurtz acknowledges, many Jewish writings describe libations exactly as they describe sin offering blood; both the sacred wine and sacrificial blood are said to be "poured into the altar's base."[78] Second, wine itself was often referred to as "blood," being called "blood of the vine" in the Jewish *Book of Wisdom*.[79] Within Scripture one finds a few allusions to and even specific references to blood in terms of wine and vice versa. For instance in his great song, Moses informs God's people that "of the blood of grapes you drank wine."[80] In Isaiah's prophecy, the treading of grapes becomes the gushing of blood. God said, "I have trodden the wine trough alone...And their lifeblood is sprinkled on my garments."[81] Third, the Jewish libation was wine, but the pagan libations involved blood. Thus the Psalmist says of pagan sacrifice, "I shall not pour out their libations of blood..."[82] Such a comparison between pagan and Jewish libations shows a perceived parallel between wine and blood.[83]

Probably the most important reason to connect blood and wine is found in the fact that wine and blood were handled almost identically in

---

[78] Kurtz, *Offerings*..., 301,302: Εξεχεεν εισ θεμελια θυσιαστηριου was the same directive for both the wine and the blood.
[79] Kurtz, *Offerings*..., 301.
[80] Deuteronomy 32:14.
[81] Isaiah 63:3. The word for *lifeblood* is literally "juice." Lifeblood is obviously the intended meaning, as attested in the LXX. See also Jeremiah 25:30; Revelation 14:17-20; 19:13.
[82] Psalm 16:4.
[83] Not all agree with this understanding of Psalm 16:4, but there is no doubt that "libation" is used to refer to blood.

temple ritual. As already noted, no priest could drink of the libation-wine in God's courts. Such a prohibition was placed upon blood as well, a prohibition that reached even beyond the priests and beyond the holy courts.[84] Probably the most profound correlation between wine and blood is that within the temple, as indicated by records at the time of Christ, they both were poured at the identical location at the foot of the altar. In the temple of Jesus' day, at the base of the Bronze Altar there were two pipes or channels into which sacred liquids were poured. Into one was poured the ceremonial water at the Feast of Tabernacles—a highly sacred event.[85] Into the other pipe, however, the *sacred blood and the libation-wine* were both poured.[86]

Though it is true that the two channels ultimately "disposed" of such liquids via the brook Kidron, yet the base of the altar was a holy location, and the rituals associated with such pouring were not incidental; the blood or wine poured at the altar's base was not simply being disposed of, else why even bring a libation? The libation wine was not brought to God's house just to be thrown out; we believe its placement at the altar's foundation indicated that in some way God was receiving this wine, even as He received all the sacrificial blood poured in the same place. The sacredness of the base of the Bronze Altar is attested to by the placement of the blood of the sin offering; God directed, "Pour out all [the rest of] the blood at the base of the altar."[87] Indeed when Moses sanctified the Bronze Altar for holy use, the blood that was shed at its base contributed in establishing its holiness.[88]

From such an understanding one recognizes how the blood of Christ,

---

[84] Leviticus 17:14.
[85] Edersheim, *The Temple*..., 220ff. Kurtz, *Offerings*..., 301 explains the two "pipes".
[86] Though such water, blood and wine ultimately flowed into the Kidron, yet we disagree with Kurtz (302) that this pouring at the base of the altar was merely for disposing of leftovers. All sacred ingredients ultimately end up disposed of, whether through the bowels of a priest, soaking into the ground, or via the brook Kidron. But the base of the Altar—holy ground—was not for mere disposal, even as the eating of sacred foods was not for mere disposal.
[87] Exodus 29:12. This verse describes sin offering blood at Aaron's ordination. This blood was poured at the Altar's base only after an initial portion was smeared on the horns of the Altar.
[88] Leviticus 8:15.

The Grain Offering, Food of Holy Communion

flowing to the base of the cross, is antitypical of the blood and wine poured at the foot of the altar. The cross of Christ was identified early in Christian history as the *altar of the cross*.[89] At the base of the cross, which is the holiest of altars, the blood of the supreme sacrifice was shed. This blood had been promised just hours before to be received under the parallel yet consumable sacrificial element of wine.[90]

To further fortify the cross and altar connection, St. John emphatically declared that both blood and water flowed from Christ's pierced side. Such a declaration would have called to mind the two channels at the base of the Bronze Altar, the one for water and the other for blood (and wine). The church from its earliest history considered St. John's cross-related reference about water and blood to be an unmistakable allusion to the sacraments of Baptism and the Lord's Supper.[91]

The three elements poured into the two channels at the base of the Bronze Altar—water, wine and blood—truly link together OT sacrifice, the cross of Christ, and the Lord's Supper. As OT sacrifice was directly related to the Passover, it made sense that the combination of wine and water at the Bronze Altar paralleled a Passover practice as well. The parallel is found in the fact that the Passover Seder prescribed that the cups of wine be cut with

---

[89] Gayford, *Sacrifice and Priesthood*, 146, traces the phrase, *Altar of the Cross* (ara crucis) as far back as Ambrose. Many have used the phrase to describe the fulfillment of OT sacrifices at the cross. Thus e.g. Alfred Cave, *The Scriptural Doctrine of Sacrifice and Atonement*, (Edinburgh: T & T Clark, 1890), 421: "The cross is the altar upon which Jesus makes His sacrifice." It should be noted, however, that Jewish sacrifices were never literally *slain upon* an altar, but the creature was slain *and then* portions placed upon the altar. In 1 Peter 2:24, "He bore our sins in His body on the tree," the Greek word for "bore" is the word for bearing a sacrifice to the altar.

[90] The Passover wine in Jesus' day was *always* red wine and *always* to be mixed with water. See Edersheim, *The Temple*, 187.

[91] Robert J. Daly, *Christian Sacrifice* (Washington, D.C.: The Catholic University of America Press, 1978), 291f: "As for Jn 19,34f, the simultaneous flowing of blood and water from the side of Christ may also be an allusion to that specific rite of the Feast of Tabernacles in which water and wine poured out simultaneously from bowls on the altar. If so, then it would serve the function of bringing in the idea of Jesus and those who follow him as the new temple, an interpretation which harmoniously supports the customary sacramental-ecclesial interpretation of the water and blood from Christ's side."

water.[92] It was this wine and water mixture in the Passover chalice that Christ declared to be His blood. The water, wine and blood conveyed by the chalice of the Eucharist almost cry out their ancient relationship to the Bronze Altar! Probably especially imitating the Passover practice—but also, perhaps inadvertently or purposely, imitating the practice of pouring water, wine and blood at the base of the Bronze Altar—the early church and many Christian churches yet today offer the communion of Christ's blood by blessing a chalice containing not simply wine, but *wine* mixed with *water*.

Thus when Kurtz disavows the wine and blood connections clearly apparent in Jewish ritual, opining that "the wine had nothing in common with the blood of expiation," we must decidedly disagree. Wine obviously had much to do with blood in OT ritual, and though the Jews themselves may have wondered why God established such an association between wine and blood, all such wondering was laid to rest when Christ instituted His Holy Supper. Now, in the NT, the wine in worship has *everything* to do with the blood of expiation, the blood of the sin offering.

In OT worship only God could partake of the libation-wine, even as only God could partake of sacrificial blood, both of which were poured at the base of His altar. As one considers such OT regulations, it is humbling to realize the tremendous privileges accorded to God's people in the NT era. The wine, which no priest could ever drink in the sacred courts, and the blood, which no Hebrew could drink *anywhere*, are now offered to God's people in the Sacrament of the Altar! This is so because Christ has now magnanimously invited, "Drink of it, all of you, for this cup is the New Testament in my blood..." The gate has truly been opened to the presence of God, for what used to be *only* His in the OT, now in the NT—through the cross of Christ—is bequeathed to *every* Christian. Christians may, even though they are priests, drink wine in His presence, and as they do so they are told that they are actually drinking the sacred blood of the Son of

---

[92] Edersheim, *The Temple...*, 187.

God. Such consuming of wine and blood was unthinkable in OT times, but now it is an important part of Christian worship because God wants all of His people to participate in the ultimate communion with Himself. When God shares that which had previously belonged solely to Him, this is a mark of the highest communion with Him. Once again we see the antitype far surpasses its type. As God shares with His NT people the blood and wine which in OT worship only belonged to Him, His NT people are truly in a wondrous fellowship with Him—as Saint Paul exclaimed in I Corinthians 10:16: "Is not the cup of blessing which we bless a sharing ("communion") in the blood of Christ?"

Wine with Peace Offerings

> "Nor will foreigners drink your new wine, for which you have labored......But those who.....gather it will drink it in the courts of my sanctuary."
> Isaiah 62:8,9

Though it is certain that Jewish priests drank no wine in the tabernacle courts, and similarly the laity could not drink the wine of the *minchah*, yet it is also evident that wine was consumed by the laity in the OT worship setting. For instance in 1 Chronicles 29:22, following the public offering of numerous sacrificial creatures, the record indicates—in peace offering fashion—that the people "ate *and drank* that day before the Lord with great gladness." The context of this verse indicates that such eating *and drinking* were no doubt drawn from the "coronation" peace offering for Solomon. The point to note here is that the people indeed *drank* in relation to worship.

Though there are scant texts that designate exactly what was drunk at these worship-related events, yet the oft-repeated description of wine in the worship context indicates that this was indeed the substance consumed.[93] One verse that does present the contents of sacrificial drinking is Isaiah 62:9. In verse 8 God initially declares, "Nor will foreigners drink your new wine, for which you have labored." Noting that wine is the subject of this verse, the next verse then explains of this wine, "But those who...gather it will drink it in the courts of My sanctuary." Drinking wine *in the courts of the sanctuary* meant that this was worship-related drinking, and clearly this verse is referring to the laity who themselves would harvest the grapes, make the wine, and then consume it in a worship setting.[94]

When the Jewish laity brought their tithe (10% to the Lord), they were privileged to drink some (all?) of the tithed wine at their sacrificial banquets. God invited, "And you shall eat in the presence of the Lord your God...the tithe...of your new wine..." (Deut. 14:23). No doubt this wine served as a main source of drink when these people of God came to Jerusalem to worship. While on duty, priests could still not drink even this wine.[95]

In Psalm 116:13 the psalmist excitedly exclaims, "I shall lift up the cup of salvation and call upon the name of the Lord." In Passover-like language, this verse connects a celebrative cup of wine to the votive offering, as verse 12 implies and as verse 14 explains: "I shall pay my vows to the Lord." Wine was thus consumed, as indicated here, with a votive peace offering.

A final reason why it makes sense to consume *wine* at the sacrifice of a peace offering is found in the fact that, as already abundantly noted, the Passover no doubt established the groundwork for the sacrificial system. Since wine was consumed at every Passover, it thus makes perfect sense that this would be the drink consumed when God's OT people would "eat and drink" in relation to the sacrifice of the peace offerings.

---

[93] The libations and the tithes involved the bringing of wine. Deuteronomy 14:22-23 indicate the drinking of the tithe-related wine in God's presence. Also in v. 26 "wine or strong drink" are directed to be consumed.

[94] These verses are predicting NT worship in OT terms. E. J. Young, *The Book of Isaiah* vol. III, (Grand Rapids: Wm. B. Eerdmans Publishing Co., 1969), 472.

[95] Kleinig, Leviticus, 225. See e.g. Numbers 18:12.

Memorial Bread Rituals

> *"This is my body which is for you; do this in remembrance of Me...This cup is the new covenant in My blood; do this as often as you drink it in remembrance of Me."*
> 1 Corinthians 11:24,25

Sacred memorial formulae were extremely common among the Jews.[96] One finds that memorial precepts were especially connected to sacred bread-rituals, and thus one observes that the bread-rituals of the Passover, the grain offering, the showbread and the Lord's Supper were each in some way memorial-oriented.

The Passover was the first bread-related memorial feast. God had declared, "Now this day will be a *memorial* for you, and you shall celebrate it as a feast."[97] Not only was unleavened bread a central ingredient of this sacred meal, but the overarching festival surrounding the Passover was called the *Feast of Unleavened Bread*.

The grain offering was also memorial-related. The handful of the grain offering burned upon God's altar was called the *memorial* portion of the offering. God directed, "The priest then shall take up from the grain offering its *memorial* portion, and shall offer it up in smoke on the altar as an offering by fire of a soothing aroma to the Lord."[98] Since the sacrificial system was related to—and perhaps even based upon—the Passover celebration, it is reasonable that the grain offering "memorial" likely reminded God's people of His Passover deliverance.

The memorial portion of grain offering was eaten by God when it was burned upon His altar. As noted earlier, such memorial sacrifices were to be

---

[96] Joachim Jeremias, *The Eucharistic Words of Jesus* (Philadelphia: Trinity Press International, 1966), 244ff. Jeremias (244) relates the important fact that within Palestinian Judaism "memorial formulae are very common in religious language." Jeremias does *not* emphasize the bread rituals as we do.
[97] Exodus 12:14. See also 13:9.
[98] Leviticus 2:9.

considered signs of God's grace, that *He remembered* His covenant to his people.[99] Thus the "memorial" terminology communicated not only the *worshipper's* recollection of God's grace, but it also conveyed *God's* gracious remembrance of His promises to His people. Such a memorial relationship is to be recognized in Holy Communion. God's people recall the death of Christ, but additionally God recalls His Son's death, and from it He graciously sees His people to the end of time.[100]

In the Lord's Supper, like the grain offering meal instituted centuries before, Jesus declared that His people were to eat and drink *in remembrance* (memorial) of Him.[101] Stephen Bedale explains that the unique memorial word contained in the record of the Lord's Supper "is definitely a ritual, or liturgical, term."[102] In the very institution of Christ's Supper, Jewish hearers would thus have realized the institution of a worship practice. Such a worship practice was not inaugurated for private use; M. F. Sadler explains that Christ's memorial wording indicated "a very solemn sacrificial memorial, and not a private act of reminding themselves, or one another."[103] The Lord's Supper was thus not intended to be like private Bible study, but it was intended to be a worship activity celebrated by a group of worshipers. Whenever such memorial meals were/are consummated—whether OT sacrificial meals or the NT Lord's Supper—God remembers His Son's sacrifice for His people, and God's people remember His acts of love and they remain in His grace.

Though the Lord's Supper "memorial" is related to OT memorials, it

---

[99] Jeremias, *The Eucharistic Words*...,244ff: "By far the more frequent practice of Judaism at the time of Jesus, however, is to use [memorial terminology]...of God's remembrance."

[100] Jeremias, *The Eucharistic Words...*, 253ff. God has an eschatological remembrance of Christ.

[101] Only Luke and Paul utilize memorial language in their Words of Institution. They both use the identical phrase, εις αναμνησιν, Paul using it for both the bread and wine but Luke using it only for the bread.

[102] Stephen Bedale, 'The Eucharistic Sacrifice', *Theology*, lvi, no. 398 (1953), 300.

[103] M.F. Sadler, *The Gospel According to St. Luke* (London: G. Bell and Sons, LTD, 1911), 560.

far transcends them. The memorial nature of the Lord's Supper is not the mere recollection of an historical event, but it is a participation in that event. Herman Sasses explains:

> It is this Real Presence of the crucified and risen Lord, who gives us his true body and blood to eat and to drink that lends to the **remembrance** of his death a reality and actuality such as we do not find otherwise in the recollection of a historical event.[104]

Even if He had not employed memorial language, simply Christ's use of *unleavened bread* in the institution of the Lord's Supper would have created a connection in the minds of Jewish participants both to the Passover and to the grain offering. By additionally using memorial language, Jesus not only magnified this connection but He also showed the continuity in the ways of God who had established memorial language for the OT Passover and the grain offering.[105]

All three of these sacred "bread rituals" (the Passover, the grain offering and the Eucharist) are eaten as memorials. These three bread rituals also find kinship in that they each are connected to a slain lamb: The unleavened bread of the Passover was obviously connected to the Passover lamb; the two go together. The unleavened bread of the grain offering was primarily offered in connection with the slaying of the daily burnt offering lambs; again lamb and unleavened bread go together. And of course the unleavened bread of the Lord's Supper is directly linked to the body of The

---

[104] Herman Sasse, *This is My Body* (Augsburg Publishing House, 1959; revised ed., Adelaide: Lutheran Publishing House, 1977), 309,310. Emphasis, Sasse.

[105] Frequently "memorial" or "remembrance" is also connected to the peace offering. The offerer recalls God's blessings and is bound to offer a peace offering. F.C.N. Hicks, *The Fullness of Sacrifice*, (First Published by Macmillan & Co., 1946, Reprinted London: S.P.C.K., 1953), 212: "....The idea of 'memorial before God' was a familiar part of the ancient sacrificial thought; and if we adopt the interpretation here it will be just so far as we are convinced on the other grounds that it is the ancient sacrifices our Lord has in mind [when He speaks of the Supper as "memorial"]." See also Hicks, 195.

Lamb that was slain but is alive forevermore; Jesus—no doubt purposely consistent with the OT—once again brought together Lamb and unleavened bread. Furthermore, each of these three bread rituals is intimately connected to the sacred use of wine. Thus one observes a consistency of ingredients as these three memorial meals each would employ unleavened bread, lamb and wine as primary and essential components.

Showbread Memorial Connected to the Eucharist

There is another memorial-related bread ritual of the OT that is also associated with the Lord's Supper. This bread ritual, explained briefly already, is the ritual surrounding the *bread of the presence* (showbread). Though this bread was not directly linked to the slaying of a lamb, yet, as noted earlier, it was side by side with wine and it was seen to prefigure the Lord's Supper. Christ's people are directed to the showbread by the memorial terminology ("in remembrance") used in the record of the Lord's Supper.[106] In the accounts of the Last Supper, the Greek word used for "memorial" is not the memorial word for the Passover, nor is it the memorial word for the grain offering.[107] But the memorial formula of the Lord's Supper is in fact a memorial formula that is found only *once* in the OT, and there it is used in conjunction with the bread of the presence.[108] Christ's memorial formula is the prepositional phrase that is translated "in remembrance."

The memorial formula (*in remembrance*) used in the Lord's Supper is found only in the text of OT Scripture in Leviticus 24:7: "And you shall put

---

[106] Such memorial terminology is only found in the accounts of Luke and Paul.

[107] Jeremias, *The Eucharistic Words...*, 244ff, considers the various cognates for "memorial" to be equivalents. Though such words have parallel meanings, the use of the relatively rare εις αναμνησιν causes one to question why the Passover memorial terminology was not utilized. In this section of our book we put forth a theory as to the meaning of this phrase.

[108] The "formula" is the prepositional phrase εις αναμνησιν, which in the OT can only be read from the LXX. This formula is also found in the titles of two Psalms (LXX 37, 69). These Psalms were likely liturgical texts used at the burning of the grain offering or at the eating of the bread of the presence. Such titles are not unimportant yet many also believe they are not part of the biblical text. See Darwell Stone, *A History...*, 10.

pure frankincense and salt on each row [with the bread], that they may be for the showbread *for remembrance* set before the Lord."[109] The salt and the frankincense are *for remembrance* (or "in remembrance"). Salt was placed upon every sacrifice that was burned on the Bronze Altar, and as a preserving element it reminded God's people of His durable covenant with them.[110] We believe frankincense is the central ingredient established to memorialize the showbread (bread of the presence), and in this reference the burning of the frankincense served to "memorialize" the bread of the presence.[111] Such memorializing, we believe, is the *highlighting* or *framing* of the *presence* of a lofty reality.[112] Thus the wafting frankincense can be said to *highlight* the showbread that is set before the Lord. We believe the rare prepositional formula, *in remembrance*—used here and in the Lord's Supper—can be translated "for framing" or "for causing to remember" or "for highlighting." The phrase explaining the burning of the frankincense can then be translated simply "*for highlighting* the bread of the presence."[113]

Though frankincense and the memorial portion of the *grain offering* were routinely burned together, when it was burned in conjunction with the *bread of the presence* the frankincense was burned *alone*.[114] The fragrance of the pure frankincense—unblended with any acrid aroma of roasting bread, as

---

[109] LXX translation by the author.

[110] The salt, a sign of God's lasting covenant, stood as a unique memorial with every sacrifice.

[111] Kleinig, *Leviticus*, 76, explains, "Whatever the reason, incense thereby came to be closely associated in the popular mind with the grain offering." This is true, but only when the showbread was eaten would the frankincense be burned by itself.

[112] Sasse, in the previous quote, seems to have a similar understanding. Hans Conzelmann, *1 Corinthians*, trans. James W. Leitch (Philadelphia: Fortress Press, 1975), 198: "Αναμνησις, 'remembrance,' is more than mere commemoration; it means a sacramental presence." We believe from its etymology and from contextual use, εις αναμνησιν emphasizes *causing* one to remember or recognize the presence of a great reality.

[113] Though not the prepositional phrase, yet the unique word for "memorial" (αναμνησις) is found in one other text in the LXX, Numbers 10:10. In this text the blowing of the silver trumpets would *highlight* or *frame* the sacrifice of burnt, peace and grain offerings. Αναμνασις, when considered in other texts (e.g. Hebrews 10:3), can consistently be understood as something that *highlights* the presence of some great thing or activity.

[114] Leviticus 2:2,15,16, etc. show the frankincense burned with the memorial portion of the minchah. However, *no* bread of the presence was burned. It was solely eaten by the priests.

The Grain Offering, Food of Holy Communion

it wafted upward once a week—*framed* (memorialized) the priestly eating of the *bread of the presence*. When the people smelled this pure frankincense, they realized (*remembered*) that the priests were consuming the most holy bread of the presence. The aromatic smoke of the pure frankincense did not draw attention to itself so much as it drew attention to the much greater bread of the presence. Such burning of the frankincense, though important, served to *frame* (memorialize) the highly sacred eating of the most holy bread of the presence. The eating of this bread was so sacred that the text declares, "And it shall be for Aaron and his sons, and they shall eat it in a holy place; for it is most holy to him from the Lord's offerings by fire, his portion forever."[115] Aaron and his sons ate *all* of this bread, even receiving "from the Lord's offerings by fire" so that God consumed none of the bread—for the frankincense was burned alone on God's table. The eating of this bread of the presence was a unique priestly meal, and it was identified as a *most holy* meal for the priests. Being a unique, most holy food of which God ate none, this priestly meal was *framed* (put "in remembrance") by the burning of frankincense.[116] The burning of the frankincense on God's altar also served to highlight the fact that God Himself—though eating none of the bread—was uniquely present with the bread of the presence; His distinctive presence was identified simply from the name of the bread: bread of *the presence*. And His presence was brought to mind as the frankincense filled the tabernacle with its sweet aroma.

The object memorialized (framed) by the frankincense, as stated in the text, is the bread of the presence.[117] The Greek translation literally states that the frankincense and salt were *for the bread for remembrance*.[118] Thus, when the *bread* of the Lord's Supper is considered primarily as a "memorial,"

---

[115] Leviticus 24:9.

[116] As far as we can discern, the only other *most holy* food eaten by priests and not by God was the leavened bread associated with the sacrifice of a thank offering. Could it be that the two breads are related?

[117] This phrase must of course be referenced in the LXX.

[118] εις αρτους εις αναμνησιν...

it is prefigured not so much by the OT *bread of the presence* but by the *frankincense* in the bread of the presence ritual. For even as the aroma of the frankincense highlighted (memorialized) the sacred eating of the showbread, so the bread of the Lord's Supper highlights (memorializes) the sacred eating of Christ's body, the ultimate bread of God's Presence. Christ's bread-related memorial formula thus enhances the reality of the true *presence* of His very body. If our understanding is correct, then Christ's memorial formula, instead of being translated, "Do this in memory of me," would be translated, "Do this *for highlighting* my presence."

Of the four records of the Words of Institution neither Matthew nor Mark use the memorial formula at all. Paul uses it for both the bread and the cup, and Luke (no doubt influenced by Paul) uses the memorial formula solely for the bread. Luke's usage *only for the bread* is intriguing since, as has been demonstrated, memorial formulae were especially common for OT *bread* rituals.

Did Christ intend His people to think of the bread of the presence in His institution of the Eucharist? Was St. Luke then, by his memorial wording, intentionally linking the bread of the Lord's Supper with the ceremony surrounding the bread of the presence?[119] On the surface such a conclusion does not appear to be very convincing, but consider the following summary of the textual and extra-textual evidence that lend credence to this theory.

First, there is the unique prepositional phrase in the Lord's Supper that directly links it to the bread of the presence ritual. Then, even as there were twelve loaves of showbread, so too there were twelve Apostles at the institution of the Supper.[120] Simply the *eating* of the bread of the presence and the *eating* of the bread (body) of Christ's Supper is an important parallel.

---

[119] It is probable that Paul supervised the writing of Luke's Gospel. Paul was uniquely and highly educated relative to Hebrew minutia; he likely was very much aware of these things.
[120] Leviticus 24:5. In Luke 6:1-4 might Christ be showing Himself to be both the new David and the High Priest with His priestly band? Jesus states, "[David] entered the house of God, and took and ate the consecrated bread which is not lawful for any to eat except the priests alone, and gave it to his companions." Isn't this what the New David did?

And again, recall that the *weekly* eating of the Lord's Supper in early Christianity may have had its origin in the *weekly* eating of the bread of the presence.[121] Additionally, in Leviticus 24:8, immediately following the memorial reference, the bread of the presence placed before God is called "an everlasting covenant."[122] This covenant wording enhances an association between the bread of the presence and the *covenant* nature of the Lord's Supper. Furthermore, the showbread ritual carried significant Christological overtones, as perceived by some in early Christianity.[123] One of those overtones was the presence of God, a presence magnified in the NT Breaking of Bread.[124] This unique presence of Christ is emphasized further if one understands "in remembrance" to be the *highlighting* of a *present* reality—that reality being the sacramental presence of Christ. Also, as pointed out earlier in this chapter, the bread of the presence was connected to the angel of God's presence who has been understood to be the pre-incarnate Christ.[125] Recall also that salt was, in early Christian communities, directly associated with the Lord's Supper, even as salt was directly associated with the frankincense that highlighted the eating of the Bread of the Presence. Finally, recall that the Jews themselves had connected the bread of the presence to the coming Messiah.[126]

---

[121] Edersheim, *The Temple....*, 145. The number 12 no doubt indicated the 12 tribes of Israel. See Matthew 19:28 where Jesus connects the NT church to these 12 tribes.

[122] The addition of "salt" in the LXX showbread text no doubt emphasized the covenant concept. Recall that sacrificial salt is called, "the salt of the covenant." (Lev. 2:13). J. Cullmann and F.J. Leenhardt, *Essays on the Lord's Supper* (London: Lutterworth Press, 1958), 12: "In the Pseudo-Clementines, as I have already mentioned, the Lord's Supper is celebrated with bread and salt, so much so that the expression 'To share the salt,' has become the technical term for 'to celebrate the Lord's Supper.'"

[123] Daly, *Christian Sacrifice,* 368, shows that for Hippolytus, "The idea of Christ's sacrifice is also clearly presented in the instructions for private prayer (AT 41, 90, 1-9; cf. ATC 62 37). For there the OT bread of proposition [presence] is seen as a type of the body and blood of Christ."

[124] Note the emphasis in Luke 24:30-35, how the Emmaus disciples recognized Jesus' presence in the breaking of bread.

[125] Edersheim, *The Temple...*, 140ff, as noted earlier in this chapter.

[126] Edersheim, *The Temple...*, 144: "Ancient symbolism, both Jewish and Christian, regarded 'the bread of the Presence' as an emblem of the Messiah."

Concluding Remarks

Even as God had commanded His OT believers to observe special rituals surrounding the grain offering and the showbread, and even as these bread rituals were associated with wine, so now Christ has lovingly commanded His NT believers to observe an extraordinary bread ritual, which once again is associated with wine. When Jesus gave His great commission, He reminded His Apostles to teach people to *observe* all that He *commanded*.[127] What had Christ *commanded* His people to *observe*? Surely one of His foremost mandates was that Christians *observe* the Lord's Supper. With this Eucharistic understanding connected to the Great Commission, it perhaps is no coincidence that Christ concluded this commission by promising, "Lo, I am with you always even to the end of the world." Is there any other identified place where Christ is so profoundly *with His people always* than in the "bread of the presence," which they eat in His Holy Supper? Let us joyfully observe this mandated sacrament, even to the end of the world: "For as often as you eat this bread and drink the cup, you proclaim the Lord's death until He comes."[128]

---

[127] Matthew 28:19ff.
[128] 1 Corinthians 11:26.

> *"For every high priest is appointed to offer both gifts and sacrifices; hence it is necessary that this high priest also have something to offer."*
> Hebrews 8:3

Chapter Eight

HEBREWS, EPISTLE OF SACRIFICE AND SACRAMENT[1]

Glancing at the title of this chapter one might immediately question the validity of studying the book of Hebrews with a view toward sacramental overtones. Additionally, one might question why a NT epistle would be considered in a book dealing with the Eucharist in the OT. The following rationale is offered.

The earliest Christian churches were comprised almost exclusively of Jews. Obviously these first-century Jews drew their theology and terminology from the OT, and thus a study of the NT epistle addressed to them cannot but help in understanding how such OT theology and terminology were used by early Hebrew Christians. These Jews grasped Christianity as the proper continuation of Judaism. As a natural consequence, most primitive Christians were fluent in Jewish sacrificial terminology, and their liturgical life was permeated with sacrificial themes.[2]

In this Jewish cloud of witnesses, even before Pentecost, Christ had

---

[1] Daniel J. Brege, "Eucharistic Overtones Created by Sacrificial Concepts in the Epistle to the Hebrews," *Concordia Theological Quarterly* 66 (January 2002): 61-81, condenses this chapter.
[2] F.C.N. Hicks, *The Fullness of Sacrifice* (London: S.P.C.K., 1956), 248, "…Sacrificial thought and language, and the underlying principles of sacrifice, were at once the inheritance of our Lord and the New Testament writers from the past, the material for much of their own thoughts and words and actions, and were capable of expressing the whole content of the Christian revelation."

instituted Holy Communion and Holy Baptism. Among these Hebrew Christians there were no immediate technical words for these sacraments because Christ had given none. Thus it made perfect sense for these Christians to harness their sacrificial language in referencing the two sacraments. Obviously the NT book addressed specifically to the Jews, bearing even "Hebrews" as its title, would be the place to look for such sacramental references veiled in sacrificial language. Moreover, since sacrificial referents clearly permeate the epistle to the Hebrews—far more than any other NT book—it is only logical to consider this epistle in our present study.

Though discussions about both the sacraments of Baptism and the Lord's Supper are, we contend, embedded within the book of Hebrews, we will concentrate especially on the Lord's Supper, which seems to underlie the entire writing.[3]

As explained in previous chapters there are many connections between the Jewish sacrificial rites and the Lord's Supper. However, in our present study of the epistle to the Hebrews, particularly the sin offering and the peace offering will be considered, simply because these two sacrifices are repeatedly referenced in the epistle. Of the peace offering we will demonstrate that several peace offering themes surface throughout the epistle. Because the sin offering sacrificed on the Day of Atonement is a core topic in the book of Hebrews, this special-occasion sin offering will be at the heart of our sin offering discussion.

As we delve into Hebrew worship concepts in relation to this epistle, it

---

[3] Herman Sasse, *This is My Body* (Augsburg Publishing House, 1959; revised edition, Adelaide: Lutheran Publishing House, 1977), 326: "[Jesus is] the Passover Lamb of the New Covenant and the Bread of Life. This understanding of the Lord's Supper we find in 1 Cor. 10:1ff and John 6. It also underlies the Epistle to the Hebrews..." John Edward Field, *The Apostolic Liturgy and the Epistle to the Hebrews* (Waterloo Place, London: Rivingtons, 1882), in his preface (p. i): "One chief purpose of this work is to trace throughout the argument of the Epistle to the Hebrews a continuous allusion to the Holy Eucharist, showing that the writer keeps this always in view as the practical centre of Christian Worship and the highest expression of the Christian Faith."

will perhaps seem strange that so much needs to be explained in order to grasp the meaning of the epistle. It should be borne in mind, however, that the Hebrews to whom the epistle was first addressed effortlessly realized what the author of the epistle was talking about when he spoke of the many OT worship practices; this epistle was not that difficult for them to grasp. In addition to readily understanding OT worship practices, most in the audience for this epistle were also conversant in NT worship practices as well.

The Centrality of Baptism and Eucharist

In primitive Christianity the Lord's Supper and Baptism were critical marks, externally identifying what it meant to be a church.[4] These two sacred ordinances were in place and being practiced over a century before the "New Testament" books of the Bible were finalized as the rule and norm of the faith. A corollary to this is that these two sacraments were consistently employed in all of the churches within early Christendom, and that without these sacraments a church was heterodox, which means it wasn't within mainstream Christianity and perhaps was not even Christian. In support of this assertion Walter Oetting writes concerning the Eucharist, "The wealth of liturgical material that remains from the celebration of the Eucharist by early Christians supports the thesis that the Eucharist was the most important element of their worship every Lord's Day."[5] Concerning Baptism, one must simply read the NT *Acts of the Apostles* to observe the prominence of this initiatory sacrament in first century Christianity.

That the two sacraments were the norm within primitive Christian

---

[4] Some deny the writer of Hebrews to have been referring to the Eucharist. They do this by denying the universal practice of the Eucharist in first century Christianity. An example of this is R. Williamson, "The Eucharist and the Epistle to the Hebrews," *New Testament Studies*, 21: 300-312. Williamson believes "that the author of Hebrews did not share in the eucharistic faith and practice of other segments of the Early Church." He continues, "It is almost incredible that the author of Hebrews should have believed what he did about the 'already' and the 'not yet', without relating those beliefs to the Eucharist, if in fact he did belong to a community in which that Sacrament was celebrated." (312).

[5] Walter Oetting, *Church of the Catacombs* (St. Louis: Concordia Publishing House, 1964), 38.

churches is entirely consistent not only with the Biblical witness but with additional historical data as well. With this in mind, it becomes increasingly clear why it is appropriate to seek sacramental overtones embedded in the sacrificial references within the book of Hebrews.

Why Isn't the Eucharist Obvious in Hebrews?

Though the two sacraments are clearly found in Acts and in 1 Corinthians, and Holy Baptism is referenced in almost every NT book, some have legitimately questioned why references to the two sacraments are not obvious in the book of Hebrews, or for that matter why the Eucharist is not detected in the other epistles of the NT. We have already given one reason for this seeming absence: the technical terminology had not been fully developed and thus there could be numerous sacramental references that remain veiled to those who are only familiar with modern Christian jargon.[6]

To first century Christians we believe the sacraments *were* obvious in the epistle to the Hebrews. A theory supported throughout our entire book is that NT sacramental discussions were initially presented in terms of Jewish worship practices. Consequently as the ignorance of these temple-related practices increased through the centuries, sacramental references became more and more obscure.

There are two additional reasons why sacramental references are not glaringly obvious in the book of Hebrews.

First, if the sacraments were basic to catechesis and worship, one would not have to directly refer to them in writing or speaking. An early Christian preacher (or writer) would assume that properly instructed Christian hearers would make the appropriate connections to the sacraments when

---

[6] James Swetnam, ""The Greater and More Perfect Tent". A Contribution to the Discussion of Hebrews 9,11," *Biblica* 47, (1966): 91-106. P. 106, Swetnam concludes, "The fact that a modern theological term like the 'Eucharist' must be imposed on the epistle for the sake of clarity for the modern reader does not mean that the author of Hebrews did not have a reflex ordering of his knowledge (i.e., a theology) about Christ's cultic body and blood. But his theology was in terms of Old Testament realities rather than in terms of philosophical analysis or of subsequent Christian thought."

listening to a sermon that didn't even specifically mention them. To speak or to write about Jesus Christ was sufficient unto itself, because the catechized Christian listeners would automatically realize that Christ and His works of salvation are received via the Sacraments. E. L. Mascall thus explains that the sacraments are not merely additional events in the life of Christ, but the life of Christ is "a permanent reality communicated to the Church under the sacramental signs." He then summarizes this thinking relative to the Eucharist in the book of Hebrews:

> Thus, if from one point of view we are bound to say that there is nothing about the Eucharist in the Epistle to the Hebrews, from another point of view we might almost say that the Epistle is about nothing else. For everything that the Epistle describes is given to us in the Eucharist; it would be a pitiful weakening of the theme to make the Eucharist one item in the series.[7]

Such a quote conveys the important reality that the sacraments were foundational, even crucial in understanding Christ and the distribution of His gifts of salvation.

Another reason why the sacraments (especially the Lord's Supper) are not clearly expressed in several NT writings is the esoteric attitude of the early Christian community. We already discussed this secretive attitude in chapter one, and there we referenced it as the *discipline of the secret*. This "discipline of the secret" dictated that in the early history of Christianity the theology of the Lord's Supper was not revealed to a person until that person was sufficiently mature in the faith. The basics of the Lord's Supper were thus *purposely* veiled to those outside the faith. This "veiling" of the Eucharist is really the definition of the esoteric attitude among early Christians. Recall that this practice followed Jesus' prescription that Christians "not give what is holy

---

[7] Alan M. Stibbs, *Sacrament, Sacrifice and Eucharist* (London: Billing and Son LTD., 1961), 18,19. Stibbs references E.L. Mascall, *Corpus Christi*, Longmans Green, 1953, 109.

to the dogs."[8] Thus the sacred theology of Holy Communion would not be paraded in public writings.

Joachim Jeremias shows how Hippolytus of Rome maintained this esoteric attitude. Jeremias explains that Hippolytus, writing around 215AD, wanted to preserve the *older usage* of catechesis: "Hippolytus of Rome in his *Apostolic Tradition* (about 215), which is concerned to portray the older usage, concludes the section on Baptism and Eucharist with the words, 'He shall not tell this to any but the faithful.'"[9] What is truly amazing in this quote is that already in 215AD keeping sacramental instruction away from the public was considered the "older usage" in Christian catechesis! Jeremias also explains that this secretive attitude is very likely the reason why NT books such as the Gospel of John and the epistle to the Hebrews are lacking in *obvious* sacramental content. Concerning the book of Hebrews he writes:

> The epistle to the Hebrews offers evidence pointing in the same direction [as the Gospel of John]. The conspicuous absence of any reference to the Eucharist in the list of subjects taught to beginners in the faith (Heb. 6.1f) is probably to be explained by the consideration that the eucharistic doctrine belonged to those elements which were reserved to the 'mature'.[10]

If indeed the sacramental details were only presented to the mature, it would also make sense that early writers would then convey sacramental

---

[8] Matthew 7:6. Some have seen this to be a specific reference to the Lord's Supper. The "holy things" in Matthew 7:6, not to be given to the dogs, may be terminology drawn from verses such as Leviticus 22:10,14, which refer to eating "holy things." Before Communion distribution within Greek churches, the liturgy declares, "Holy Things for Holy Ones." Sasse, *This is My Body*, 320: "'Ta hagia tois hagiois' (sancta sanctis, 'the holy things [body and blood of the Lord][sic] to the saints') was an exclamation of the Greek liturgies, still in use today."
[9] Joachim Jeremias, *The Eucharistic Words of Jesus* (London: SCM Press, 1966), 136. James Swetnam, ""The Greater and More Perfect Tent," 96: "The fact that the early Church was under the 'Discipline of the Secret', i.e., was not allowed to speak openly about the cult of the Church, seems to be at least partially responsible for the vagueness of references [in Hebrews] where reference are found, and the relative lack of testimony in general."
[10] Jeremias, *The Eucharistic...*, 134.

"hints" so that the mature Christian reader or hearer would readily recognize and be instructed by such hints. These sacramental "hints," we believe, are scattered throughout the book of Hebrews, and are purposely veiled under Jewish sacrificial terminology; mature Hebrew Christians would have easily identified them. Moreover such Eucharistic "hints" are not merely scattered throughout Hebrews as if they were simply incidental remarks, but they are, as will be shown in this chapter, the very bedrock of the epistle.

Reviewing Two Sacrificial Basics

Recall the important fact that in Jewish sacrifice the blood was never burned within the tabernacle precincts.[11] It was placed upon a person or upon the outer parts of one of the two altars, or it was sacredly sprinkled toward a holy place or a person, or it was poured at the base of the Bronze Altar.[12] Blood was *the* most sacred element of sacrifice. It was the atoning element. It was life.[13] This understanding of sacrificial blood will be essential in rightly discerning the epistle to the Hebrews.

It should also be borne in mind, as frequently explained already in previous chapters, that when a Jew spoke of sacrifice, all of the sacrifices

---

[11] This is true of all blood in the sacred ritual *within* the Tabernacle. There was however one exception concerning the burning of blood. The sacred ashes of the Red Heifer, prepared *outside* the Tabernacle, were obtained partly by the burning of its blood! (Numbers 19:5). This peculiar part of OT sacrifice is referenced in Hebrews 9:13 where it is perhaps utilized to connect the sprinkling of "sacrificial blood" with God's people, via the water combined with the ashes of the Red Heifer. Or possibly this is again a reference in Hebrews to the Day of Atonement, for which the high priest was to be sprinkled with the Red Heifer ashes and water. See Alfred Edersheim, *The Temple, Its Ministry and Services* (Peabody, MS: Hendrickson Publishers, 1994), 245,282.

[12] Brooke Westcott, *The Epistle to the Hebrews* (Grand Rapids: Eerdmans Publishing Company, 1973), 291f has a good summary of the Jewish blood rites.

[13] Westcott, *The Epistle...*, 293,294: "I have endeavoured to shew elsewhere that the Scriptural idea of Blood is essentially an idea of life and not of death...The Blood...represents the energy of the physical, earthly, life as it is. The use of the term in the Epistle to the Hebrews becomes first fully intelligible by taking account of this truth." Also S.C. Gayford, *Sacrifice and Priesthood* (London: Mathuen & Co., 1924; second ed. 1953), 68.

were often blended together.[14] One could almost say that the different sacrifices were perceived not so much as different sacrifices but as stages of sacrifice.[15] The first stage of sacrifice was the sin/guilt offering. The second stage was the burnt offering. The third and final stage was the peace offering. These three stages are observed frequently in this order in the OT, and even though only one stage may be mentioned yet the other stages can often be assumed to be present as well. Such an understanding will be important in our study of the epistle to the Hebrews, because the author of this epistle frequently blends the various sacrifices, speaking one moment of one type of sacrifice then, without warning, switching his discussion to another type. This was both natural for a temple-familiar Jew and it also showed how all of the sacrifices were, as a unified concept, fulfilled in Jesus Christ.

The Author of Hebrews Identifies His Purpose

> *"Now the main point in what has been said is this: We have such a high priest..."*
> **Hebrews 8:1**

Unlike numerous other biblical writers the author of the book of Hebrews actually states the main point (or *a* main point) of his writing:[16]

Now the main point in what has been said is this: we have such a

---

[14] Hicks, *The Fullness...*, 311: "In practice they [types of sacrifice] were offered together: and if, under the exigencies of language the word sacrifice could be applied to each, it is still true that each contained several of the essential acts of the whole procedure. There is no warrant for applying the word "sacrifice" to the death of the victim alone, or to the use of the blood, or to the offering; but if there were, it would be equally applicable to the act of eating with which the complete sacrificial action ended."

[15] Hicks, *The Fullness...*. Throughout Hicks relates the different sacrifices as "stages" within the single concept of sacrifice.

[16] Though we refer to the Epistle as a "writing" yet many consider it to have originally been a sermon. E.g. William Lane, *Hebrews 9-13*; also Albert Vanhoye, "Structure and Message of the Epistle to the Hebrews," trans. James Swetnam, *Subsidia Biblica* 12 (Rome: Editrice Pontificio Instituto Biblico, 1989).

high priest who has taken His seat at the right hand of the throne of the Majesty in the heavens, a minister in the sanctuary, and in the true tabernacle, which the Lord pitched, not man. For every high priest is appointed to offer both gifts and sacrifices; hence it is necessary that this high priest also have something to offer. (Hebrews 8:1-3).[17]

Three verses after this statement, the writer then compares Jesus to the Levitical priests who served the Temple: "But now He [Jesus] has obtained a more excellent ministry [than the Levitical priests], by as much as He is also the mediator of a better covenant." (Hebrews 8:6)

As the author of Hebrews in these few verses summarizes his main point, questions are generated. We now list four of these questions, which will serve to outline our present chapter: *What does it mean that Christ is a priest mediating a better covenant? What does it mean that Christ is at the right hand in the tabernacle pitched by God? What does it mean that Christ is a "minister"? What are the gifts and sacrifices offered by Christ and how does He offer them?* The answers to these questions, it will be shown, relate the Jewish sacrificial system to the Sacrament of the Altar. The answers also permeate and interconnect the entire epistle to the Hebrews.

What Does it Mean That Christ is a Priest, Mediating a Better Covenant?

> *"[You have come] to Jesus, the mediator of a new covenant, and to the sprinkled blood..."*
> *Hebrews 12:24.*

As a priest, Christ would be responsible to administer the sacrifices,

---

[17] We will frequently note the specific Hebrews references in the text rather than in footnotes, so the reader can more clearly perceive the relationship and context of certain verses.

and as such to mediate between God and man. It is obvious to Christians, and it is clearly stated throughout Hebrews, that Christ is both *the* priest and *the* sacrifice.[18] The author of Hebrews relates Christ's priestly work particularly in terms of the peace offering and the sin offering. We will now penetrate these priestly sacrifices and present their probable relationship to the Lord's Supper in the epistle.

Christ, Priest of the Peace Offering

Recall that the two main marks of peace offerings were that they were eaten, and that such eating was joined with joyful celebration. These main marks will be sufficient for understanding the peace offering in the epistle to the Hebrews. Because of its emphasis on sacred feasting, the peace offering has been recognized by Bible students to be the most natural sacrifice used to explain the Lord's Supper. Andrew Jukes summarizes, "The peace-offering remains our food until the resurrection."[19]

Peace Offering: "Confession" Sacrifice

We begin with a rather obscure reference to Christ's priestly work as it relates to peace offerings. Hebrews 3:1 labels Jesus as the "high priest of our *confession*." It appears to be a little known fact that the Greek word used here for "confession" was also a technical word used by Jews for the peace offering.[20] The peace offering was not associated with confession of sins but rather with confession of praise and thanksgiving. This is likely why the peace offering was at times called a "confession." To call Jesus the "high priest of our *confession*" makes perfect sense because he administers and mediates this sacrifice of Himself, distributing the peace offering feast to His

---

[18] See e.g. Hebrews 7:27; 9:11,12,26; 10:10-12.
[19] Andrew Jukes, *The Law of the Offerings in Leviticus I.-VII, Considered as the Appointed Figure of the Various Aspects of the Offering of the Body of Jesus Christ* (London: James Nisbet & Co., 1883), 109. Field, *The Apostolic...*, 41,42, says that the Lord's Supper "is, in fact, the continuance of the ceremonial of the Mosaic peace-offering."
[20] We label it a "little known fact" because the only theologian this writer has found to point this out is Field, *The Apostolic Liturgy...*.

people. When Jesus is here called "*high priest* of our confession" the title *high priest* is especially appropriate when "confession" is understood to be a sacrifice.

John Field explains that the word *confession* was indeed used for *peace offering*: "And accordingly, this word *Confession,* like the word *Eucharist* or *Thanksgiving,* was one of the terms in the Jewish Church for the peace-offering, or, as it was frequently called, the Sacrifice of Praise."[21] Thus, for example, the Septuagint, the official Jewish Greek translation of the Hebrew Bible, used the Greek word "confession" in Leviticus 22:18 to translate the votive peace offering. Field also shows how Clement of Rome, who wrote around the year 100—writing as if he "had the Epistle to the Hebrews before him"—obviously references Hebrews 3:1 by calling Jesus "the high priest of our *offerings.*" The context of this statement by Clement is the peace offering, which Clement has just cited as the "Sacrifice of Praise."[22] Field, who is convinced Saint Paul is the author of Hebrews, comments about this quote from Clement: "It is evident, therefore, that S. Clement is paraphrasing S. Paul's words [in Hebrews 3:1], and that he uses the word *offerings* as a substitute for the *confession* in S. Paul."[23] Thus it is apparent that Clement believed that the Greek word for "confession" in Hebrews 3:1 was being utilized to refer to the peace offering.

Field connects this with the Christian Eucharist by concluding, "Now the peace-offering, which this word *Confession* represents, is the form of sacrifice under the Mosaic Law which corresponds most closely with the Christian Eucharist."[24] Christ Jesus is indeed the *high priest* of our *confession,* for He offers up Himself as our peace offering, and then He again serves as priest by mediating the meal. As He performs this priestly mediation we may feast upon Him, confessing our praise in the celebration of Holy

---

[21] Field, *The Apostolic...*, 92.
[22] Field, *The Apostolic...*, 94.
[23] Ibid., 95. Emphasis added.
[24] Ibid., 95.

Communion.²⁵ As we here consider whether the Greek word for *confession* was used in the epistle to the Hebrews for the peace offering, bear in mind that frequently these *confession* references are nesting in verses that are rich in Eucharistic language, thus supporting the use of *confession* as a peace offering reference to the Lord's Supper.

If *confession* is a sacrificial term referencing the Lord's Supper in the epistle to the Hebrews, then several other related passages in Hebrews are almost certainly referring to the Eucharist as well.²⁶ Hebrews 4:14 reads: "Since then we have a great high priest who has passed through the heavens, Jesus the Son of God, let us *hold fast our confession*." Observe here, as in the previous Hebrews reference, that Jesus' *priestly* activity is appropriately associated again with this "confession." This is apt if indeed *confession* is understood to be a reference to *peace offering*. Later this verse in Hebrews will be shown to have other Eucharistic innuendo as well. The Hebrew Christians are encouraged in this verse to *hold fast* to their *confession*. To *hold fast* to the Lord's Supper and to the praise surrounding it is an appropriate exhortation to Jewish believers who were prone to "hold fast" to the temple rituals and OT sacrifices instead.

As another example, consider the use of "confession" in Hebrews 10:23. As will be discussed in a later portion of our present chapter, this verse is also nestled in a section of Hebrews that has much sacramental language. Hebrews 10:21,23 explain that "...since we have a great priest over the house of God...Let us *hold fast the confession* of our hope without wavering, for He who promised is faithful..." Once again Christ's *priestly*

---

²⁵ Hicks, *The Fullness*..., 326: In the context of the Lord's Supper, Hicks pointedly remarks: "But our alms, the elements [bread and wine], our own lives: to say that these are worthy to be offered to God [as praise] in themselves is either pagan or Pelagian. It is not Christian. Nothing that we have, no offering that we can make...can be brought to God otherwise than 'through Jesus Christ our Lord'."

²⁶ Westcott, *The Epistle*..., 323. Westcott explains that ομολογεω "was used specially of the confession at Baptism." Field, *The Apostolic*..., 268, neatly connects the two sacraments under the "confession": "And the 'fulfillment' of the Baptismal 'Faith' is obviously the Eucharistic 'Confession.'"

activity is directly linked to this *confession*, the peace offering sacrifice. Also, as in Hebrews 4:14, the Hebrew recipients of this epistle are exhorted to *hold fast the confession*.

As a final example, Hebrews 13:15 not only contains the word "confession" but many translators reflect the Jewish eucharistic flavor and actually translate "confession" as giving "thanks": "Through Him then, let us continually offer up a sacrifice of praise to God, that is, the fruit of lips that give thanks ["confession"] to His name." Though this passage does not refer to Christ as priest, yet it verifies "confession" as peace offering in another way by calling it a "sacrifice of praise." Recall that this too was terminology used for the peace offering. As with the other passages in Hebrews related to "confession," this passage also will be more thoroughly investigated later as it too contains other sacrificial themes that clearly relate it to the Lord's Supper.

Peace Offering: Covenant Sacrifice

In the epistle to the Hebrews Christ's priestly work relative to the peace offering is repeatedly related to the theme of *covenant*.[27] Recall that a covenant (or "testament"[28]) was sealed with peace offering blood and ratified by a meal drawn from a peace offering.[29]

As we discussed the peace offering in chapter six, the prophet Jeremiah's prediction of a *new covenant* was shown to have noteworthy correlations with the Lord's Supper. Recall that Jeremiah's prediction especially connected the peace offering and the sin offering to God's new covenant in Christ. Since covenant theology permeates the epistle to the Hebrews, it is no coincidence, we believe, that the author of Hebrews quotes

---

[27] William L. Lane, *A Call to Commitment* (Peabody: Hendrickson Publishers, 1985), 139. See our discussion in chapter six.
[28] Much could be considered pertaining to the differences, real and perceived, between the words "covenant" and "testament." This chapter simply treats them as synonymous.
[29] Roland De Vaux, *Studies in Old Testament Sacrifices* (Cardiff University of Wales Press, 1964), 38.

this entire "new covenant" prophecy from the thirty-first chapter of Jeremiah.[30] This quote from Jeremiah is the longest OT quote found in the NT, and it makes sense that it would be found in Hebrews since the two main sacrifices in Jeremiah's prediction (peace and sin offerings) are the two sacrifices emphasized in the epistle to the Hebrews as well.

Covenant Inauguration

The primary example of a covenant being sealed by both blood and a communion meal is found in God's institution of the covenant through Moses as recorded in Exodus 24. Exodus 24:5 explains that after Moses built an altar, "they offered burnt offerings and sacrificed young bulls as *peace offerings* to the Lord." Verse 8 describes how Moses "took the blood and sprinkled it on the people, and said, 'Behold the blood of the covenant, which the Lord has made with you in accordance with all these words.'" This covenant blood that Moses sprinkled was the blood from the peace offering just sacrificed. Concerning this covenant, inaugurated through Moses, Hebrews 9:18 relates that "even the first covenant was not inaugurated without blood."[31] Since the peace offerings were to be eaten in the sealing of a covenant, Exodus 24:11 presents the communion meal of Moses' peace offering by stating, "they beheld God, and *they ate and drank*."[32] In this record, we observe God—through Moses—inaugurating the covenant by both the sprinkled blood and the communion meal that followed.[33] This was standard procedure for establishing a covenant. Keep in mind Moses' words, "Behold the blood of the covenant."

---

[30] Hebrews 8:7-13
[31] As reflected in this verse, the author of Hebrews considered this covenant established through Moses (Ex. 24) to be the *first* covenant, and that Christ's covenant is the new covenant.
[32] Jeremias, *The Eucharistic...*, 235: "Concerning Exodus 24:11 ["the elders ate and drank"]: In these last words the thought is of a covenant meal: the fact that God grants to the envoys the fellowship of his table is the pledge of the covenant."
[33] Hicks, *The Fullness...*, 22: "It must be realized that when a Jew thought of a covenant he thought of a sacrifice." 325: "No covenant-meal was other than sacrificial." Westcott, *The Epistle...*, 440: "His [Christ's] blood became the blood of a New Covenant (x.29)...and the Covenant sacrifice became the groundwork of a feast."

Christ is compared to Moses in the book of Hebrews almost from the beginning.[34] As God *inaugurated* the first covenant through Moses, even so God in Christ *inaugurated* the second covenant.[35] Christ, however, inaugurated the second covenant with His own blood, shed upon the cross. When God through Moses inaugurated the old covenant, Moses referred to the blood as the "The blood of the covenant." The only place where Christ calls His blood "The blood of the covenant" is in His Holy Supper. Unlike Moses who sprinkled the blood upon the people, Christ applies the blood of His new covenant by drinking. Keep this relationship between sprinkling and drinking in mind.

When Moses sprinkled the testamental blood he declared, "*Behold*, the blood of the covenant." (Ex. 24:8). It may seem unimportant to some and strange to others that in Hebrews 9:20 the author of the epistle changes Moses' words to, "*This* is the blood of the covenant." Many, noting this change, have correctly observed that when Christ instituted the Lord's Supper He used exactly these words, "*This* is the blood of the covenant. (Matthew 26:28)." Could changing "*Behold*, the blood..." to "*This* is the blood..." be a clever (or perhaps common!) means utilized by the author of Hebrews to direct his hearers to the Lord's Supper?[36] William Lane, who appears to approach the Lord's Supper from a reformed viewpoint, must nevertheless concede, "It is widely held that the substitution [of "This" for "Behold"]...shows that the quotation [in Hebrews 9:20] has been brought into conformity with the

---

[34] Observe the initial specific comparison in Hebrews 3:1ff.

[35] "Inaugurated"(εγκαινιζειν) appears to be used in Hebrews, as in other Jewish writings, in a technical way. See discussion below on Hebrews 10:19ff.

[36] Field, *The Apostolic*..., 236: "In Exodus xxiv.8 we read: '*Behold* the Blood of the Covenant which the Lord hath covenanted unto you.' But S. Paul [whom Field believes wrote Hebrews] writes, '*This* [is] the Blood," evidently to bring out the parallel with the words of Christ." Swetnam, ""The Greater...,98: "The mere change in wording in itself would not be more than suggestive were it not for the context: in the context Moses is pictured as "inaugurating" the Sinai διαθηκη with blood (9:18). And the implication is that he is foreshadowing Christ, who is the mediator of the new testament just as Moses was the mediator of the old. This at once evokes the scene of the institution of the Eucharist by Christ at the Last Supper; the change in wording of Ex. 24,8 to conform to the Eucharistic formula can then hardly be a matter of chance."

eucharistic words of Christ, perhaps under the influence of a local liturgical tradition."[37] Even as God inaugurated his first covenant through Moses, God inaugurated his second covenant through His Son. Both testamental inaugurations involved participation in the blood of the covenant—one by sprinkling and the other by drinking—and both covenants were sealed by eating the covenant-sealing peace offering flesh.

Covenant Mediation

After God through Moses *inaugurated* the first covenant, Aaron and his sons then *mediated* it. These men were the priests of the first covenant. As the covenant of Moses was *inaugurated* by the sprinkling of blood, so the sprinkling of sacrificial blood continued as the sign of the priestly *mediation* of the old covenant.[38] No longer would this covenant of Moses need to be *inaugurated*, however it would have to be *mediated*. Such mediation meant the continued application and participation in the covenant already inaugurated through Moses. This mediation was the main purpose for the Jewish priesthood, and it was actuated as they serviced the divinely directed sacrificial system.

Hebrews 9:1 describes such priestly mediation of the first covenant: "Now even the first covenant had regulations of *divine worship* and the earthly sanctuary." This verse describes the mediation of the first covenant as the OT priests led the people in "divine worship" via the prescribed rituals and liturgy of the tabernacle—the "earthly sanctuary." In the subsequent verses of Hebrews 9, this "earthly sanctuary" is described in detail. The divine worship in this earthly tabernacle involved sacrifice, which meant that certain animal portions would be burned upon the altar. However, beyond such sacrificial

---

[37] William L. Lane, *Hebrews 9-13*, Word Biblical Commentary, vol. 47b (Dallas: Word Books, 1991), 245. Lane, however, does not believe this to be necessarily the case.

[38] Robert J. Daly, *Christian Sacrifice* (Washington, D.C.: The Catholic University of America Press, 1978), 90,93: Daly concludes that "selamim," the word for peace offering, should really be understood as "covenant-sacrifice." Daly (89) maintains that the priestly mediation ("Mosaic cult") was founded upon the sacrifice of Isaac, the Passover and the Covenant Sacrifice of Exodus 24.

burning, the priestly "divine worship" primarily meant the sacred sprinkling (or other application) of blood, the cleansing with water, *and especially* the eating of the sacred meals. Hebrews 9:10 emphasizes the eating aspect of the priestly work by explaining that the priests were thus occupied with "*food and drink* and washings." Such "food and drink and washings," to be further discussed in relation to Hebrews 9:10, summarized the "gifts and sacrifices" mediated by the priests. As both the laity and the priests *ate* the peace offerings, the "old covenant" was continuously mediated.

Christ then comes as the "great high priest," and in a far greater way than Aaron and his sons He now *mediates* the final covenant. Hebrews 8:6 describes this divine worship led by Christ: "But now He [Jesus] has obtained a more excellent ministry [than the Levitical priests], by as much as He is also the *mediator* of a better covenant..." Not only does this verse reflect Christ's priestly work as "mediator" wherein He replaces the Aaronic priesthood, but the Greek word used here for "ministry" was a technical worship-word among the Jews. We will consider this word shortly.

The Sprinkled Blood

If the Aaronic priesthood mediated the "first" divine covenant by sprinkled blood and by communion meals drawn from the sacrificial flesh, how then does the great high priest, Jesus, mediate the New Covenant? Christ takes the concepts of the old covenant, keeps the continuity recognizable, but then He incorporates radical changes into the rite. For instance, the blood of the old covenant, which was never to be eaten, was mediated by sprinkling, daubing or pouring—usually at God's altar.[39] Recall that Moses sprinkled the covenant blood upon the people as he declared, "Behold the blood of the covenant." Christ, like Moses and the first covenant, also now directs His people to the blood of the covenant, but now it is mediated by drinking. John Edward Field is convinced that the references to "sprinkling of blood" in

---

[39] Such blood would be sprinkled or daubed upon a human being when Moses inaugurated the covenant, and also on special occasions such as the ordination of the priests.

Hebrews are really references to the Blood of the Eucharist that Christians now drink:

> In chapter ix. he [the writer of Hebrews] had spoken of Moses 'sprinkling the people' with 'the Blood of the Testament,' regarding this as a type of the Eucharist. Now again [in Hebrews 12:24] he [the author of Hebrews] speaks of the 'Blood of sprinkling,' with the 'Mediator of a New Testament'; and it is plain that he is thinking of the Blood of the New Testament. The thought conveyed by the sprinkling no doubt is that the reception of the Eucharistic cup is a spiritual sprinkling of the heart with the Blood of Christ to fit it for the worship of God, just as the old ritual sprinklings removed the various kinds of legal defilement."[40]

We believe Field's application is correct, for the evidence throughout the epistle to the Hebrews indicates a *real* participation in the blood of Christ, and this participation is frequently spoken of in terms of *sprinkled blood*.

It is important to realize that even as the various Hebrew sacrifices had a certain connectedness from one kind of sacrifice to another, the OT covenant was mediated not merely by the peace offering but also by participation in sin offerings. As we demonstrated in chapter five, the sin offering blood was uniquely *sprinkled* in the tabernacle regulations; other sacrifices in the tabernacle did not involve such *sprinkling*.[41] When the priests continually sprinkled the sin offering blood in the sacrificial rites, this was not only a reminder of the original blood-sprinkling when Moses inaugurated the

---

[40] Field, *The Apostolic*..., 380. Kleinig, *Leviticus*, 371: "By giving his blood to drink, he sprinkles their hearts, their consciences (Heb 9:13-14; 10:22; 12:24; 1 Pet 1:2). ...In the light of all this, it comes as no surprise that the description of the Divine Service in Heb 12:22-24 culminates in 'the blood for the sprinkling.' Our involvement in the heavenly liturgy is only possible through the blood of Jesus. Through his blood the risen Lord Jesus gives God's holy people access to the heavenly city here on earth."

[41] Though English translations may use the word "sprinkle" for various blood applications, it was only the blood of the sin offering that was truly sprinkled.

covenant with the unique *peace offering* sacrifice, but it was a continued mediation of the Mosaic covenant via the *sin offering* blood. Brooke Westcott explains, "It follows from the general idea of the Jewish sacrifices that they were ruled by the conception of the Covenant."[42]

Westcott also then divides Jewish sacrifices into two categories: Sacrifices made while the covenant relation is valid and those made in regard to violations of the covenant. This second category of sacrifice—that which was sacrificed because of *violations of the covenant*—is describing the sin offering. Recall that the sin offering was established uniquely for the nation of Israel shortly after Moses had sprinkled the blood drawn from the covenant-sealing peace offering. Thus, appropriately, the sin offering blood was sprinkled, like the peace offering blood on Mt. Sinai, because it involved the continued *mediation* of God's covenant. Though the *peace offering* blood was initially sprinkled in the *inauguration* of the Mosaic covenant, such peace offering blood was *not* sprinkled when the OT priests *mediated* this covenant. Nonetheless the OT covenant was truly *mediated* by the sprinkling of blood, blood drawn from the *sin offerings* in the OT sacrificial rituals. Thus references to sprinkled blood in the epistle to the Hebrews call to mind both the *peace offering* blood that Moses sprinkled at the *inauguration* of the first covenant and the *sin offering* blood that the OT priests sprinkled in the *mediation* of that covenant.

In addition to the sin offering blood, the ashes of the red heifer were also sacredly sprinkled in order to offer cleansing and forgiveness.[43] The sacrifice of the red heifer was considered the most intense of sin offerings, and the sprinkling of its ashes was considered a most potent remedy for sin/uncleanness. Hebrews 9:13,14 review this sprinkling of blood and ashes:

For if the blood of [sin offering] goats and [sin offering] bulls and the

---

[42] Westcott, *The Epistle*..., 288
[43] Edersheim, *The Temple*..., 281, says the Red Heifer was the most intense sin offering. The week before the Day of Atonement the high priest was twice cleansed with these ashes (245).

ashes of a heifer sprinkling those who have been defiled, sanctify for the cleansing of the flesh, how much more will the blood of Christ, who through the eternal Spirit offered Himself without blemish to God, cleanse your conscience from dead works to serve the living God?

The obvious implication here is that the blood of Christ is now the antitype of the OT "sprinkled blood [and ashes]," and Christ's blood totally cleanses the conscience. Where then do Christians encounter this "sprinkled blood" of Christ? The next verse, Hebrews 9:15, continues the line of thinking:

> And *for this reason* He is the *mediator of a new covenant*, in order that since a death has taken place for the redemption of the transgressions that were committed under the first covenant, those who have been called may receive the promise of the eternal inheritance [emphasis added].

"For this reason," this verse begins; for what reason? The reason Christ mediates the new covenant is to cleanse a Christian's conscience that he/she might serve the living God. As this verse explains, Christ is the *mediator of a new covenant*. Simply referring to Christ's new covenant would have triggered Eucharistic thinking in the minds of the early Christians, but this verse magnifies this relationship by explaining that Jesus *mediates* the new covenant. Where else but in the Eucharist do we find such mediation! Jesus mediates the new covenant not by sprinkling His blood but by offering it to drink: "Drink of it, all of you, for this cup is the *new covenant in my blood*."[44]

The author of Hebrews emphasizes the Christian's approach to this sprinkled blood of Jesus. Hebrews 10:22, embedded in rich Eucharistic references, invites, "Let us draw near with a sincere heart and full assurance

---

[44] Combined wording from Luke 22:20 and Matthew 26:27,28.

of faith, having our hearts *sprinkled clean* from an evil conscience..." Hebrews 12:24, again nestled in Eucharistic references, encourages Christians to approach Jesus, "the mediator of a new covenant, and to the *sprinkled blood*..." Strangely, even though there was technically no "sprinkled" blood in the Passover, yet the author of the epistle to the Hebrews refers to Passover blood as having been sprinkled.[45] Hebrews 11:28: "By faith he [Moses] kept the Passover and the *sprinkling of the blood*, so that he who destroyed the firstborn might not touch them." Why all this talk about sprinkled blood, even connecting it to the Passover? With such connections to the mediation of a new covenant, we agree with Field, that the "sprinkled blood" in Hebrews is the way the author of the epistle directed his audience to the blood of Jesus received in the Lord's Supper. Such sprinkled blood in the epistle to the Hebrews is not merely remembered, nor is it simply symbolic terminology, but Christ's sprinkled blood, as referenced in the epistle, is truly encountered. This blood of the Savior is now a blood that is not sprinkled outwardly but sprinkled inwardly as it is encountered in the Eucharist by drinking.

In some transcendent way Christ now mediates His blood of the covenant, offering it to His people as true drink. Observe the continuity of testamental blood, but then also perceive the incorporation of something radically different: *drinking*. As Hicks explains: "His [Christ's] blood itself, the very Life of the sacrifice, too holy in the old days ever to be received, and never imparted to any offerer, priest, or layman, more closely than by an external sprinkling, is given to every Christian worshipper to drink."[46]

Concerning the sacrificial meals, though there was indeed eating of the sacrificial flesh in the Jewish peace offerings and in the "regular" sin offerings, yet from the most sacred sin offerings no one, not even the priests, were allowed to eat. When this is discussed later in this chapter it will be

---

[45] The reference is likely to the blood placed on the original Passover doorposts and lintel. But why use the word, "sprinkle?" Such use fit the discussion of the Eucharist!

[46] Hicks, *The Fullness*..., 237; 245: "They will realise their corporate unity alike with all the children of God and with their Father; and still more the blood, which is the Life of mankind, and will be theirs, not in a mere outward sprinkling, but in themselves by the act of drinking."

observed that here Christ again incorporates another of His radical changes; for His people are given the privilege to eat of even *the* most sacred sin offering. In some transcendent way, certainly not as cannibals consume flesh, Christ offers His people His flesh as true food. In the Lord's Supper there is continuity with the OT, but there are also radically new and profound things as well. It does not work to take new wine and put it into old wineskins.

Ancient Liturgical Connections to Hebrews 12

The writer of Hebrews in a single verse vividly unites in Christ the liturgical themes of priestly mediation, covenant and sprinkled blood: "[You have come] to Jesus, the mediator of a new covenant, and to the sprinkled blood...(Hebrews 12:24)." As just explained, such sprinkled blood finds its application in the eucharistic drinking of Christ's blood, and clearly such a covenantal reference here in Hebrews 12:24 would have stirred the minds of early Christians to recall Christ's Supper as well. Thus, even standing alone, Hebrews 12:24 has eucharistic overtones. Lending support to this eucharistic argument is the context of Hebrews 12:24. The verses preceding this verse describe the Christian approach to God:

> But you have come to Mount Zion and to the city of the living God, the heavenly Jerusalem, and to myriads of angels, to the general assembly and church of the first-born who are enrolled in heaven, and to God, the Judge of all, and to the spirits of righteous men made perfect. (Hebrews 12:22,23).

The Jews, who in the first century were very familiar with their official Greek Bible (Septuagint), would likely have associated these verses with Holy Communion simply from the fact that the word for "general assembly" was usually used in the Septuagint for the festal assembly at worship-related feasts!⁴⁷ A spiritually mature Christian might also consider these verses to be referring to Holy Communion simply because they speak of a place where Christians approach Mount Zion, myriads of angels, saints who are already in glory and The Judge Himself. Where could such a place be except the "festal assembly" at Holy Communion?

The relationship of these verses to Holy Communion was certainly realized by early worshipers, as attested by ancient Christian liturgies. Perhaps the most ancient of Christian liturgies is the *Liturgy of Saint James*. This liturgy for Holy Communion is so ancient that some believe it predates the writing of the New Testament!⁴⁸ Field contends that the writer of Hebrews had this liturgy in mind as he penned his epistle.⁴⁹

This ancient liturgy connects the elements of Hebrews 12:22,23 to the celebration of the Eucharist. Shortly before the consecration of the bread and wine, the *Liturgy of Saint James*—and indeed other ancient liturgies—had a common introduction called *The Prayer of the Veil*. This prayer has such an important relationship to the book of Hebrews it will later be further explored. *The Prayer of the Veil* in the *Liturgy of Saint James* prefaces Holy Communion with these words [Italics added],

> It is very meet...to give thanks unto Thee...whom the heavens are hymning, ... *the heavenly Jerusalem, the general assembly and church of the firstborn written in heaven, spirits of righteous men* and

---

[47] The "general assembly" (πανηγυρις), only found here in the NT, should surely be translated "festal assembly". This is so because in the LXX πανηγυρις was almost exclusively associated with worship-related feasts! See e.g. Hosea 2:11; 9:5; Amos 5:21; Ezekiel 46:11. Heinrich Seesmann "πανηγυρις," in vol. V, *Theological Dictionary of the New Testament*, ed. Gerhard Kittel and Gerhard Friedrich, trans. Geoffrey W. Bromiley (Grand Rapids: Wm. B. Eerdmans Publishing Co., 1968), 722.

[48] There really was no other liturgy than for Holy Communion.

[49] Field, *The Apostolic...*, Throughout his book, Field presents reasons why the Liturgy of Saint James should be understood to have preceded the New Testament documents. In his preface, p. iii, Field states that his secondary purpose is to "examine the important subject of alleged quotations from the Greek Liturgy of S. James in the New Testament."

prophets, *souls of martyrs and Apostles, angels and archangels.*[50]

Compare this liturgical phrase with Hebrews 12:22,23 just quoted above. With so many matching words, phrases and themes there can be little doubt that either the *Liturgy of Saint James* had Hebrews 12:22,23 in mind or vice versa. Either way, the *Liturgy of Saint James* uses the wording of Hebrews 12:22,23 to introduce the Holy Eucharist. Thus it appears likely that the author of Hebrews considered Hebrews 12:22,23 to be speaking of the Lord's Supper. Thus the verse that follows these verses (12:24), which speaks of the Christian approach to "Jesus, the mediator of a new covenant, and to the sprinkled blood," was almost certainly associated with the Eucharist in the early church as well.

Summarizing what has been said thus far, the priestly work of Jesus as administrator of the peace offering is clearly prevalent in Hebrews. Peace offerings were closely connected both to inaugurating and mediating a covenant (testament). However the mediation of the Mosaic covenant also involved the sin offerings. Christ is observed to be performing his priestly liturgy towards His people as He inaugurates His covenant meal, sheds His blood to seal the covenant, then mediates the covenant in His blood and flesh by His peace offering meal, the Holy Eucharist. The early church had this understanding portrayed in her ancient liturgies. As Christ's priestly work relative to the sin offering is presented next, we will again return to the peace offering as the two are woven together.

Christ, Priest of the Sin Offering

Basic Sin Offering Rubrics

Even as Christ is observed in the epistle to the Hebrews as priestly mediator of the peace offering, so too as High Priest He mediates the sin

---

[50] Field, *The Apostolic...*, 376.

offering. The main characteristics of the OT sin offering included the following. First the offerer confessed his sins as he laid his hands upon the animal to be sacrificed. After the offerer slew the sacrifice the priest sprinkled, daubed and shed the sacrificial blood upon and around one of the altars (but never burned the blood). The fatty portions, considered nearly as sacred as the blood of the creature, were burned upon the Bronze Altar. Finally the flesh of the sin offering was cooked and eaten by the priest, thus bestowing absolution upon the offerer. However, for the most sacred sin offerings the sacrificial flesh was not eaten, because the sacrificial flesh for these sin offerings was totally burned outside the camp.[51] For these holiest of sin offerings God had also prescribed that the blood be sprinkled either before the inner veil or toward the mercy seat within the Most Holy Place.

Christ, the Sin Offering

Hebrews 9:26b portrays Christ as the sin offering by declaring, "He has been manifested to *put away sin by the sacrifice of Himself*." Hebrews ten continues this topic stating that Christ, "having offered *one sacrifice for sins* for all time, sat down at the right hand of God." (v.12). As a final example, Hebrews 10:18 speaks of Christ by using a Jewish technical term for sin offering: "Now where there is forgiveness of these things, there is no longer any *offering for sin* [literally, "sin offering"]."[52] The Christian realizes this to be a central tenet of Christ's death, that He is the sin offering. But unlike the OT sin offerings, which had to be repeated, Christ's sacrifice is final, never needing repetition. And unlike the sin offerings in the OT, which only atoned for sins already committed, Christ's sin offering even atones for

---

[51] Edersheim, *The Temple...*, 80ff.
[52] This verse uses the technical terminology for sin offering, περι αμαρτιας. See also Hebrews 5:3; 7:12.

all future sins.[53] However, when God's people fall into sin after Christ's sin offering on the cross, which of course includes every sin committed in our present era, there still must be a way to approach and appropriate this sin offering. The ultimate sin offering is regularly approached and appropriated as one partakes of the Sacrament of the Altar.

Part of the procedure of the private sin offering that relates it with the Lord's Supper is, as with the peace offering, the fact that the regular sin offering was eaten. In such offerings, brought by the laity, it was the *obligation* of the priest to eat of such a sin offering, and by this eating he was bestowing an "absolution" upon the offerer.[54]

Such eating by the priests was their privilege alone. The laity were never to eat of the sin offering. The "Priesthood of Believers" is thus an underlying doctrine in the book of Hebrews, a doctrine presupposed by the Christian's priestly privilege of eating Christ's sin offering, a privilege performed as a Christian partakes of the Lord's Supper.[55]

---

[53] Many theologians have noted that the OT sacrifices only looked backward, but that Christ's sacrifice also looks forward, atoning for even future sins. E.g. Gayford, *Sacrifice...*, 55: "Note some significant limitations in the scope and purpose of the Jewish Sacrifices. First, that none of those Sacrifices had any grace-giving power...No Sacrifice looked forward to the future, far less contained any promise of grace to meet future temptations. In this respect they stand in strong contrast with the Christian Sacrifice."

[54] Washburn, *The Import...*, 74,75: "The expression, 'to bear the iniquity of the congregation,' clearly indicates that the priests here filled a mediatorial office; they took the sins of the people, to bear them away by the divinely appointed method [of eating the sin offering]." Jeremias, *The Eucharistic...*, 236, footnote to Siphra Lev. on 10:17 (ed. Princ., Venice, 1545, 24d.38-40): "Where (is it said) that the eating of the sacred sacrifices brings atonement to Israel? The Scripture teaches: 'And He (Yahweh) hath given it (the sin offering) to you to bear the iniquity of the congregation, to make atonement for them before the Lord.' (Lev. 10.17). How so? The priests eat, and for the masters (who provide the sacrifice) atonement is made."

[55] By comparing the high priest's approach to the Holy of Holies with our approach to the Lord's Supper, the author of Hebrews is clearly inferring the priesthood of believers. Swetnam, "The Greater...," 103, summarizes this priestly inference: "The whole passage [Hebrews 10:19ff] uses Old Testament terminology to imply that the Christians are priests, primarily because of the allusions to purification through sprinkling and ritual washing. The work of priests is prayer and worship. The Christian is priestly through baptism and should draw near to the worship of the Christian economy, the Eucharist. [...] Those who are urged to "draw near" in 10,19-25 are considered to be priestly: the Christian priesthood of all Christians is the fulfillment of the Old Testament priesthood of the Levites." See also Westcott, *The Epistle...*, 322, 323.

Recall, as explained in chapter five, how Isaiah 53 with its peculiar use of the word "many" is perceived by some to have a direct link to the Lord's Supper.[56] Isaiah 53:10 is a prediction of Christ as guilt offering (sin offering in the LXX).[57] The writer of the epistle to the Hebrews makes the connection with Isaiah 53 by stating in Hebrews 9:28 that Christ "was offered to *bear the sins of many*."[58] This verse of Hebrews has nearly identical wording with the Septuagint translation of Isaiah 53:12. Isaiah therein predicts of Christ, "He Himself *bore the sin of many*." If, as Jeremias maintains, "without Isaiah 53 the eucharist words remain incomprehensible,"[59] then it is nearly certain that the clear reference to Isaiah 53:12 in Hebrews 9:28 is really another cleverly concealed reference to the Lord's Supper. Thus Hebrews 9:28—through just a few well-chosen words—describes Christ as the sin offering, consumed by the priesthood of believers in the Lord's Supper.

The 'Day of Atonement' Sin Offering

The sacrifice of a public sin offering was the central ritual for the Day of Atonement. This Jewish High Holy Day is a primary topic of the epistle to the Hebrews.[60] Only once a year, on the Day of Atonement, could the high priest, alone, enter into the Holy of Holies in the tabernacle. The blood of a

---

[56] Concerning "for many" Daly, *Christian Sacrifice*, 217: "The phrase seems to be an allusion to Isa 53,10-12." 222: "[...] the words of institution themselves carry unmistakable references to it [Isaiah 53]."

[57] Isaiah 53:10 uses the technical Hebrew word for "guilt offering," but the LXX employs the technical Greek wording for "sin offering."

[58] To the Hebrew mind the word "many" usually meant "all." Joachim Jeremias, "πολλοι," in vol. VI, *Theological Dictionary of the New Testament*, ed. Gerhard Kittel and Gerhard Friedrich, trans. Geoffrey W. Bromiley (Grand Rapids: Wm. B. Eerdmans Publishing Co., 1968), 536-545. Jeremias (536) explains concerning Jewish usage of πολλοι: "The inclusive use is due to the fact that Heb. and Aram. have no word for "all.""

[59] Jeremias, *New Testament Theology* (New York: Scribner's, 1971), 291.

[60] Hicks, *Sacrifice...*, 236: "[The author of Hebrews] has been stressing the analogy of our Lord's sacrifice with one special aspect of Jewish sacrifice, namely, the sin offering, and in particular the great sin-offering of the Day of Atonement." 238: "The one special form of Jewish sacrifice that is dwelt upon [in Hebrews] is the sin-offering in its fullest form on the Day of Atonement."

special sin offering enabled him to do this, and he sprinkled such blood within this Most Holy place. The flesh of the sin offering was then burned outside the camp. No one ate of such sacred sin offering flesh; the laity, the Levite, the priest and even the high priest could not eat of the flesh of this sin offering. As will be explained later, however, Christ's people have now been given God's invitation to eat even of this most sacred sin offering.

The Holy of Holies—where but once a year the OT high priest entered on the Day of Atonement—was truly the most holy place because God Himself declared this to be His throne room. This then leads us to the next question.

What Does it Mean that Christ is at the Right Hand in the Tabernacle Pitched by God?

> *"Since therefore, brethren, we have confidence to enter the holy place [Holy of Holies] by the blood of Jesus, by a new and living way which He inaugurated for us through the veil, that is, His flesh, and since we have a great high priest over the house of God, let us draw near in full assurance of faith, having our hearts sprinkled clean from an evil conscience and our bodies washed with pure water."*
> **Hebrews 10:19-22**

The Heavenly Tabernacle

The writer of Hebrews conveys in several places the Jewish belief that the earthly tabernacle had its heavenly counterpart.[61] In Hebrews 8:5 the priests are said to "serve a copy of *the heavenly things*." Hebrews 9:11 explains that "when Christ appeared as a high priest of the good things to come, He entered through the *greater and more perfect tabernacle, not made with hands, that is to say, not of this creation*." The same theme is found in Hebrews 9:23: "Therefore it was necessary for the copies of the *things in the*

---

[61] James L. Kugel, *The Bible As It Was* (London: Belknap Press, 1997), 420: Kugel gives several Jewish references showing a common belief in a heavenly tabernacle.

heavens to be cleansed with these [animal sacrifices], but *the heavenly things themselves with better sacrifices than these.*"[62] The "things in the heavens" are the *heavenly* "tabernacle and all the vessels" (9:21). The heavenly tabernacle has been cleansed by the holiest of sacrifices, Christ-crucified. Hebrews 9:24 describes it this way: "For Christ did not enter a holy place[63] made with hands, a mere copy of the true one, but into heaven itself, now to appear in the presence of God for us." Christ has entered the heavenly tabernacle, the heavenly Holy of Holies, presenting His body and blood as *the* sacrificial elements. Why are there so many references in this epistle to God's heavenly tabernacle? We believe, as will be demonstrated, that such references stood as reminders to those listening/reading that the heavenly tabernacle was precisely what they were approaching when they approached to eat the Eucharist.

There have been numerous discussions and descriptions concerning this heavenly tabernacle. It has been related to Christ's flesh and even specifically to the Eucharist.[64] In this chapter it will be identified simply as the heavenly dwelling "place" of God.[65] Relative to the earthly tabernacle, God was understood to have been enthroned in the Holy of Holies, between the two gold Cherubim. Thus the psalmist prays in Psalm 80:1, "Oh give ear, Shepherd of Israel [...] Thou who art *enthroned between the Cherubim*, shine forth!" Even as in the earthly tabernacle, so too in the heavenly tabernacle—yet outside the time and space of this creation—God is understood to be *enthroned in the Holy of Holies*, surrounded by myriads of angels. It is into

---

[62] Why does the heavenly tabernacle need cleansing? Perhaps this is the eternal "place" of worship for mankind, cleansed by Christ. Maybe this describes Christ Himself as mankind's eternal Tabernacle/Temple, having been made sin for us, He then had to be cleansed.
[63] The author of Hebrews speaks of the Holy of Holies as simply the Holy Place.
[64] Swetnam, "'The Greater...'", 104: Swetnam presents some of the theories concerning the "more perfect tent," but he concludes that there is ample evidence "in favor of the Eucharistic body of Christ as being the "greater and more perfect tent not made with hands.""
[65] It is conceivable that even as He is omnipresent on earth and yet chooses to be found in the Jewish Holy of Holies, so God may choose to allow himself to be found by his creation in such a heavenly place. To be found in such a place does not mean confinement to it. This heavenly place is surely beyond human imagination, as it is apparently not bound to space and time.

this Holy of Holies that the Great High Priest, Jesus, has entered. Of necessity the writer of the epistle to the Hebrews, and indeed all writers, must describe this dwelling place of God as if it is a specific "location" like unto our places in space and time. Such a heavenly location is no more to be found than the specific throne upon which Christ is seated at God's right hand. Bear this in mind as we too must treat of this heavenly Holy of Holies as if it were a location in space and time.

Christ's 'Day of Atonement' Work

God set the stage for His people to grasp Jesus' entry into the heavenly Holy of Holies when He instituted the Day of Atonement to be celebrated in the earthly tabernacle of the Jews. Uniquely on this great day the high priest was obligated to enter the Holy of Holies, the sacred place behind the veil, where God Himself was enthroned among men.

At specified times in the liturgy of that day the high priest had to perform several washings or "baptisms."[66] The first sin offering he sacrificed was for himself, and then he could enter the Holy of Holies for the first time under a cloud of incense. Then, after sacrificing a sin offering for the nation, the high priest entered the Holy of Holies a second time, sprinkling the blood of that sacrifice upon the Mercy Seat. Recall again that this Mercy Seat in the Holy of Holies within the earthly tabernacle was perceived to be the throne of God. This is where the King of the universe was seated.[67] After the ritual of the "Scapegoat,"[68] the Day of Atonement sin offerings were burned outside the camp. Two main marks of the great atonement sin offering were that the blood was sprinkled in the Most Holy Place, and the remainder of the sacrifice was burned outside the camp. This is only a skeletal description of the divine

---

[66] George Wesley Buchanan, *To the Hebrews*, The Anchor Bible (Garden City, NY: Doubleday & Company, 1972), 128: "On the Day of Atonement, the high priest bathed five times and washed his hands and feet ten times (Yoma 3:3)."

[67] Several Jewish writings identify the Ark as God's footstool. With this understanding, His throne is just above the Ark of the Covenant.

[68] Edersheim, *The Temple...*, 247-258 offers a good summary of the Scapegoat ritual.

service on the Day of Atonement, but it should be sufficient for the reader to make the proper connections in the epistle to the Hebrews.[69]

With the writer to the Hebrews constantly returning to the priestly actions surrounding the Day of Atonement, many theologians have concluded that a discussion of the Day of Atonement is the author's main purpose. Most likely the first reference to Christ's entrance into the Holy of Holies is already in Hebrews 1:3b: "When He had made purification of sins, He sat down at the right hand of the Majesty on high."[70] Observe first of all in this verse the atoning "purification of sins," and then observe Christ taking His *seat* in the very presence of the Majesty of God—understood to be the heavenly Holy of Holies.

Jesus entered the heavenly Holy of Holies and sat down; He remains seated there. It is clear in other parallel references that Christ, unlike the OT high priests, entered the Holy of Holies to reside there, not merely to present the sacrificial blood and then exit.

Christ, Seated at the Right Hand in the Holy of Holies

As Christ then resides in the Holy of Holies, He is appropriately described here in Hebrews 1:3 as being "seated" at the right of His Father's majesty. Such a description not only shows the fact that Christ remains there (being *seated*), but the author of the epistle also presents this "position" of Christ as that place which may be approached in the Eucharist.[71] Shortly, when we consider especially Hebrews 10:19ff, it will be demonstrated that in the Lord's Supper Christians are privileged to supernaturally enter behind the veil into this Most Holy Place, the place of God's throne, the place where the

---

[69] For a succinct summary of the Day of Atonement see Westcott, *The Epistle...*, 279f.
[70] Field, *The Apostolic......*, 10-21, 258-260. 209: "We learnt subsequently (Heb. 1:3) that in taking this place at the right hand of God Christ entered as a Forerunner "within the veil" of heaven to be the New Priest..."
[71] Christ at God's right hand—particularly in the epistle to the Hebrews but perhaps throughout the entire NT—perhaps frequently identifies that heavenly place, behind the veil, which may be approached in the Eucharist. Thus also such "right hand" expressions in the Christian creeds may be references to the approachableness of Christ in the Eucharist.

Great High Priest is seated. With this in mind, consider the Eucharistic flavor of the following "seated at the right hand" excerpts. From Hebrews 8:1: "...we have a high priest, who has *taken His seat at the right hand* at the throne of the majesty in the heavens." From Hebrews 10:12: "He, having offered one sacrifice for sins for all time, *sat down at the right hand* of God." From Hebrews 12:2: "[Jesus], for the joy that was set before Him endured the cross, despising the shame, and has *sat down at the right hand* of the throne of God."

In Hebrews 4:14, even though Christ is not described as being seated at God's right, yet the picture is still focused on the same theme as Christ, the high priest, passes through the heavens for us: "Since we then have a great high priest who has passed through the heavens, Jesus the Son of God, let us hold fast our confession." Passing *through the heavens* no doubt meant ending up at the very dwelling place of God, the Most Holy Place. Remember also that the "confession" spoken of in this verse may be a reference to the Lord's Supper, which Christians appropriately *hold fast* to when they approach the *great high priest*. The next verse, Hebrews 4:15, again repeats Christ's identity as the "high priest," then verse 16 elaborates by inviting: "Let us therefore *draw near* with confidence to the throne of grace that we may *receive mercy* and may find grace to help in time of need." The invitation here is to "draw near" and "receive *mercy*" at the "throne of grace." By inviting Christians to *draw near* the author of Hebrews utilizes technical worship language, which we will discuss shortly. When Christians are invited to *receive mercy*, such an invitation fits well if Christ is enthroned with His Father on the *Mercy* Seat; this is the *throne of grace*.

Concerning Christ's entrance into the Holy of Holies, it is clarified even more in chapter nine of the epistle. Hebrews 9:24 explains that "Christ did not enter a holy place [here meaning "Holy of Holies"] made with hands, a mere copy of the true one, but into heaven itself, now to appear in the presence of God for us." Christ only needed to perform His "Day of Atonement" sacrifice once, unlike the Jewish high priests who year-by-year had to enter the earthly tabernacle on the Day of Atonement. Thus verses 25 and 26 inform the reader that Christ did not need to "offer Himself often, as the high priest enters the holy place [Holy of Holies] year by year with blood not his own. [...] but now once at the consummation of the ages He has been manifested to put away sin by the sacrifice of Himself." When Christ finally exits the Holy of Holies, it will be time for Judgment Day![72] The following verses (27,28) clearly present this scenario: "And inasmuch as it is appointed for men to die once and after this comes judgment, so Christ also, having been offered once to bear the sins of many shall appear [exit the Most Holy place] a second time for salvation without reference to sin, to those who eagerly await Him." When in verse 28 Christ is said to appear the second time "without reference to sin," this is because as He exits the Holy of Holies He will have completed His Day of Atonement liturgy, and the people of God will then be ready to enter His glory, forever free from sin. He will never have to refer to sin again!

Hebrews 10:19-22; "Drawing Near"

In the meantime, what shall God's people do? What is Christ doing? A clue to the answers to these questions is given by the invitation, "Let us draw near." The word for "draw near" was a common worship-word used especially for the priests who drew near to present and participate in the sacrifices.[73] Chapter ten of Hebrews begins by explaining that the OT

---

[72] Westcott, *The Epistle...*, 280.
[73] Jon Scholer, *Proleptic Priests, Priesthood in the Epistle to the Hebrews* (Sheffield: Sheffield Academic Press, 1991), 91-149. Scholer here spends an entire chapter outlining the technical nature of "drawing near." (προσερχεσθαι) He shows it to be a worship-word for both laity and priests. He concludes: "Since the earthly situation of the readers is in view, this would again allude not to an actual approach through the heavenly curtain by corporeal beings, but a 'drawing near' through worship, prayer or the eucharist." 127. Daly, *Christian Sacrifice*, footnote on p. 375: "Cf. In this connection the use of the cultic προσερχεσθαι in Heb 4,16; 7,25; 10,1; 10,19-22; 12,18.22-24 where the word seems to signify participation in the act or the benefits of Christ's high-priestly sacrifice. In Did. 10,6 the word signifies reception of the Eucharist." Westcott, *The Epistle...*, 108, says of προσερχωμεθα: "It is used in the LXX for the priestly approach to God in service [...] That right of priestly approach is now extended to all Christians."

sacrifices, particularly on the yearly Day of Atonement, were "only a shadow of the good things to come."[74] This is type/antitype language. The verse then explains that such sacrificial shadows could not "make perfect those who *draw near.*" In OT worship, as this verse explains, the worshipers who drew near could not be perfected. Christ's one sacrifice, however, can make perfect those who draw near! Hebrews 10:12 again returns the reader to the Holy of Holies, the right hand of God, reminding God's people that Christ, "having offered one sacrifice for sins for all time, sat down at the right hand of God." By His sacrifice upon the cross Christ "has perfected for all time those who are sanctified." (Heb. 10:14). Now, however, one finds again another of Christ's radical changes: Christ's faithful people are *all* invited to *draw near* and enter the Holy of Holies behind the veil! The author of Hebrews speaks not to Jewish priests but to all Christians, reminding them of this grandest of invitations:

> Since therefore, brethren, *we have confidence to enter the holy place* [Holy of Holies] by the blood of Jesus, by a new and living way which He inaugurated for us *through the veil*, that is, His flesh, and since we have a great high priest over the house of God, *let us draw near* in full assurance of faith, having our hearts sprinkled clean from an evil conscience and our bodies washed with pure water [italics added]. (Hebrews 10:19-22)

The initial verse of this text conveys the startling revelation that brothers and sisters in Christ—"we"—can "have confidence to enter the holy place!" The holy place into which Christ's people are here invited was understood by the Jews to be the Holy of Holies, the place in the earthly tabernacle reserved only for the high priest, once a year. Lo and behold,

---

[74] Field, *The Apostolic...*, 250,252: "And these are the same "good things that were to come" of which Christ has just been called the 'high priest [9:11]];' and therefore they are to be identified with the Eucharistic 'Confession' of which He was called 'the high priest'..."

Christians are invited to enter behind the veil into the *heavenly* Holy of Holies! The final verse in the above quote similarly encourages Christians, "Let us *draw near* with full assurance of faith." Such "drawing near" to the Holy of Holies was formerly a right reserved only for the Jewish high priest. Now Christians have the right of the Jewish high priest because they have the great high priest, Jesus, who has presented His blood to His Father upon the Mercy Seat. Through that blood the catechized are invited into God's presence.

What then is the tangible means for this entrance? Is this text of Hebrews merely describing the Christian's faith which appropriates Christ's high priestly work? Closer examination reveals that the privileged entrance into the Holy of Holies is indeed that which is at the heart of Christian worship: the celebration of the Lord's Supper.

In support of this, observe that the two means named in verses 19 and 20 enabling a Christian's entrance into the Holy of Holies are the *blood* and *flesh* of Christ. "We have confidence to *enter the most holy place by the blood* of Jesus," verse 19 explains. Verse 20 states furthermore that the entranceway *through the veil* into the Holy of Holies is precisely *His flesh*! Just the proximity of *blood* and *flesh* would surely have caused early Christians to think of the Lord's Supper, but to speak of these as means by which a Christian has access to the heavenly tabernacle would have nearly clinched this as a reference to the Eucharist.

Then, sandwiched between Christ's blood and flesh are the words, "by a new and living way which He inaugurated for us." The word "new" originally meant, "newly sacrificed." It is true that at the time of Christ it usually meant simply "new," yet some Greek scholars are convinced that the more ancient connotation of "newly slain" was still understood, and in this context in Hebrews 10 such understanding would have been appropriate.[75]

---

[75] Field, *The Apostolic...*, 297.

Jesus truly remains perpetually *newly slain*, for after three short days He rose from the grave to become also the "living way." Christ's flesh has been newly slain, and the resultant blood and flesh are Christ's new and living way given to God's people that they may find entrance into the Holy of Holies! When considering such verses as Hebrews 10:19,20, where else are Christ's people invited to thus participate in His body and blood but in the Sacrament of the Altar?

The altar of the cross is the altar from which Christians are then in communion with God.[76] When these verses in Hebrews combine "living way" to "newly slain," one perceives also the foundational doctrines of the death (newly slain) and resurrection (living way) of Christ. This crucified and risen Christ is the one whose flesh and blood give access to heaven itself!

Inaugurated

This "newly slain and living way" has been "inaugurated" by Christ. The word "inaugurate" was already used in Hebrews to describe God's institution of the former covenant through Moses.[77] Recall that this inauguration upon Mt. Sinai involved the sprinkling of blood and the peace offering meal. After the *inauguration* through Moses, as already explained, the Jewish priesthood then *mediated* the continuation of this covenant.

The Greek word "inaugurate" describes the institution of a religious

---

[76] Westcott, *The Epistle...*, 438: Commenting on Heb. 13:10, "...the only earthly 'altar' is the Cross on which Christ offered Himself: Christ is the offering: He is Himself the feast of the believer...When the idea of the one act of sacrifice predominates, the image of the Cross rises before us; when the idea of our continuous support, then the image of Christ living through death prevails." Gayford, *Sacrifice...*, 166: "It [Heb. 13:10ff] is also a precious biblical witness to the 'glorious interchange' of Heaven and earth in the Eucharist. All is lost when the altar is regarded as the place of slaughter and identified with the Cross. It was probably from this passage [Heb. 13:10ff] so interpreted that the expression 'ara crucis' arose. A truer conception and a richer vein of teaching are found in Irenaeus, and Origen who place this Christian altar in the Heavenly Sanctuary. Origen, in particular, identifies it with the 'heavenly altar' of Revelation vi.9." We prefer the precision of Gayford's concept of "altar," but for simplicity of discussion, Westcott's "altar of the cross" works well. In support of Gayford see also Hicks, 240ff. In support of Westcott see also Alfred Cave, *The Scriptural Doctrine of Sacrifice and Atonement*, (Edinburgh: T & T Clark, 1890), 421.

[77] Hebrews 9:18ff

thing for future sacred use. The word was thus used in the Greek OT to describe the dedication of both the sacred altar and the holy temple.[78] As a noun, the word had come to be used for the Jewish *Feast of Dedication*. Delitzsch says that the verbal form, as used here in Hebrews, "is the term for dedicating or setting apart *for future use*."[79] If Christ has thus set something sacred "apart for future use," how is it to be used? It is apparent that the word "inaugurate" is being utilized here in Hebrews to explain Christ's institution of the Lord's Supper, to present a sacred thing enjoined *for future use*.

As already stated, "drawing near" was technical worship language among the Jews. John Field is convinced that the author of Hebrews, whom he believes to be the Apostle Paul, consistently used the term to describe the Christian approach to God through the Eucharist. Thus Field writes, "The 'drawing nigh to God' is the same as that 'coming unto' God which we have already seen to be intimately connected in the Apostle's mind with the celebration of the Holy Eucharist."[80] How else would the author of the epistle to the Hebrews describe the Christian's approach to God in the Eucharist except through official Jewish worship words? "Let us *draw near* with a true heart," certain liturgies yet echo today.[81]

Many are convinced the author of Hebrews had the sacraments in mind when he penned Hebrews 10:19ff. Albert Vanhoye speaks as one representing this viewpoint:

> Speaking of faith, the author alludes to the Sacraments which lead to faith's fullness: baptism (10:22) and the eucharistic "blood" and "flesh" of Christ (10:19-20). There are no more rites in the ancient

---

[78] Westcott, *The Epistle...*, 319.
[79] Franz Delitzsch, *Epistle to the Hebrews*, trans. Thomas Kingsbury (Minneapolis: Klock and Klock, 1978), 170. Italics added.
[80] Field, *The Liturgy* ..., 192.
[81] This KJV wording from Hebrews 10:22 has appropriately found its way into various liturgical settings. E.g. *The Lutheran Hymnal*, "The Order for Holy Communion," p. 15ff.

meaning of the word, for the Christian sacraments are closely linked with the personal offering of Christ. It is from it alone that they draw all their worth. They make the offering present and active in the existence of the believers so that this existence is transformed."[82]

Ancient Liturgical Connections to Hebrews 10

A fact that nearly seals the Eucharistic nature of Hebrews 10:19ff is that the text is clearly integrated into the ancient liturgical *Prayer of the Veil*. Recall that this ancient prayer, as recorded in the most ancient of Christian liturgies, was either paraphrased by the author of Hebrews or the prayer drew from Hebrews. One or the other must be true since the parallels are undeniable. Since the ancient *Prayer of the Veil* was basically the ancient preface to the rite of Holy Communion, it is nearly certain that the early church connected the elements of Hebrews 10:19ff to the Eucharist. Observe even in its ancient liturgical name, *Prayer of the Veil*, that it indicates the *veil*, the curtain marking the entrance into the Most Holy Place.

In delving into the *Liturgy of Saint James*, it is beyond doubt that those who worshipped with this liturgy understood that in Holy Communion God's people are truly entering behind the heavenly veil, drawing near to the Lord in the Holy of Holies as described in Hebrews 10:19,20. Field states "that the liturgy of S. James, from which S. Paul makes a quotation in Hebrews x. 19,20, may be traced in every [ancient] liturgy." Field demonstrates that this liturgical portion was originally positioned "at the Great Entrance, when the priest passes with the sacramental elements into the sanctuary."[83] Two main points made by Field, as drawn from this liturgy are:

1. We give thanks for the boldness with which we enter through the veil into the most holy place of the Glory of God;

---

[82] Vanhoye, *Structure and Message...*, 72. Lane, *Hebrews 9-13*, 310: "The exhortations in 10:22-25 appear to rest on a pattern of worship influenced by the peace offering."
[83] Field, *The Apostolic...*, 478.

2. We have this entrance by virtue of the flesh which Christ assumed in His Incarnation and which is sacramentally given to us in the Holy Eucharist.[84]

The words "boldness," "flesh of Christ," "veil," and "Holy of Holies" are obvious highlights in numerous ancient Eucharistic liturgies. Observe how the following excerpts from the *Prayer of the Veil* clearly have these thoughts along with the tenth chapter of Hebrews in mind. The following are excerpts from the *Prayer of the Veil* as found in several ancient liturgies, vividly revealing the imprint of the more ancient *Liturgy of Saint James*. Phrases in the following liturgical excerpts are italicized to show the unmistakable parallels to Hebrews 10:19ff which, in summary, says, "We have confidence to enter the holy place by the blood of Jesus...through the veil, that is His flesh...let us draw near with full assurance of faith":

> We give thanks to Thee, O Lord our God, that Thou hast given *us boldness for the entrance of Thy holy place*, which [entrance] Thou hast newly *dedicated* for us [to be] *a new and living way through the veil of the Flesh of Christ*. Therefore being counted worthy to come into the place where Thy glory dwelleth, and to *be within the Veil*, and *to behold the holy of holies*, we fall down before Thy goodness.[85]

> Grant us to offer unto Thee the reasonable oblation and sacrifice of thanksgiving and the spiritual incense, that *we may enter within the Veil, into the place of the holy of holies*.[86]

> I have entered *into Thy house*, and *before Thy holy throne* have I fallen down, O heavenly King: forgive me all my sins against Thee.

---
[84] Ibid., 478
[85] Ibid., 438.
[86] Ibid., 486, From an Alexandrine remnant.

[Recall the Mercy Seat was considered God's throne.][87]

To the table of Thy most sweet feast, good Lord Jesus Christ, ...with *confidence [boldness] in Thy mercy* and goodness, *I draw near* in fear and trembling...Take from me then, most merciful Father, all my iniquities and sins, that being cleansed in mind and body, I may be counted worthy fitly *to taste the holy of holies*. [The holy of holies is tasted!][88]

O God Almighty, the Lord whose name is great, who hast given us an *entrance into the holy of holies through the Flesh of Christ*...We supplicate and beseech Thy goodness, since we are fearful and trembling, being about to stand before Thy holy altar...[89]

Prerequisites for Drawing Near to Christ in the Eucharist

Recall that to "draw near" was a near-technical term particularly reserved for OT priests as they drew near to God by servicing the sacrifices.[90] How is it then that God's NT people are eligible to *draw near*? They certainly do it through Christ in prayer, but clearly also through the Eucharist wherein Christ mediates the covenant to us. Hebrews 10:22 gives Christians the encouragement to "draw near in full assurance of faith." This is the first thing that makes a person eligible for drawing near to the Eucharist: *full assurance of faith*. The verse then continues, "having our hearts sprinkled clean from an evil conscience and our bodies washed with pure water." This statement, and those surrounding it, present multiple facets on the diamond of the Eucharist. The Eucharist is truly a diamond; it is solid, beautiful, shimmering with the

---

[87] Ibid., 480, From a Syriac remnant.
[88] Ibid., 498, From a Western remnant. Psalm 34:8a was also quoted in ancient liturgies.
[89] Ibid., 493
[90] Delitzsch, *Epistle to the Hebrews*, 177: "προσερχεσθαι is a technical liturgical word, and sprinkling and washing are liturgical acts of preparation." The term was also occasionally used for the worshipful drawing near of the laity in the OT.

light of Christ, and its many facets reflect much Christian doctrine.

Two of these Eucharistic facets are Christian Baptism and the priesthood of believers. Consider the priesthood of believers. As expressed already, by comparing the high priest's "drawing near" into the Holy of Holies with a Christian's "drawing near" to the Lord's Supper, the author of Hebrews is clearly implying the priesthood of believers. James Swetnam summarizes this priestly implication conveyed by Hebrews 10:19ff:

> The whole passage [Hebrews 10:19ff] uses Old Testament terminology to imply that the Christians are priests, primarily because of the allusions to purification through sprinkling and ritual washing. The work of priests is prayer and worship. The Christian is priestly through baptism and should draw near to the worship of the Christian economy, the Eucharist. [...] Those who are urged to "draw near" in 10,19-25 are considered to be priestly: the Christian priesthood of all Christians is the fulfillment of the Old Testament priesthood of the Levites.[91]

Not only does the technical reference to "drawing near" imply the Christian's priestliness, but Swetnam also shows that the priestliness of believers is implied in verse 22 as Christians have been "sprinkled clean" and their "bodies washed with pure water." On the Day of Atonement, in the Temple at the time of Christ, the high priest would not only wash his feet at the laver—as the other priests did daily—but he would then bathe his entire body in a special golden basin near the Court of the Priests. He performed this cleansing ritual with both the laver and golden basin five times on that sacred day![92] Concerning such sacred washing referenced in Hebrews 10, Brooke Westcott comments, "In the latter clause there is a reference both to

---

[91] Swetnam, "The Greater...," 103.
[92] Kevin Howard and Marvin Rosenthal, *The Feasts of the Lord*, (Nashville: Thomas Nelson, 1997), 122.

the consecration of priests (Ex. xxix.4), and to the bathing of the High-priest on the Day of Atonement (Lev. xvi.4)."[93] Thus a Christian's priestly privilege presented here in Hebrews is not simply that of a common priest, but of the OT high priest. Westcott explains: "Each Christian in virtue of his fellowship with Christ is now a high-priest, and is able to come to the very presence of God."[94] No wonder the author of Hebrews would describe the Christian's privilege in terms of entering the Holy of Holies; this was a privilege only accorded the high priest, and every Christian is now granted this lofty privilege in the approach of the Eucharist!

Not only do such references imply the priesthood of believers, but the "washing" description also implies that Christ's people have a water-prerequisite that makes them eligible to approach the Holy of Holies. Even as OT priests had to be ceremonially "baptized" at the laver to encounter the Holy, so does every Christian. Concerning a Christian's washing-prerequisite, which is Holy Baptism, Westcott concludes, "The two phrases [here in Hebrews 10:22] appear to contain allusions to the Christian sacraments. That to the Eucharist is veiled: that to Baptism is unquestionable."[95] Even as the priests would ceremonially wash at the laver, so it is no coincidence that two NT texts actually employ the Greek word for laver when speaking of Baptism (Eph. 5:26, "He saved her by the laver of water"; Titus 3:5, "laver of regeneration."). This is consistent with the laver implications here in Hebrews 10:22, wherein the high priestly washing is described.

Recall again Hebrews 10:22: "Let us draw near in full assurance of faith, having our hearts sprinkled clean from an evil conscience and our bodies washed with pure water." A Christian's faith together with having a cleansed conscience with his/her body lavered in the water of Baptism, are the eligibility requirements for such a priestly person to draw near to the NT Holy of Holies. This NT Holy of Holies is approached through Christ's flesh

---

[93] Westcott, *The Epistle...*, 322, 323.
[94] Ibid., 318.
[95] Ibid., 323.

and blood, the two heavenly elements consumed in the Holy Eucharist.

Additionally, Hebrews 10:22 points to the Eucharist because, like the verses preceding it, it is clearly incorporated in the ancient Communion liturgies. For example, note the exact parallels to Hebrews 10:22 in the Syriac remnant of the *Prayer of the Veil*:

> Grant, O Lord God, that *with our hearts sprinkled and cleansed from an evil conscience* and unclean thoughts, we may be counted *worthy to enter into the holy of holies* on high, and may stand before Thy holy altar chastely and purely [emphasis mine].[96]

This ancient liturgy again brings one to the conclusion that Hebrews 10:19ff were written with the Lord's Supper in mind.

Compounding this clear liturgical reference in Hebrews 10:19-22, verses 23-25 present even more facets for the Eucharistic diamond unearthed in Hebrews ten:

> Let us hold fast the confession of our hope without wavering, for He who promised is faithful; and let us consider how to stimulate one another to love and good deeds, not forsaking our own assembling together, as is the habit of some, but encouraging one another; and all the more, as you see the day drawing near. (Hebrews 10:23-25).

The Eucharist, Our "Hope"

Read again the first line of the verses just cited. Recall how we demonstrated that in Hebrews 10:23 the word "confession" is very possibly a cryptic reference to the Lord's Supper, utilizing peace offering terminology. As it is here called, "the confession of our hope," the word "hope" may itself be, in the book of Hebrews, another reference to the Lord's Supper. Indeed,

---

[96] Field, *The Apostolic...*, 481.

an important facet of the diamond of the Holy Eucharist is that it gives unwavering *hope* to the downtrodden, sin-laden people of God. In the above phrase ("the confession of our hope") *our hope* could very possibly be a further description of *the confession*. Thus both *confession* and *hope* may be hidden references to the Lord's Supper in the epistle to the Hebrews. At first glance this may seem far-fetched. However as one reviews the previous—and abundant—references to "hope" in the book of Hebrews, the theory not only becomes plausible but likely.

Hebrews 6:18b says of such hope that we Christians "may have strong encouragement, we who have fled for refuge in laying hold of the *hope set before us*." Literally the final phrase is the *set-before hope*. There is significance in the Greek word translated, "set before." The word was used in the OT for the showbread that was "set before" God and was to be eaten weekly by the priests.[97] If "set before hope" is being paralleled with the OT "set before bread," then there enters a shred of evidence that "hope" refers to the Lord's Supper in the book of Hebrews.

In the very next verses—which immediately follow the words, "hope set before us"—the evidence becomes stronger: "This hope we have as an anchor of the soul, a hope both sure and steadfast and one which *enters within the veil*, where Jesus has entered as a forerunner for us, having become a high priest forever..." (Hebrews 6:19,20a). Somehow this unusual "hope" is one "which enters within the veil." Recall how the author of Hebrews parallels the approach behind the veil with the liturgical approach of the Lord's Supper. Now when the Christian's hope is described as that "which enters within the veil," the possibility that "hope" in Hebrews refers to

---

[97] Ibid., 170, 171. Field explains how the word προκειμενος was used in the LXX in Lev. 24:7,8 and in Ex. 34:36 for the showbread "set before" the Lord. Num. 4:7 renders "Table of Showbread" as "Table of 'what is set before'". Esther 1:8 uses the word in connection with feasting. The Word is repeated in Hebrews at 12:1,2, perhaps to remind readers/hearers of the Eucharist, as they are surrounded by a cloud of witnesses....all the company of heaven. It is only used once elsewhere in the NT, in 2 Cor. 8:11,12, which can be understood to have sacrificial overtones.

the Lord's Supper is enhanced. Note also the high priestly office of Christ in these verses, and the fact that He enters the Holy of Holies as a "forerunner." A forerunner implies that someone else is following to the same destination, and here the destination is behind the veil. Christians indeed follow, and already in this life they find their Lord behind the veil as they approach and partake of the Lord's Supper!

The likelihood of "hope" being a reference to the Lord's Supper increases again as its use is observed in Hebrews 7:19. Here the author to the Hebrews explains the new worship "laws" created by the new high priest, Jesus, from whom "there is a bringing in of a better hope, through which we draw near to God." We as Christians *draw near to God* through the Eucharist, but here in Hebrews 7:19 such drawing near occurs *through* "a better hope," thus again presenting the use of *hope* in this epistle in terms that seem to imply the Holy Eucharist. Observe also that this phrase "better hope" dovetails quite nicely with "better covenant" just three verses later. The Eucharist is our covenant meal. As one considers the connections existing between covenant-sacrifices and the Lord's Supper then again another possible link to the Eucharist is uncovered, for a Christian's better hope is the better covenant, from which there is participation in the blood of the covenant and in the sacred covenant meal.

Returning to Hebrews 10

As we further consider Hebrews 10, verses 23-25a present another facet that glimmers on the diamond of the Eucharist, as these verses simply encourage Christians to attend worship:

> Let us *hold fast the confession of our hope* without wavering, for He who promised is faithful; and let us consider how to stimulate one another to love and good deeds, *not forsaking our own assembling together...* [italics added]

Christians are thus admonished to be *not forsaking the assembling together.* [98] If our original premise is correct—that early Christians assembled together with the Lord's Supper being central to all such gatherings—then clearly Hebrews 10:23-25 also refer to the Lord's Supper within the greater Eucharistic context of Hebrews 10:19ff. Observe the statement preceding such encouragement to worship, "Let us hold fast the *confession of our hope.*" From such a phrase the partaking of the Eucharist in worship is even more enhanced if *hope* is understood to be a word used to refer to the Eucharist. Holding fast to the Eucharist is indeed holding fast to the confession of hope that exists in the Lord Jesus.

Finally, skip to verse 29: "How much severer punishment do you think he will deserve who has trampled under foot the Son of God, and has regarded as unclean the *blood of the covenant* by which he was sanctified, and has insulted the Spirit of grace?" How does one "regard as unclean the blood of the covenant?" Firstly, the reference here to *blood of the covenant* is precisely the wording used by Christ when instituting Holy Communion. Secondly, the word "unclean" is the Greek word usually translated "common." To regard such *blood of the covenant* as "unclean" ("common") is explained in verse 26: "For if we *go on sinning willfully* after receiving the knowledge of the truth, there no longer remains a sacrifice for sins." Such "sinning willfully" is the deliberate persistence in sin, and by such willful sinning a person profanes the sin offering of Jesus, a sin offering that is uniquely encountered in the Eucharist. When a Christian sins persistently and yet claims to remain under the blood of the covenant then he treats such blood as unclean or "common." The Lord's Supper has, for such a person, become merely a *common* meal of bread and wine. With such a dismissive attitude, the Lord's Supper is not being treated as the real participation in the very body and

---

[98] Gayford, *Sacrifice*..., 166: "If (as is of course true) in Heb. x. 19-25 the prime reason for the 'assembling of ourselves together' is the Breaking of Bread, we have in that passage also the same interchange of Earth and Heaven and the same interweaving of Communion and Sacrifice as in Heb. xiii. 10ff."

blood of Christ, and thus His body and blood are then profaned. If indeed Hebrews 10:29 is a reference to participation in the blood of the covenant as found in the Lord's Supper, then it perfectly parallels Paul's warnings in I Corinthians 11:27: "Therefore whoever eats the bread or drinks the cup of the Lord in an unworthy manner, shall be guilty of the body and the blood of the Lord." Paul here warns the unrepentant Christian ("unworthy" person) not to treat the Eucharist as common bread and wine, and if a person does so—especially by persisting in unrepentant sin—he profanes that which is truly present...Christ's body and blood.

The Lord's Supper is truly for sinners, as was participation in OT sacrificial rites. However God's covenantal grace never implies license to sin. One who thinks he has such license to sin abandons the faith, for he tramples under foot the Son of God, and thus treats the blood of the covenant as common or unclean. Consistent with this thought, in the OT there was also a distinction made between such "willful sinning" and unintentional sinning. For example, Moses warns in Numbers 15:30: "But the person who does anything defiantly...that one is blaspheming the Lord; and that person shall be cut off [excommunicated] from among his people."[99]

Hebrews 13; Eating the Most Sacred Sin Offering

The author of Hebrews has returned repeatedly to the themes surrounding the Day of Atonement. Move now to his final chapter where again he references this High Holy Day. Before specifically returning to the

---

[99] Lane, *Hebrews 9-13*, 292, shows the parallel here with OT warnings concerning intentional sinning. Lev. 4:1-2,13,22,27; 5:14-15 LXX refer to the forgivable nature of "unintentional" sins. Numbers 15:22-31 reflects what is also here in Hebrews where "a deliberate and calculated violation of the commandments placed the offender beyond forgiveness." Such thinking certainly has bearing on the "ban" or excommunication.

Day of Atonement, he first warns his Jewish readers, "It is good for the heart to be strengthened by grace, not by foods, through which those who were thus occupied were not benefited." It was and still is a spiritual fact that those who merely *eat* sacred foods, occupying themselves with such eating as if it is the goal rather than the means, are "not benefited." The heart of man must be strengthened by grace, not by foods. If one only treats such sacred eating as a law, a regulation for godly living, then his heart is not strengthened by grace.

Though the OT sacrificial rituals truly required faith, they were especially understood as laws, regulations for the flesh (Heb. 9:10). It thus is apparent that such legalistic OT religious meals were likely in the mind of the author of Hebrews 13:9 as he here encourages his readers not to be strengthened by foods, "through which those who were thus occupied were not benefited." The people "who were thus occupied" were no doubt the Jews who were legalistically occupied with sacrificial and kosher foods.[100] To re-introduce such teachings into Christianity would truly be the "varied and strange teachings" referred to in the first half of Hebrews 13:9.

Such "food" here in Hebrews 13:9 is obviously parallel to the Jewish "food and drink and washings" mentioned in Hebrews 9:10. Are then such sacred food and drink and baptisms to be ignored or shuffled aside as useless? God forbid! When these were properly combined with faith even in OT times they were pleasing to God and conveyed a certain encouragement. It has always been true that "without faith it is impossible to please Him."[101] Thus when such foods, drinks and washings are properly combined with faith, they are truly God's "means of grace."

The NT foods and washing are far superior to those of the old, for the

---

[100] Field, *The Apostolic...* 415,416: "Here we have an obvious reference to the Holy Communion. The unprofitable 'meats,' clearly meaning those of the old covenant, are distinguished from the 'grace' of the Lord Jesus Christ which is the appointed means of 'establishing the heart' of Christians [...] Our Christian 'meats,' he [the author of Hebrews] would say, are the very means by which the grace of God establishes the heart."

[101] Hebrews 11:6

Lord's Supper and Baptism are based upon and draw from Christ's sacrifice, the only sacrifice able to cure a troubled conscience.[102] They are not, as in the OT, based upon laws and regulations pertaining to the sacrifice of animals. The NT sacraments are not God's "goals" but His "means."

We Have an Altar

Such sacred eating (and washing) is so important (when united with faith), that immediately after warning his readers *not* to be "occupied" by foods, the author of Hebrews continues with a description of the most sacred Christian eating. He states, "We have an altar, from which those who serve the tabernacle have no right to eat."[103]

This "altar," as will be shown, is the Day of Atonement altar for the Christian. In the Jewish tabernacle there really was no such Day of Atonement altar for the Jews, because that sacrifice was burned outside the camp, and thus it was not to be eaten by anyone. Many have specifically identified this altar here in Hebrews with the cross of Jesus. We believe the author of Hebrews here uses "altar" to create a mental picture of sacrifice, of worship and of God's presence. The "altar" here is not so much a place or an event, but a figure identifying what is to be associated with eating the Lord's Supper. It is the Sacrament of the *Altar*.[104] "We have an altar" therefore means that we Christians have a sacrament drawn from a sacrifice, and we

---

[102] Westcott, *The Epistle...*, 293, gives a good summary of the use of συνειδησις in the NT.

[103] Lane, *Hebrews 9-13*, 538: Though Lane himself is doubtful of the eucharistic nature of this verse, yet he summarizes some of the scholarly opinion supporting it: "It has frequently been claimed that the confessional statements, εχομεν θυσιαστηριον, "we have an altar," is an allusion to the Eucharist or to the eucharistic table (Schroger, MTZ 19 [1968] 170, lists twenty scholars holding this opinion;...more recent proponents of the eucharistic interpretation of v 10 include Swetnam, *Bib* 70 [1989] 909, and especially Thuren, *Lobopfer*, 83-91, 204, who concludes that the Lord's Supper is the theme of Hebrews in its entirety, arguing that the writer's intention was to defend the Lord's Supper as the genuine sacrificial meal time against the strange meal celebrations to which reference is made in v 9)."

[104] Return to chapter two, wherein we discussed altar-related concepts.

thus have the means of worship and we are guaranteed God's presence.[105]

"Those who serve the tabernacle have no right to eat" from the Christian altar. Such who "serve the tabernacle" are no doubt the Jewish priestly order. There are basically two reasons why the Jewish priests have no right to eat of the Christian altar. First, if they do not hold to Christian tenets then they do not belong at the same "altar" as Christians. Joining in a sacrificial feast presupposes oneness of belief.[106] The second reason why those who serve the tabernacle have no right to eat from the Christian altar is found in the radically new nature of Christianity's sacred meal. The Christian observance of Holy Communion is the antitype of all Jewish sacrificial meals, and then, as something radically new, it is even a meal drawn from the Day of Atonement sin offering! This is explained in the next verse in Hebrews 13:11: "For the bodies of those animals whose blood is brought into the holy place by the high priest as an offering for sin, are burned outside the camp." This is plainly describing the most holy sin offering, finding its loftiest OT use on the Jewish Day of Atonement. Observe in this verse the basics of the Day of Atonement as it describes the ritual blood being brought into the most holy place by the high priest, and the sacrifice being burned outside the camp. Recall that on that Holy Day no one, not even the high priest, had a right to eat of the sin offering.

The next verse then describes Jesus to be precisely that sin offering on the Day of Atonement: "Therefore Jesus also, that He might sanctify the people through His own blood, suffered outside the gate." Jesus' death, as described in this verse, is able to "sanctify the people," and thus it is a sin offering. His death upon the cross, occurring "outside the gate" of Jerusalem, is also here portrayed as fulfillment of the Day of Atonement liturgy. Being also the Great High Priest, Jesus—as has often been shown—has brought

---

[105] It seems clear that Ignatius already around 100AD spoke of the Lord's Supper in relation to an altar: "Let no one be led astray: except a man be within the altar, he is deprived of the Bread of God." To the Ephesians, v. Quoted from Field, *The Apostolic...*, 416.

[106] See 1 Corinthians 10:17; Romans 16:16,17; 1 Corinthians 5:11; and 2 John 10,11 where such "closed" Communion is inferred. See also e.g. Psalm 101:5 (LXX).

His sacrificial blood into the Most Holy Place, into the very presence of God in the heavenly tabernacle. Thus those who serve the earthly tabernacle, as they remain under their OT regulations, have no right to eat of the atoning sacrifice of Jesus. They have no right to eat of the Lord's Supper because His sacrifice is that from *the* Day of Atonement, and they have been bound by OT law not to eat of such a sacrifice. If they desire to eat of it, they must remove themselves from the OT regulations, for under those Levitical regulations no one could eat of the sin offering on the Day of Atonement.

This then is the final radical change inaugurated by the Savior: *Every catechized, penitent Christian may eat of the most sacred sacrifice!* In the former covenant, being based upon the flesh of animals, no one could eat of the Day of Atonement sacrifice. Westcott, commenting on this Hebrews 13:10ff, summarizes the thought well:

> The superiority which the Christian enjoyed over the Jew became most conspicuous when the highest point in each order was reached. The great sacrifice for sin on the Day of Atonement was wholly consumed [by fire]. Though they 'who served the tabernacle' 'were partakers with the altar,' even those who were most privileged had no right to eat of this offering. But Christ who is our sacrifice for sins, the perfect antitype of that symbol, is our food also [...] The Christian enjoys in substance that which the Jew did not enjoy even in shadow [...] We Christians *have* an altar, from which we draw the material for our feast. In respect of this, our privilege is greater than that of priest or high-priest under the Levitical system. Our great sin-offering, consumed in one sense outside the gate, is given to us as our food. The Christian therefore who can partake of Christ, offered for sins, is admitted to a privilege unknown under the old Covenant.[107]

---

[107] Westcott, *The Epistle...*, 439.

The Christian "altar" is "outside the camp."[108] It is thus outside of the Jewish tabernacle and regulations. Hence when God's NT people approach their holy meal, it is not in Jerusalem or on Mount Gerazim,[109] but rather it is in Spirit and in truth that they approach Christ's sacrifice at the "heavenly Jerusalem." (Heb. 12:22). Christians now approach His sacrifice *outside the camp*, which of course is not a literal location, but it turns out to be wherever the Sacrament of the Altar is rightly celebrated. Outside the camp Christ's people find, among other things, these three experiences: a meal, the same rejection He encountered, and the preview of their eternal dwelling: "Hence, let us go out to Him outside the camp, bearing His reproach. For here we do not have a lasting city, but we are seeking the city which is to come." (Hebrews 13:13,14)

Combining Sin and Peace Offerings in Hebrews 13

Elaborating the thought of *eating* of Christ's sacrifice, the author of Hebrews next subtly, but clearly to the Jewish reader, reiterates the fact that Christ's sacrifice is a meal, drawn from a peace offering: "Through Him then, let us *continually* offer up a *sacrifice of praise* to God, that is, *the fruit of lips* that give *thanks to ["Confess"]* His name. And do not neglect doing good and *sharing*; for with such sacrifices God is pleased." (Hebrews 13:15,16).

Through Christ's sacrifice upon the cross His people may now offer a *sacrifice of praise*, the *fruit of lips,* as they *confess* His name while being involved with *sharing*. It is true that all of these are definitely *actions* specifically connected to the peace offering, however each of these are also specifically *terms for* the peace offering as well. F.C.N. Hicks succinctly states the observation of many a scholar: "The 'sacrifice of praise' was the peace-

---

[108] "Outside the camp" was a pregnant phrase associated especially with the Day of Atonement, and also with the sacrifice of the Red Heifer. In addition, it was associated with the place to which the unclean were banned, as well as the place where a blasphemer was put to death. Probably the most interesting—applying all of these to Christ—is the fact that when the children of Israel rejected God, He had Moses erect a "tent" [Tabernacle?] "outside the camp" (Ex. 33:7-10)! See Lane, *Hebrews 9-13*, 541-546.
[109] John 4:20ff.

offering."[110] The *confession*, as already explained earlier in this chapter, was also a technical term used for the peace offering. William Lane conveys the fact that the *fruit of lips* "came to be associated with thank offerings."[111] Recall that the thank offering was a type of peace offering. The final technical word, *sharing*, was a technical term even among pagans, describing the peace offering meal by which the worshipper "shared" (koinonia) the same meal his god was eating. The word was then soon adopted by Christianity to label the genuine communion meal, the Lord's Supper. Tibor Horbath, realizing the Eucharistic use of this word, says that here in Hebrews 13:16, "The 'koinonia' ['sharing'] might mean not only sharing goods with others, but also the gathering where Eucharistic celebrations were held."[112] Even the word *continually* "connotes simply and succinctly that the whole continuous liturgy of the old covenant is fulfilled in the continual praise offering of Christians."[113] Standing alone, *Sacrifice of Praise*, *Fruit of Lips*, *Giving Thanks* [Confession] or *Sharing* [koinonia] would not give a certain witness to the concept of peace offering, but standing together, they give powerful reference to the peace offering. In addition to the terms used for the peace offering, the Greek word for "sacrifice" used in these verses "appears to have been understood in the early Church of the prayers and thanksgivings connected with the Eucharist."[114]

---

[110] Hicks, *The Fullness...*, 294. Westcott, *The Epistle...*, 443, says that the *sacrifice of praise* "occurs in Lev. vii.12...of the highest form of peace-offering." Lane, *Hebrews 9-13*, 551: "A number of scholars have found in v 15 an undisguised reference to the Christian Eucharist. They assert that the 'sacrifice of praise' is nothing else but the praising answer of the Church to the sacrifice of Jesus, which is celebrated in the Lord's Supper." Lane doesn't fully agree.

[111] Lane, *Hebrews 9-13*, 550. Lane also here explains that such terminology referred to songs of thanksgiving as well. Field, *The Apostolic...*, 420, shows how the "fruit of our lips" was taken from the LXX. The Hebrew literally is "calves of our lips," perhaps bringing out the sacrificial nature of the expression.

[112] Tibor Horbath, *The Sacrificial Interpretation of Jesus' Achievement in the New Testament* (New York: Philosophical Library, Inc., 1979), 71.

[113] Lane, *Hebrews 9-13*, 550. On pp. 449,450, Lane explains that δια παντος was also used regularly for the daily burnt offering. "It occurs fourteen times in Num 28:10-29 LXX in reference to the daily sacrifices." Thus the burnt offering enters the sacrificial picture along with the sin offering and peace offering here in Hebrews 13:10ff.

[114] Westcott, *The Epistle...*, 443.

Remember that the main activity associated with the peace offering was the communion meal. Thus the writer to the Hebrews is obviously, in a manifold way, drawing the Hebrew Christian reader to think of worshipful feasting in the Lord's Supper.

Some might object to the thought that the author of Hebrews is mixing the sin offering on the Day of Atonement with the peace offering. Recall that often the different sacrifices were considered a unit, and each sacrifice was considered a "stage" in the sacrificial process. The final stage of sacrifice was indeed the peace offering.[115] Having presented the radical sacramental eating of the Day of Atonement sin offering, the author of Hebrews then encourages such sacrifice-related eating by describing Christian worship also in terms of the final stage of sacrifice, the peace offering. "The third stage in the Sacrifice, once more for Christ and for us, ...is the stage of the Communion-meal."[116]

What does it Mean that Christ is a "Minister"?

> "Now the main point in what has been said is this: we have such a high priest, who has taken His seat at the right hand of the throne of the Majesty in the heavens, a minister in the sanctuary..."
> Hebrews 8:1,2

Before one can discern how Jesus is a "minister" (Heb. 8:2), there must first be a consideration of the preceding verse (8:1). Here the author of Hebrews declares that Christ has "taken His seat at the right hand of the throne of the Majesty in the heavens." This is—as discussed previously and as explained in the next verse—a description of Christ's presence in the

---

[115] Hicks, *The Fullness...*, 251: "And, without doubt, it [NT] leaves us with the Eucharist in so many words described as constituting...the last of the six stages in the Sacrifice ["the meal"]."
[116] Hicks, *The Fullness...*, 341.

heavenly Holy of Holies. Christ does not, like the Jewish high priests of old, enter the Holy of Holies then exit. He enters and then takes His seat at the right hand of the Majesty.

Does He then remain out of contact with His people? Certainly it would be agreed among all denominations in Christendom that Christ can be approached by prayer, and thus at least in this way Christians approach the presence of God in the Holy of Holies. However, as clearly demonstrated throughout the OT, worship of God primarily meant that God was distributing His gifts of salvation through *active and tangible participation* in the official sacrifices. This brings us to the meaning of Christ as "minister."

God's distribution of His OT gifts was performed by His priests. One of the technical words for this priestly work was the Greek word "leitourgein" ("lightorgine"). The word "liturgy" is not only derived from this word but in Christian worship liturgy directly relates to this OT priestly service. Frequently "leitourgein" is translated *ministry* or *service*. In Kittel's *Theological Dictionary of the New Testament* the unique use of this word "leitourgein" is explained: "Apart from the two pagan [biblical] instances, ...the [Septuagint] reference is always to the worship of Yahweh performed by the priests and Levites either in the tabernacle or in the temple."[117] With this unvarying use of the word "leitourgein," it is clear that the Jewish people considered the word to be one of the most specific technical terms used to describe worship led by priests.[118]

Henceforth we will transliterate the Greek word "leitourgein"—which conveyed the unique priestly ministry—as "liturgy". The priests, as they did liturgy, were receiving *and distributing* God's gifts of salvation to His people.

---

[117] Hermann Strathmann, "λειτουργεω," in vol. IV, *Theological Dictionary of the New Testament*, ed. Gerhard Kittel and Gerhard Friedrich, trans. Geoffrey W. Bromiley (Grand Rapids: Wm. B. Eerdmans Publishing Co., 1968, 220.

[118] Besides λειτουργεω, the Jews also used λατρευω seemingly as a synonym. Strathmann, "λατρευω," vol. IV, *Theological Dictionary of the New Testament*, ed. Gerhard Kittel and Gerhard Friedrich, trans. Geoffrey W. Bromiley (Grand Rapids: Wm. B. Eerdmans Publishing Co., 1968, 61: "λατρευειν is ...very closely related to the term λειτουργειν. But only apparently! The two words are very clearly distinguished, for λατρευειν always denotes the religious conduct of the people generally, including, of course, that of the priesthood, whereas λειτουργειν is wholly restricted to the priestly functions and is even a tt. for them."

Thus, as one would expect, when Saint Luke described Zecharias' entrance into the temple to perform his priestly *service*, this service was called "liturgy."[119] And when the book of Hebrews discusses the *ministry* of the priests, again, as one would expect, it is described as "liturgy."[120] An apparent exception to this is Hebrews 1:14 where angels are said to be "*ministering* spirits, sent out to render service for the sake of those who will inherit salvation." Here the "ministering" of the angels is described as "liturgy." The apparent difficulty is easily resolved when one understands that "liturgy" involves a distribution of God's gifts to His people. Indeed, both priests *and* angels performed this service of worship, distributing God's gifts to His people, and thus it is quite common to find angels present in both Old and New Testament descriptions of worship.[121] God's people must never forget that God was and is worshiped as His gifts are distributed to His people. Such worship would automatically illicit offerings of praise and thanksgiving, which are indeed the essential secondary part of worship.

Return now to Christ, the "high priest who has taken His seat at the right hand of the throne of the Majesty in the heavens." He does not merely "sit" there, but the next verse explains that he is "a minister [*liturgist*] in the sanctuary, and in the true tabernacle, which the Lord pitched, not man." (Hebrews 8:2). Is Christ then "ministering" like the angels in 1:14 or like the OT priests? It is apparent that He is ministering a little like both! He is liturgically like the angels in that we cannot directly observe Him liturgizing on this side of heaven, yet He is truly distributing God's holy gifts.

With the emphasis on priestly service in the epistle to the Hebrews, the use of "liturgy" in the epistle emphasizes that Jesus ministers not so much like an angel but as a priest—the High Priest par excellence. It is important to realize that such "ministry" (liturgy) is not a passive work but it means an active fulfillment of the duties of one's high priestly office. Westcott thus

---

[119] Luke 1:23
[120] Hebrews 10:11
[121] E.g. Hebrews 12:22, and recall excerpts from the *Prayer of the Veil*.

comments on the word: "The Leitourgia is the fulfillment of an office: it has a definite representative character, and corresponds with a *function to be discharged* [emphasis added]."[122] Thus, according to the common Jewish use of "leitourgein," Jesus as the high priest not only holds the office of high priest but He, from the right hand of the Majesty, has a "function to be discharged." Jesus is thus seen, after His ascension, to be continuing in the performance of God's priestly functions.[123]

What does it mean, then, that Christ is a minister ("liturgist")? It means simply that He, like the OT priests, is tangibly distributing God's gifts of salvation to His people. This is exclusively Christ's liturgy! Christ performs this liturgy through the office of the public ministry—the office of pastor—which He instituted to represent Himself. Pastors thus represent Christ as they rightly (and ritely) administer His Word and Sacraments.[124] It is then not surprising that the early church would speak of pastors as "liturgists," because through them Christ is doing His liturgy.[125]

Hebrews 8:3 describes Christ's priestly functions: "For every high priest is appointed to *offer both gifts and sacrifices*; hence it is necessary that this high priest [Jesus] also have something to offer." Here observe that the high priests offered "both gifts and sacrifices," and thus Christ—performing His liturgy—must "also have something to offer." This leads us to our next question.

---

[122] Westcott, *The Epistle*..., 230.
[123] Gayford, *Sacrifice*..., 138ff. Gayford maintains Christ was the victim and the offerer, but He was not the priest until He entered the heavenly temple at His ascension.
[124] Luke 10:16; John 20:21-23; Ephesians 4:11,12
[125] It should be borne in mind that the NT does not have a priestly office paralleling the OT priestly office. Field, *The Apostolic*..., 211-224, explains that the early church (e.g. Clement) uses the word "liturgus" to describe the work of the Pastor, whereas "Priest" is applied to all believers. All participate in the liturgy, but one who leads it is the "liturgus."

What are the Gifts and Sacrifices Offered by Christ and How Does He Offer Them?

> "...gifts and sacrifices are offered [by the priests] which cannot make the worshipper perfect in conscience, since they relate only to food and drink and various washings [lit. Baptisms], regulations for the body imposed until a time of reformation."
> Hebrews 9:9,10

Priestly Gifts and Sacrifices

The terms "gifts and sacrifices" are used more than once in Hebrews to describe the "liturgy" work of the priests. The priestly offering of "gifts and sacrifices" was spoken of in Hebrews 5:1 as "gifts and sacrifices for sins."

Some wrongly conclude that the OT "gifts and sacrifices" must mean that which was slain and placed on the altar. As one investigates the OT use of the word "gifts," it becomes apparent that it was usually used in the OT for those sacrificial portions to be *eaten* by the priests.[126] The author of Hebrews apparently agrees with this observation, for in Hebrews 9:9,10 he explains that "gifts and sacrifices are offered [by the priests] which cannot make the worshipper perfect in conscience, since *they relate only to food and drink and various washings* [lit. Baptisms], regulations for the body imposed until a time of reformation." "Gifts and sacrifices" relate especially to "food and drink"!

The best OT parallel to the "gifts and sacrifices" spoken of here in Hebrews appears to be found in Numbers 18, where, for instance, in verse 9 the words "gifts" and "sacrifices"[127] are not only found together but they relate to eating. God directed the OT priests [italics added]:

---

[126] The word δωρον is the translation of either Minchah or Qorban. See Cave, *The Scriptural...*, 510-520. The Minchah was usually the grain offering, and was almost always eaten of by the priests. Qorban (Equated with "gift" in Mark 7:11) was used for any type of offering, but of all the offerings only the burnt offering did not involve eating by humans.

[127] The Greek word for "gifts" (δωρον) is the same in Heb. 9:9.10 and Num. 18:9. The words for "sacrifice" are different (θυσιαι, θυσιασματων), yet they are from the same root.

And let this be to you from all the holy things that are consecrated to me, even the burnt-offerings, from all their *gifts and from all their sacrifices,* and from every guilt offering of theirs, and from all their sin offerings, whatever things they give to me of all their holy things, they shall be yours and your sons' [to eat!].

As sin and guilt offerings were to be eaten by the priests, God in the next verse (Numbers 18:10) then directs the priests, "In the most holy place shall you *eat them.* Every male shall *eat them*, you and your sons: they shall be holy to you."[128] Observe the importance of *eating* the priestly *gifts and sacrifices*; this certainly is significant in recognizing the Eucharist in the epistle to the Hebrews.

Supporting this theory that the author of Hebrews 9:9,10 has Numbers 18 in mind, is the fact that Numbers 19:1ff follows with descriptions of certain sacred washings—particularly washings related to the Red Heifer. This fits with the "food and drink *and washings*" of Hebrews 9:10. Then even as Hebrews 9:9,10 appear to be drawing upon Numbers 18, Hebrews 9:13, in referencing the cleansing from the Red Heifer, is drawing from Numbers 19. It is apparent that Hebrews 9:9ff are directly referencing both Numbers 18 and 19 where "gifts and sacrifices" are displayed as both priestly food and sacred washings, and where the sacred washings are related to the Red Heifer.

Truly Hebrew "gifts and sacrifices" were generally related sacrificial rituals. However, the author of Hebrews relates the "gifts and sacrifices" specifically to "food and drink and various washings." Some scholars confess to be baffled as to why the author of Hebrews here includes *drink* with "food" relative to "gifts and sacrifices."[129] It is baffling because the Jews had

---

[128] *The Septuagint Version of the Old Testament with an English Translation* (Grand Rapids: Zondervan, 7th printing 1975), 200.

[129] Westcott, *The Epistle...*, 254: "The mention of 'drinks' has caused difficulty, for the Law gave no universal directions in this respect..."

practically no directives concerning "drink" within the sacrificial procedures, and the "drink offerings" were not for human consumption but were to be poured at the base of the altar. Once again Numbers 18 comes to the rescue. In Numbers 18:30,31, God speaks of "the product of the wine vat," informing the priests, "You may eat it anywhere."[130] So once again, Numbers 18 appears to be in the mind of the author of Hebrews 9:9,10.

Though Numbers 18 may give a clue concerning the inclusion of "drink" with food, and Numbers 19 may give a clue concerning the inclusion of "washings" with food and drink, yet ultimately combining "food and drink and washings" seems to be a poor way to explain "gifts and sacrifices," simply because it is difficult to find such a combination outside of Numbers 18 & 19. To the non-Christian there seems to be little rhyme or reason why the author of Hebrews 9:10 would summarize priestly liturgy by speaking of "food and drink and various washings." To the Hebrew Christians of the early church, however, such a summary is custom-made to create the thought of the Christian sacraments, which include precisely *food and drink* and *washings!*[131] Thus once again the author of Hebrews, by using "food and drink and washings" to describe the priestly "gifts and sacrifices," is directing his readers (or hearers) to their Christian sacraments.[132]

Christ Reforms the Old

This understanding becomes even more pronounced when the word "reformation" is properly understood. Recall from Hebrews 9:9,10 that the Jewish priestly rites utilizing "food and drink and various washings" were to exist until a "time of *reformation*." The word used here for "reformation" does

---

[130] Obviously such wine could be drunk anywhere but the Tabernacle courts. Drinking wine there was forbidden (Lev. 10:9).

[131] Concerning such "washings," the author of Hebrews uses this word, βαπτισμων, to describe Christian baptism in 6:2.

[132] Field, *The Apostolic...*, 234: "So again we may see the same contrast implied between the 'meats and drinks and diverse baptisms' of the old covenant (v. 10) and the 'good things' which belong to the Priesthood of Christ (v. 11)." Field concludes: "Nothing, therefore, seems to be wanting to place the present allusion to the Holy Eucharist beyond doubt."

not mean cancellation. The use of food and drink and baptisms was not to be *cancelled* but *reformed*. Concerning this word for "reformation" William Lane summarizes, "The use of the word in the papyri and in the hellenistic Greek indicates that it expresses the notions of correction, reconstruction, improvement, or amendment."[133] Thus the "food and drink and various washings," which stood primarily as legal regulations for the Jews in OT liturgy, would be *reconstructed, improved and amended*. Christ now serves as high priest, ministering gifts and sacrifices under the *reconstructed and improved* sacraments of the NT. God did not do away with the use of *food and drink and baptisms*, He *reformed* their use! This is precisely a type/antitype line of thinking.

This *reformation* performed by Christ runs parallel with the description set forth in Hebrews 7:12: "For when the priesthood is changed, of necessity there takes place a change of law also." Christ thus took the "law"—here referring to the worship statutes instituted through Moses—and He did not cancel or destroy it, but he *changed* this worship "law" by *reforming* it. The Sacraments of Holy Baptism and Holy Communion are truly the results of changing/reforming the tabernacle rites; in God's NT ordinances there still exist food, drink and washings—as observed also in God's OT tabernacle ordinances—but now they are on a much higher plane.

Is this understanding, that Christ was reforming temple practices, found anywhere else in the New Testament? We believe so. For instance, recall Stephen—the first Christian martyr. The initial accusation leveled against Stephen was, "This man incessantly speaks against this holy place [the temple] and the Law; for we have heard him say that this Nazarene, Jesus, will destroy this place and *alter the customs which Moses handed down to us*. [italics added]"[134] Though there were certainly falsehoods in this accusation—for Stephen would never have spoken against the temple or against the Law of Moses—yet there is a ring of Christian truth in this

---

[133] Lane, *Hebrews 9-13...*, 217.
[134] Acts 6:13,14

accusation. The temple would indeed be destroyed in 70AD, as Christ had predicted; and upon its destruction the sacrificial rites would cease. Such rites were supposed to cease because they were types, but their antitypes would continue; those antitypes are particularly Baptism and the Sacrament of the Altar. It thus makes sense that Stephen was informing the Jews that Christ Jesus was indeed *altering* the customs of Moses, taking the temple washings and sacred meals and *altering* (changing/reforming) them.

Food, Drink and Washings that Cleanse the Conscience

NT believers now have "food and drink and...washings" which are not legal *requirements* for the flesh, but *means* by which the conscience is cleansed. Hebrews 9:9,10 makes the following two important points concerning the OT priestly ministry:

> 1. The gifts and sacrifices of the Old Testament related merely to food, drink and washings, and thus they could not "make the worshiper perfect in conscience."
> 2. This is so because such food and drink and washings were "regulations for the body imposed until a time of reformation."

Simply stated, the Old Testament food and drink and washings were legal, fleshly requirements based upon the sacrifice of animals and grain. Such food, drink and washings would indeed *salve* the conscience of an OT believer, but they would not *perfect* the conscience.[135] Thus Hebrews 10:1 explains: "For the Law, since it has only a shadow of the good things to come and not the very form of things, can never by the same sacrifices year by year, which they offer continually, make perfect those who draw near." The OT shadow could not perfect the conscience, but that which it foreshadowed could! Such perfection of the conscience can only happen through the cross,

---

[135] See Hebrews 9:9,14; 10:2,22; 13:18 for references to a purged, perfect conscience in Christ.

upon which *the* Lamb of God was sacrificed. The gifts of salvation earned at the cross are directly found in the NT sacraments. In these sacraments— the amended and reformed food and drink and washings foreshadowed in the OT—Christians receive the perfect conscience purchased for them at the cross of Christ.

In the NT era, God's people know the historical reality and completion of the center of their faith: Christ's self-sacrifice. They know this Ultimate Sacrifice was validated by His resurrection. Now, in the Christian era, Christ's crucifixion finds its application in the food and drink and washings of the sacraments.

Legal Requirements vs. NT Sacraments

The OT regulations were legal requirements and thus they were in and of themselves the *goal* of OT worship. The NT regulations of Baptism and Eucharist are *not* legal requirements; they are *not* the goal of worship, but they are *means* whereby God's people directly encounter the cross and the empty tomb. Such an encounter is the goal of NT worship, for in such an encounter the conscience is made white as snow.

As legal requirements, the OT "sacraments" of food and drink and washings were twice removed from the reality of the cross. First, they were distanced from the cross in that they were based upon animal sacrifices; and second, they were removed from the reality of the cross because the Jews who participated in them really had no clear understanding that it all centered in the cross of Christ.[136] Their food and drink and washings were thus regulations *for the flesh*—mechanical movements of the body through which God bestowed atonement based upon Christ's future crucifixion. Faith in OT

---

[136] John Leighton, *The Jewish Altar: An Inquiry into the Spirit and Intent of the Expiatory Offerings of the Mosaic Ritual* (New York: Funk and Wagnalls, 1886), 27: "Nay, if Israel saw Christ at all in their service, they must, because of its many details, have seen nearly everything about Him; and we should find them again and again saying so. But their silence is conclusive of the fact that they saw him not." The Jews knew Christ was coming, and it was taught that their worship related to Him, but when He came unto His own, they did not know Him, and His cross became their stumbling block.

worshippers would cling to God's gracious *promise* of forgiveness conveyed in the animal gifts and sacrifices that He ordained, but it did not really grasp the fact that such forgiveness was founded upon Christ's cross. Through the OT priestly work, God distributed a sort of *promissory note* to the Jews, a promissory note of forgiveness that, unbeknownst to the OT Jews, was backed already by the cross of Christ.

When Christ's work of salvation was completed, the food and drink and washings of the OT were reformed and the NT sacraments of Communion and Baptism then became established as direct links to the cross of Christ. These NT sacraments are not based upon animal sacrifices, like their OT counterparts, but they are solely based upon Christ's once-for-all sacrifice.[137] Similarly, unlike the OT food and drink and washings that did not fully inform OT believers of Christ's death, the NT food and drink and washings are not rightly used by congregations ignorant of Christ's sacrifice for sin! Christ's cross is now, in the Christian era, perceived and believed to be the center of the NT Sacraments as well as the source of forgiveness behind the OT "sacraments."[138] Now faith clings to the full *payment* of Christ's cross, not merely to God's *promissory note* of OT sacrificial rites.

Christ's Liturgy

Unlike the OT priests, Christ, the great high priest, never needs to perform another sacrifice. But this then means that the NT sacraments are His sole priestly liturgy through which His people are invited in this era to enter behind the veil. Christians partake of the sacraments now, awaiting the time when no more sacraments shall be needed, for they will then see Him as He is, basking in His unveiled presence. Then, in heaven, Christ's liturgy will be an eternal, personal distribution of their every need, and they will respond

---

[137] It is clear in Hebrews that Christ is not re-sacrificed in the sense that He is not re-slain. Often the author of Hebrews reminds us of the fact that Christ was sacrificed "once." Heb. 7:27; 9:12,26,28; 10:10.

[138] If we define a sacrament loosely as something through which God offers grace, then the OT sacrificial rites were indeed sacraments.

with perfect praise.

In the meantime, however, God's people in this present era have a high priest who is sitting in the heavenly Holy of Holies, distributing the gifts drawn from His atoning blood. Every time there is a Baptism, it is His liturgy—His service to the people. Every time the Lord's Supper is celebrated and His people partake of the body and blood given and shed on the cross, it is His liturgy—His service to the people. His Divine Liturgy, like that of the OT, flows from sacrifice, only now the sacrifice is "the offering of the body of Jesus Christ once for all." (Hebrews 10:10).

Sanctification Flowing From the Eucharist

Through His sacraments the Great High Priest distributes forgiveness and salvation. Certainly the epistle to the Hebrews emphasizes this "cleansing" nature of Christ's body and blood received in the Sacrament. Through the Eucharist a Christian's conscience is indeed cleansed; he/she is forgiven through faithful participation in the holy sin offering meal. However, the changes in a Christian do not stop with the miracle of forgiveness.

The author of the epistle to the Hebrews also conveys the important truth that Christians are called to lead God-pleasing lives. In order for Christians to accomplish this, God must enable them to will and do it.[139] In short, God must work any good works that flow from Christians. This miracle is often called sanctification.

To accomplish sanctification in a Christian, God uses means, and a primary means is the Sacrament of the Altar. Thus, in Hebrews 9:13-15—after the author of Hebrews explained that the OT sacrificial rites could sanctify for the cleansing of the flesh—he then goes on to say, "how much more will the blood of Christ who through the eternal Spirit offered Himself without blemish to God, cleanse your conscience from dead works *to serve the living God*. And for this reason He is the mediator of a new covenant...

---

[139] Philippians 2:13.

[emphasis added]" The blood of Christ, mediated by Christ in the Eucharist, indeed gives to every Christian the ability to *serve the living God*.

In the midst of the Eucharistically saturated section of Hebrews 10:19-29, again the author of the epistle writes of sanctification when he says, "And let us consider how to stimulate one another to *love and good deeds*. (10:24)" How is this accomplished? The next verse (v. 25) explains that it is done by "not forsaking our own assembling together..." So, assembling together can stimulate Christians to love and good deeds. Why do Christians assemble together? Certainly to pray and praise God, but particularly the early church realized that Christians assembled together to celebrate Holy Communion, and this is, we are convinced, the very topic of the verses surrounding this admonition to accomplish love and good deeds. It is truly in the reception of the Holy Eucharist that a Christian is stimulated to love and good deeds. For faithful reception of Holy Communion causes Christians to fix their eyes upon Jesus—and to literally take in Jesus—without whom a Christian can do nothing.[140]

A third time the author of Hebrews points to Christ and His Supper as the source of strength to do God's will is in Hebrews 13:20,21. These verses exhort:

> Now may the God of peace who brought up our Lord Jesus from the dead, that great Shepherd of the sheep, *through the blood of the everlasting covenant, make you complete in every good work to do His will, working in you what is pleasing in His sight...* [italics added][141]

How then can Christians live the sanctified life and thus be *complete in every good work*? God accomplishes this completion *through the blood of the everlasting covenant*. Where is that *blood of the covenant* found? The

---

[140] John 15:4,5.
[141] NKJV, Thomas Nelson Publishers.

only Scriptural reference to Christ's *blood of the covenant* is, outside of the epistle to the Hebrews, in the Words of Institution for Holy Communion. We have observed the abundant references to the covenant nature of Holy Communion, and thus it makes sense that this *blood of the covenant* described in Hebrews 13:20 is indeed a reference to the sanctifying power of Christ through His Holy Supper. It is only through the *blood of the covenant* that Christians can begin to be *complete in every good work*!

Concluding Remark

We pray that every Christian may realize that they uniquely abide in Christ and He in them whenever they partake of His once-sacrificed body and blood.[142] In the supreme feasting fellowship this side of heaven, He wants His people to realize that He is both joining them in the feast and He is their food. Strangely, He is also the one who serves the meal![143] He longs to dine with His people: "Behold, I stand at the door and knock; if any one hears My voice and opens the door, I will come in to him, *and will dine with him, and he with Me.*"[144] He earnestly desires believers not only to dine *with* Him, but *upon* Him—as the ultimate burnt offering, sin offering, guilt offering, peace offering and grain offering—that through Him they would overcome the evils of this world and then join Him at His lavish eternal banquet.[145]

SDG

---

[142] John 6:56.
[143] Luke 12:37; 22:27. Note the context of Luke 22:17 is the Eucharist. This likely speaks of the representative nature of the Office of the Holy Ministry. Pastors represent Christ, and He works through them. "He who hears you, hears me." Luke 10:16.
[144] Revelation 3:20. Italics added.
[145] Luke 12:35-40; 13:29.

Bibliography

"The Babylonian Captivity". Vol. 2, in *Works of Martin Luther*, translated by A. T. W. Steinhaeuser. Philadelphia: Muhlenberg Press, 1915, renewed 1943.

Bauer, Walter, William F. Arndt, and Wilbur Gingrich, . *A Greek-English Lexicon of the New Testament and other Christian Literature.* 2nd. Chicago: University of Chicago Press, 1979.

Beck, William F., trans. *The Holy Bible, An American Translation.* New Haven, MO: Leader Publishing Company, 1976.

Bedale, Stephen. ""The Eucharistic Sacrifice"." *Theology* 1vi, no. 398 (1953): 300.

Behm, Johannes. θυω, θυσια. θυσοαστηριον. Vol. III, in *Theological Dictionary of the New Testament*, edited by Gerhard Kittel and Gerhard Friedrich, translated by Geoffrey W. Bromily, 180ff. Grand Rapids: Wm. B. Eerdmans Publishing Co., 1968.

Beri, Elwood Sylvester. *Commentary on the Psalms.* New York: Benziger Brothers, 1915.

Brege, Daniel J. ""Eucharistic Overtones Created by Sacrificial Concepts in the Epistle to the Hebrews"." *Concordia Theological Quarterly* 66:1 (January, 2002): 61-81.

Brege, Daniel J. *"The learning of Old Testament sacrificial concepts will enhance one's appreciation for the Lord's Supper".* Doctor of Ministry, Concordia Theological Seminary, Ft. Wayne, IN: Concordia Theological Seminary, 2002.

Brown, William. *The Tabernacle: Its Priests and Its Services.* Peabody, MS: Hendrickson Publishers, Inc., 1966.

Buchanan, George Wesley. *To the Hebrews, The Anchor Bible.* Garden City, NY: Doubleday & Company, 1972.

Buchler, Adolph. *Types of Jewish and Palestinian Piety from 70 B.C.E. to 70 C.E.* London: Jews' College, 1922.

BIBLIOGRAPHY

Cameron, Bruce. *Luther's Summary of the Psalms (1531)--a Model for Contemporary Psalm Interpretation, STM.* St. Louis: Concordia Theological Seminary, 1991.

Cave, Alfred. *The Scriptural Doctrine of Sacrifice and Atonement.* Edinburgh: T & T Clark, 1890.

Conzelmann, Hans. *1 Corinthians.* Translated by James W. Leitch. Philadelphia: Fortress Press, 1975.

Conzelmann, Hans. Ευχαριστεω. Vol. IX, in *Theological Dictionary of the New Testament*, edited by Gerhard Kittel and Gerhard Friedrich, translated by Geoffrey W. Bromiley. Grand Rapids: Wm. B. Eerdmans Publishing Co., 1968.

Cullmann, O., and F.J. Leenhardt. *Essays on the Lord's Supper.* London: Lutterworth Press, 1958.

Daly, Robert J. *Christian Sacrifice.* Washington D.C.: The Catholic University of America Press, 1978.

Delitzsch, F. *Commentary on the Old Testament, Psalms.* Translated by Francis Bolton. Vol. V. Grand Rapids: Eerdmans Publishing Co., reprinted 1978.

Delitzsch, Franz. *Epistle to the Hebrews.* Translated by Thomas Kingsbury. Minneapolis: Klock and Klock Christian Publishers, 1978.

DeWitt, Roy Lee. *Teaching from the Tabernacle.* Grand Rapids: Baker Book House, 1988.

Edersheim, Alfred. *The Life and Times of Jesus the Messiah.* McLean, VA: MacDonald Publishing Company, nd.

—. *The Temple, Its Ministry and Services.* updated edition. Translated by unknown. Peabody, MS: Hendrickson Publishers, 1994.

Falls, Thomas B., trans. *Writings of Saint Justin Martyr.* New York: Christian Heritage, Inc., 1948.

BIBLIOGRAPHY

Fohrer, Georg. Σωτηριον *in the LXX.* Vol. VII, in *Theological Dictionary of the New Testament*, edited by Gerhard Kittel and Gerhard Friedrich, translated by Geoffrey W. Bromiley, 1022, 1023. Wm. B. Eerdmans Publishing Co., 1968.

Gavin, F. *The Jewish Antecedents of the Christian Sacraments.* New York: The Macmillan Co., 1928.

Gayford, S.C. *Sacrifice and Priesthood.* 2nd. London: Methuen & Co. LTD, 1953.

Gieschen, Charles A. *Angelomorphic Christology.* Leiden: Brill, 1998.

Grundmann, Walter. Ετοιμαζω. Vol. II, in *Theological Dictionary of the New Testament*, edited by Gerhard Kittel and Gerhard Friedrich, translated by Geoffrey W. Bromiley, 704-706. Grand Rapids: Wm. B. Eerdmans Publishing Co., 1968.

Hauck, Friedrich. Κοινονια. Vol. III, in *Theological Dictionary of the New Testament*, edited by Gerhard Kittel and Gerhard Friedrich, translated by Geoffrey W. Brimiley, 797-809. Grand Rapids: Wm. B. Eerdmans Publishing Co., 1968.

Hicks, F. C. N. *The Fullness of Sacrifice.* London: Macmillan & Co., 1946.

Horbath, Tibor. *The Sacrificial Interpretation of Jesus' Achievemnt in the New Testament.* New York: Philosophical Library, 1979.

Howard, Kevin, and Marvin Rosenthal. *The Feasts of the Lord.* Printed in the U.S.: No printer specified, 1977.

James, K.E.O. *Sacrifice and Sacrament.* New York: Barnes and Noble, Inc., 1962.

Jeremias, Joachim. *New Testament Theology.* New York: Charles Scribner's Sons, 1971.

Jeremias, Joachim. Πολλοι. Vol. VI, in *Theological Dictionary of the New Testament*, edited by Gerhard Kittel and Gerhard Friedrich, translated by Geoffrey W. Bromiley, 536-545. Grand Rapids: Wm. B. Eerdmans Publishing Co., 1968.

BIBLIOGRAPHY

—. *The Eucharistic Words of Jesus.* Translated by Norman Perrin. Philadelphia: Trinity Press International, 1966.

Jukes, Andrew. *The Law of the Offerings in Leviticus I. - VII Considered as the Appointed figure of the Various Aspects of the offering of the Body of Jesus Christ.* 13th . London: James Nisbet & Co., 1883.

Kavanagh, Aidan. *On Liturgical Theology.* Collegeville, MN: The Liturgical Press, 1984.

Keil, C. F., and F. Delitzsch. *Commentary on the Old Testament in Ten Volumes.* Translated by James Martin. Vols. I, The Pentateuch. Grand Rapids: Wm. B. Eerdmans Publishing Company, 1978.

Kirkpatrick, A. F., ed. *The Book of Psalms.* Cambridge: University Press, 1957.

Kleinig, John W. *Leviticus.* St. Louis: Concordia Publishing House, 2003.

Kodell, Jerome. *The Eucharist in the New Testament.* Collegeville, MN: The Liturgical Press, 1988.

Krauth, Charles Porterfield. *The Conservative Reformation and Its Theology: as represented in the Augsburg Confession, and in the History and Literature of the Evangelical Lutheran Church.* Philiadelphia: The United Lutheran Publication House, n.d.

Kugel, James L. *The Bible As It Was.* London: Belknap Press, 1997.

Kurtz, J. H. *Offerings, Sacrifices and the Worship of the Old Testament,.* Translated by James Martin. Peabody, MA: Hendrickson Publishers, Inc., 1998.

Lane, William L. *A Call to Commitment.* Peabody: Hendrickson Publishers, 1985.

—. *Hebrews 9-13, Word Biblical Commentary.* Vol. 47b. Dallas: Word Books, 1991.

Leighton, John. *The Jewish Altar: An Inquiry into the Spirit and Intent of the Mosaic Ritual.* New York: Funk & Wagnalls, 1886.

Lenski, R. C. H. *The Interpretation of St. Paul's First and Second Epistles to the Corinthians.* Minneapolis: Augsburg Publishing House, 1963.

Lenski, R.C.H. *The Interpretation of St. Matthew's Gospel.* Minneapolis: Augsburg Publishing House, 1943.

Lightfoot, J. B., ed. *The Apostolic Fathers Clement, Ignatius, and Polycarp .* Translated by J. B. Lightfoot. Vol. 2. Grand Rapids: Baker Book House, 1981.

McCauley, Leo P., and Anthony A Stephenson, . *The Works of Saint Cyril of Jerusalem.* Vol. 1. Washington, D.C.: The Catholic University of America Press, 1969.

Michel, Otto. Ομολογεω *[and cognates].* Vol. V, in *Theological Dictionary of the New Testament*, edited by Gerhard Kittel and Gerhard Friedrich, translated by Geoffrey W. Bromiley, 199-220. Grand Rapids: Wm. B. Eerdmans Publishing Co.

Moenkemoeller, William. *The Festivals and Sacrifices of Israel Compiled from the Mosaic Regulations.* Saint Louis: Concordia, 1932.

Neale, J. M., and R. F. Littledale, . *The Liturgies of SS. Mark, James, Clement, Chrysostom, and Basil, and of the Church of Malabar .* London: Griffith Farran & Co., 1869, 2nd ed.; n.d. 7th ed.

Neyrey, Jerome H., ed. *The Social World of Luke-Acts, (Peabody, MS: Hendrickson Publishers, 1991).* Peabody, MS: Hendrickson Publishers, 1991.

Oetting, Walter. *Church of the Catacombs.* St. Louis: Concordia Publishing House, 1964.

Plass, Edward M., ed. *What Luther Says.* Vol. 2. 3 vols. St. Louis: Concordia Publishing House, 1959.

Plaut, W. Gunther. *The Torah: A Modern Commentary, Exodus Commentary.* New York: Jewish Publication Society, 1983.

Quasten, Johannes, and Joseph C. Plumpe, . *Ancient Christian Writers, the Works of the Fathers in Translation.* Translated by James Kleist. Vol. 6. Mahwah, NJ: Paulist Press, n.d. copyright 1948.

BIBLIOGRAPHY

Rodriguez, Angel Manuel. *Substitution in the Hebrew Cultus, Andrews University Doctoral Dissertation Series 3.* Berrien Springs, MI: Andrews University Press, 1979.

Sadler, M. F. *The First and Second Epistles to the Corinthians.* London: George Bell and Sons, 1898.

Sadler, M.F. *The Gospel According to St. Luke.* London: G. Bell and Sons, LTD, 1911.

Sasse, Herman. *This is My Body.* Adelaide: Lutheran Publishing House, 1977.

Scholer, Jon. *Proleptic Priests, the Priesthood in the Epistle to the Hebrews.* Sheffield: Sheffield Academic Press, 1991.

Seesemann, Heinrich. Πανηγυρις. Vol. V, in *Theological Dictionary of the New Testament*, edited by Gerhard Kittel and Gerhard Friedrich, translated by Geofrey W. Bromiley, 722. Grand Rapids: Wm. B. Eerdmans Publishing Co., 1968.

Steinmann, Andrew E. *Daniel.* St. Louis: Concordia Publishing House, 2008.

Stephenson, John R. *The Lord's Supper.* St. Louis: The Luther Academy, 2003.

Stibbs, Alan M. *Sacrament, Sacrifice and Eucharist.* London: Billing and Son LTD., 1961.

Stoeckhardt, George. *Epistle to the Romans.* Translated by Erwin Koehlinger. Fort Wayne, IN: Concordia Theological Seminary Press, 1980.

Stone, Darwell. *A History of the Doctrine of the Holy Eucharist.* London: Rivingtons, 1909.

Strathmann, Hermann. Λατρεια. Vol. IV, in *Theological Dictionary of the New Testament*, edited by Gerhard Kittel and Gerhard Friedrich, translated by Geoffrey W. Bromiley, 58-65. Grand Rapids: Wm. B. Eerdmans Publishing Co., 1968.

BIBLIOGRAPHY

Strathmann, Hermann. Λειτουργια. Vol. IV, in *Theological Dictionary of the New Testament*, edited by Gerhard Kittel and Gerhard Friedrich, translated by Geoffrey Bromilly, 220. Grand Rapids: Wm. b. Eerdmans Publishing Co.,, 1968.

Swetnam, James. ""The Greater and More Perfect Tent," a Contribution to the Discussion of Hebrews 9,11." *Biblica* 47 (1966): 91-106.

Tappert, T., ed. *The Book of Concord*. Translated by T. Tappert. Philadelphia: Fortress Press, 1959.

The Holy Bible, New American Standard Version. La Habra, CA: William Collins, World Publishing Co., Inc., Copyright 1975 The Lockman Foundation.

The Holy Bible, New King James Version. Nashville, Atlanta, London, Vancouver: Thomas Nelson Publishers, Copyright 1994.

The Lutheran Hymnal. St. Louis: Concordia Publishing House, 1941.

The Septuagint Version of the Old Testament with an English Translation. Grand Rapids: Zondervan, by special arrangement with Samuel Bagster & Sons, Ltd., London, 1970.

Vanhoye, Albert. ""Structure and Message of the Epistle to the Hebrews" (trans. James Swetnam)." *Subsidia Biblica* (Editrice Pontificio Instituto Biblico) 12 (1989).

Vaux, Roland De. *Studies in Old Testament Sacrifice*. Wales: Cardiff University of Wales Press, 1964.

Wakefield, Gordon S. *An Outline of Christian Worship*. Edinburgh: T & T Clark, 1998.

Washburn, W. W. *The Import of Sacrifice in the Ancient Jewish Service*. New York: Phillips & Hunt, 1883.

Westcott, Brooke. *The Epistle to the Hebrews*. Grand Rapids: Wm. B. Erdmans Publishing Co., 1973.

Williamson, R. ""The Eucharist and the Epistle to the Hebrews"." *New Testament Studies* 21: 300-312.

BIBLIOGRAPHY

Young, E. J. *The Book of Isaiah.* Vol. III. Grand Rapids: Wm. B. Eerdmans Publishing Co., 1969.

—. *The Book of Isaiah.* Vol. II. Grand Rapids: Wm. B. Eerdmans Publishing Co., 1969.

BIBLIOGRAPHY

Glossary with Index[1]

Aaron: Brother of *Moses*, descendant of Levi; first *high priest*; only his male descendants could be priests in God's house. (196, 383)

Absolution: The lifting off of sins (pronouncement of forgiveness) on God's behalf; the second part of *confession*. (221ff)

Agape Meal: Greek for "love" meal; meal that preceded (or followed?) *Holy Communion* in early Christian tradition; meal shared with the poor. (327f)

Allegory (allegorize): In Biblical interpretation, a method whereby elements of stories or of things are seen as symbolic or instructive. Not the same as *type*; *allegory* often employs imagination to obtain interpretation. (33)

Altar: A table/platform associated with worship-related *sacrifice*, God's name, God's presence, forgiveness, unity and sacred eating; sacrificial portions were often burned upon it, and blood was often placed on its walls, *horns* and at its base. (122ff)

Altar for Burnt Offering: See *Bronze Altar*.

Altar of Incense: Gold-plated, horned altar in the *Tabernacle Holy Place* upon which *incense* was burned and the most sacred *blood* applied to its *horns*; associated with prayer ascending heavenward. (135, 139ff)

Angel of the Lord: Heavenly messenger frequently appearing in the OT; considered to be the pre-incarnate Son of God. (111ff, 146, 187, 348ff)

Anointing: Pouring of liquid upon a person or object; in the OT the application of the special anointing oil, which—in a religious sense—identified something as appointed by God for His use. (147f) See *Christ*.

Anointing Oil: Special oil recipe ordained by God for *anointing* those things or people appointed by Him. (147)

Antitype: A person, place, object or activity which was foreshadowed. A Biblical antitype has something to do with *Christ*, and often is *Christ*. That which does the foreshadowing is called a *type*. (32ff)

Apostles: The men commissioned and sent by *Christ* to be the foundation of His NT Church; originally twelve men, but a couple of others were also appointed by *Christ*; they all died within 100 years; pastors continue their work in leading congregations, but not in being Apostles; there is no need for additional Apostles—the *Church* does not have to be re-founded. (94ff)

---

[1] The Index only cites major or key references.

GLOSSARY WITH INDEX

Ark of the Covenant: Gold-plated chest in the *Most Holy Place*; its cover was the solid gold *Mercy Seat*, on which were two gold *cherubim*; OT location of God's throne among men; main contents were the two tablets of the *Ten Commandments*. (142, 144f, 204)

Baptism: A sacred, ceremonial washing associated with spiritual cleansing; now identified as a Christian *sacrament*. (19, 60, 131ff)

Blood: Identified by God as the life of a creature; loftiest element in the sacrificial process; key element (Christ's blood) of the *Lord's Supper*. (128f, 160ff)

Body: That which tangibly identified a creature; key ingredient of OT *sacrifice*; term used by some Rabbis for the *Passover lamb*; key element (Christ's body) of the *Lord's Supper*; at times interchanged with *flesh*. (70ff)

Book of Concord (also **Concordia**): Confessional statement of Lutherans compiled in 1580AD, delineating key beliefs and practice. (14)

Bread of the Presence: Also called *showbread*; twelve loaves on the *Table of Showbread* in the *Holy Place* associated with God's presence; a *most holy* food consumed by priests once a week. (135ff, 346ff)

Breaking Bread: Action preceding most any Jewish meal; immediately became the most common way of referencing the *Lord's Supper*. (59, 265f)

Bronze Altar: Bronze, horned *altar* in the *Tabernacle Outer Court*; viewed as the hub of sacrificial activity, as well as the table and hearth of the Lord; also called the *Altar for Burnt Offering*; had in Christ's day two channels at its base: *Water* was poured into one, and *blood* and *wine* were poured into the other. (117ff, 121ff)

Bull: Largest sacrificial creature sacrificed in the *Tabernacle*; offered on the *Day of Atonement* and on other special occasions. (203, 381, 386)

Burnt Offering: Kind of *sacrifice* completely burned on the *Bronze Altar*, except for its *blood* and hide; common referent for *holocaust sacrifice*; especially signified dedication; offered after the *sin offering* but before the *peace offering*. (27f, 43, 149ff [Chapter Four])

Candelabrum (Candelabra): Solid gold, seven-branched, olive-oil-fired lamp in the *Holy Place*. (135, 138)

Catechize: To thoroughly instruct in the basics of the faith; such instruction is catechesis. (25, 45, 371ff)

GLOSSARY WITH INDEX

Chagigah: Special *peace offering* in Christ's day sacrificed usually the day after the *Passover*, was described as "sacrificing the Passover". (270ff)

Cherubim: A high rank of angels; gold cherubim were mounted on the *Ark of the Covenant*. It is uncertain what these gold figures looked like. (142f)

Christ: Greek for "anointed one"; Hebrew "*Messiah*"; the Savior awaited by the Jews, predicted and foreshadowed throughout their Scriptures. (147f)

Chrysostom, John: Patriarch of Constantinople, born 345; wrote much and was known as a great preacher. (250) See *Liturgy of Chrysostom*.

Church: Collectively identifies all believers in *Christ* both before and after His incarnation; visibly, a congregation gathered around Word and *Sacrament*. (222, 284)

Clean/Unclean: Of worshipers, it described a ceremonial status identifying whether one could approach God in worship—the unclean could not; of animals, it identified which ones could be eaten—the unclean were not to be eaten or sacrificed; "unclean" relates things/actions to man's fall. (233ff)

Clement of Rome: Pastor/Bishop considered by *Roman Catholicism* to be third successor of Peter as "Pope"; likely knew the Apostle Peter; wrote earliest example of Christian literature around 96AD. (274, 279)

Communion: "Fellowship" or "point of contact"; worship word used to indicate contact with one's god; usually associated with eating. (173ff, 237, 248ff, 254ff)

Communion Sacrifice: Another name for *peace offering*; sometimes associated with the *burnt offering* on God's table; *sacrifice* associated with being in fellowship with God—usually such fellowship involved eating. (155ff, 173ff). In contrast see *Holocaust Sacrifice*.

Completion Sacrifice: A name for the *peace offering*; *sacrifice* that was the finale of the sacrificial process, culminating in a sacred meal. (306ff)

Confession: First admitting one's sins (*confession of sin*) and second receiving *absolution*; also describes voicing praise (*confession of praise*); also describes stating one's faith. (224ff)

Confession of Praise: Voicing praise; especially associated with the *peace offering*; as opposed to confession of sin for a *sin offering*. (312f, 377)

Confession of Sin(s): Speaking aloud one's sins or sinfulness, either privately or generally; preceded the slaying of a *sin offering*. (224ff)

GLOSSARY WITH INDEX

Confession Sacrifice: Another name for the *peace offering*, likely emphasizing the *confession of praise* rather than the *confession of sin*. The Greek word used for "confession" is often translated "thanksgiving" in English. (312ff)

Consecration Sacrifice: A *peace offering* that marked the *ordination* of priests or the coronation of kings in Israel. (317ff)

Corban: See **Qorban**.

Covenant: At times synonymous with *testament*; an agreement or testament between God and man established by a *peace offering*, sealed with *blood* and a *communion* meal drawn from the *sacrifice*. (296ff)

Covenant of Salt: Identification of an enduring *covenant*, even as *salt* preserves; *salt* was thus put on all Jewish sacrifices. (190ff)

Covenant Sacrifice: Another name for *peace offering*, identifying that it sealed a *covenant* with sacrificial *blood* and a *communion* meal. (296ff)

Cup of Blessing: Liturgical term used for the third official cup of wine at *Passover*; came to be associated with *wine* blessed in the *Lord's Supper*; identifying source of blessing in the *Lord's Supper*. (71)

Cyprian: Pastor/Bishop of Carthage born around 200AD; espoused high church view of clergy offices. (275)

Cyril of Jerusalem: Pastor/Bishop, born 315AD; known for catechetical lectures. (132)

Day of Atonement: The one day per year when the *high priest*, with public *sin offering* blood, entered the *Holy of Holies* to do the atonement *liturgy* for the nation of Israel; only time *blood* was *sprinkled* on the *Mercy Seat*; involved scapegoat ceremony. (204f, 393f)

Didache: Greek for "teaching"; abbreviation for "Teaching of the Apostles"; ancient document some believe was penned partly by *Apostles*, discovered in 1883. (46, 227)

Discipline of the Secret: Early church attitude of holding the *Lord's Supper* in such high regard that only those sufficiently catechized could be taught its secrets; discipline of withholding teachings of the *Lord's Supper* to outsiders. (45ff, 372ff)

Drink Offering: See **Libation**.

GLOSSARY WITH INDEX

Easter: The name given to the day Christ rose from the dead; also name used by some to identify the Jewish *Passover*. (87f)

Eucharist: Greek for "thanks"; when the *Temple* stood, commonly used to identify the Jewish *thank offering*; became the technical term for the *Lord's Supper* within a century of *Christ*. (253, 272ff)

Fat: Associated with blessing/wealth; forbidden for Jews to eat; important sacrificial element; consumed by God when burned on the *Bronze Altar*. (22ff, 179f, 239)

Fat (Fatty) Portions: Fat-laced organs burned with the fat on the *Bronze Altar*, possessed a degree of sacredness; used by pagans for divining. (179ff)

Feast of Booths (Feast of Tabernacles): Jewish festival commemorating their wandering in the wilderness when God provided food/water before they entered the *Promised Land*; involved an important *water* ceremony in Christ's day, culminating with *water* poured into a channel at the base of the *Bronze Altar*. The feasts are described in Lev.23, Num. 28,29 and in Deut.16. (21)

Feast of Unleavened Bread: Jewish festival days that begin with *Passover* during which all *leaven* was purged from every Jewish home. During this feast Jesus instituted the *Lord's Supper*. The feasts are described in Lev.23, Num. 28,29 and in Deut.16. (21,62)

Feast of Weeks: Also called *Pentecost*; Jewish festival celebrated 50 days after *Passover*, marked the official beginning of the fall harvest; day the NT Church was established, when the Holy Spirit was poured forth. The feasts are described in Lev.23, Num. 28,29 and in Deut.16. (21)

First-born (firstborn): The first to open a womb, whether of man or beast; all first-born of man (especially sons) and of beast were owned by God because He delivered the first-born at the *Passover*; livestock were sacrificed to God with *peace offering* status; sons—except Levite sons who were bound to serve in the *Temple*—were redeemed at the . (77ff, 242, 315ff, 389f)

First-fruits: Initial portion of a harvest, to be dedicated to God; treated as a *grain offering*; Jewish spring feast—marking the beginning of barley harvest—occurring on the third day of *Passover*, which was the day *Christ* rose from the dead (I Cor. 15:20). (335f)

Fish: Common food in Christ's day; chosen by the early church as a symbol of Christianity and as a symbol for the *Lord's Supper*. (266f)

GLOSSARY WITH INDEX

Flesh: Sacrificial portion of an animal either eaten by God (burned on His *altar*) or eaten by man in worship; common sacrificial *communion* food; at times equated with *body*. (24f, 258f, 262ff)

Flour: Common *grain offering* ingredient; *sin offering* element that could be offered by the poor instead of livestock. (202, 331)

Frankincense: *Incense* that rested on the *Table of Showbread*; burned with *grain offerings*; burned by itself when the priests ate the *Showbread*. (362ff)

Free Will (Free-will) Offering: Category of private *peace offering* given of one's free will, apparently indicating thanks for some deliverance. (259, 295)

Fruit of Lips: Verbal praise; used also of the *peace offering*. (419f)

General Confession: Confession of sins that specifies none; often spoken publicly; observed in the OT on the *Day of Atonement*; common liturgical practice in preparation for receiving *Holy Communion*. (226ff). In contrast see *Private Confession*.

General Sacramental Eating: See *Sacramental Eating*.

Gifts and Sacrifices: Summary of the worship elements derived from priestly work; employed in the epistle to the Hebrews to indicate the food, drink and washings involved in worship. (383, 424ff)

Glory of the Lord: Majesty and power possessed solely by God; often revealed as a bright light or fire. (109, 145ff)

Goat: Common sacrificial creature; frequently associated with the *Day of Atonement*. (216, 225, 233)

Good Friday: The day *Christ* was crucified; center of the Christian faith and the day when OT *sacrifice* found its absolute *antitype*.

Grain Offering: Called *Minchah of the Outer Court*; included various forms of *unleavened bread*, part of which was burned as a *memorial* on the *Bronze Altar*; unburned portion was eaten as a *most holy* meal by priests; upon entrance into the *Promised Land*, included grape *wine* as a *libation* poured at the *Bronze Altar*'s base; also called *Unbloody Sacrifice*. (28f, 44, 329ff [Chapter Seven])

Guilt Offering: Subordinate species of *sin offering*; associated with specific sin or sense of guilt; obligated repayment of debt to God or man; always a *ram*; always of a private nature; *flesh* always eaten as a *most holy* meal by priests; commonly called *trespass offering*. (26f, 43, 193ff [Chapter Five])

GLOSSARY WITH INDEX

Haggadah: Official proclamation of God's deliverance recited at every *Passover* celebration; used by Paul for *Lord's Supper* proclamation. (82f)

Heave Offering: Right thigh of a *peace offering* given to priests and their families for a *holy* meal; heaving likely indicated God gifting it to the priests; major source of sustenance for priests' families. (244ff). See also *Wave Offering*.

Heavenly Tabernacle: Heavenly dwelling place of God; "pattern" for earthly *Tabernacle*. (105ff)

Hebrews: Ancient word for "Jews"; also the epistle of the NT addressed to early Christians who were Jewish. (368ff [Chapter Eight])

High Priest: The only Jewish priest privileged to enter the *Most Holy Place*; viewed by many as the sin-bearer for the nation of Israel. (143f, 376ff)

Hippolytus of Rome: Church father who wrote "The Apostolic Tradition" around 220AD. (137, 293)

Holocaust Sacrifice: Any sacrifice totally burned up; usually identifies the *burnt offering*. (155ff, 205). In contrast, see also *Communion Sacrifice*.

Holy: An identification of God as separate, unique, the standard of the universe; contact with God is the only way anything can be *holy*; identifies the food of the *peace offering* from which all clean Jews could eat. (25, 215ff, 244ff). See also *Most Holy*.

Holy Communion: A technical term for the *Lord's Supper*; used also of the *communion* of God's OT people with Him and with one another. (248, 254ff)

Holy Gifts: Used to refer to sacrificial portions; at times just *gifts*; often the same as *holy things*; see *Qorban*. (246ff)

Holy Kiss: Liturgical ritual in early Christianity preceding the reception of the *Sacrament*; also "kiss of peace" and "kiss of love". (124f)

Holy of Holies: See *Most Holy Place*.

Holy Place: The enclosed rectangular-based room having two gilded walls with two curtain doorways—one leading to the *Most Holy Place*, the other leading to the *Outer Court*; housed the *Table of Showbread*, the *Candelabrum* and the *Altar of incense*; off-limits to the *laity*. (134ff)

GLOSSARY WITH INDEX

Holy Things: OT sacrificial portions, especially those that were eaten; often same as *holy gifts*; employed in the NT liturgical phrase, "Holy things for holy people." (246ff)

Holy Supper: Name for the *Lord's Supper*.

Horns (on Altars): Found on the four corners of both the *Bronze Altar* and the *Altar of Incense*; symbols of power; on the altars, associated with proximity to God. (117f, 128, 135, 140)

Icon: A visible representation of God. E.g.: "The fire of the Bronze Altar was an icon of God's presence." (23, 158)

Ignatius of Antioch: Pastor/bishop; wrote several epistles to congregations around 107AD; knew the Apostle John and perhaps other *Apostles*. (184)

In Remembrance: The phrase used by Jesus in the *Words of Institution*; in Greek, a prepositional phrase rarely found in Scripture, except to refer to the *frankincense* burned when *showbread* was eaten by priests. (360ff)

Incarnation: The "becoming flesh" of the Son of God in the womb of Mary, enabling *Christ* to be the *sacrifice*. (54, 170, 173)

Incense: Burned on the *Altar of Incense* daily by select priests; its fragrant smoke portrayed prayers ascending to God. (135f, 139ff)

Irenaeus: Church father who wrote letters and defended the faith around 180AD. (290)

Justin Martyr: Greek layman who defended the faith around 150AD; wrote of Christ's identity in his letters to Trypho, a Jew. (76)

Kidron: The stream that flowed next to the Jewish *Temple*; ultimately received the *blood, wine* and water poured into the two channels at the base of the *Bronze Altar*. (354)

Keys: The authority Christ gave His church to lock (bind) and unlock (loose) sins; *typified* by OT priestly eating or not eating of *sin/guilt offerings*. (222f)

Koinonia: Greek for "fellowship" or "communion" or "common point"; used by pagans for their *communion* meals; used now by Christians to indicate *Holy Communion*, or to indicate worship-fellowship. (178ff, 255ff)

Laity: OT worshipers who were not priests; NT worshipers who are not pastors; individually "layman" or plural "laymen". (e.g. 39)

GLOSSARY WITH INDEX

Lamb: Most common sacrificial creature of Judaism; sacrificed twice daily as a *burnt offering*; uniquely part of *Passover*, and frequently sacrificed at other Jewish feasts, and in association with other kinds of *sacrifice*. (21, 33f, 63, 72)

Laver: Bronze basin between the *Bronze Altar* and the curtain-entrance (veil) of the *Holy Place*; water-filled font used for ceremonial washing of priest's hands and especially their feet, enabling them to encounter God's holy things; *type* of NT *Baptism*. (119, 131ff)

Layman: See *Laity*.

Leaven: *Yeast*; a symbol of evil; not allowed on God's *altar*. (332)

Leavened Bread: Bread baked with *yeast*; kind of *bread* not burned on God's *altar*, usually not involved with God's rituals, except in connection with the *thank offering*, *Pentecost* and a priest's *ordination*. (276ff, 332, 342ff)

Levitical: That which was associated with the *Levites* and the regulations surrounding their work in the *Tabernacle/Temple*; laws associated with ceremonial actions and cleanliness. (77, 215, 376, 417)

Levite: Descendant of Levi; men allowed to work in God's house; included Aaron's sons who alone could do priestly work. (e.g. 77)

Libation: A liquid offered to a god; also called *drink offering*. Jewish libations were usually grape *wine*, poured at the base of the *Bronze Altar*. (331, 333, 350ff)

Liturgist: Leader of a *liturgy*; used in OT especially of priests; used in NT of *Christ* and the men who represent Him as pastors. (47ff, 421ff)

Liturgy: Greek word meaning "service"; especially used for OT priestly procedures and actions; regular "formula" for doing worship; administrated and standardized all God's worship rituals; mostly mandated by God for OT worship, but not for NT worship; NT liturgy flows from OT liturgy. (47ff, 421ff)

Liturgy of Chrysostom: *Liturgy* associated with John Chrysostom (born 345); basic *liturgy* still used in *Orthodox* churches today. (250)

Liturgy of St. James: Ancient *liturgy* that contains foundational forms for later liturgies; perhaps established by James, brother of Jesus, or by other *Apostles*. (390ff, 405)

Lord's Supper: Common name for the *Sacrament of the Altar*, instituted by *Christ* on the *Passover* before His death; conveys Christ's *body* and *blood* to all who eat; *typified* by OT sacrificial meals. (58f)

GLOSSARY WITH INDEX

Luther, Martin: German reformer (1483-1546); father of Protestantism, founder of Lutheranism; questioned Rome's non-biblical doctrines; re-emphasized the centrality of justification by grace through faith in *Christ* alone. (e.g. 9)

LXX: See *Septuagint*.

Maimonides: Jewish scholar (b. 1135AD); wrote significantly about Jewish *Temple* worship. (225)

Marcion: Gnostic heretic born around 100AD; excommunicated by his father; wanted to free Christianity from OT and Jewish influences; believed the "God" of the OT was different than the "God" of the NT. (9)

Mass: Name for the *Lord's Supper* used especially by *Roman Catholicism*; probably derived from the Latin for "dismissal", which occurred immediately before and after the *Eucharist*. (59)

Maundy Thursday: The day *Christ* instituted the *Lord's Supper*; "Maundy" probably from the Latin "mandatum", an official command. (62)

Memorial: That which is done to commemorate or recall an event or person; many sacred meals are memorial meals, especially associated with *bread* rituals; often indicates that God remembers. (81ff, 359ff)

Mercy Seat: Solid gold cover (lid) of the *Ark of the Covenant*; had two gold *cherubim* mounted upon it; location where God condescended to dwell ("sit") with His people; God's throne; God's footstool. (115, 142, 144f, 392, 397ff)

Messiah: Hebrew word for *Christ* transliterated into English; see *Christ*.

Minchah: A Jewish word for the *sacrifice* usually involving *bread* and *wine*; some would include *incense* and olive oil as part of the minchah; earlier it was a more general word for *sacrifice*. (333ff, 346ff)

Minchah of the Inner Court: Included the *Showbread* and the *wine* in flagons, both on the *Table of Showbread*; some would include also the *frankincense* and *salt* as well. (346ff)

Minchah of the Outer Court: See *Grain Offering*.

Mosaic: That which is associated with *Moses*. (e.g. 221)

Moses: Great(est) prophet of the OT; received God's primary OT revelation; prophet through whom God instituted His OT worship; author of the *Pentateuch*. (e.g. 17ff)

GLOSSARY WITH INDEX

Most Holy: Highest degree of holiness ascribed to a person, place or thing; as opposed to *holy*, the most holy was that only handled by the priests; often identified that OT food consumed solely by priests. (215ff). See also *Holy*.

Most Holy Place: Also called *Holy of Holies*; specific location of God's dwelling in the *Tabernacle*; cubicle room approximately 15 feet on a side with three gold-plated walls; curtain (*veil*) separated it from the *Holy Place*; entered only once a year by the *high priest* on the *Day of Atonement*; only content was the *Ark of the Covenant*. (141ff)

New Covenant: Predicted by Jeremiah to displace the *Mosaic covenant*; fulfilled in *Christ*; associated particularly with the *Lord's Supper* in Luke's and Paul's accounts; another way of saying *New Testament*. (296, 300ff, 380ff)

New Moon: Time of the month when Jews sacrificed their required monthly sacrifices to God. (21)

New Testament (NT): Is used as the equivalent of *New Covenant*; usually identifies the Biblical books written after *Christ*; also used to identify the era after *Christ*. (e.g. 10)

Office of the Keys: That office held by pastors, who officially handle the keys *Christ* gave His *Church* to "lock" and "unlock" sins. See *Keys*. (222)

Old Testament (OT): Can identify the *covenant* before *Christ*; usually identifies the Biblical books preceding *Christ*; also used to identify the era before *Christ*. (e.g. 9)

Ordination: The official induction into a sacred office; especially the induction into the OT office of *priest*. (317f)

Origen: Early church pastor/catechist, born around 182AD. (403)

Orthodox Church: One of two main branches of Christianity tracing roots to the *Apostles*; employ *leavened bread* in Holy Communion; believe in the *Real Presence*. (10, 277). The other branch is *Roman Catholicism*.

Outer Court: Open, roofless area outside the enclosed *Holy* and *Most Holy Places*; was the only area of the *Tabernacle* seen by laity; contained the *Bronze Altar* and the *Laver*. (116ff)

Pasch: Also "paschal" or "pascha"; identified the *Passover* feast or specifically the *Passover lamb*. The *Lord's Supper* is called the New Pasch, and paschal candles are lit by Christians at *Easter*. (77)

GLOSSARY WITH INDEX

Passover: Jewish family celebration commemorating their deliverance from the Egyptians, when death passed over; a feast instituted by God occurring at the beginning of the *Feast of Unleavened Bread*. (62ff [Chapter Two])

Passover Seder: The *liturgy* used in Jewish homes to celebrate the *Passover*. (71f)

Pastor: Latin for "shepherd"; an official title for one called to the Christ-ordained office of the public ministry; also referred to in the NT as elders and bishops; NT leader of Word and *Sacraments* both publicly and privately. (220)

Paterfamilias: Latin for "family father"; technical term for that man who officially led and blessed Jewish feasts—especially *Passover*—in Jewish homes or other "family" gatherings. (93ff)

Peace Offering: *Sacrifice* that culminated the sacrificial process; emphasized a *communion* meal and Godly celebration/thanksgiving; sacrificed on many special occasions—e.g. sealing a *covenant*, ordaining *priest*s, dedicating the *Temple*. (28, 41, 237ff [Chapter Six], 369ff)

Pentateuch: First five books of the OT; written by *Moses*; foundation of God's revelation to man. (11f)

Pentecost: See *Feast of Weeks*.

Prayer of the Veil: Ancient liturgical prayer preceding the reception of the *Lord's Supper*, found in several ancient liturgies; implied entrance through the *veil* into the *Most Holy Place*. (390f, 405ff)

Priest: Probably derived from "presbyter" (Greek word for "elder"); male descendant of Aaron ordained by God to mediate between God and man; handled God's *holy things* in His *holy* places; led the *liturgy*; word used by many to reference NT pastors. (194ff)

Private Burnt Offering: *Burnt offering* brought by a *layman*. (159ff)

Private Confession: Confession of specific sins before a *priest* or a *pastor*, heard by OT priests when a *blood sacrifice* was brought; heard by a NT *pastor* privately; not to be divulged; finalized by absolution, which in the OT was the sacrifice of a creature and priestly consumption of the creature's flesh, and in the NT is forgiveness spoken in Christ's name. (224f)

Private Grain Offering: All *grain offerings* except that associated with the *high priest*'s ordination; *memorial* portion burned and the rest eaten as a *most holy* meal by priests. (341)

GLOSSARY WITH INDEX

Private Peace Offering: *Peace offering* brought by or for a *layman* and his family/friends; eaten by *clean* priests and by *clean laymen* as a *holy* meal; the final *sacrifice* in the "stages" of sacrifice, following the *burnt offering*. (259f)

Private Sin Offering: *Sin offering* that did not include the *high priest*; *blood* daubed on horns of the *Bronze Altar*; *fat* burned on the *Bronze Altar*; no part was brought into *Holy* or *Most Holy Place*s; *flesh* had to be eaten by *clean* priests as a most *holy* meal; could be flour if offerer was poor; the first in the "stages" of *sacrifice*, preceding the *burnt offering*. (203ff, 393)

Promised Land: That land promised to Abraham, to which *Moses* led the people of Israel; after settling there, livestock did not have to be sacrificed in the *Tabernacle* as a *peace offering*; after settling there, God required *wine* to be a *libation* part of the *grain offering*, and, apparently, part of the *Passover* meals. (24, 29, 99, 251)

Public Burnt Offering: *Burnt offering* for the nation; sacrificed twice daily and at special festivals; eaten by no human. (159ff)

Public Grain Offering: *Grain offering* sacrificed at the high priest's *ordination*; eaten by no human. (341f)

Public Peace Offering: *Peace offering* sacrificed at national events; indicated national thanksgiving and celebration; eaten by all who were clean. (259ff)

Public Sin Offering: *Sin offering* on behalf of the *high priest*; usually offered for the entire nation; its *blood* was brought into the *Holy Place* and daubed on the *horns* of *Altar of Incense*; on the *Day of Atonement* its *blood* was sprinkled on the *Mercy Seat* in the *Most Holy Place*; remaining *blood* was shed at base of the *Bronze Altar*; creature burned outside the camp, not on *Bronze Altar*; eaten by no human. (203ff, 394)

Qorban (or **Corban**): General Hebrew word for *sacrifice*; equated at times with *gifts*. (314, 425).

Ram: Common sacrificial creature; required sacrificial creature of the *guilt offering*. (202)

Real Presence: Belief that Christ's *body* and *blood* are actually present and consumed with the mouth in the *Lord's Supper*; nearly unanimously held by ancient Christendom; understood from Christ's words and by Paul's explanation, as well as from OT *types*. (10)

Redeem: To buy back; to buy out of slavery; to buy *first-born* back from God. (66, 70, 77)

Remembrance: In a worship sense frequently identifying God's recollection, resulting in bestowal of His grace; also indicates people recalling God's deliverance/salvation; caused by a *memorial*. (359ff)

Ritual: Habitual, regular bodily action; in worship often associated with eating. (50f)

Roman Catholicism: One of two main branches of Christianity tracing roots to the *Apostles*; employ *unleavened bread* in *Holy Communion*; believe in the *Real Presence*. The other branch is the *Orthodox Church*. (10, 337)

Sabbath: Seventh day of the week; Jewish day of rest; day of required weekly sacrifice and other worship observances; also seventh month and seventh year. (21)

Sacrament: Defined by Lutherans as a sacred ordinance instituted by God involving visible elements, offering forgiveness; not defined in Scripture; especially used of *Baptism* and the *Lord's Supper*. (18ff)

Sacrament of the Altar: Way of referring to the *Lord's Supper*, connecting it to the concept of *altar*, and thus to *sacrifice*. (123ff)

Sacramental Eating: Eating associated with the miraculous, sacred; *Specific Sacramental Eating* is the eating of the *Lord's Supper*; *General Sacramental Eating* is any other miracle-related eating; of the *Lord's Supper*, it is the literal—albeit miraculous—eating of Christ's body and blood as one eats and drinks the sacramental *bread* and *wine*. (18ff). See also *Spiritual Eating*.

Sacrifice: That which is offered to God involving forgiveness, dedication or thanksgiving; in OT worship especially livestock and grain. (20ff)

Sacrifice of Praise: Less common way of referring to *peace offering*; also can refer to voicing one's praise. (309ff, 378ff, 419f)

Salt: Food preservative; symbolically identified preservation, endurance; associated with God's OT *covenant*; Identified in early Christianity with the *Lord's Supper*. (190ff, 362f). See *Covenant of Salt*.

Salvation Sacrifice: Name for the *peace offering*; in Greek, it employed a unique word for "salvation"; the Greek for these words was the most common way of translating the Hebrew word for *peace offering*. (307ff)

Seder: Hebrew word for "order"; employed especially by Jews to identify their household *liturgy* used at *Passover*. (71f)

GLOSSARY WITH INDEX

Septuagint: Official Greek translation of the Hebrew Old Testament; abbreviated as LXX (Roman numeral for "70", for the reputed 70 who translated it); usual source of quotes for NT writers. (e.g. 189)

Shed: To pour out or spill; final application of *sin offering* blood (both public and private) at the *Bronze Altar*'s base; word used by *Christ* when instituting the blood-related portion of *The Supper*. (197ff, 204ff)

Sheep: Most common sacrificial creature; see *Lamb*.

Showbread: Another name for *Bread of the Presence*, which see.

Sin Offering: Category of sacrifice specifically involving *confession* of sin and forgiveness; no pagan parallel found—unique to Israel; vast differences between *public sin offering* and *private sin offering*, which see. (26f, 42, 193ff [Chapter Five], 391ff). See also *guilt offering*.

Sinai: The mountain of God located in the Sinai peninsula; also called "Horeb"; location of God's 40-day revelation to Moses, including the *Ten Commandments* and the OT worship statutes. (41f)

Specific Sacramental Eating: See *Sacramental Eating*.

Spiritual Eating: Simply believing in Christ's *body* and *blood* given and shed for one's salvation; necessary before *sacramental eating*; does not involve literal eating; some believe this to be the only meaning of the *Lord's Supper*, thus rejecting belief in the *Real Presence*. (267). In contrast see also *Sacramental Eating*.

Sprinkling: Unique application of *public sin offering* blood; seen as *typical* of the drinking of the *blood* of *Christ*. (205, 207ff, 232, 383ff, 403)

Tabernacle: In Hebrew or Greek, "tent"; God's first prescribed dwelling place; consisted of *Outer Court*, *Holy Place* and *Most Holy Place*; often identifying only the *Holy* and *Most Holy Places*. (102ff [Chapter 3], 115 [diagram], 147ff)

Table of Presence: See *Table of Showbread*.

Table of Showbread: Also called "Table of Presence"; sacred table in the *Holy Place* across from the *Candelabrum*; held the *showbread*, flagons of wine, and *frankincense*. (135ff)

Table of the Lord: Name for the *Bronze Altar*; name used by Paul for the *Lord's Supper*. (125f)

GLOSSARY WITH INDEX

Temple: The much larger, non-mobile version of the *Tabernacle*; destroyed for a final time in 70AD; used in NT times to describe Christ's *body* as well as God's dwelling "in" His people collectively and individually. (104, 113f)

Ten Commandments: Law given by God to Moses on Sinai on two stone tablets; main content of the *Ark of the Covenant*; foundational OT revelation. (142, 145)

Testament: Used as equivalent of *Covenant*; associated with one's legal will, thus necessitating the death of the *testator* to be put into force. (296, 304f)

Testator: One who endows a testament or legal will. (304f)

Thank Offering: Category of private *peace offering*; indicated thanks for blessings; called *eucharist* in Greek. (272ff)

The Sacrament: Name for the *Lord's Supper*.

The Supper: Name for the *Lord's Supper*.

Tithe: Ten percent of a person's income; commanded by God to be given to Him by OT believers; often involved eating and celebrating by the giver; considered a category of *peace offering*. (315f)

Torah: Hebrew for "teaching"; often translated *law*; used for *Pentateuch*. (11)

Trespass Offering: See *Guilt Offering*.

Type: A person, place, object or event that foreshadowed something with similar but greater qualities; that being foreshadowed is an *antitype*; identified explicitly or implicitly in Scripture; OT types usually pointed to something about *Christ* or to *Christ* himself. (32ff)

Typical: That which forms a *type*, pointing to an *antitype*. E.g.: "Eating the peace offering was typical of eating the Lord's Supper." (32ff)

Unbloody Sacrifice: The *grain offering*; also a term used by *Roman Catholicism* for the re-sacrifice of *Christ* in the *Lord's Supper*. (339)

Unclean: See Clean/Unclean

Unleavened Bread: Flat bread baked without *yeast*; only bread allowed on God's altar; bread eaten at a *Passover* feast, which is held during the *Feast of Unleavened Bread*. (e.g. 86)

GLOSSARY WITH INDEX

Veil: Curtain separating the *Holy Place* from the *Most Holy Place*; less often, curtain separating the *Holy Place* from the *Outer Court*. (145ff, 390ff, 397f, 401ff)

Votive Offering: Category of private *peace offering*; vowed *peace offering* sacrificed after God granted specified deliverance. (280ff). See *Vow*.

Vow: Promise to sacrifice a quality creature to God if He gave deliverance; initiated the votive offering process; had to be approved by the head of the household; at times involved vowing other things/people to God. (280ff). See *Votive Offering*.

Water: Significant sacrificial element; found in the *laver*, for priestly cleansing; poured at the base of the *Bronze Altar* during *Feast of Booths* ceremony; combined with *wine* in the chalice of the *Passover*. (119, 129ff, 355)

Wave Offering: Breast of a *peace offering* given to priests and their families for a *holy* meal; waving likely indicated God gifting it to the priests; major source of sustenance for priests' families. (244ff). See also *Heave Offering*.

Wine: Most common Jewish *libation* and festival drink (grape wine); considered part of the *grain offering* after entrance into the Promised Land; forbidden, as well as other alcohol, to priests in God's courts; critical ingredient of the *Lord's Supper*. (71, 89f, 94f, 129f, 329ff, 346ff)

Words of Institution: Words of Jesus inaugurating and giving the meaning of the *Lord's Supper*; summarized in Matthew, Mark, Luke and I Corinthians; observed as words of blessing and consecration when celebrating the *Lord's Supper*. (e.g. 40)

Index of Bible References

Genesis
2,3...19
2:17...80
3:15...32
3:19...329
3:21...37
4:2-8...38
8:20...122, 151
8:8,21-25...38
9:4...162
9:20ff...329
12:8...103, 122
13:4...122
14:18-20...329
15:13,14...66
15:17...158
26:26-30...38
26:30...296
31:54...37, 38, 41, 65, 296, 320
32:24ff...111
32:32...155
35:1...180
46:1...38

Exodus
3:2,4,14...348
3:18...37, 38, 65
4:22...77
5:1...37, 65
5:3,8,17...38, 65
7:5...66
8:1,20...65
8:8, 21-25...38, 65
9:1...65
10:23-26...65
12:1-13...64, 66, 70
12:5...99
12:8...70
12:14...64, 65, 66, 81, 82, 359
12:22...75
12:43,44,47,48...100
12:46...71
12:47,48...100
13:9...359
13:12-15...77
13:13...70,77
13:14...82
13:13-15...66
13:47-50...189
14...85
16,17...19
16:7,10...109
16:31-34...142
20:1,2...67
20:24...82, 108, 311
23:14...65
23:21...348
24...67
24:1-9...346
24:4-8...42, 300
24:5...155, 196, 262, 300, 381
24:5,9...347
24:8...209, 296, 299, 300, 381, 382
24:11...300, 381
24:12-32:19...104
24:16,17...109
24:23,29,30...346
25:8,9...114
25:10ff...143
25:22...116, 142
25:23-30...135, 346
25:29...350
25:29,30...350
25:30...347, 349
25:31-40...135, 138
25:37...138
25:40...105
26:33...135
26:34...141
27:2...117
27:9...116
27:9-19...116
28:38...220, 227
29...196
29:4...409
29:12...354
29:14,18,28...118
29:32...317, 345
29:38,39,42...152
29:39...43, 189
29:44,45...102
29:46...98
30:1-10...135
30:17-21...119
30:22-25...147
30:26-30...147
31:18...142
32:6...321
32:9...78
33:3...78
33:7-10...419
34:10,19...134
34:14,15...323
34:27,28...142
34:36...411
35:13...349
37:17-24...135
37:25-28...135
38:9-20...116
39:36...349
40:9-11...148
40:30...60
40:35...109

Leviticus
1...152
1-3...171
1:3...149
1:1-17...30
1:2...26, 159
1:2-4...159
1:3...149
1:4...224
1:5,15...154
1:9...119
2:1-16...30
2:2...189
2:2,4,14...331

BIBLE REFERENCES

2:2,15,16...363
2:4...332
2:4ff...29
2:9...359
2:9,10...330
2:11...332
2:13...190, 191, 366
3:1-4...247
3:1-17...30
3:2...224
3:5...173
3:5,11...251
3:11...171, 172, 251
3:16,17...179
3:17...23
4,5...202
4-7...194, 206
4:1,2,13,22,27...414
4:1-3,13-21...204
4:1-21...30, 204
4:3-12...204
4:7,18,25...128
4:7,18,25,30,34..197, 206
4:8-10,19-20,26, 31,35...216
4:13,14,27-29...203
4:15...226
4:20,26,31,35...194
4:21-5:13...30
4:24...224
4:25,26...42, 197
4:25,30,34...207
4:27ff...205
4:31...194
5:1...194
5:3-5...216
5:5...221, 224
5:6...205

5:8,10...118
5:9...197
5:10,13...194
5:11...26
5:11ff...26, 202
5:13...202, 216
5:14...194
5:14,15...414
5:14-6:7...30
5:16...199
5:16,18...194
5:17,18...198
5:18...202
6:1-5...199
6:1-7...199
6:6...202
6:7...194, 335
6:8-13...30
6:9,13...158
6:10...172
6:14-18...30
6:16...29, 40, 337
6:16,17...344
6:16,23...352
6:17...335
6:19ff...342
6:23...341, 342, 345
6:24-30...30
6:25,26...193, 215, 216
6:26...39, 218
6:26,29...216
6:30...204, 211
7,22...218
7:1-6...30
7:3-5...22
7:6...39, 202, 216, 218
7:6,7,9,10,31, 32...157
7:7...194
7:8...27, 155

7:9,10...330, 339
7;10...216
7:11...307
7:11,14...162
7:11-34...30
7:12...272, 276, 310, 420
7:13...276
7:15...272
7:15,16...242, 243, 247
7:16...295
7:19-21...233, 326
7:27...161
7:28-34...239
7:30-32...245
7:31...245
7:32,33...245
8:14...196
8:14,18...118
8:15...197, 206, 354
8:30...209
8:31...317
9:1-4...240
9:6,23...109
9:7...43, 189
9:7,8,12,22...118
9:9...197
9:24...157, 172
10:1ff...217, 221
10:1-3...50
10:9...29, 331, 352, 427
10:9,10...233
10:12...343, 344
10:12ff...330
10:12,13...352
10:16,17...216
10:17...219, 393
10:19...221
11...233
12,15...233

463

BIBLE REFERENCES

12:6,7...234
13,14...233
13:45...233
14:4,6...75
14:12...199, 202
14:12,13,19...234
14:13...217, 233
14:19,20,22,31...118
15:15,30...118, 234
16...143, 204, 210
16:4...409
16:11,24...118
16:24...213
16:26...233
17:1-6...24
17:3,5,6...252
17:5...249
17:6,11...179
17:11...75, 117, 160, 168
17:11,14...22
17:14...354
18:11...244
19:5,6...39, 237
19:5-8...247
19:6...247
19:8...248
19:20-22...199
19:22...194
21:6...30, 39, 171
21:22...246
22:4...246
22:6...223
22:10,14...46, 373
22:11,13...246
22:18...378
22:30...247
23...21

23:9-23...336
23:10...335
23:14...336
23:15-21...336
23:17...342
23:17ff...276
24:1-9...346
24:5...365
24:5-9...135, 347
24:7...43, 189, 362
24:7,8...411
24:8...366
24:9...347, 364

Numbers
1:53...142
3:12,13...67, 77
3:44-51...66
4:7...411
4:21-28...49
5:7...224
6:11,16,17...118
6:12...202
6:14...201
7...118
8:12...118
9:1-14...66
9:12...71
10:10...43, 189, 363
14:10,21...109
15:2ff...29, 351
15:2,5...331, 351
15:4,5...329
15:22-31...414
15:25,28...194
15:30...414
16:19,42...109
17:10...142
18...426, 427
18:1...220, 221
18:7...47, 49

18:9...425
18:10...426
18:11...239
18:12...358
18:30,31...427
19:1ff...211, 426, 427
19:4,5...165
19:5...374
19:7...233
21:6-9...80
25:2...320
25:2,3...323
28,29...21, 159, 350-352
28:1-15...21
28:2...172, 339
28:3...99
28:7...351, 352
28:8...352
28:10-29...420
28:12-14...352
28:26...336
30...282

Deuteronomy
12:5...108, 114, 122, 224
12:5-7...122, 311
12:5,7...268, 315
12:6,7...20, 315
12:7...268
12:17,18...315
12:18...269
12:20-23...24
12:21...252
12:26...280
14:22,23...358
14:22,23,28,29...25, 325
14:23...358
14:26...358
14:29...325

BIBLE REFERENCES

16:2...75,96
16:3,6...69
16:10...295
16:16...21
23:23...281
26:2...122
27:6,7...239
27:7...241
31:20...22
32:14...353
32:17...322
32:38...171

Joshua
5:13ff...111
9:14...296

Judges
13:13ff...111
13:20,22...186, 187
20:26...306
21:4...306

Ruth

1 Samuel
1:11...282
1:21...260, 282
2:1,10...118
2:19...260
9:12,13...323
11:15...319
16:2,3...319
16:5...319
20:6,29...260
21:3ff...347

2 Samuel
6:2...143

1 Kings
1:9,25...319
1:19...319
1:39...148
8:29,30,35-38...108
8:62,63...261
8:63...259
12:32,33...323
18:38...158
19:21...319

2 Kings

1 Chronicles
21:26...158
29:22...29, 268, 357

2 Chronicles
4:6...132
7:1...158
13:5...190
29:31-35...306
30:2,15
35:12,16...309

Ezra
2:62,63...218
3:1-6...119

Nehemiah
8:4,5,9...120

Esther
1:8...411

Job
1:1ff...123
1:5...38

Psalms
16:4...353
19:12,13...200
20:3...83
22...282ff
22:17...71
22:22...284
22:24...283, 285
22:25ff...314
22:25...284
22:25,26...282
22:26...241, 284, 287
22:27,28...286
22:29...287
23...285
26:4-7...297
26:6-8,12...314
27:1,4-6...314
30:9...165
32:3-6...58
34:8...407
34:20...71
37, LXX title...362
40...150
42...314
42:4,5...313
43...314
43:4,5...313
44:22...133
50:5...297
50:5,14,16,23...297
50:7ff...57
50:7-13...297
50:7-15...173
50:12,13...173
50:14...273
50:14,23...311
50:16...298
51:5...78
51:7...75
51:16-19...57
51:17...58
51:19...249
54:6...314
56:12f...314
66:15...43, 189

BIBLE REFERENCES

69, LXX title ... 362
69:31...273
76:10...312
76:10,11...314
80:1...145, 396
81:10...314
87:7...314
89:20...148
92...314
95:2...314
95:2,7...314
100:3...314
100:4...314
101:5 LXX...417
103:3-5...314
107:9,17-22... 314
107:22...273, 310, 311
110...103, 329
111:5...314
113-118...71,72
113:5,6...175
116...311, 314
116:12...358
116:13...358
116:14...358
116:10ff...311
116:12,13...279
116:12-19...297
116:13...152
116:17,18...311
118...314
118:27...270
119:103,108... 314
119:49...83
138:1,2...314
141:2...140, 278
146:7...273
150:4...268

Proverbs
14:31...325
15:8...57

Ecclesiastes

Song of Solomon

Isaiah
1:11,13...154
6:6,7...123
9:6...92
19:19,21...294
24:23...319
25:6...319
40:5...146, 147
52:13-53:12... 231
52:15...232
53...229-232
53:10...34, 229, 230, 394
53:10-12...394
53:12...43, 231, 232, 394
56:6,7...294
60:3,7...293, 294
61:1...147
62:8,9...357, 358
62:9...29, 358
63:3...353
63:9...348, 349
66:1,2...58

Jeremiah
6:20...57
7:4...56,57
7:8-10...57
25:30...353
31:31...301
31:31-34...303
31:31,33,34...30

Lamentations

Ezekiel
1:26-28...146
43:19,27...118
43:24...190
44:6,7...46
44:7...172
44:7-9...124
44:16...124
45:19...98
46:11...390

Daniel
6:10...108
9:24...197, 229
9:27...34, 231, 299

Hosea
2:11...390
6:6...57
8:12-14...57
9:5...390

Joel
1:9,13...333
2:14...333

Amos
4:4,5...57
4:5...273
5:21...390
5:21,22...57
5:22,23...251
9:11...107, 113

Obadiah

Jonah
2:9,10...284

BIBLE REFERENCES

Micah
3:11...120
6:6-8...57

Nahum
1:15...281

Habakkuk
2:20...105

Zephaniah

Haggai
2:7...113

Zechariah
2:10...107
3:8,9...103
6:12...113
6:12,13...103

Malachi
1:7,12...125, 126
1:11...126, 289, 290-293, 333
1:11-13...291
1:11-14...292
1:12...126, 290
1:13...289, 291
1:14...289, 291, 292
2:7...120

Matthew
1:23...108
3:17...176
5:3-6...58
5:17...85
5:23,24...126, 127, 200, 314
7:6...59, 45, 46, 246, 373
12:3ff...347
12:28...91
12:39-41...284
13:3-23...46
14:19...265
16:4...284
16:9,10...265
16:18ff...284
16:19...222
17:5...176
18:18...222
18:20...114, 123
19:28...366
20:28...166
22:32...170
23:18,19...217, 123
26:17...62
26:26...72, 211, 343
26:26-28...40, 93, 210
26:27...76
26:27,28...163, 296, 387
26:28...41, 42, 128, 197, 210, 231, 299, 302, 303, 382
26:29...89, 90, 91
26:30...72
28:19,20...101
28:19ff...367

Mark
6:41...265
7:11...200, 314, 425
9:50...191
14:12...21
14;24...231
14:25...91

Luke

1:9,11...140
1:23...423
1:44...171
2:14...309
2:29-31...308
2:30...308
3:6...308
4:18...147
6:1-4...365
9:16...265
9:28ff...109
10:16...424, 434
11:31...261
12:1...332
12:35-40...434
12:37...48, 434
13:29...92, 434
15:11ff...24
15:23...25
16:29...11
16:31...11
22:15...62, 63
22:15,16...90
22:17...63
22:18...88, 89
22:19...188, 210, 266
22:20...387
22:27...48, 434
22:30...288
24:27...11, 136
24:30-35...366
24:35...266
24:39...169

John
1:1,14...92, 112
1:14...107, 109
1:18...111
1:29...70, 96, 98, 196
2:19ff...96
2:19-22...113, 261

2:22...113
4:20ff...419
4:23...96
5:39...10
5:46...9, 11
6...262ff, 369
6:1-14...20, 74
6:11...266
6:23...266
6:39,40,54...268
6:51ff...267, 343
6:51-58...264
6:53-56...59, 257, 263
6:54,55...262
6:55...162, 267
6:56...434
6:60...264
7:37-39...91
12:24...336
13:3ff...119
13:29...270
14:20...61
15;4,5...433
15:5...177
15:13...184
17:5...110
17:24...169
18:28...270, 271
19:30...306
19:34...71, 130
19:34,35...130, 355
19:35...130
19:36...71
20:12...116
20:21-23...222, 424
20:22,23...91
21:9-13...267

Acts
1:4...191
2:14...91
2:27...244
2:38...91
2:42...58, 59, 91
2:48...265
6:13,14...428
10:41...244
13:2...53
15:16-18...113
15:29...324
20:7,11...59
20:11...95
20:28...128, 164
21:25...324
28:28...308

Romans
1:8...276
3:20ff...58
3:24,25...144
3:25...143
4...305
5:6-11...197
5:14...33
6:1ff...61
6:34...61
7:7...58
8:2..196
8:14...78
8:16,17...78
8:19...235
8:36...133
9:4...53
12:1...133, 278
16:16...124
16:16,17...417
16:17...123, 124, 125

1 Corinthians
1:4...276
1:27...80
3:16...96, 114
4:1...59
5...86

5:7...32, 34, 71, 85
5:7,8...86, 87
5:8...332, 341
5:11...417
6:19...114
8:10...322
10:1ff...255, 369
10:1,2...60, 85
10:3,4,16...18
10:7...255, 321
10:16...59, 95, 166, 181, 254, 255, 265, 321, 340, 357
10:16,17...254, 255
10:17...417
10:18...17, 59, 174, 180, 255, 339
10:18-21...256
10:19-21...322
10:21...59, 123, 125, 255, 290
11:20...59
11:20-22...328
11:21,22...182
11:23ff...266
11:23-25...81
11:23-29...83
11:24...81, 188
11:24,25...359
11:25...303
11:26...40, 82, 367
11:27...341, 414
11:27-29...47
11:28...341
11:30...55
12:27...114
14:34,35...182

BIBLE REFERENCES

15:4...243
15:20...336
15:35ff...170
15:36...336
15:45...111
15:56...58
16:20...124

2 Corinthians
1:11...276
2:14...177
4:6...147
5:21...197
8:11,12...411
9:11-15...59
13:12...124

Galatians
3,4...305
3:13...197
3:26,27...78
3:27...61
4:4,5,7...78
4:14...348

Ephesians
1:4...169
1:7...166
2:6...187
2:13...166
2:13-15...257
4:5...223
4:11,12...424
5:1,2...340
5:2...175, 176, 182, 183
5:18...182
5:20...276
5:25,26...187
5:26...132, 223, 338, 409
5:28-32...114
5:32...188
6:17...308

Philippians
1:3...276
2:13...432
4:18...177

Colossians
1:9...108
1:12...276
1:18...316
1:20,22...257
1:20-22...257
2:9...265
2:11ff...101
2:12...61, 223
2:16,17...33,63, 68
2:17...120
3:5-10...223

1 Thessalonians
1:2...276
5:26...124

2 Thessalonians
1:3...276

1 Timothy
2:5...140, 182
2:11...182
3:16...53

2 Timothy

Titus
2:11...308
3:5...132, 223, 338, 409

Philemon

Hebrews
1:3...398
1:6...77

1:14...423
2:14...257
3:1...377, 378
3:1ff...382
3:5...104
4:14...318, 379, 380, 399
4:15...70, 399
4:16...399, 400
5:1...425
5:3...392
5,7...329
5:7...283
6:1,2...373
6:1-8...58
6:2...427
6:18...411
6:19,20...411
7:12...392, 428
7:19...412
7:25...400
7:26,27...92
7:27...377, 431
8:1...375, 399, 421
8:2...421, 423
8:1,2...421
8:1-3...376
8:3...368, 424
8:5...105, 395
8:6...121, 376, 384
8:7-13...381
9...305
9:1...300, 383
9:1,2...104
9:4...142
9:8-12...303
9:9,10...425, 426, 427, 429
9:9,14...429
9:9ff...426
9:10...384, 415, 426, 427

469

9:11...45, 105, 395, 401, 427
9:11,12...109, 143
9:11,12,26...377
9:12,24...213
9:12,26,28...431
9:13...211, 374, 426
9:13-14...208, 385, 386
9:13-15...432
9:14...128
9:15...387
9:16...304
9:16,17...304
9:16ff...257
9:16-20...304
9:18...299, 381, 382
9:18ff...403
9:18-20...42
9:20...299, 382
9:21...396
9:23...395
9:23,24...106
9:24...105, 396, 399
9:25,26...400
9:26...392
9:27,28...400
9:28...394
10:1...400, 429
10:1-12...257
10:2,22...429
10:3...363
10:4-10...149, 150
10:10...431, 432
10:10-12...377
10:11...423
10:12...196, 392, 399, 401
10:14...401

10:18...392
10:19...213, 402
10:19ff...214, 223, 382, 393, 398, 404-408, 410, 413
10:19,20...59, 109, 214, 257, 403, 404, 405
10:19-22...132, 133, 212, 395, 400, 401, 410
10:19-25...185, 393, 408, 413
10:19-29...433
10:21,23...379
10:22...80, 119, 133, 208, 338, 385, 387, 404, 407- 410
10:22-25...405
10:23...379, 410
10:23-25...410, 412, 413
10:24...433
10:24,25...185
10:25...433
10:26...413
10:26-29...154
10:29...109, 381, 413, 414
11:6...80, 415
11:28...388
12:1,2...411
12:2...399
12:4...129
12:18,22-24... 400
12:22...419, 423

12:22,23...77, 389-391
12:22-24...53, 208, 385
12:23...78, 79
12:24...206, 208, 376, 385, 388, 389, 391
13:8...148
13:9...415, 416
13:10ff...185, 413, 418, 420
13:10...59, 123, 403, 416
13:10-12...212
13:11...417
13:11,12...257
13:12...211
13:13,14...419
13:15...59, 278, 380, 420
13:15,16...277, 419
13;16...420
13:18...429
13:20...257, 434
13:20,21...433

James

1 Peter
1:2...208, 209, 385
1:2,3...257
1:2,18,20...128
1:10,11...102
1:18,19...70, 166
1:19,20...110, 169
2:1-10...113
2:4-10...318
2:5...327
2:9...133, 320
2:24...220, 355

3:21...33
5:14...124

2 Peter
1:3,4...187
2:12-22...58
2:13...327

1 John
1:7...128, 197
1:7-10...58
2;1f...197
3:2...170
3:16...183
4:10...197
5:6-8...130

2 John
10,11...417

3 John

Jude
10-13...58
12...327

Revelation
1:5...166, 257
1:5,6...320
1:6...133 338,
1:12,13...138
1:18...74
1:20...138
2:14...178, 323
2:20...30, 324
3:20...93, 434
5,6:1-8...145
5:8...140
5:9,10...133
6:9...165, 403
7:14-16, 106
7:17...92
13:8...74, 110, 169

14:17-20...353
19:13...353
21,22...145
21:3...139
21:22,23...139
21:23...114, 139
22:1...145

www.ingramcontent.com/pod-product-compliance
Lightning Source LLC
Chambersburg PA
CBHW020727160426
43192CB00006B/144